NAPOLEON'S ADMIRALS

NAPOLEON'S ADMIRALS

Flag officers of the *Arc de Triomphe*, 1789–1815

Richard Humble

CASEMATE

Oxford & Philadelphia

Published in Great Britain and the United States of America in 2019 by
CASEMATE PUBLISHERS
The Old Music Hall, 106–108 Cowley Road, Oxford OX4 1JE, UK
and
1950 Lawrence Road, Havertown, PA 19083, USA

Hardcover Edition: ISBN 978-1-61200-808-0
Digital Edition: ISBN 978-1-61200-809-7

A CIP record for this book is available from the British Library

Printed and bound in the United Kingdom by TJ International

Typeset in India for Casemate Publishing Services. www.casematepublishingservices.com

For a complete list of Casemate titles, please contact:

CASEMATE PUBLISHERS (UK)
Telephone (01865) 241249
Email: casemate-uk@casematepublishers.co.uk
www.casematepublishers.co.uk

CASEMATE PUBLISHERS (US)
Telephone (610) 853-9131
Fax (610) 853-9146
Email: casemate@casematepublishers.com
www.casematepublishers.com

Contents

Introduction	ix
Naval Ranks	xv
A Note on Ship Nomenclature	xvii
Naval Chronology	xix

Part 1: The Constitutional Monarchy, 1789–1792

Admiral Laurent-Jean-François Truguet	3

Part 2: The Convention, 1792–1795

Vice-Admiral Louis-René-Madeleine-Levassor, *Comte de* Latouche-Tréville	9
Vice-Admiral Edouard-Thomas de Burgues, *Comte de* Missiessy	15
Vice-Admiral Louis-Thomas, *Comte* Villaret-Joyeuse	19
Vice-Admiral François-Etienne de Rosily-Mesros	25
Vice-Admiral Pierre, *Comte* Martin	31
Rear-Admiral Jean-François Renaudin	35
Vice-Admiral Pierre-César-Charles-Guillaume, *Marquis de* Sercey	39

Part 3: The Directory, 1795–1799

Vice-Admiral Etienne-Eustache Bruix	49
Vice-Admiral Pierre-Charles-Jean-Baptiste-Silvestre de Villeneuve	55
Vice-Admiral François-Paul, *Comte de* Brueys d'Aigalliers	65
Vice-Admiral Honoré-Joseph Ganteaume	71
Rear-Admiral Jean-Baptiste-Emmanuel Perrée	79
Vice-Admiral Denis, Duke Decrès	87

Part 4: The Consulate, 1799–1804

Vice-Admiral Carel Hendrik, Count Ver Huell	95
Vice-Admiral Maxime-Julien Émeriau, *Comte de* Beauverger	101
Rear-Admiral Charles-René Magon de Médine	107
Vice-Admiral Charles-Alexandre Léon Durand, *Comte de* Linois	115

Part 5: The Empire, 1804–1814/15

Rear-Admiral Julien-Marie Cosmao-Kerjulien 129
Rear-Admiral Jacques-Félix-Emmanuel Hamelin 139
Jérôme Bonaparte 149
Vice-Admiral Jean-Baptiste-Philibert, *Comte* Willaumez 159
Rear-Admiral Count Pierre Baste 169
Vice-Admiral Guy-Victor, Baron Duperré 183
Rear-Admiral Jean-Mathieu-Adrien Lhermitte 197
Rear-Admiral Amable-Gilles Troude 203

Appendix 1: Admirals of the Tricolour 211
Appendix 2: Admirals of the Arc 213
Appendix 3: Absentees from the Arc 215
Bibliography 223
Index 225
Index of Ships 243

The *Arc de Triomphe*. The names of 26 admirals who served in the Revolutionary and Napoleonic Wars are inscribed on the columns inside its four pillars. (Shutterstock, Perig)

Introduction

Second only to the Eiffel Tower as the most famous landmark of Paris, the *Arc de Triomphe* was begun by France's first emperor and completed by her last king. Commenced while the glory of Napoleon's Empire was rising to its brief zenith, it was finished 21 years after his overthrow and the humiliation of the nation which he had led to utter defeat.

This makes the *Arc de Triomphe* very different from the great triumphal arches of imperial Rome, whose emperors – Titus, Trajan, Constantine, and the like – were obsessed with building monuments to their own living glory, not to bygone victories and lost dominion. Although it came into being as a megalomaniac's brainchild, the *Arc de Triomphe* became a symbol greater than any dreamed of by Napoleon. It shelters the Eternal Flame and France's Unknown Warrior. It is the supreme monument to the military genius of the French nation.

The *Arc de Triomphe* is also a thanksgiving in stone to the men who made possible – as Conan Doyle has put it – 'that inconceivable Napoleonic past when France, like an angel of wrath, rose up, splendid and terrible, before a cowering continent'.[1] On its four sides – north, east, south, and west – are inscribed the names of 660 leaders and commanders from the wars of the First Republic and Empire. The vast majority of those names, 634 in all, are those of soldiers: generals and marshals. But 26 of them are the names of admirals, commanders of the fleets of Republican and Imperial France. This book tells their story.

From the North Sea to the western Pyrenees, from the eastern Pyrenees to the Maritime Alps, France has considerably more sea coast than land frontiers. French seaports grant immediate access to the entire length of the English Channel, the wild 'Atlantic corner' of the Brittany peninsula, the Bay of Biscay and the western Mediterranean basin. Each of these coasts has produced a crop of famous sailors.

Not every sailor draws his first breath of sea air (Vice-Admiral Lord Horatio Nelson was born at an inland Norfolk parsonage), but it is hardly possible to ignore the maritime environment of the 26 'Admirals of the *Arc*'. Excluding the Dutchman Ver Huell and Corsican-born Jérôme Bonaparte, no less than eight of the remaining

24 hailed from Brittany and the Atlantic coast, four from the Channel coast, and three from the Mediterranean coast. Two were colonial-born: Martin in French Canada, and Bruix at Saint-Domingue in the Caribbean. Only seven were born inland and central France.

The naval war fought by Britain against Republican and Napoleonic France was the longest maritime conflict of modern history. With only one 14-month intermission, the Peace of Amiens in 1802–3, it lasted 21 years, from 1793 to 1814. (The 'Hundred Days' of March–June 1815 were cut short by the Battle of Waterloo, before naval strategy could play any effective part.)

A genuine epic, both in its scope and its duration, this great naval war is only dimly remembered today, and such memories of it that endure are usually blurred. For the British in particular, this eclipse is mostly due to the giant shadow cast by Vice-Admiral Lord Horatio Nelson. The Battle of Trafalgar, in which Nelson died, is popularly believed to have saved England from invasion, ending the war at sea by destroying the last great Franco-Spanish fleet. But on 21 October 1805, the day of Trafalgar, the French invasion camps on the Channel had been empty since the last week of August, and Napoleon was celebrating his latest victory over the Austrians at Ulm, on the upper Danube, more than 400 miles from the Channel.

Nor did Trafalgar achieve the end of the naval war. It dragged on for nine more years, keeping Britain's thinly stretched naval resources ever more extended. In its latter stages, it blossomed into a parallel naval conflict with France's last potential maritime ally, the United States. There was no rest, no respite; even admirals were kept at sea for years, dying from sheer exhaustion. In March 1810, Vice-Admiral Sir Cuthbert Collingwood, Nelson's second-in-command at Trafalgar, died at sea, utterly worn out, as the British Admiralty had not dared to relieve him. Five months later (August 1810), the French handed the British Navy its most humiliating defeat of the entire naval war: the loss of four frigates, with great loss of life, in the Battle of Grand-Port, Mauritius (pp. 181–93). This interminable naval war had no crashing finale, no Waterloo at sea. It was ended only by the attrition of Napoleon's last land armies, and by the invasion and capitulation of France.

Historical attention has always concentrated on Britain's six famous victories over the fleets of France and her allies. These were the First of June against the French, in 1794; Cape St Vincent against the Spanish and Camperdown against the Dutch, in 1797; Aboukir Bay or 'the Nile', against the French, in 1798; Copenhagen against the Danes, in 1801; and Trafalgar against the French and Spanish, in 1805. But for all their drama, courage, and slaughter, none of these great battles were war-winners. They were only gory interludes in the long and weary story of blockade and breakouts, encounters and chases, privateer cruises and raids, while the unabated French subjugation of mainland Europe gave the French Navy more and more shipbuilding bases and havens for the British Navy to cover. Like Waterloo, the British victory at sea was a near-run thing; unlike Waterloo, the British Navy had no loyal ally to come to its aid in the nick of time. By any standard, it is surely time that the French Navy, which imposed such a strain on the greatest naval power on earth during these years, is given more consideration than it has had to date.

Whole libraries have been devoted to the generals and Marshals of the French First Republic and Empire and, to repeat, the names of 634 military heroes of the First Republic and Empire are listed on the *Arc de Triomphe*. This book is an attempt to redress the balance by telling the stories of the 26 French naval officers who reached the rank of admiral between 1789 and 1814, whose names are similarly honoured.

After completing a study of *Napoleon's Peninsular Marshals,* I planned a sequel on *Napoleon's Admirals,* but this soon encountered difficulties. The barest initial research showed that only 22 French admirals were created under Napoleon's Consulate and Empire (1799–1815). But no fewer than 45 had reached flag rank under the Republican Convention and the Directory, between January 1793 and November 1799, and among these were the most famous names: Villaret-Joyeuse, Latouche-Tréville, Missiessy, Brueys, Villeneuve, Bruix, Decrès, and Ganteaume. Another ten admirals had been promoted during the Revolution's opening phase, the doomed experiment with constitutional monarchy (July 1789–August 1792). All their stories are clearly of the utmost importance in judging the effect of the Revolution on the French Navy.

The case histories of the first French admirals promoted after the Fall of the Bastille, dispel one myth at the outset. The Revolution did *not* prompt a mass emigration of aristocratic naval officers, leaving an executive vacuum to be filled with inexperienced landsmen, and so making a string of French defeats at sea a foregone conclusion. The best of them stayed, and loyally tried to serve their country as the Revolution followed its unpredictable course.

After the fall of the monarchy on 10 August 1792, these former King's officers took the required oath of loyalty to the nation and addressed themselves to serving the new Republic. Neither the horrific 'September Massacres' of the following month, nor even the execution of King Louis XVI in January 1793, led them to revoke their oath and abandon the Republic. For four of them this loyalty proved fatal: Rear-Admiral Marquis Joseph de Flottes, cut to pieces by a mob at the Toulon Dockyard gates, Admiral *Comte d'*Estaing, Vice-Admiral Nicolas-René, *Comte de* Grimouard, and Vice-Admiral Armand-Guy Kersaint, guillotined under the Jacobin Terror.[2]

Time and again, the admirals' stories throw new light on what a deadly and wasteful lottery the French Revolution was. An impressive 'survivors' club' could have been formed by naval officers who, languishing in prison under the guillotine's shadow, were only saved by the fall of Robespierre and the end of the Terror. There were 27 all told, including eight of the 26 future 'Admirals of the *Arc*'. By no means all of them were restored to the Active List after their release. But while the Revolution squandered so much available naval talent with one hand, it made abundant use of it with the other.

Between January 1793 and October 1794, a total of 28 naval officers were promoted to flag rank (of whom only one, Kersaint, was guillotined). Not one of them was a Republican fanatic, or an accelerated promotion from the lower deck prompted by Revolutionary dogma. All 16 of the captains promoted to rear-admiral in the remarkable New Year's Day list of 1793 were veterans of the American Revolutionary War, and eight of them had also served in the Seven Years War. As for fighting talent, one of the latter group, Latouche-Tréville, deserves better remembrance as the only French admiral to have defeated Nelson.

Pre-Revolutionary naval careers also characterized the 22 'imperial admirals' promoted during Napoleon's Consulate and Empire. Only one of them, Napoleon's youngest brother, Jérôme Bonaparte, owed his admiral's flag to unashamed imperial patronage, and even he was not promoted admiral before he had had his own independent command. (In this he resembled most members of the British royal family who had served in the Navy.) In short, Jérôme excepted, all the admirals of the French Republic and Empire had learned their trade in the French royal navy or merchant service of the *Ancien Régime*.

Before considering this navy and the changes it underwent in the Revolution, another point should be remembered. This was the sharp drop in the average age of French admirals under Republic and Empire:

REGIME	ADMIRALS PROMOTED	AVERAGE AGE
CONSTITUTIONAL MONARCHY, 1789–92	10	52.1
CONVENTION, 1792–95	31	47.8
DIRECTORY, 1795–99	14	41.9
CONSULATE, 1799–1804	6	40.8
EMPIRE, 1804–14	16	42.25

These figures invite comparison with the ages of the admirals who had fought the major Franco-British sea battles of the Seven Years War and the American Revolutionary War:

BATTLE	BRITISH	Age	FRENCH	Age
LAGOS, 1759	Boscawen	48	de la Clue	56
QUIBERON, 1759	Hawke	54	Conflans	69
GRENADA, 1779	Byron	56	d'Estaing	50
CHESAPEAKE, 1781	Graves	56	de Grasse	59
SAINTS, 1782	Rodney	63	de Grasse	60
PROVÉDIEN, 1782	Hughes	62	Suffren	53

The age reduction showed through in the major Anglo-French sea battles of the Revolutionary and Napoleonic Wars:

BATTLE	BRITISH	Age	FRENCH	Age
1st OF JUNE, 1794	Howe	68	Villaret-Joyeuse	46
ABOUKIR BAY, 1798	Nelson	40	Brueys	45
TRAFALGAR, 1805	Nelson	47	Villeneuve	42

(The youngest French-allied admiral to command a fleet in battle was the Dutchman De Winter at Camperdown in 1797, who at 36 was some 30 years younger than his British opponent, Duncan.)

Here, then, is one French Revolutionary myth that is at least partly true. The Republican governments *did* make a deliberate effort to promote younger captains to flag rank and give them seagoing commands. At the same time, none of the Republican regimes could do without older flag officers to superintend the ports, dockyards and general administration of the Navy. Of the 28 promotions to rear-admiral made in 1793, 11 were over 50 (Rear-Admiral Pierre Landais and Rear-Admiral Pierre-François Cornic were both 62) and only two – Vice-Admiral Edouard-Thomas de Burgues, *Comte de* Missiessy (37) and Rear-Admiral Corentin-Urbain Leissegues (35) – were under 40.

The Revolution, and the long ensuing naval war between Britain and the new France of Republic and Empire, left one international custom of naval warfare completely untouched. This was the long-established wartime practice of 'trading with the enemy' in the matter of officer prisoners. As in the courtly days of the *Ancien Régime,* Britain and France continued to negotiate for the exchange or release on parole of captured officers. This had little to do with chivalry: it suited both sides, and the practice continued until the Crimean War of 1854–56. As Emperor, however, Napoleon suspended officer exchanges from 1806, which resulted in Linois remaining a prisoner of the British from March 1806 until Napoleon's abdication in April 1814.

Of the 26 admirals whose names adorn the *Arc de Triomphe,* six (Latouche-Tréville, Magon, Missiessy, Rosily-Mesros, Sercey, and Willaumez) had been prisoners of war during the American War of 1778–83. But another 13 – Baste, Decrès, Duperré, Émeriau, Ganteaume, Hamelin, Lhermitte, Linois, Perrée, Renaudin, Rosily-Mesros, Villeneuve, and Willaumez – experienced captivity between 1792 and 1814 (twice, in the cases of Perrée and Villeneuve, and three times in that of Linois). Three were killed on their quarterdecks in battle: Brueys, Perrée, and Magon. (Rear-Admiral Baste also died in action, but that was as an Army brigade commander in the brief-lived land campaign of 1814.)

The careers of the 26 'Admirals of the *Arc*' tell the story of a professional class striving with mixed success to come to terms with a period of cataclysmic change. It is time that their stories were told, for the benefit not only of naval history enthusiasts, but also of all students of the French Revolution and the Napoleonic imperium. The admirals' all-important pre-Revolutionary service is a reminder that the Revolution was not an isolated explosion. This book explores a decidedly neglected aspect of pre-Revolutionary France in its last three decades, which alone merits far more research and attention than has so far been bestowed on it by historians.

'The French Revolution', wrote Alexis de Tocqueville, 'will only be the darkness of night to those who merely regard itself; only the times which preceded it will give the light to illuminate it.'[3] The French national crisis which triggered the Revolution in 1789 was itself precipitated by the nation's inability to pay for the war of 1778–83, the most successful naval conflict, and the last, fought by the Navy of the *Ancien Régime*.

Notes

1 Doyle, C. 1900. 'How the Brigadier Slew the Fox', *The Adventures of Brigadier Gerard*.
2 Under the Terror 42 French Army generals were executed in 1793–94, nearly all by the guillotine.
3 Tocqueville, Alexis de. 1856. *L'Ancien Régime*, Book III, Chapter VIII.

Naval Ranks

BRITISH	FRENCH
Vice-admiral	Vice-amiral
Rear-admiral	Contre-amiral
Commodore	Chef de division
Captain	Capitaine de vaisseau
Commander	Lieutenant de vaisseau
Lieutenant-commander	Lieutenant de frégate
Lieutenant	Enseigne de vaisseau
Midshipman	Garde/Aspirant de la marine

A Note on Ship Nomenclature

In descending order of firepower, three-masted warships in both the British and French fleets were classified as ships of the line (*vaisseaux*), frigates (*frégates),* and sloops (*avisos*). History makes frequent reference to three other ship-types which may not be familiar to English readers: the xebec, the corvette, and the *flûte*.

Xebecs

Of unmistakable Arab descent, and much employed by the North African Barbary Corsairs, the xebec featured a single main deck topped by a poop deck aft. It carried triangular lateen sails on three masts and the smaller ones were light enough to be rowed in a calm. French xebecs were extensively used by the Toulon fleet for inshore work and were only occasionally employed outside the Mediterranean.

Corvettes

Usually attached to frigate squadrons, corvettes were ocean-going, three-masted warships – there were also two-masted brig-corvettes – with a single tier of guns, usually of a heavier calibre than those mounted in British sloops. They often provided the first command of a newly promoted *lieutenant de vaisseau.*

Flûtes

A *flûte* was an armed ship partially disarmed to carry troops, stores, or both. Taking out alternate guns to create more accommodation and storage space left an interrupted row of empty gun ports, like the finger holes on a flute. An *armée en flûte* was a warship which could have its full broadside of guns restored once its transportation role had been fulfilled (see p. 41–42).

Naval Chronology

1740   Outbreak of War of the Austrian Succession

1745   Birth of future admiral Latouche-Tréville

1748   Treaty of Aix-la-Chapelle ends Austrian Succession War.
         Birth of future admiral Rosily-Mesros

1750   Birth of future admiral Renaudin

1752   Birth of future admirals Martin and Truguet

1753   Birth of future admirals Brueys and Sercey

1755   Birth of future admiral Ganteaume

1756   Outbreak of Seven Years War.
         Birth of future admiral Missiessy

1757   Birth of future admiral Villaret-Joyeuse

1759   20 November: Battle of Quiberon Bay – Latouche-Tréville
         Birth of future admiral Bruix

1761   Birth of future admirals Cosmao-Kerjulien, Decrès, Linois and Perrée

1762   Birth of future admirals Émeriau and Troude

1763   Peace of Paris ends Seven Years War.
         Birth of future admirals Magon, Villeneuve and Willaumez

1764   Birth of future admiral Ver Huell

1766   Birth of future admiral Lhermitte

1768   Birth of future admirals Baste and Hamelin

1769   Birth of future Emperor Napoleon

1774   Accession of King Louis XVI

1775   Birth of future admiral Duperré

1778   France enters American Revolutionary War against Britain.
         27 July: Battle of Ushant – Émeriau and Magon
         18 December: Battle of St Lucia – Truguet

1779   4 July: French capture of Grenada – Émeriau
         6 July: Battle of Grenada – Émeriau, Ganteaume, Martin and Missiessy
         9 October: French repulse at Savannah – Émeriau, Ganteaume, Martin, Missiessy and Truguet

1780   17 April, 26 June: Battle of Martinique – Sercey and Troude
1781   5 August: Battle of Dogger Bank – Ver Huell
            5 September: Battle of Chesapeake Bay – Brueys, Bruix, Decrès,
            Lhermitte, Magon and Villeneuve
1782   27 January: French capture of St Kitts – Brueys, Émeriau
            17 February: Battle of Madras – Villaret-Joyeuse
            12 April: Battle of Provédien – Villaret-Joyeuse
            12 April: Battle of the Saints – Bruix, Decrès, Émeriau, Magon and
            Villeneuve
            6 July: Battle of Negapatam – Villaret-Joyeuse
            3 September: French capture of Trincomalee – Villaret-Joyeuse
1782–83   Franco-Spanish 'Great Siege' of Gibraltar – Missiessy, Troude
1783   Peace of Paris ends American Revolutionary War
1784   Birth of future admiral Jérôme Bonaparte
1789   14 July: French Revolution begins; fall of the Bastille
1792   10 August: French monarchy overthrown
            22 September: First Republic proclaimed
            26 September: Toulon fleet attacks Nice, Montalban, Villafranca,
            Oneglia – Brueys, Cosmao-Kerjulien, Hamelin, Latouche-Tréville,
            Truguet and Villeneuve
1793   15–16 February: Failure of Toulon fleet's attack on Cagliari, Sardinia
            – Brueys, Cosmao-Kerjulien, Hamelin, Latouche-Tréville, Truguet and
            Villeneuve
            September: Mutinies in French Atlantic fleet – Villaret-Joyeuse
            24 October: Capture of first British warship in home waters, frigate
            Thames – Lhermitte
1794   Campaign and Battle of First of June – Émeriau, Ganteaume, Hamelin,
            Lhermitte, Linois, Renaudin, Troude and Villaret-Joyeuse
1795   14 March: Battle of Cape Noli, Genoa Gulf – Cosmao-Kerjulien,
            Hamelin, Martin and Perrée
            23 June: Battle of Groix – Bruix, Linois, Villaret-Joyeuse
            13 July: Battle of Fréjus [*Hyères*] – Cosmao-Kerjulien, Ganteaume,
            Martin and Renaudin
            7 September: Capture of British Levant convoy, recapture of *Censeur*
            – Hamelin
1796   Toulon fleet sends battle squadron to Atlantic – Decrès, Émeriau,
            Ganteaume and Villeneuve
            December: Failed French invasion of Ireland – Bruix, Émeriau, Linois
            and Truguet
1796–99   Indian Ocean cruise of French frigate squadron – Lhermitte, Magon,
            Sercey and Willaumez

1797   July: French capture of Ionian Islands – Brueys and Perrée

1798   June: French capture of Malta – Brueys and Émeriau

1 August: Battle of Aboukir Bay ['The Nile'] – Decrès, Ganteaume, Émeriau and Villeneuve; Brueys killed in action

July–November: Bonaparte's conquest of Egypt supported by Nile flotilla under Perrée

1799   February–May: Bonaparte's invasion of Syria supported by frigate squadron under Perrée

April–August: 'Bruix's Cruise' from Brest to Mediterranean and back – Bruix, Cosmao-Kerjulien and Linois

18 June: Perrée's frigate squadron captured off Toulon

August–October: Bonaparte's return from Egypt to France achieved by Ganteaume

24 December: Bonaparte becomes First Consul after the *coup d'état* of *Brumaire*

1800   18 February: Perrée killed during failed relief of Malta

31 March: Decrès captured in last fight of *Guillaume-Tell*

March–July: Prolonged cruise by Toulon fleet fails to relieve Army of Egypt – Bonaparte, Ganteaume and Troude

Surrender of Malta garrison – Baste and Villeneuve

1801   6 July: Repulse of Saumarez and capture of *Hannibal* at Algeciras;

12–13 July: Battle of the Gut of Gibraltar – Linois and Troude

15–16 August: Repulse of Nelson at Boulogne – Latouche-Tréville

1 October: Anglo-French preliminary peace treaty signed

1802–3   Treaty of Amiens

1801–3   Nicolas Baudin's scientific expedition to Australia – Hamelin

1801–3   All French fleets support campaign to reconquer Saint-Domingue – Baste, Bonaparte, Cosmao-Kerjulien, Duperré, Émeriau, Ganteaume, Latouche-Tréville, Magon, Troude, Villaret-Joyeuse and Willaumez

1803   6 March: French squadron sails for Indian Ocean under Linois

1803–5   French flotilla for the invasion of England concentrated at Boulogne – Baste, Duperré, Hamelin, Magon and Ver Huell

1805   2 June: Capture of Diamond Rock – Cosmao-Kerjulien

22 July: Battle of Cape Finisterre Villeneuve, Magon and Cosmao-Kerjulien

21 October: Battle of Trafalgar – Villeneuve, Magon and Cosmao-Kerjulien

1805–7   Atlantic war cruise by Brest fleet squadron – Bonaparte, Duperré, Willaumez; and by Lorient squadron – Lhermitte

1806   13 March: Capture of *Marengo* – Linois

xxii • NAPOLEON'S ADMIRALS

1808   22 March: Frigate action off Île de Groix – Duperré
1809   14–17 April: Battle of Îles des Saintes, Guadeloupe – Troude
1810   20–28 August: Battle of Grand-Port, Mauritius – Duperré, Hamelin
1813   December: Defence of Rotterdam – Truguet
1814   April: Defence of Den Helder – Ver Huell – and Venice – Duperré

The admirals' names are listed against the actions and battles they were involved in.

The Constitutional Monarchy, 1789–1792

Admiral Laurent-Jean-François Truguet (1752–1839)

Between Louis XVI's acceptance of the Tricolour on 17 July 1789, and the fall of the monarchy on 10 August 1792, ten French naval captains – le Gardeur de Tilly, d'Entrecasteaux, Morard de Galles, Thévenard, Flottes, Grimouard, Lavilléon, Rivière, Saint-Félix, and Truguet – were promoted to admiral's rank. They were the last admirals promoted in the pre-Republican French *marine d'état*, and Laurent-Jean-François Truguet was by far the most successful of them.

By 1789 Truguet had already made his name as a gallant and intelligent junior officer. He went on to carry out the first French naval operation of the Revolutionary

Truguet. Lithograph by Antoine Maurin, c.1835. (Wikimedia Commons)

War. Truguet survived imprisonment and the threat of the guillotine under the Terror, became Navy Minister and Ambassador to Madrid under the Directory, then a Councillor of State and combined Atlantic fleet commander under the Consulate, and resigned in protest against the proclamation of the Empire in 1804. Although captured by the Allies while defending Rotterdam for the Emperor in 1813, he was showered with honours by the returning Bourbons in 1814. In his later years Truguet became the Grand Old Man of the French Navy, emulating the aged Marshal Soult with the Army: a revered living link with the great years of the Republic and Empire.

Truguet was one of several future French admirals who had a naval father, a commodore in Louis XV's *marine d'état*. Truguet was born at Toulon on 10 January 1752, which made him too young to experience the French defeats and humiliations of the Seven Years War (1756–63), and in his prime for the British defeats and humiliations of the American Revolutionary War (1778–83). He had to pay for this timing with slow promotion in the 15 years of peace between the latter wars. He first went to sea as a cadet *garde de la marine* in June 1765, but despite an unbroken run of appointments to a sequence of frigates and ships of the line, it was not until October 1773 that he was commissioned lieutenant (*enseigne de vaisseau*), attached to the Toulon naval base.

As with many other young French naval officers, Truguet's career took off with France's entry into the American war against Britain. In the ship of the line *Hector*, he served in American waters under the leading French commanders – d'Estaing, de Guichen, de Grasse, Vaudreuil – and was promoted commander (*lieutenant de vaisseau*) on 13 March 1779. Fighting at his commander's side, Truguet was badly wounded and created *Chevalier de Saint-Louis* for saving d'Estaing's life during the desperate French attempt to storm Savannah in October 1779, and was invalided home. After serving in the ships of the line *Languedoc* and *Citoyen* from June 1780 to June 1783, Truguet was promoted *major de vaisseau*, senior commander: that hybrid rank of the Navy between frigate captain (*capitaine de frégate*) and Post Captain (*capitaine de vaisseau*).

On 30 August 1784, Truguet took command of the brig *Tartelon*, bound for an 18-month hydrographic survey cruise in the Dardanelles and the Sea of Marmara. When he had completed this work, Truguet made his first essays in diplomacy, negotiating with Egypt's Mameluke rulers for French trade privileges on the overland route to Suez and the Red Sea route to India. While at Constantinople in 1787, Truguet published a naval service treatise (*Traité de la Marine Pratique*) before leaving *Tartelon* in December 1788, after four creative and fulfilling years.

When it came, Truguet's advancement to flag rank came fast. On 21 September 1791 he was promoted Captain Second Class, with effect from 1 January 1792, and was promoted again, to rear-admiral, on 1 July 1792. At Toulon he hoisted his flag in *Tonnant* on 30 August 1792, and after the provisional republican government's declaration of war on the Kingdom of Sardinia[1] (16 September) he sailed with nine of the line to bombard and land troops at Nice, Montalban, Villafranca, and Oneglia.

But these were comparatively easy targets, well within the capability of the Toulon fleet. The capture of the Sardinian capital Cagliari, ordered by the new Republican Convention and dutifully attempted by Truguet in February 1793, failed, and he was replaced in command of the Toulon fleet by the newly-promoted Rear-Admiral Trogoff. At least this spared Truguet from the agonizing decision of which side to back during the revolt and reconquest of his native city, Toulon (August–December 1793), but not from being stripped of his rank and imprisoned by the Committee of Public Safety in February 1794. He was not released until the fall of Robespierre on ninth *Thermidor* (27 July) of that year.

The newly-formed Directorate not only restored Truguet to his rank, but advanced him to vice-admiral on 26 May 1795 and then (11 November 1795) appointed him

Minister for the Navy and the Colonies. In this post he was ordered to plan the most audacious operation ever envisaged for the Republican French Navy: a concerted blow at the two most vulnerable sectors of the British Empire, Ireland and India. Villaret-Joyeuse was to sortie from Brest and carry the army of General Hoche to a landing in Ireland. Villaret was then to sail for the Indian Ocean with his eight best ships of the line; embark the troops taken out to Île-de-France (Mauritius) by Sercey; land them in India to reinforce Tipu Sultan in his war with the British; join forces with Sercey to mop up Britain's trade on the Malabar and Coromandel coasts; and finally assist the Republican Dutch in their efforts to reconquer the East Indies.

It is easy to ridicule this scheme as pure fantasy, but, if attempted, it would certainly have stretched Britain's naval resources to the limit. In the early 1780s, Suffren and his modest battle fleet had proved how vulnerable the British could be to energetic French naval pressure in Indian waters. On their showing, Sercey, in partnership with Villaret, might have proved worthy successors to Suffren. But in Villaret, Truguet had to deal with a seasoned fleet commander who was – as the First of June campaign had proved in 1794 – acutely aware of the art of the possible, given the French Navy's chronic inexperience in long-term operations at sea. Caught between the sound professional objections of Villaret and the demands of his political masters for a great naval *coup*, Truguet compromised. He cancelled the Indies operation, replaced Villaret with Morard de Galles, and concentrated on the invasion of Ireland.

Morard proved to have even less faith in the Irish venture (December 1796–January 1797) than Villaret, but the real cause of its failure was weather of an unprecedented vileness, even for the season, which made it impossible to land a single French soldier on Irish soil. Although Truguet escaped direct censure for the fiasco, he was replaced as Navy Minister in July 1797, by Pléville le Pelley, and in October was appointed French Ambassador to Madrid. This was a post in which he did well, with his diplomatic skills and *Ancien Régime* manners proving highly acceptable to the Spanish authorities.

On being relieved in July 1798, however, Truguet took his time in returning to France. This proved unwise, for with an allied Second Coalition already formed to bring down the Republic, and Austrian and Russian armies poised to overrun Italy, capture Switzerland and invade France in the crisis year of 1799, any unauthorized behaviour by senior French officers was suspicious. Truguet paid for his leisurely return from Spain by having his name struck from the Navy List and being temporarily exiled to Holland.

After Bonaparte's accession to power as First Consul (November 1799) Truguet was recalled to France, and, on 28 June 1801, he was appointed to command the Franco-Spanish combined fleet at Cadiz. He also received a political mark of favour from the new *régime*: his appointment as Councillor of State (20 September 1801). Any hopes Truguet had of taking his fleet into battle were wrecked by the

Treaty of Amiens (1802–3), after which younger men were chosen for the major fleet commands.

Napoleon appointed Truguet Commander of Naval Forces at Brest in September 1803, and promoted him full admiral in March 1804. Two months later, however, Truguet resigned from his duties with a courageous letter protesting at the proclamation of the new French Empire. As he handed over the Brest fleet to Ganteaume, Truguet laconically assured Napoleon that it was ready to sail whenever the Emperor gave the word – *'un mot, et l'armée est à voile'* – 'one word, and the fleet's under way'.

This should have been the end of Truguet's career, but in July 1809 he was recalled from retirement to take over the remnants of the Rochefort squadron from Rear-Admiral Zacharie Allemand, after the devastating British fireship attack in the Île d'Aix roads. Truguet was subsequently appointed Maritime Prefect of the Dutch Coast (March 1811), in which post he was taken prisoner during the defence of Rotterdam in December 1813.

The first Bourbon Restoration of 1814 brought Truguet the award of the Grand Cordon of the Legion of Honour and the title of *Comte*. He remained in France during the 'Hundred Days' of Napoleon's return in March–June 1815, but Napoleon left him without employment. Back on the throne after Waterloo, Louis XVIII appointed Truguet supreme commander at Brest, awarded him the Grand Cross of Saint-Louis, and made him a Peer of France. The old admiral's final honours came from the hand of King Louis-Philippe, who made Truguet a full admiral in November 1831 and, on 10 October 1832, awarded him the baton of a Marshal of France with Admiral's insignia.

Truguet was the only one of the ten admirals appointed by the Constitutional Monarchy of 1789–92 to have his name inscribed on the *Arc de Triomphe*. This monument to the great commanders of the Republic and Empire was completed in 1836 – three years before Truguet's death on 26 December 1839.

Note

1 Ruled by the House of Savoy with its Piedmontese heartland astride the Ligurian Alps, its capital at Turin and Sardinia as its largest offshore province.

PART 2

The Convention, 1792–1795

Vice-Admiral Louis-René-Madeleine-Levassor, *Comte de* Latouche-Tréville (1745–1804)

The career of Latouche-Tréville, the inheritor of not one, but two aristocratic titles, a Count of the *Ancien Régime* and Knight of the Order of Saint-Louis, goes far to disprove the myth that the French Navy was decerebrated by the emigration of all its aristocratic officers in the early years of the French Revolution. He was unique: the only French admiral to hand Nelson a defeat and, by 1804, the fleet commander entrusted with making possible Napoleon's invasion of England. But for his unexpected death later that year, Latouche-Tréville, not Villeneuve, would have been Nelson's opponent in the last great encounter between the French and British battle fleets.

Latouche-Tréville. Lithograph by Maurin, c.1835. (Wikimedia Commons)

For Louis-René-Madeleine-Levassor, the future *comte* de Latouche-Tréville, born at Rochefort on 3 June 1745, a naval career was virtually inevitable. His father and his uncle were both navy captains, and both subsequently became admirals. Yet, despite these powerful family connections, it still took Latouche-Tréville ten years to reach the lowest commissioned officer's rank. The professional demands of the service, most obviously the mathematics required for navigation, meant that nepotism alone only played a minor part in nudging a young officer up the ladder of naval promotion (although it might certainly help increase his experience of time at sea). In this respect, the French and British navies were similar.

Latouche-Tréville joined the Navy as a 13-year-old cadet *garde de la marine* in February 1758, and first went to sea in his uncle's ship of the line *Dragon*. In her he saw his first battle: the shattering defeat inflicted on the French by Admiral Lord Edward Hawke in Quiberon Bay (20 November 1759), in which *Dragon* escaped from the wreck of the French fleet. As a Boy First Class (*garçon major*), he transferred to his uncle's next command, the ship of the line *Louise*, which spent six months (July 1760–January 1761) under British blockade in the Charente estuary at Rochefort. Further service in the ships of the line *Intrépide* and *Tonnant* (1762) was interspersed with an exciting summer in the gunboats *Mélanide* and *Couleuvre*, in which he took part in two actions against blockading British warships.

After the Peace of Paris ended the Seven Years War in 1763, Latouche-Tréville, still under his uncle's eye, had the luck to be constantly employed. The next five busy years included a cruise to Guiana and Saint-Domingue in the *flûte Garonne* (September 1763–July 1764). He got in a second Caribbean voyage to Martinique in 1767, before his commission as *enseigne de vaisseau* finally came through in September 1768. By this time Latouche-Tréville had already decided on a spell of service with the colonial army, first with the infantry, then the cavalry. He served as *aide-de-camp* to the Governors of Martinique and the Windward and Leeward Islands, and became a captain of dragoons in the *régiment de la Rochefoucauld,* before transferring back to the Navy in September 1772 with the rank of fireship captain (*capitaine de brûlot).*

Two years of port duty at Rochefort (1773–75) were followed by a posting to the *flûte Courtier* (February 1776) and a 'cloak and dagger' voyage: running 100,000 *livres* of gunpowder to the rebel American colonists (a premature fruit of the Franco-American alliance formally signed two years later). Promoted *lieutenant de vaisseau* in May 1777, Latouche-Tréville got as his first warship command the 20-gun corvette *Rossignol* (April 1778–January 1779), escorting merchant shipping in the Gulf of Gascony. For his capture of two privateers and three merchant ships, he was created *Chevalier de Saint-Louis* in October 1779.

Further recognition came with a frigate command: the 32-gun *Hermione*, in which Latouche-Tréville sailed with the squadron of Rear-Admiral Charles-René Sochet Destouches, returning Lafayette to America in March–April 1780. *Hermione* was then detached to patrol off Long Island and prey on shipping bound for the British northern base of New York. After taking two easy prizes, Latouche-Tréville sighted four more sails on 7 June, and steered to intercept. They turned out to be the British frigate *Iris* with three sloops in company. A brisk action ensued at close range, with Latouche-Tréville taking a wound in the arm from a musket ball. He fought *Hermione* clear by dint of adroit ship-handling, but not before she had lost ten men killed and 37 wounded.

Back with Destouches' squadron based on Newport, Rhode Island, Latouche-Tréville got his next taste of action in March 1781. The focus of the war had shifted to Virginia where Washington's Patriot army, with its French allies ashore and afloat, was trying to prevent Lord Cornwallis from completing the British conquest of Virginia. The efforts of both sides to reinforce their armies in Virginia depended on the control of Chesapeake Bay, contested for the first time when Destouches sailed to support Lafayette with eight of the line, and *Hermione* in company. Intercepted off Cape Henry on 26 March by nine of the line from Long Island, Destouches extricated his force by excellent manoeuvring, but his withdrawal enabled Cornwallis to receive his last reinforcements across Chesapeake Bay.

Months of stalemate ensued before the arrival of Admiral *Comte de* Grasse's battle fleet from the Caribbean in September won control of Chesapeake Bay, sealing the fate of Cornwallis's army at Yorktown. During this waiting time the French squadron at Newport was not idle. It despatched a two-frigate force – Commodore Jean-François La Pérouse's *Astrée* and Latouche-Tréville's *Hermione* – to raid the British convoy route to Canada. On 21 July 1781, off Cape Breton, Nova Scotia, they attacked a convoy of 13 ships sent to collect coal for shipment to Halifax. Although totally outmatched, the five-strong British escort fought back manfully and managed to save ten of their charges, with La Pérouse and Latouche-Tréville delivering their three prizes to Boston. This was Latouche-Tréville's last action in *Hermione.* He was recalled to France, his promotion to *capitaine de vaisseau* having been confirmed on 20 June 1781.

In the New Year of 1782, the French Navy purchased the 38-gun frigate *Aigle,* built at Saint-Malo as a privateer, and appointed Latouche-Tréville as her first captain. With the frigate *Gloire* as consort, he was entrusted in June 1782 with carrying 3 million *livres* in gold to America, as well as privateer officers and urgent despatches for Admiral *Marquis de* Vaudreuil's squadron. Having completed this mission, *Aigle* and *Gloire* fell in with the lone British 74 *Hector* on 5 September, and Latouche-Tréville attacked.[1] After a two-day running battle, *Hector* was left in a sinking condition by the two frigates, which were chased off their prey by the intervention of a British squadron.

Promisingly begun, the war cruise of *Aigle* and *Gloire* ended abruptly. On 15 September they were chased into the mouth of the Delaware by two British 74s, a frigate and two sloops. Refusing to accept blockade, Latouche-Tréville boldly ordered a breakout across the sand bars of the estuary on a falling tide. *Gloire* made it to the open sea but *Aigle* ran firmly aground, leaving Latouche-Tréville with no option but to strike his colours. He remained a prisoner of the British, first at New York and later in England, until the conclusion of peace in September 1783.[2]

Although Latouche-Tréville received no further seagoing commands in the six years before the Revolution, his career continued to advance. He was honoured with the Order of Cincinnatus in 1784 and successively appointed Adjutant Director of Ports and Arsenals, and Director General of Naval Auxiliary Gunners. When Louis XVI inaugurated the new naval base at Cherbourg in 1786, Latouche-Tréville had the honour of commanding the corvette which carried the King from Honfleur to Le Havre.

High on the Captains' List with an impressive fighting record, twice decorated and marked by royal favour, Latouche-Tréville was a respected ornament of France's *noblesse d'epée* (Nobles of the Sword) by the spring of 1789. In the elections for the *États généraux* (Estates General) he was returned as sole deputy for the nobility for

Montargis, and, on the night of 4 August 1789, he effectively embraced the cause of the Third Estate – now the self-styled 'National Assembly' – by voting for the abolition of the nobility's feudal privileges. He also sat in the Constituent Assembly but, unlike his naval contemporary Kersaint (subsequently guillotined), Latouche-Tréville took no further interest in Revolutionary politics. He returned to the Navy when the King accepted the constitution in September 1791 and the Constituent Assembly dissolved. A week after the fall of the monarchy, on 17 August 1792, Latouche-Tréville was appointed to command the ship of the line *Languedoc* at Brest.

On 4 September 1792, Latouche-Tréville sailed from Brest with four of the line to join Truguet's fleet at Toulon. He was promoted rear-admiral in the New Year's List of 1793, having taken part in the capture of Nice and the bombardment of Oneglia, and served as one of Truguet's squadron commanders during the subsequent failure at Cagliari (February 1793). He was next earmarked for the fleet command at Brest, but this was vetoed by 'People's Representatives' Laignelot and Lequinic. Latouche-Tréville was arrested as a suspect 'aristo' and imprisoned in La Force (15 September 1793–20 September 1794) throughout the zenith of the Jacobin Terror. He was reinstated by decree of the rump Committee of Public Safety in June 1795, and fully restored to his rear-admiral's rank by the new government, the Directory, in December of that year.

Although thus pronounced politically acceptable to the new regime, Latouche-Tréville was left without any active employment for the next four years. This spared him from any responsibility for the Irish fiasco of 1796–97, or for the annihilation of the Egyptian expeditionary battle fleet at the Nile in 1798. Given subsequent events, it is intriguing to speculate how Nelson would have fared if Latouche-Tréville, not Brueys, had commanded the French fleet and deployed it for battle on 1 August 1798. (Latouche-Tréville is unlikely to have left the fateful gap through which Nelson enveloped and crushed Brueys's battle line.) But by autumn 1799, Latouche-Tréville had been reduced to advertising himself for hire as a privateer captain.

Five months after the establishment of Bonaparte's Consulate in November 1799, Latouche-Tréville was finally recalled to active service. After a few weeks as a divisional commander in the Brest fleet, he was appointed (30 April 1800) to the command of the entire 'naval army' at Brest: the appointment of which he had been robbed seven years earlier. With the main French effort for 1800 being the land offensives against Austria in Italy and southern Germany, there was no prospect of any naval ventures against England. But once Austria had been knocked out of the war by the French victories at Marengo and Hohenlinden, Bonaparte intensified the pressure on an isolated and war-weary Britain.

By making ostentatious preparations for a cross-Channel assault in the Dover Narrows, Bonaparte hoped to push the British into negotiating for the temporary peace which was now his main objective. He ordered an 'invasion force' to assemble at Boulogne with maximum publicity, giving the command of this flotilla of brigs and gunboats to Latouche-Tréville. The British Government took it seriously, forming a special service squadron under Nelson to cope with this apparent invasion threat.

Not content with waiting for the Boulogne flotilla to put to sea, Nelson determined to destroy it at its anchorage. Latouche-Tréville had made excellent preparations, however, chaining his line of 24 gunboats together and insisting on maximum vigilance – heightened after Nelson's abortive shelling of the Boulogne defences on 3–4 August – by day and night. When Nelson pressed ahead with his attack on the night of 15–16 August, it was decisively beaten off: 12 British boats sunk, 44 men killed and 126 wounded. Not a single French craft was taken, and the defenders lost only ten killed and 30 wounded. Latouche-Tréville had handed Bonaparte a victory out of all proportion to its modest scope. By the end of August 1801, the despondent British Government had entered peace negotiations, a cessation of hostilities being agreed on 31 October.

Napoleon's intention was to exploit this breathing-space by taking up the options won from Spain in his San Ildefonso Treaty of October 1800. This treaty's centrepiece was the transfer of Spanish Louisiana to France, giving Napoleon the vision of a new French transatlantic empire. Former French colonies such as Martinique and Guadeloupe could be recovered from Britain by negotiation. The establishment of the new empire would begin with a French expedition to recover Saint-Domingue from the *regime* of freed slaves headed by Toussaint l'Ouverture and return them to slavery.

Preparations for the Saint-Domingue expedition began as soon as the British blockade ended with the 1801 armistice. Latouche-Tréville's contribution to the armada commanded by Villaret-Joyeuse was the Rochefort squadron, of which he took command in December 1801. On the 14th of that month, General Leclerc's expeditionary force sailed for Saint-Domingue in two divisions. The main body of 23,000 troops was conveyed by Villaret's fleet: ten French and five Spanish ships of the line (the latter commanded by Admiral Gravina), six frigates, four corvettes and two transports. The remaining 3,000 troops sailed in Latouche-Tréville's Rochefort squadron: six of the line, six frigates, two corvettes and two dispatch vessels – the biggest force he had yet commanded. His senior captains included future admirals Daniel Savary, Pierre-François Violette, and Jean-Baptiste-Philibert Willaumez, with a fourth in the person of the 17-year-old Midshipman (*aspirant*) Jérôme Bonaparte, serving in the ship of the line *Foudroyant*.

After making a separate passage, Latouche-Tréville's squadron joined the main body off Saint-Domingue on 29 January 1802. The main landings went in on 6 February and secured the capital, Port-au-Prince. Once the troops were ashore, they found themselves trapped in the purgatory of an endless guerrilla campaign, scourged by yellow fever. Leclerc himself died of it in November 1802; Latouche-Tréville nearly followed him, but his recovery was not complete and left him with lingering symptoms which helped kill him 12 months later.

From this fateful sideshow of a campaign, Latouche-Tréville was liberated by his appointment (6 July 1803) of the Toulon fleet. Returning to France in October, he took up his new command in the knowledge that the Toulon fleet would be making no more grandiose forays into the eastern Mediterranean. When it next sailed its destination would be the Atlantic, the ultimate objective being a massive concentration of naval force in the Channel for the invasion of England. In the meantime, Latouche-Tréville must avoid any unnecessary encounters with Nelson's blockading warships, unless he could do so in overwhelming force.

By spring 1804, despite his worsening health, Latouche-Tréville had taught Nelson to take no risks with his inshore frigates, on 24 May chasing off a close British reconnaissance of Toulon by sailing progressively stronger forces. On 14 June, to bring in two frigates and a corvette threatened by Nelson off the Hyères Islands, Latouche-Tréville sortied from Toulon with eight of the line and five frigates. As he only had five of the line in company, Nelson hoped to lure the French onto the rest of his force over the horizon, but Latouche-Tréville refused to oblige. After making a feint in Nelson's direction, he withdrew to Toulon, publishing a despatch stating that 'I pursued until nightfall; he ran to the south-east'. Implying that he had made the British admiral run away was a deliberate exaggeration, made to provoke Nelson still further, and in this it succeeded beyond expectation. With his vanity outraged, Nelson volleyed angry denials in all directions and kept a copy of the offending dispatch, vowing to make Latouche-Tréville eat it if he captured him.

Nelson's anger did not abate when Napoleon made Latouche-Tréville a Grand Officer of the Legion of Honour on 14 June 1804. A further honour followed on 6 July: the title of Inspector of the Mediterranean Coasts. The duel of vigilance between the rival admirals was still in full swing when, on 19 August 1804, Latouche-Tréville died of his illness aboard his flagship, the new 80-gun *Bucentaure*. He was 59 years old.

Notes

1 A decision to be compared with Sercey's six-frigate attack on two British 74s in July 1796 (p. 42).
2 Vaudreuil reported Latouche-Tréville to the Navy Ministry for having a kept woman (*'créature'*) on board with him, passing her off as his wife to his British captors. Such immorality, Vaudreuil feared, could well be offensive to France's staid American allies (*'un pays aux bonnes moeurs'*).

Vice-Admiral Edouard-Thomas de Burgues, *Comte de* Missiessy (1756–1837)

Respectively aged 37 and 35, Missiessy and Leissegues were by far the youngest captains promoted to Flag Rank under the Convention. They were the first of the 'second generation' of French Revolutionary admirals: those born too late to see service in the Seven Years War of 1756–63. Edouard-Thomas de Burgues, *Comte de* Missiessy, was born at Toulon on 23 April 1756. His father was a naval officer, and it was in his father's ship of the line *Altier* that the young Missiessy was entered as a 10-year-old Volunteer in April 1766.

Most of Missiessy's first ten years of service were spent within the Mediterranean, in the Toulon fleet's frigates. As a Boy First Class

Missiessy. Lithograph by Maurin, c.1835. (Wikimedia Commons)

(*garçon-major*) he experienced two prolonged cruises to the Levant in *Engageante* (April 1773–January 1774 and May 1774–February 1775). A third Levant cruise (October 1775–September 1776) followed in the frigate *Flore*, with Missiessy serving as Guard to the Colours (*garde du pavillon*). In April 1777, newly commissioned lieutenant (*enseigne de vaisseau*), he sailed in the frigate *Sultane* on a mission charged with protecting merchant commerce from those perennial pests of the Mediterranean sea lanes, the Barbary Corsairs of Tunisia, Algeria and Morocco.

One of the most crucial appointments in Missiessy's career came in March 1778, when he transferred to the ship of the line *Vaillant*, bound for America with the battle fleet of d'Estaing. In *Vaillant* he served in all the early actions of the American Revolutionary War – off Newport, St Lucia, Grenada, and the ill-fated attack on Savannah – before returning to Lorient in December 1779. In February 1780 he sailed again for American waters in the frigate *Surveillante*. This was another important commission during which Missiessy received his promotion to commander (*lieutenant de vaisseau*) on 9 May 1781.

Missiessy's first command followed his return to Brest in December 1781: the cutter *Pygmée*, in March 1782. It was abruptly cut short by his capture by the British on 27 July 1782, but he had the luck to be exchanged after a brief spell of imprisonment at Deal, and sent back to France.

In September 1782 he went back to sea as Second Officer in the ship of the line *Réfléchi*, transferring to the ship of the line *Censeur* off Cadiz, in the dying stages of the 'Great Siege' of Gibraltar. Home at Toulon in April 1783, Missiessy returned to sea in command of the transports *Guyane* and *Durance*, supporting the French naval squadron sent to the Baltic in May 1786, and from August 1789 to January 1792 he commanded the frigates *Belette* and *Modeste* in the Mediterranean. Crowned on 1 January 1791 by promotion to Post Rank as *capitaine de vaisseau*, honoured in April 1785 by being created *Chevalier de Saint-Louis*, Missiessy's busy and effective career had returned after 20 years to its beginnings, with the frigates of the Mediterranean fleet.

After his promotion to rear-admiral on 1 January 1793, Missiessy was appointed to Truguet's fleet at Toulon, flying his flag in the ship of the line *Centaure*. The other squadrons were commanded by Latouche-Tréville and Trogoff, who had been seven years senior to Missiessy on the Captains' List. On 21 May 1793, Missiessy was ordered ashore and jailed, as an 'aristo' and political suspect, but was released on 30 June. During his imprisonment, on 25 May, Truguet had been replaced in command of the Toulon fleet by Trogoff.

In August 1793 Toulon revolted against Republican rule, declared for the dead King's son, Louis XVII, and called on the British for help. It was a traumatic event in Missiessy's life, but he did not side with his native city and abandon the cause of the Republic. Instead he abandoned his command and adopted the life of an exile in Italy. He did not return to France until May 1795, when he was arrested again, and his conduct was subjected to a court of enquiry. Although acquitted and released on 25 August 1795, Missiessy was denied a seagoing command and spent the next five years in Paris, first attached to the Department of Charts and Maps, and from 1796 as Director of the School of Naval Construction.

In 1801–1802 Missiessy became the object of a tug of war between his former chief Truguet and the Navy Ministry in Paris. In June 1801 Truguet, commanding the combined Franco-Spanish fleet at Cadiz, chose Missiessy as his chief of staff. But during the Treaty of Amiens, Missiessy was recalled to Paris and appointed 'Maritime Prefect', responsible for all port facility works servicing the Cadiz fleet. Maritime Prefects were subsequently appointed for all naval bases. In July 1802 Missiessy was appointed Maritime Prefect for the second *arrondissement* at Le Havre, but, on 24 October, Truguet successfully indented for Missiessy's services again, this time as commander of the Brest fleet's second squadron. In this post he remained until 10 September 1804, when he was appointed commander-in-chief of the Rochefort squadron.

Although dwarfed in size by the fleets of Brest and Toulon, the modest battle fleet at Rochefort was the trigger of Napoleon's grand design to make possible the invasion of England. The idea was to repeat the concentration of ships of the line achieved by Bruix in 1799, delivering a force of 40-odd battleships to the Dover Straits to safeguard the crossing of the invasion fleet. The Rochefort squadron's objective was the West Indies, there to reinforce the French garrisons of Martinique, Guadeloupe and Saint-Domingue, then to launch the conquest of British Dominica, St Lucia and St Kitts-Nevis. Within 35 days of his arrival in the West Indies, Missiessy would be joined by Villeneuve's Franco-Spanish battle fleet from Toulon, Cartagena, and Cadiz. Once they had been joined by Ganteaume's fleet from Brest, they would recross the Atlantic and arrive off Boulogne in overwhelming strength.

Missiessy sailed from Rochefort on 11 January 1805 with five ships of the line, three frigates and two brig-corvettes. His force included General Lagrange and 3500 troops with their artillery, extra stocks of weapons and other military stores for the French garrisons in the West Indies. The gales which had blown the British blockaders off station kept the Rochefort squadron pinned to the French coast for five days before it could get out to sea, but it then made an unmolested Atlantic crossing, arriving at Martinique on 20 February.

Once the troops, weapons and stores had been landed, Missiessy and Lagrange conferred with Villaret-Joyeuse, Captain-General of Martinique since April 1802, on the most suitable plan of campaign. The Diamond Rock, only 2 miles off the coast of Martinique, had been held by the British since January 1804. The heavy naval guns mounted on HMS *Diamond Rock*, as this impudent outpost was rated in the British Navy List, forced French shipping to and from Martinique to make wide detours, and its continued retention by the British exasperated Napoleon. Unfortunately for himself, Missiessy failed to persuade Lagrange and Villaret to open the campaign by recapturing the Diamond Rock. They decided instead to assault Dominica, where Missiessy landed Lagrange's troops on 22 February. The tiny British garrison put up a ferocious resistance, and when Lagrange failed to storm Prince Rupert Fort, he decided on evacuation rather than a prolonged siege – in spite of the defenders being outnumbered by over three to one. The crestfallen French reembarked on 25 February, after destroying all the British defences within reach, spiking all captured guns and burning the warehouses.

The next objective was the reinforcement of Guadeloupe, where Missiessy landed more troops and stores on the 28th. He sailed again on 2 March, and between the 5th and the 10th landed troops which destroyed defences and extorted sizeable ransoms from the British settlers of St Kitts, Nevis, and Montserrat. This foray gained little more than a useful cash windfall of £25,000, which at least temporarily ensured the pay of the French garrisons in the West Indies; but when he returned to Martinique Missiessy found the brig *Palinure* waiting for him with gloomy despatches. The assault on England was back on the shelf, Villeneuve having returned to Toulon on 20 January, and the Rochefort squadron was recalled.

Even then, Missiessy did not sail for France before visiting Saint-Domingue and landing the last spare battalion of troops to reinforce the hard-pressed garrison of General Ferrand. He then set out to run the unbroken British blockade and did so with perfect success, returning to Rochefort with his force intact on 20 May. Missiessy had carried out his part of the campaign to the letter and had not been responsible for the outcome of the military operations, facts which Napoleon chose to ignore. Instead of putting the lion's share of the blame on Villeneuve for having failed to escape from the Mediterranean on schedule, the frustrated Emperor blamed Missiessy for not having recaptured the Diamond Rock. Missiessy was dismissed from command of the Rochefort squadron and replaced by Allemand, his second-in-command during the cruise.

Missiessy remained unemployed until February 1808, when he was appointed to command the Scheldt Flotilla. He was promoted vice-admiral on 9 March 1809 and successfully beat off the British attacks on Antwerp in July–September 1809. For this achievement he was appointed commander-in-chief of the Northern Coasts and created a Count of the Empire, with an annual rent of 20,000 francs from the imperial domains of Illyria and Piedmont, on 23 February 1811.

Ironically, Missiessy's very success in this last command helped seal the fate of the Empire as the allies closed in on France in the New Year of 1814. Even after the natural frontiers of the Rhine and Pyrenees had been breached, Napoleon was offered the chance of remaining Emperor if he surrendered the Low Countries and Antwerp – but as long as Antwerp held out under Missiessy, Napoleon was determined to fight on for the retention of this strategic lynchpin. The returning Bourbons did not condemn Missiessy for having thus contributed to prolonging the war. Louis XVIII awarded him the Grand Cross of the Legion of Honour in August 1814.

Missiessy was not employed during the 'Hundred Days' of March–June 1815, and further honours and appointments followed after the second Bourbon restoration. His first appointment after Waterloo was as Maritime Prefect of Toulon, where he served as naval commander-in-chief from January 1816. After service on the Council of Admiralty, he ended his active career as Commander-in-Chief of the Navy on 17 September 1824. Created Knight Commander of the Holy Spirit in June 1827, he was finally placed on the Retired List on 23 April 1832, enjoying five years of retirement before dying at his birthplace of Toulon, aged 81, on 24 March 1837.

Vice-Admiral Louis-Thomas, *Comte* Villaret-Joyeuse (1748–1812)

During the height of the Jacobin Terror (1793–94), one of the deadliest accusations which could be levelled at a French serving officer was that he was an 'aristo' – of aristocratic birth – and that his loyalty to the Republic must therefore be suspect. This was doubly ironic in the case of Louis-Thomas Villaret de Joyeuse, who down to the outbreak of the French Revolution had assiduously polished his claims to aristocratic lineage – and yet who, in the high summer of 1794, became the man who lost a great sea battle and in so doing saved the French Republic.

His family was Gascon, from Auch (Gers), where he was born on 29 May 1748. Louis-Thomas's grandfather had worked at

Villaret-Joyeuse. Lithograph by Maurin, c.1835. (Wikimedia Commons)

Auch as a skilled artisan, a cabinetmaker, under the name of Villaret. His father, a soldier who had prospered in the royal service, had added 'de Joyeuse' to the family name. Down to 1789 Louis-Thomas usually signed himself 'Dejoyeuse', abbreviating his surname to 'Villaret-Joyeuse' and finally to the original 'Villaret' after 1792 and the birth of the Republic.

French researchers have failed to unearth any documentary evidence for the dramatic tale of how the 15-year-old Villaret-Joyeuse joined the *Gendarmes du Roi* as a cadet in 1763, only to leave hastily, very much under a cloud, after fighting a duel in which he killed his opponent. The source of the story, concocted 20-odd years after the event, could well have been Villaret himself. By the early 1780s he was already a naval officer of proven worth, hungry for promotion, and could plausibly have felt that the aura of having emerged victorious from a teenage 'affair of honour' could do his reputation in aristocratic circles nothing but good. The duel story would also help explain why he had to lie low before joining the Navy at Rochefort – not as a gentleman cadet *garde de la marine* but as a Volunteer – on 2 May 1765.

Villaret's first two voyages in Navy service were to South America and the Caribbean – to Cayenne in the *flûte Nourrice* (1765–66), and carrying troops to the West Indies garrisons in the *flûte Éléphant* (1766–67). He then obtained a sub-lieutenant's commission in the *Compagnie des Indes,* in which service he made two further Caribbean voyages, to Saint-Domingue, between 1768 and 1770. These early voyages gave Villaret the accumulation of sea time necessary to pass the examinations qualifying him as a watchkeeping officer: the essential foundation for a career leading to independent command, Post Rank, and – ultimately – to an admiral's flag.

Villaret's return to Navy service in the spring of 1773 took him to the Indian Ocean for the next eight years, there to emerge as one of Suffren's most trusted officers in the epic sea battles of 1781–83. Still lacking any naval commissioned rank, Villaret's company service had made him a competent watchkeeping officer with the status of a naval *enseigne de vaisseau,* or sub-lieutenant. On 20 April 1773 he embarked at Brest in the Navy *flûte Fortune,* bound for Île-de-France, Mauritius, remaining with her until January 1774. 11 years were to pass before he saw France again.

In June 1774, he was appointed second officer in the *Coromandel,* flying the pendant of the naval commander at Île-de-France, the future admiral Armand Saint-Félix, who kept Villaret as his second officer in the frigate *Atalante* (1775–76). It was thanks to the recommendation of Saint-Félix that Villaret received his first naval promotion, to *lieutenant de frégate* (lieutenant-commander). In this rank, he served in the frigate *Pintade* (June–November 1778), before briefly commanding *Dauphine* from 10 November 1778 to 20 January 1779.

Villaret was serving in the ship of the line *Brillant* when, in October 1781, the battle fleet of the aggressive Bailli de Suffren arrived in the Indian Ocean. Within a week of his arrival at Île-de-France, Suffren appointed Villaret Fireship Captain (*capitaine des brûlots*), special duty requiring qualities of daring and ingenuity; and Villaret commanded the resoundingly-named fireship *Pulvérisateur* from 27 October 1781 to 26 September 1782. He took part in all three of the hard-fought battles with the British Admiral Hughes which preceded Suffren's capture of Trincomalee, Ceylon, on 31 August 1782: Madras (17 February), Provédien (12 April), and Negapatam (5 July). After Suffren's fourth battle, off Trincomalee on 3 September, he appointed Villaret captain of the frigate *Bellone* (26 September 1782).

On 7 April 1783 Villaret was picked by Suffren for a special mission. Suffren needed to alert the French squadron blockading Madras to the danger of being cut off by a more powerful British force. He gave Villaret the frigate *Naïade* and told him to get through to Madras at all costs, which meant running the gauntlet of the main British fleet. On 12 April Villaret had succeeded in getting within sight of his objective when he was brought to battle by the 64-gun British ship of the line *Sceptre*. After a five-hour ferocious action Villaret was forced to strike his colours, but he had achieved his mission and the French squadron escaped. Overwhelmed by the gallantry of *Naïade's* resistance, the British released Villaret who was promptly awarded the Grand Cross of the Order of Saint-Louis by Suffren and recommended for promotion to commander (*lieutenant de vaisseau*). On 29 June 1783, a ship under flag of truce from Madras brought Suffren the news that peace had been signed in Paris.

Before sailing from Trincomalee for Île-de-France and home on 6 October 1783, Suffren gave Villaret command of the frigate *Coventry* (12 September), which he brought back to Brest on 6 January 1785. With his promotion to *lieutenant de vaisseau* confirmed (15 July 1784), Villaret was appointed to command the frigate *Railleuse* at Brest (29 June–3 October 1785). But France's bankruptcy had been cemented by the cost of her five-year war with Britain and Villaret's career now fell victim to service cutbacks. He got no further command until October 1790, when he took the frigate *Prudente* on a voyage from Lorient to Saint-Domingue; and his long-awaited promotion to *capitaine de vaisseau* did not come through until 1 January 1792.

Now qualified for battleship command, Villaret was appointed to the 74-gun ship of the line *Trajan* (3 December 1792–26 October 1793), under Morard de Galles in the Brest fleet, in which all was far from well. Inactivity spread demoralisation through the fleet and Morard could do nothing to check it, particularly after his refusal to engage Lord Howe's fleet off Belle-Île on 31 July 1793. In September, Morard's fleet, still at anchorage inshore of Belle-Île, mutinied. The predictable result was Morard's dismissal as the Republican government suppressed the mutiny; and the all-powerful 'People's Representative' Jeanbon Saint-André recommended Villaret, as one of the very few captains to have kept his crew under firm discipline throughout the mutiny, to replace Morard in command of the Brest fleet. Villaret became Brest fleet commander on 14 October 1793, with his promotion to rear-admiral following on 16 December.

By the spring of 1794, Robespierre's dictatorship had become brilliantly successful at liquidating its political enemies and a total failure at keeping the nation fed. Disastrous harvests in 1793 had made nationwide famine imminent, and the Navy was the only state instrument capable of saving the regime by bringing in vital food supplies from America. The assembly of a relief convoy, laden primarily with grain, began in the late autumn of 1793 and in December Rear-Admiral Pierre-Jean Vanstabel was ordered to the Chesapeake with two of the line to command and escort the convoy. Numbering 117 sail, the convoy sailed on 11 April 1794. On 6 May, Rear-Admiral Nielly sailed from Rochefort with five of the line (including Villaret's former ship, *Trajan*) to act as a spearhead for Vanstabel and the convoy. Finally, on 16 May, flying his flag in the 120-gun *Montagne,* Villaret sailed from Brest with

25 of the line, charged with the mission of keeping the main British battle fleet under Lord Howe as far from the track of the convoy as possible.

Only two years before taking command at Brest, Villaret had still been awaiting his promotion to captain. That fact alone makes his supreme achievement in 1794 – nothing less than the salvation of the French Republic from famine, collapse and anarchy – all the more astonishing. Like Admiral Jellicoe with Britain's Grand Fleet in 1914, Villaret had become the only man who could 'lose the war in an afternoon' for France. Yet he had, in only six months of command, transformed an unseaworthy fleet shot through with mutiny into a fighting force capable of

- conducting an 11-day ocean cruise over 400 miles out into the Atlantic, then;
- fighting two days of sporadic actions followed by a major battle, then;
- spending another ten days of deliberate manoeuvring at sea, in ships crammed with sick and wounded, then;
- returning to base in triumph with its nation-saving mission fully accomplished.

It must also be remembered that Villaret sailed in May 1794 with Robespierre's personal assurance that failure would cost him his head. As if that were not burden enough, Villaret also sailed with the Republic's most ruthless political commissar, Jeanbon Saint-André, breathing down his neck as a passenger in his flagship *Montagne* – a day-to-day encumbrance which would have tested to destruction the mettle of Nelson himself. Saint-André had staked his own reputation in appointing Villaret, and knew that Villaret's was not the only head in danger. For both of them, it was a case of triumph or death.

From the moment that the rival fleets first clashed on 28 May, Villaret proved that he was not going to act merely as a passive decoy to Howe. He kept the French fleet together, manoeuvred with skill and vigour, and in the action of the 29th intervened in person to save two of his disabled ships, *Indomptable* and *Tyannicide,* from otherwise certain capture. At least he was spared any interference from Saint-André once the guns started firing. *'Ah! Le coquin!'* recalled Villaret years later. *'The moment the Queen [Queen Charlotte, Howe's flagship] attacked us, he went down below, and we didn't see him again for the whole battle.'*[2] On 30 May, Villaret was joined by Nielly's battle squadron, making good the detachment of three battle-damaged ships after the fighting of the 28th and 29th, and bringing the French fleet back up to 26 of the line. But Villaret now learned that Nielly had never made contact with Vanstabel's oncoming convoy, and that all was still to play for. The French were greatly helped by the problems Howe was having with several of his captains, leaving the fleets in contact but with no renewal of battle on the 30th or 31st. At last, on 1 June, Howe got what he wanted, a day of clear visibility, and headed in to attack at 0915 with the French fleet, deployed in line-ahead,[2] greeting him with a spirited fire.

When the main action petered out around 1230, the British had 11 ships which had lost at least one mast and the French 12. None of the latter had surrendered (some struck their colours to obtain a respite from fire, only to re-hoist them later); all were gamely trying to rejoin the main fleet under jury rig and continuing to fire at any British ship which came within range. Only one sank: Renaudin's *Vengeur*, battered, defenceless and flooding after a brutal four-hour duel with the *Brunswick*. As on the 29th, Villaret did all he could to support his disabled ships and managed to save half. Howe, 68 years old and physically exhausted after the past four days, concentrated on making sure of his six prizes rather than on pursuing Villaret's fleet which, nursing its cripples, drew off in good order.

The last act of the campaign came on 9 June, when Villaret's battered fleet was intercepted off Ushant by Rear-Admiral Montagu's intact battle squadron of eight 74s. Believing that Howe was still in pursuit, which would have caught him between two fires, Villaret chased off Montagu with an aggressive thrust by his least damaged ships before continuing his withdrawal to Brest. Aware that the fleet was returning from an undoubted defeat while the fate of Vanstabel's all-important convoy was still unknown, Saint-André ordered Villaret not to enter Brest and land his sick and wounded, but to anchor in Berthaume Roads, which the fleet reached on the 11th. But on the following night a dense cluster of lights was seen approaching through the Raz du Sein: the convoy. Stage-managed by Saint-André, fleet and convoy triumphantly dropped anchor in Brest on the 14th. Villaret, to quote his own words, 'had saved the convoy – and his head'.

The 1 June campaign made Villaret a national hero of the Republic and on 27 September 1794 he was promoted vice-admiral (his record of advancement from commander to vice-admiral in three years being broken only by Martin). In June 1795 he sailed from Brest with nine of the line to raise the blockade of Belle-Île in a clash with the British squadron off the Ile de Groix. But in a second engagement off Groix (23 June), several of his captains disobeyed orders and he was unable to prevent the loss of three ships. Villaret's command of the Brest fleet ended in November 1796 when he protested that political neglect of the fleet made the plan to invade Ireland an absurdity. Navy Minister Truguet replaced Villaret with Morard de Galles, but the total failure of the Irish expedition (December 1796–January 1797), with its ruinous effect on the Brest fleet, proved Villaret's case.

In April 1797, he was elected as Deputy for Morbihan in the Directory's lower chamber, the Council of Five Hundred, his fame winning him the appointment as Secretary to the House. No politician, Villaret continued to speak out bluntly on controversial issues, most notably during the trial of maverick privateer Robert Surcouf. The latter had returned to France to clear his name after having made a slave-trading voyage in defiance of the Republic's anti-slavery policy, and for having waged a privateering campaign without the requisite letter of marque. Surcouf won his case with the emphatic support of Villaret (who also strongly pleaded the case against slave emancipation), but Villaret's outspoken stance won him no friends in high places. On 4 September 1797, Villaret was proscribed after the *coup d'état* which purged the Directory of royalist suspects. He escaped deportation to French Guiana (which had replaced the guillotine as the way of disposing of political opponents of the regime), but spent the next three years as an exile on the Île d'Oléron.

Retrieved from exile and restored to favour by Bonaparte's Consulate (February 1800), Villaret was also restored to command of the Brest fleet. On 14 December 1801, he sailed for Saint-Domingue with the main body of the expeditionary force sent to recover the island from the rebel black slaves. He carried out this mission with complete success and was rewarded (3 April 1802) with the appointment as Captain-General of Martinique. There, in the dramatic days of 1805, Villaret provided what support he could for the Caribbean forays of Missiessy and Villeneuve.

Villaret was decorated with the Grand Eagle of the Legion of Honour on 2 February 1805, and three years later the cabinetmaker's grandson finally joined the ranks of the French nobility when Napoleon made him a Count of the Empire. But the New Year of 1809 brought Villaret nothing but the British invasion of Martinique. Despite Villaret's defiant three-week defence of Fort Desaix, he was forced to capitulate on 24 February 1809, with an English ship courteously returning him to France on 27 April.

Napoleon ordered a court of enquiry into the loss of Martinique, which removed Villaret from the Active List and restricted him to Rouen. The Emperor did not relent until 10 April 1811, when he appointed Villaret Governor-General and commander of the 6th Military District of the Kingdom of Italy at Venice. But Villaret was already a sick man, suffering from œdema, and he died in harness at Venice on 24 July 1812.

Notes

1 In conversation with Captain Brenton of *Belleisle*, who repatriated Villaret to France from Martinique in 1809; quoted in Oliver Warner's *The Glorious First of June*, p. 70.
2 From van to rear, *Trajan, Éole, América, Téméraire, Terrible, Impétueux, Mucius, Tourville, Gasparin, Convention, Trente-et-un Mai, Tyrannicide, Juste, Montagne (FLAG), Jacobin, Achille, Vengeur, Patriote, Northumberland, Entreprenant, Jemappes, Neptune, Peletier, Républicain, Sans-Pareil, Scipion.*

Vice-Admiral François-Etienne de Rosily-Mesros (1748–1832)

If the roads between Paris and Cadiz had been less atrocious in 1805, Rosily-Mesros, not Villeneuve, would have been Nelson's opponent at Trafalgar. With Villeneuve under the blackest imperial disfavour for having ruined Napoleon's master plan for the invasion of England, Rosily had been ordered south to take over the Franco-Spanish Combined Fleet. But by the time he finally reached Cadiz Villeneuve had already sailed, and there was nothing left for Rosily to command but the remnants of Trafalgar.

Napoleon's choice of Rosily to replace Villeneuve was all the more remarkable because Rosily had not spent a moment at sea since his promotion to rear-admiral in 1793. When he was ordered to Spain in

Rosily-Mesros. (Wikimedia Commons)

September 1805, he had spent the last ten years as Inspector-General of Charts and Maps: a strange fate for an officer who had had an active and highly successful career in the pre-Revolutionary Navy.

Rosily was the elder of two sons – distinguished in convenient French style as Rosily-Mesros and Rosily-Vieuxbourg – of Navy Captain François-Joseph de Rosily. Both brothers eventually became admirals on the same day, a unique achievement even in the most dedicated naval families. (The nearest British equivalents were the famous Pellew brothers, Edward and Israel, to the latter of whom Villeneuve surrendered at Trafalgar.)

François-Etienne de Rosily-Mesros was born at Brest on 13 January 1748. Having a Navy Captain for a father helped decide François-Etienne's career, but – unusually, given such a ready source of service patronage – he did not first go to sea in his father's ship. Entered as a cadet *garde de la marine* at Brest in July 1762, the last year of the Seven Years War, he joined the ship of the line *Sage*. Two months later she sailed as part of the abortive French expedition which, between September 1762 and April 1763, tried to repeat Duguay-Trouin's brief-lived conquest of Rio de Janeiro in 1711. During this voyage Rosily transferred to the ship of the line *Six-Corps*, in which he returned to France in October 1763.

Rosily was immediately transferred to the frigate *Malicieuse,* in which, under the command of la Motte-Picquet, he saw action against the 'Sallee Rovers': the Muslim pirates of Salé (Rabat) in Morocco, among the most notorious corsairs of the North African 'Barbary Coast' (October 1763–March 1764). A sequence of virtually unbroken service kept him employed on both sides of the Atlantic for the next six years: in the ship of the line *Amphion* off Newfoundland, in the frigate *Terpsichore* at Martinique and Saint-Domingue, in the corvette *Hirondelle* along the Spanish-Portuguese coasts, then back to the West Indies in the corvette *Perle*. All this sea time secured Rosily his commission as lieutenant (*enseigne de vaisseau*) on 1 February 1770.

Rosily began to make a name for himself under the wing of the ocean explorer Kerguelen, under whom, in the *Aber-Vrach*, he first served on a surveying mission between Brest and Dunkirk (June–November 1770). When Kerguelen sailed for the Indian Ocean in the following year, he chose Rosily as one of his junior officers. On discovering a desolate archipelago (still bearing his name) in February 1772, Kerguelen left Rosily to explore and survey the islands in a ship's launch, sending back the store ship *Gros-Ventre* to pick up the survey party. The *Gros-Ventre* conveyed Rosily-Mesros and his men to Batavia in the Dutch East Indies, that invaluable supply base and haven for all Southern Hemisphere voyages of exploration in the eighteenth century. From Batavia, Rosily sailed for the Cape of Good Hope in the *flûte Île-de-France,* returning to Brest in April 1773.

Thanks to this protracted return voyage, Rosily missed the departure of Kerguelen on his second voyage in March 1773, but in May he sailed with the merchantman *Vicomte-Talleyrand* for Île-de-France, Mauritius. There he should have taken command of the corvette *Ambition,* earmarked to join Kerguelen in his search for the elusive 'Southern Continent'. But after Kerguelen's second voyage ended in ignominy, with Kerguelen denounced by his own officers for gross professional misconduct, Rosily headed for home in the *flûte Laverdy*. After returning to France in August 1774, he was given a diplomatic posting as an attaché to the French Embassy in London – a mark of favour, but one which delayed his promotion to commander (*lieutenant de vaisseau*) until February 1778.

Back in France in December 1777, Rosily returned to service afloat in command of the lugger *Coureur*. He was now to fall victim to the niceties of going to war in the eighteenth century. On 13 March 1778, France formally notified Britain that she had not only recognised the American 'United States' with whom Britain

was at war, but had concluded a defensive alliance with them. Britain recalled her ambassador from France but there was no immediate formal declaration of war, and the warships of the rival navies eyed each other tensely for months in the 'No Man's Land' of the English Channel. The shooting war was eventually opened by Admiral Keppel of the British Channel Fleet, who fired on two French frigates in June, and on 5 July Rosily was attacked and captured by the British cutter *Alert*. Declining to place himself at the top of the list for exchange under cartel, he informed his captors that he refused to consider himself a prisoner on the grounds that there had been no formal declaration of war. Unimpressed, the British kept Rosily captive for 20 months before finally negotiating his exchange in February 1780. This spirited if unorthodox stance earned Rosily his creation as *Chevalier de Saint-Louis*.

From May 1780 to March 1781, Rosily served in home waters, protecting coastal convoys in the Gulf of Gascony, first in the ship of the line *Sage* and from late September 1780 in the frigate *Lively*, which he commanded. After six months' service in American waters under de Guichen in the ship of the line *Dauphin-Royal*, he was posted to the India station in the ship of the line *Fendant* (October 1781). Rosily ended the war as one of Suffren's frigate captains, commanding the *Cléopatre* from December 1782 to March 1784. The latter service, in the most prestigious naval theatre of the war, earned Rosily his promotion to *capitaine de vaisseau* in July 1784 – unlike his comrade and similar recipient of Suffren's favour, the lowly-born Villaret-Joyeuse, who had to wait over seven years for the same promotion.

Rosily spent the next seven years on the India station, starting with a prodigiou 42-month surveying voyage (December 1784–June 1788) in command of the *flû Vénus*. On this painstaking odyssey he followed the entire coastline of East Afric the Red Sea, Arabia and the Gulf, and the Indian subcontinent. He then to command of the new frigate *Méduse,* at Pondichéry, remaining her captain u November 1791. During this commission he was appointed commanding off of the India station, (November 1790), carrying the new Tricolour flag as far a coasts of Cochin-China, China, and the Philippines.

When he returned to France in 1792, Rosily had completed an unbroken d of service which earned him one of the best-deserved promotions to rear-adm the New Year's List of 1793. Yet the only use of his talents which the Repu Navy could find was to appoint him Naval Commander at Rochefort (24 1793). In this post he served for the next two and a half years, surviving th and the fall of the Jacobins without the slightest political molestation. His s experience made him eminently suitable for his next appointment: Dire Inspector-General of Naval Charts and Maps (23 August 1795), with the a honour of being promoted vice-admiral on 22 September 1796. But nine passed before Rosily was snatched from his office by Napoleon to replace at Cadiz (23 September 1805).

Setting aside the length of time since Rosily's last seagoing service, this was a strange appointment by any standard. It came only nine days after Napoleon had ordered Villeneuve to sail from Cadiz for the Mediterranean, and land troops to reinforce Naples before returning to Toulon. Napoleon was naturally anxious to reinforce his southern flank while he marched against the Austro-Russian coalition in southern Germany. At the same time he had clearly lost confidence in Villeneuve, and his decision to replace Villeneuve seems to have been a snap decision, made during the welter of preparations for the Emperor's departure from Paris for the campaign of Ulm and Austerlitz.

The choice of Rosily as Villeneuve's replacement was straightforward enough on paper, because Rosily was the senior vice-admiral. Far harder to explain is the glare of publicity attending the command change, which was even known in the British fleet by the eve of Trafalgar. Blackwood, Nelson's frigate commander, believed that Villeneuve had already been replaced, and that the oncoming Combined Fleet was commanded by the French Navy Minister, Decrès. There seems little doubt that the news of Rosily's arrival at Madrid (12 October) was the spur that drove Villeneuve to sea a week later. But although this news was passed at once to Cadiz, reaching Villeneuve on the 18th, the French ambassador at Madrid pressed Rosily not to continue his journey until a suitable escort for him could be found. If this was the method chosen by Napoleon (or more probably Decrès) to give Villeneuve one last chance – prompting him to sail at once, before Rosily could arrive – it was an extraordinary way of going about it.

Whatever the truth may have been, the outcome was the same. Rosily reached Cadiz on 22 October to find that Trafalgar had slashed his new command from 33 ships of the line to a tightly blockaded five, deprived of any strategic potential. He became in effect Truguet's successor as naval ambassador to Spain, and in this role did much to repair much of the damage done by the hapless Villeneuve. But no ambassadorial skills could offset Napoleon's growing belligerence towards Spain in 1807–8. This was caused by Portugal's refusal to join the 'Continental System' proclaimed by Napoleon in November 1806: the closure of European ports to British trade. Napoleon bullied Spain into permitting the transit of a French army to invade Portugal, which entered Lisbon in November 1807.

By the New Year of 1808 Napoleon had decided to take direct action against Spain, occupying Madrid in March and deposing the Spanish royal family on 30 April. But on 1 May Madrid erupted in nationalist riots, brutally crushed by the French, and by the end of the month the provincial *juntas*, declaring for their deposed king, were urging a national resistance to French domination. On 4 June 1808 the *junta* of Seville declared war on France, and nemesis finally descended on Rosily and his crews at Cadiz.

With ten British ships of the line waiting hungrily outside Cadiz, Rosily's position was hopeless, but he did everything possible to achieve an honourable solution.

As soon as he heard of the *junta's* declaration of war, he moved his force – the ships of the line *Neptune, Algésiras, Argonaute, Héros,* and *Pluton,* with the frigate *Cornélie* – out of range of the nearest shore batteries. But by the afternoon of the 9th new batteries had been set up, and a long-range bombardment of the French ships began. The French fired back and, having made a decent demonstration of their ability to defend themselves, Rosily hoisted a flag of truce on the afternoon of the 10th. To the Spanish commander at Cadiz, General Morla, he offered to keep his crews afloat but lower the French colours and land his guns and ammunition. Morla rejected this offer, established a new battery of 30 long 24-pounders, and prepared confidently to destroy the French ships at anchor. On the morning of 14 June, as the Spaniards prepared to renew their bombardment, Rosily ordered his ships to strike their colours.

Returning the Spanish fire at Cadiz proved to be Rosily's last taste of action. Having returned to France under the terms of the capitulation, he took up his old post at the Inspectorate of Naval Charts. So far from blaming Rosily for the humiliation of Cadiz, Napoleon made him a Count of the Empire in 1809, and two years later appointed him President of the Council of Naval Construction. When the veteran explorer Bougainville died in October 1811, Rosily replaced him on the Board of Longitude.

After Napoleon's abdication in 1814 Rosily was honoured by the returning Bourbons with the Grand Cordon of the Legion of Honour, and after the second restoration in 1815 he became an associate of the Academy of Sciences. Rosily's final honour, the Grand Cross of Saint-Louis, came in August 1822, but he was not placed on the Retired List until April 1832. Seven months later, on 11 November 1832, Rosily died in Paris at the age of 84.

Vice-Admiral Pierre,
Comte Martin (1752–1820)

Many French admirals came from the famous maritime centres of France – Saint-Malo, Brest, Lorient, Rochefort, Toulon – but Pierre Martin was Canadian by birth, born at Louisbourg, Nova Scotia, on 29 January 1752. Louisbourg was the great anchor-fortress of French Canada, the 'Gibraltar of the North', sited to protect the Grand Banks fishery and the Gulf of St Lawrence. As such it was a vital objective for the British in their campaigns against French Canada in the Seven Years War (1756–63), and its fate depended on the vagaries of sea power.

Pierre Martin. Lithograph by Maurin, c.1835. (Wikimedia Commons)

The French Navy managed to provide enough naval support to foil a British assault on Louisbourg in 1757 but not in the following year, and on 26 July 1758 the unsupported fortress fell to a British amphibious operation. Rather than remain in Canada under British rule Martin's family finally relocated to Rochefort in 1764, but the 12-year-old Pierre had no taste for the formal schooling awaiting him in France. He chose to remain aboard the *flute Saint-Esprit,* which had brought him from Canada, as a *pilotin,* or merchant service apprentice, in which quality he began the first five years of his career at sea.

On 1 January 1769 Martin joined the regular Navy as an ordinary seaman (*matelot*), and over the next 22 years his long climb towards commissioned rank and his admiral's flag bore many similarities to that of Villaret-Joyeuse (both were eventually promoted rear-admiral within weeks of each other at the end of 1793). By December 1771 he had risen to assistant pilot and served in the *flûte Bricole,* having become second pilot, from 20 January to 22 November 1774.

In the following year he was posted to the frigate *Terpsichore* during which commission (15 March–21 September 1775) he lost his left eye in a shipboard accident. On 25 March 1778, one month after France cast in her lot with the struggle of the American colonies for independence from British rule, Martin became master pilot in the ship of the line *Magnifique*.

Martin sailed for America in the battle fleet of the *Comte d'*Estaing and remained with *Magnifique* until 11 January 1781, serving in the actions off Grenada and Martinique, the capture of Dominica, and the ill-fated attack on Savannah. He then transferred to the frigate *Cérès* and returned to French home waters in the fleet of the *Marquis de* Vaudreuil, qualifying in 1782 as an auxiliary officer cadet *(officier bleu auxiliaire)*. Master pilot in the store ship *Vigilante* in French waters (February–September 1784), Martin was transferred to the *flûte Desirée,* returning to the West Indies from September 1784 to May 1785. He remained in colonial waters in the corvette *Rossignol* from 22 June 1785 to 21 August 1786.

On 16 December 1786, Martin's impressive accumulation of sea time and watchkeeping experience won him his first command: the corvette *Cousine,* bound for the West African station of Senegal, where he was appointed port lieutenant at Gorée. His long period in command of *Cousine* paralleled Truguet's command of *Tartelon* and on 28 March 1788 Martin was promoted *sous-lieutenant de vaisseau,* or sub-commander. After returning to France to get *Cousine* overhauled at Rochefort (September–December 1789), Martin returned in her to the West African station until August 1791, being honoured as *Chevalier de Saint-Louis* on 15 October 1791. Promoted full *lieutenant de vaisseau* in February 1792, he returned yet again to Senegal where he spent the rest of the year in command of the corvette *Espoir.*

Although Martin's rise from ordinary seaman to commander met all the criteria of the Republican ideal, the pace of his subsequent advance from commander to flag rank and fleet command – 12 months – was still breath-taking. In the New Year of 1793 he led *Espoir,* with the frigates *Hermione* and *Pomone,* on defensive patrols in French coastal waters, capturing a privateer off Jersey, and on 10 February was promoted *capitaine de vaisseau.* After brief spells in command of the ship of the line *América* and the frigate *Tortue* at Rochefort, Martin was promoted rear-admiral on 16 November 1793 after only ten months as a Post Captain. At first he commanded one of the divisions of the Brest fleet under Villaret-Joyeuse, but on 1 February 1794 he was given command of the Toulon fleet.

Seldom has a fleet commander been handed a more ruinous heritage. Toulon's brief-lived defiance of the Republic and declaration for the boy-King Louis XVII, a prisoner in the Temple (August 1793), calling in British and Spanish naval support, had been brutally crushed by the Republicans in December. The fighting had left the Toulon port complex a burned and battered wreck and reduced the fleet to a shred. Martin's supreme achievement in command at Toulon (February 1794–October 1797) was to restore this crucial naval base and rebuild the Toulon fleet to its former power. By November 1796, less than three years after the shattering Republican conquest of the port, the Toulon fleet was strong enough for Martin to detach a powerful battle squadron under Villeneuve to reinforce the Brest fleet.

Apart from the all-important work of restoration at Toulon, Martin proved himself to be an aggressive fleet commander, willing to exploit the mistakes and hesitation of his British opponents. He could do nothing to prevent the British invasion and conquest of Corsica (January–June 1794), but by 5 June he was able to put to sea in his flagship, the 120-gun *Sans-Culottes,* and head for Corsica with six of the line to test the mettle of Lord Hood's fleet. When Hood reacted forcibly with 13 of the line, Martin prudently withdrew inside the forts protecting Gourjon Bay, and subsequently returned to Toulon with his force intact. In November, Hood was replaced by the far less aggressive Vice-Admiral Hotham.

By February 1795, Martin's fleet was strong enough to take the offensive and on the 28th he sailed from Toulon with 15 of the line, carrying 3,500 troops intended for the reconquest of Corsica. Despite foul weather he had battled to within sight of Corsica by 2 March, only to be driven back in the direction of Genoa by a gale (reminiscent of Truguet's failure at Cagliari two years before). Hotham sailed from his anchorage in Livorno roads on the 9th with 14 of the line, hoping to bring his strength up to that of the French by retrieving the detached 74-gun *Berwick.* But the latter, heading for Livorno under jury rig after being dismasted in a gale on 16 January, encountered the French frigate squadron under Perrée and was captured on 7 March.

The fleets sighted each other off Cape Noli, to the south-west of Genoa on 12 March, and battle was joined on the 13th, but Martin's slight advantage in firepower was lost at the outset when the 80-gun *Ça Ira* was crippled by a collision and had to be taken in tow, first by the frigate *Vestale* and later by the 74-gun *Censeur.* The confused fighting on the 13th and 14th was concentrated against *Ça Ira* (one of whose assailants was Captain Nelson, experiencing his first fleet action in the grossly outmatched 64-gun *Agamemnon*). By dawn on the 14th *Ça Ira* and *Censeur* had dropped far behind the French main body and Martin, who had shifted his flag to the frigate *Friponne* to control the battle more effectively, was prevented by light winds from bringing his van ships to their aid. The action on the 14th was dominated by the heroic last fight of the *Ça Ira* and *Censeur.* By the time they surrendered they had battered the 74-gun *Captain* defenceless while the 74-gun *Illustrious,* having lost her mainmast and mizzenmast, was driven ashore and had to be burned. Satisfied with his two prizes, Hotham declined to press further attacks on the French fleet (telling a furious Nelson *'We have done very well. We must be contented'*)[1] and allowing Martin to withdraw to Toulon via the bay of Hyères.

By early June – reinforced on 3 April by the arrival of Renaudin from Brest with six of the line – Martin's exertions had restored the Toulon fleet to 17 seaworthy ships of the line, and on the 7th he led it back to sea. Hotham, now based on San Fiorenzo Bay in Corsica, had detached Nelson's *Agamemnon* with a reconnaissance flotilla of a frigate and two sloops, and on 6 July it ran straight into the oncoming Toulon fleet. In a 23-hour chase Martin pursued Nelson back to San Fiorenzo, but stood off when he sighted Hotham's fleet, now numbering 21 of the line, most of which were watering and refitting ship. Hotham managed to get to sea on the night of the 7th, but it was not until the 13th that he caught up with Martin off the Hyères islands. The leading ships of the British van managed to engage the French rear and forced the 74-gun *Alcide* to strike (she blew up after surrender), but a lucky shift of wind enabled Martin to get his fleet safely into Fréjus bay and Hotham withdrew.

It was Martin's last action with the Toulon fleet which he had done so much to rebuild. Promoted vice-admiral on 22 March 1796, he finally handed over the Toulon fleet to Rear-Admiral Brueys, recent captor of the Ionian Islands, on 23 October 1797. Martin returned to Rochefort as port commander and, from 27 September 1801, as Maritime Prefect. Napoleon created him a Grand Officer of the Legion of Honour on 27 May 1805 and (4 June 1810) a Count of the Empire.

Placed on the Retired List by the restored Bourbons on 27 December 1814, Martin was briefly restored to activity during the Hundred Days but returned to the Retired List after the second Bourbon restoration, with effect from 1 August 1815. On 2 February 1817, King Louis XVIII confirmed Martin's title of Count by letters patent. It was at Rochefort, where his naval career had begun at the age of 12, that Martin died on 1 November 1820.

Note

1 Quoted in Mahan, A. T. 1897. *Life of Nelson.*

Rear-Admiral Jean-François Renaudin (1750–1809)

Jean-François Renaudin was to French Revolutionary legend what Sir Richard Grenville of the *Revenge* was to late Elizabethan England: the hero-commander of a gallant ship (of the same name), lost in battle against overwhelming odds, with the difference that Renaudin survived to hoist his admiral's flag. His name will always be linked with the last fight of the *Vengeur,* sunk in the battle of the First of June 1794 in which the fleet of Villaret-Joyeuse saved the First Republic.

Among the roll of French admirals Renaudin counts as an 'inlander', born at Le Gua, south of Grenoble, on 13 July

Renaudin. Portrait by Giraudin, 1794. (Wikimedia Commons)

1750. Details of his early life are sparse, but his seagoing debut and subsequent career closely resembled that of his close contemporary, Martin: another reminder that the French Navy of the *Ancien Régime* needed no Revolution to make possible a career which could take a man from the lower deck to the officers' wardroom and command of a warship.

By the age of 17, Renaudin had joined the merchant service as a boy entrant (*mousse*), his first ship being the *Saint-Joseph,* voyaging to Saint-Domingue from September 1767 to July 1768. After two further voyages to Saint-Domingue and one to Guadeloupe (1768–72), he became *second capitaine* or first mate in the *Hazard* (December 1772–February 1774). Two more Caribbean voyages followed in the merchantman *Volage* (1774–75) before Renaudin joined the regular Navy as a probationary officer *(officier bleu)* on 1 April 1776, with eight years of sea time and watchkeeping experience behind him.

Renaudin's first three years in Navy service were spent in store ships and *flûtes* attached to the fleet, in which his merchant service experience served him well. Promoted acting lieutenant-commander (*lieutenant de frégate auxiliaire*) in 1779 while serving in the *flûte Dorade,* he was appointed her captain on 1 January 1780 and remained in command of her until 15 July 1782. This commission confirmed his rank as *lieutenant de frégate* and earned him his second command, the *flûte Mulet* (16 July 1782–25 February 1783).

While service in supply ships lacked the glamour of service in frigates and ships of the line, with the chance of winning distinction in battle, it had the advantage – as the service department for the Navy and colonies – of providing officers of Renaudin's experience with continuous employment throughout the peacetime years after 1783, and after the coming of the Revolution in 1789. Commanding the *Gave,* Renaudin made his first voyage to the North and Baltic Seas (April–September 1785) and on 1 May 1786 was advanced to the rank of *sous-lieutenant de vaisseau.* He set foot in a ship of the line for the first time when appointed to the 74-gun *Orion* (destined for a Revolutionary re-christening as the *Trente-et-un Mai*) in the Brest squadron (23 June 1790–4 February 1791).

From *Orion,* Renaudin was transferred to command the corvette *Lutine,* escorting a convoy to Saint-Domingue (March 1791–November 1792), with his promotion to *lieutenant de vaisseau* coming through on 1 January. When Renaudin returned to France from this his last peacetime commission in late November 1792, France was not only at war but had been a Republic since 22 September. His first wartime command, in the corvette *Perdrix* (9 December 1792–12 January 1793), was spent in French coastal waters. Within 43 days of his promotion to *capitaine de vaisseau* on 1 January 1793, Renaudin was given command of the frigate *Andromaque* (13 February 1793–4 March 1794).

On 5 March 1794, Renaudin's next command – his fourth ship in three years – was to the 74–gun ship of the line *Vengeur* in the Brest fleet commanded by Villaret-Joyeuse, who by the spring of 1794 held the fate of the Republic in his hands(details of the naval campaign of May–June 1794 are given on pp. 22–23). When, after the skirmishing of 28–29 May, Villaret finally accepted battle with Lord Howe's fleet on the morning of 1 June, *Vengeur* was stationed three ships astern of Villaret's flagship *Montagne* in the centre of the French line. The main action began shortly after 0915 and petered out around 1230, by which time all attention in both fleets was centred on the continuing savage ordeal of the *Vengeur.*

At about 1000, intent on repeating Howe's piercing of the French line in his flagship *Queen Charlotte,* Captain Harvey of the *Brunswick* steered to pass astern of the *Achille,* the ship immediately ahead of Renaudin's *Vengeur.* The French line was so tightly deployed that *Brunswick's* starboard anchors hooked into *Vengeur's* foremast shrouds. Locked side by side, so closely that several of their gun ports could not be opened and the gunners blew them off by firing through them, the two ships dropped out of the line and commenced a furious mutual battering. Renaudin had musketeers on his upper deck and his poop carronades loaded with scrap iron. Together they wrought havoc on *Brunswick's* quarterdeck, mortally wounding Captain Harvey at 1130. The blazing wads from *Vengeur's* guns started three separate fires aboard *Brunswick,* which had 23 guns knocked out during the action.

The ordeal continued for four hours and at 1400 was as intense as ever, with *Vengeur* bringing down *Brunswick's* mainmast shortly before her own foremast and mainmast fell. This caused *Vengeur* to roll so heavily that *Brunswick's* anchors tore loose, and the exhausted ships drifted apart at last. With his ship totally defenceless and flooding through her gun ports and numerous shot-holes, Renaudin finally surrendered at 1415 by hanging a Union Jack over the side. He had the grim satisfaction of seeing *Brunswick* lose her last remaining mast and, equally helpless, signal for aid. The British *Culloden* tried to take *Vengeur* in tow and brought off Renaudin and about 130 survivors of her crew, many of them mortally wounded, but many were still aboard when *Vengeur* finally sank shortly after 1730.

The notorious 'People's Representative' or commissar, Jeanbon Saint-André, had sailed as an ominous passenger in Villaret's flagship (and passed the battle, to Villaret's contempt, safely below deck). After the battle Saint-André wrote a bombastic report of how *Vengeur* had gone down with all hands cheering and shouting *'Vive la République!'* and her colours nailed to the (by then non-existent) mast. Although given the lie by the list of surviving prisoners subsequently exchanged with Renaudin, this gaudy propaganda was the true stuff of Republican legend and was genuinely believed for many years. The truth was simply that the heroism of Renaudin and his crew on 1 June 1794 needed no such tawdry enhancement.

Exchanged after the battle, Renaudin returned to France on 11 August and was promptly given command of the ship of the line *Jemappes* in Villaret's fleet. This was to prove Renaudin's longest command (18 August 1794–19 December 1797). *Jemappes* remained his flagship after his promotion to rear-admiral on 29 October 1794, and in the following year he sailed in her with five of the line to reinforce Martin's fleet at Toulon. There he saw his last action in the battle between Martin and Hotham off the Hyères Islands (13 July 1795).

Renaudin's last command afloat was that of the second squadron of the Brest fleet, flying his flag in the *Républicain* (24 March 1798–19 March 1799). He was then transferred to command the naval forces at Naples, and from 19 June to 23 September 1799 served as military commander at Toulon. His last post was as inspector-general of all naval bases between Cherbourg and Bayonne, before being placed on the Retired List (4 February 1801) with a pension of 4,000 francs. Receiving no further honours from Napoleon – not even admission to the Legion of Honour – Renaudin died in obscurity at St Martin, near his birthplace of Le Gua, on 29 April 1809. Twenty-seven years were to pass before his name received lasting honour on the *Arc de Triomphe.*

Vice-Admiral Pierre-César-Charles-Guillaume, *Marquis de* Sercey (1753–1836)

From 1796 to 1806, Sercey and Linois were the admirals who kept the Tricolour flying in Indian and Far Eastern seas, posing a constant threat to Britain's lucrative East Indian trade routes. Of the two, Sercey's was easily the most impressive achievement. Sailing from Brest in 1796, operating from France's colonial base of Île-de-France (Mauritius) in the southern Indian Ocean, he made repeated raiding cruises from the East African coast to the Dutch East Indies until 1799, staying on station until his force had dwindled to a single frigate.

Sercey. Lithograph by Maurin, c.1835. (Wikimedia Commons)

Pierre-César-Charles-Guillaume, *Marquis de* Sercey, was born at the Château de Jeu, near Autun, on 26 April 1753. Entered as a Volunteer at Brest, he first went to sea at the age of 13 in the frigate *Légère,* serving nine months in the West Indies (1766–67). He then transferred to the corvette *Heure du Berger,* bound for the Indies station. This two-year commission (1767–69) began Sercey's long association with the Indian seas, and it sealed his commitment to the Navy. On returning to France he became a cadet *garde de la marine,* with his first three years of sea time giving him a flying start. He then sailed for the West Indies on another two-year commission in the frigate *Ambuscade* (1770–72).

Between 1772 and 1774 five future admirals – the other four being Rivière, Rochegude, Rosily-Mesros, and Trogoff – sailed for the South Seas with Kerguelen, but Sercey was the only one of the five who took part in both of Kerguelen's voyages. On the first, he served in the *Gros-Ventre,* sent back to retrieve the survey party commanded by Rosily-Mesros; on the second he served in the frigate *Oiseau.*

Three more years of frigate service followed in the *Amphitrite* and the *Boudeuse*, the latter commission taking Sercey back to the West Indies. When *Boudeuse* returned to Brest in June 1778, Sercey commanded a skeleton crew charged with sailing the damaged frigate *Belle-Poule* from Plouescat to Brest. This achievement, in the first year of the American Revolutionary War, won Sercey his commission as lieutenant (*enseigne de vaisseau*) in May 1779.

Sercey's varied and eventful combat experience in the American War was concentrated in the West Indies theatre. He got his first taste of battle fleet service in the ships of the line *Triton, Couronne,* and *Ville de Paris,* and was in de Guichen's fleet during its fierce clash with Rodney off Martinique on 17 April 1780. In command of the cutter *Sans Pareil* he was captured by the British on 26 June 1780, exchanged in August, and given another cutter, the *Serpent.* In the winter of 1780–81 Sercey's third cutter, *Levrette,* sank in wild weather off the Azores while escorting a homeward-bound convoy.

Back in the Caribbean after this near-fatal mishap, Sercey was attached to the French naval squadron reinforcing the Spanish siege of Pensacola. On 5 May 1781, four days before the fall of Pensacola, he was promoted *lieutenant de vaisseau,* ending the war as a successful frigate commander. He was first officer of the frigate *Nymphe* when she and *Concorde* recaptured the *Cérès,* which had been taken by Hood's fleet. In the New Year of 1783 Sercey was promoted to command the *Nymphe* in which, assisted by *Amphitrite,* he captured the British West Indiaman *Argo,* having on board the retiring Governor-General of the British West Indies.

Still only 30 years old when the war ended, Sercey had to wait another nine years for his next promotion. After bringing *Nymphe* back to Brest he served in the ship of the line *Séduisant* before being given two more frigate commands, *Ariel* in 1785–87 and *Surveillante* in 1790, both in the familiar waters of the West Indies. He was finally posted *capitaine de vaisseau* on 1 January 1792, a promotion as eminently deserved as it was long overdue; but the Navy Ministry of the new Republic atoned for the delay by promoting him rear-admiral on 1 January 1793.

Sercey was one of the relatively few newly promoted admirals to be given immediate employment appropriate to his experience and talents. In April 1793 he sailed from Brest for Saint-Domingue with the ships of the line *Éole, América,* and *Jupiter.* His mission was to gather in all homeward-bound French merchant shipping in the West Indies to return to France in convoy, but the immediate problem confronting him when he arrived off Saint-Domingue was the rebellion of the black slaves. Sercey did what he could for the colonists, concentrating them at Cap Haïtien where they could be better defended by the hard-pressed garrison. He then mustered the West Indies merchant shipping with commendable speed and in June escorted it to Norfolk, Virginia, passing north to show the flag off the Chesapeake, New York and Newfoundland before returning to Brest on 4 November.

Sercey's cruise laid the groundwork for the sailing of the great American grain convoy by Vanstabel which saved the Republic in June 1794. When it arrived Sercey was in prison: a political suspect, threatened with the same fate that had already befallen fellow-admirals Kersaint, d'Estaing, and Grimouard – the guillotine. Less than four weeks after his return from America, Sercey had been denounced as an 'aristo', stripped of his rank and thrown into the Luxembourg prison. Even after the fall of Robespierre in July 1794, Sercey remained in prison until he obtained both release and reinstatement in rank on 30 January 1795.

In the winter of 1795–96, Navy Minister Truguet gave Sercey an appointment that could have been invented for him: command of the squadron of frigates and corvettes which the new Directory proposed to unleash on Britain's Indian and Far Eastern trade routes. Truguet envisaged Sercey sweeping the eastern seas at the head of the most powerful frigate squadron ever sent to sea by the Republic, but persistent bad luck dogged the venture from the outset. Sercey lost one of his four frigates, *Cocarde*, by accidental grounding before the squadron even left La Rochelle. The only available replacement, *Vertu*, was not ready for sea and Sercey sailed without her on 4 March 1796. His squadron consisted of the 40-gun *Forte* (flag), 36-gun *Régénérée* (commanded by Willaumez), the 40-gun *Seine* (armed *en flûte* as a part-transport, with alternate guns dismounted), and the corvettes *Bonne-Citoyenne* and *Mutine*). Lhermitte was to follow with *Vertu* and join the main force in the Canaries.

Sercey's frigates and corvettes carried 800 troops with artillery and stores, not only to reinforce the Île-de-France garrison but to serve in such expeditions on the Indian mainland as might prove practicable. They also carried two political passengers: René-Gaston Baco and Etienne-Laurent Burnel, charged with carrying through the abolition of slavery throughout the Mascarene plantations. Sercey could have had no idea of how close their mission would come to ruining his.

The outward voyage began with the loss of the two corvettes. Storm-damaged and separated from the main body by a Biscay gale, *Bonne-Citoyenne* and *Mutine* were both captured by a British frigate squadron (7–8 March). Pressing on, Sercey reached Palma in the Canaries on 17 March, and waited there for Lhermitte to join him before resuming the voyage. On 25 May, while rounding South Africa, Sercey's force sighted and chased the British sloop *Sphynx*, whose captain only escaped by throwing his guns overboard. The French squadron arrived at Île-de-France on 18 June and Sercey took under his command the frigates *Cybèle* and *Prudente* with Magon, *Prudente's* captain, becoming Sercey's second-in-command.

Sercey was immediately confronted with the hostile attitude to his arrival of Governor Malartic and the colonial assembly. The Île-de-France planters refused point-blank to wreck their economy by freeing their slaves. They also rejected the Republican deputies, whom Malartic tried to ship to the Philippines in the corvette *Moineau*. (Once aboard, however, Baco and Burnel browbeat *Moineau's* captain into sailing for France instead, where their eventual arrival laid down a store of future trouble for Sercey and his captains.) But by the second week of July 1796, having landed his troops and with *Seine* re-equipped with her full broadside, Sercey was ready to commence active operations.

The cruise began in earnest on 14 July, when Sercey sailed from Île-de-France with his six frigates and headed north for India, sending the privateer schooner *Alerte* ahead to scout – but on 19 August *Alerte,* with all her papers and Sercey's plans for the cruise, was captured by the British frigate *Carysfort.* The British made good use of this captured intelligence. When Sercey arrived off the virtually defenceless Coromandel coast in the third week of August, he was warned off by the news of a non-existent British battle squadron, and decided to seek easier meat in East Indian waters, heading east for the Malacca Strait.

It now fell to Sercey's squadron to fight one of the most remarkable actions of the age of fighting sail. It was axiomatic that, ship for ship, a frigate was no match for a ship of the line and could flee from one without dishonour. But the prospects for a *group* of frigates against a ship of the line had always been debatable, and on the morning of 8 September 1796, off the north coast of Sumatra, Sercey's six frigates fell in with the British 74-gun ships of the line *Arrogant* and *Victorious.* In normal weather conditions favouring the 74s' sailing qualities, Sercey's course would have been clear: to race for the horizon and disappear into the open ocean, continuing his raiding cruise with his force intact. But on 8 and 9 September the very light prevailing winds left the two 74s virtually becalmed and Sercey decided to attack, exploiting the superior manoeuvrability and long-range firepower (*Forte* had a broadside of 30 long 24-pounders) of his frigates.

The action took place on the morning of 9 September and was bedevilled on both sides by communication problems (in the calm conditions the signal flags tended to hang limp instead of blowing out so that they could be clearly read). As a result the two British 74s failed to close up to fight as a single unit, making the task of Sercey's frigates all the easier. Despite the light airs they managed to avoid the 74s' broadsides and inflict a battering which left *Arrogant* virtually unmanageable and severely damaged *Victorious.* The punishment was certainly not one-sided; the British defensive fire inflicted considerable damage on the frigates' spars and rigging, which required V*ertu* to be taken in tow until her crew could complete running repairs. When a breeze sprang up at about 11 am and *Victorious* was able to manoeuvre at last, Sercey broke off the action, but there was no question of a British pursuit. Sercey had won a clear-cut victory on points, but the damage to his ships marked the beginning of the steady attrition of his squadron that was to continue unabated for the next two years.

Sercey now headed for Île-du-Roi in the Mergui Archipelago, which he reached on 15 September, to make repairs and take on fresh provisions. By the first week of October he was ready to resume his cruise. Given the unabated hostility of Governor Malartic back at Île-de-France, Sercey pinned his hopes on finding more co-operation from the Republican Dutch authorities at Batavia, Java, where he arrived on 18 December. Sercey also hoped that Batavia would be a good base from which to approach the Philippines, the main Pacific colony of Spain, but in the latter regard Spain, by 1797 France's increasingly reluctant ally, proved less than helpful. At Batavia Sercey not only re-equipped and reprovisioned his ships, but negotiated a treaty by which the Batavia regency undertook to supply Île-de-France with rice, cordage and canvas. He then sailed for Île-de-France to get the treaty ratified.

It was in the Bali Strait, on 28 January 1797, that Sercey encountered any French commerce-raider's dream: an unescorted British East India convoy. But he was totally unprepared for the superb performance of the convoy commodore, Charles Lennox, who manoeuvred the convoy like a well-ordered battle fleet preparing for close action. *Cybèle,* scouting ahead, signalled to Sercey that 'ENEMY IS SUPERIOR IN FORCE'. Unwilling to risk one of his precious frigates by making a close reconnaissance – which would have revealed that most of the East Indiamen's apparently gaping 'gun-ports' were painted imitations – Sercey hastily withdrew and missed the chance of a lifetime. When the news of Lennox's feat reached Britain later in the year, the predictable exultation of the British press did nothing to enhance Sercey's reputation in Paris.

Sercey's retreat from the East India convoy was a classic wasted opportunity, and that phrase bleakly describes the fate of his squadron over the next two years. Monthly wear and tear on the frigates' sails, rigging and spars was an unceasing and accumulating problem. In the 15 years since Suffren's time, French crews had lost the experience of their British counterparts in maintaining their ships at sea. A bonus was waiting for Sercey when he returned to Île-de-France in February 1797: the 36-gun frigate *Preneuse* and the corvette *Brûle-Gueule,* which had been detached on a cruise in the Mozambique Channel when Sercey reached Île-de-France in the previous June. But although his force had now risen to seven frigates and a large corvette, Sercey was not let loose with them in 1797. A fateful legacy of his Batavia treaty was a Dutch request for French troops, and transporting the bulk of the Île-de-France garrison to Java was the main task of Sercey's squadron that year.

The New Year of 1798 brought urgent messages to Île-de-France from Tipu Sultan of Mysore, asking for French troops to support his renewed war with the British East India Company. Thanks to the troop transfers to Batavia in the previous year, Governor Malartic had none to spare for India, but promised to pass on Tipu's request to the French Government. Simultaneously, there arrived at Île-de-France two large merchantmen of the Spanish Philippine Company, whose immensely rich cargoes were valued at 4 million *piastres.* For a commission of 60,000 *piastres* Malartic undertook to see the two ships safely home to Spain and ordered Sercey to provide two frigates as escorts. This deprived Sercey of *Vertu* and *Régénérée,* captained respectively by Magon and Willaumez, who sailed from Île-de-France on 23 January 1798.

The final attrition of Sercey's squadron had begun and was soon increased by the need to lay up *Cybèle,* unfit for further service after five years on the East Indies station. Sercey now decided that his best course was to shift his base from Île-de-France to Batavia. Before sailing for the Dutch East Indies in *Brûle-Gueule* he dispatched Lhermitte in *Preneuse* (8 March 1798) to return Tipu Sultan's envoys, with the sorry reinforcement of 150 French colonial volunteers, to Mangalore. Off Tellicherry Lhermitte captured two British East Indiamen (21 April), sending them off to Île-de-France under prize crews before returning Tipu's envoys to Mangalore (24 April), then heading east to rejoin Sercey at Batavia in mid-June 1798.

In April 1798 – unknown to him – Sercey had lost a fourth frigate. This was *Seine,* commandeered by Malartic to convey 280 mutinous troops, demanding to be returned to France with their women, children, and baggage. *Seine* sailed from Île-de-France on 24 April 1798 but, after a remarkably successful homeward voyage, was captured on 30 June, within sight of the Brittany coast, by the British frigates *Jason* and *Pique.*

Sercey lost his next two frigates to a wholly unpredictable cause. Sent back to Île-de-France to reprovision, *Forte* and *Prudente* were requisitioned by Governor Malartic, who had decided to make his fortune as a privateering owner. Recommissioned as privateers, these two fine frigates were entrusted to a pair of captains who, instead of enriching Malartic and his syndicate, had lost both ships by the spring of 1799. *Prudente* was the first to go, captured off the South African coast by the British frigate *Daedalus* on 9 February 1799. Less than three weeks later *Forte,* raiding the northern Bay of Bengal, was captured on 1 March after a dramatic night action with the 36-gun frigate *Sibylle.* Sercey's force was thus reduced to *Brûle-Gueule* and Lhermitte's *Preneuse.* In September Lhermitte cruised to the Mozambique coast, but failed to repeat his success of April 1798, and by this time the British net was closing; Île-de-France was under blockade by two British ships of the line and two frigates under Admiral Hotham (Martin's former adversary of 1794–95 in the western Mediterranean). When *Preneuse* was trapped and captured in Île-de-France's Bay of Tombeau on 11 December 1799, Sercey's oriental cruise was finally brought to its end.

When Sercey returned to France after the signing of the Treaty of Amiens (March 1802–May 1803) it was a less than happy homecoming. Taking no account of Sercey's difficulties from the moment of his arrival at Île-de-France, nor of the extensive British naval resources sent east to counter Sercey's presence in the Indian Ocean, Navy Minister Decrès censured him for having frittered his squadron away to no good purpose. Sercey was even blamed for having returned the two Republican deputies to France and was denied any further command. In the end (5 August 1804), Sercey demanded to be placed on the Retired List. Refusing to live in the France which had treated him so churlishly, Sercey returned to Île-de-France, France's most remote colony. There he married into a colonial family and began a new life as a Mauritius planter.

Sercey's last taste of action came in 1810 when he volunteered to support the defence of Île-de-France against the British invasion. After the surrender (3 December 1810) Sercey returned to France. He was not returned to the Active List until after Napoleon's abdication in April 1814.

Sercey was promoted vice-admiral under the first Bourbon restoration (28 May 1814) but his sea-going days were over. King Charles X honoured Sercey in October 1828 with the double award of the Grand Cross of the Legion of Honour and the Grand Cross of Saint-Louis, and when he finally retired (28 August 1832), King Louis-Philippe created him a Peer of France. Aged 83, Sercey died at Paris on 10 August 1836.

PART 3
The Directory, 1795–1799

Vice-Admiral Etienne-Eustache Bruix (1759–1805)

In the War of the Second Coalition against France (1798–1800), Vice-Admiral Etienne-Eustache Bruix earned a unique distinction with his dramatic foray from Brest to the Mediterranean and back in April–August 1799. Historians still remember this, one of the most remarkable achievements of the French Navy in the interminable naval war of 1793–1814, as 'Bruix's Cruise'. The name of no other Republican or Imperial French admiral is so associated with a single naval operation.

Bruix. Lithograph by Maurin, c.1835. (Wikimedia Commons)

The family of Bruix came from Béarn, but his father was an Army captain in the infantry *régiment de Foix,* and Etienne-Eustache was born at Fort Dauphin, Saint-Domingue, on 17 July 1759. He joined the Navy as a cadet *garde de la marine* in the first year of France's commitment to the American Revolutionary War, on 14 November 1778. Bruix's first ship was the frigate *Fox,* which he joined at Brest, but this introduction to life at sea ended dramatically when *Fox* was wrecked off the Brittany coast (21 March 1779).

Back at sea in the frigate *Concorde* (May–September 1779), Bruix first saw action on 10 August when the squadron to which *Concorde* was attached captured the British *King George.* Further frigate appointments followed: to *Medée* (October 1779–April 1780), and *Boudeuse* (April–November 1780), in which Bruix made his first Atlantic crossing when *Boudeuse* was posted to Martinique.

Bruix's experience of battle fleet service began after the return of *Boudeuse* to Brest in early 1781. He was first posted to the ship of the line *Héros* (2 March 1781), but 13 days later he was transferred to *Auguste,* earmarked for service in the Caribbean battle fleet of de Grasse. In *Auguste,* Bruix took part in de Grasse's greatest victory: the Battle of Chesapeake Bay (5 September 1781) which compelled the surrender of the British army of Cornwallis at Yorktown and sealed the victory of the rebel Americans. Bruix's first promotion, to lieutenant (*enseigne de vaisseau*) followed on 17 November 1781. Like Villeneuve in *Marseillais,* Bruix in *Auguste* escaped capture in the defeat of de Grasse by Rodney in the Battle of the Saints (12 April 1782). In the redistribution of officers in the French fleet after the battle, Bruix was transferred to the frigate *Railleuse* (28 June–24 December 1782).

Back at Brest, Bruix served ashore as Sub-Brigadier of the Marine Guards (April–October 1783) before returning to the Caribbean in the corvette *Fauvette* (October 1783–June 1784). On 12 June 1784 he was given his first command, the corvette *Pivert,* and spent the next four years conveying the oceanographer *Comte* Antoine de Puységur on a detailed circumnavigation of Saint-Domingue, surveying and re-mapping the coasts and harbours of the island – a mission reminiscent of Truguet's eastern Mediterranean survey cruise in *Tartelon.* While engaged on this mission Bruix was promoted to *lieutenant de vaisseau,* second class (1 May 1786).

For the next five years after his return from the Caribbean, Bruix's career followed an erratic but steadily upward path which accelerated with the pace of the Revolution. Attached to the First Squadron of the Brest fleet, he was promoted *lieutenant de vaisseau,* first class, on 1 January 1790 and served in the ship of the line *Superbe* until 31 January 1791. Later that year his survey cruise in *Pivert* earned his election to the Academy of the Navy. After less than a month commanding the brig *Fanfaron* in the Channel, Bruix was appointed to command the frigate *Sémillante* on a voyage to Île-de-France in the Indian Ocean (June 1792–March 1793). His promotion to *capitaine de vaisseau,* second class, was announced in the New Year's List of 1 January 1793.

Bruix then became one of the eight future 'Admirals of the *Arc*' – the other seven being Truguet, Latouche-Tréville, Missiessy, Sercey, Villeneuve, Brueys, and Decrès – to fall foul, as political suspects, of the all-powerful 'People's Representatives' of the Jacobin dictatorship. On 24 October 1793, he was stripped of his rank – *destitué* – on the orders of the 'People's Representatives' at Brest. He spent the ensuing seven months of compulsory retirement in writing a treatise (*Moyens d'approvisionner la marine par les seules productions du territoire français*) on how, as a response to the British blockade, the French fleet should be provisioned solely from the resources of metropolitan France.

This document appeared in the months when the fate of the Jacobin regime depended on the safe arrival of a massive grain convoy, which only the Navy could guarantee – as it did, thanks to admirals Villaret-Joyeuse, Nielly, and Vanstabel, in May–June 1794. In a manner wholly typical of the Revolution's unpredictability, Bruix was abruptly restored to active service by the 'People's Representatives' on 11 June 1794, *before* the grain convoy arrived safely at Brest, with his rank as *capitaine de vaisseau,* 1st class, back-dated to 1 January of that year, and given command of the ship of the line *Éole.* In the following month the 'Representatives' went even further in making amends to Bruix by naming him 'Major-General of the Naval Army of Brest' under Villaret's command.

The visionaries of the First Republic claimed that they were creating a new heaven and earth in France to serve as a model for the world. But their delusions were never more typified than in clinging to the antique concept of the Navy as an 'army-by-sea', which stretched back far beyond the days of the Spanish Armada into the Middle Ages.

It was therefore with the anomalous double rank of major-general and captain 1st class that Bruix served under Villaret, proving himself one of the attenuated Brest fleet's most reliable captains in the abortive action off Groix on 23 June 1795. When Villaret was replaced as C-in-C of the Brest fleet by Morard de Galles in November 1796, Bruix was promoted commodore *(chef de division),* flying his broad pendant in the ship of the line *Océan,* and took part in the ill-fated Irish expedition of December 1796–January 1797. On 20 May 1797 Bruix was promoted rear-admiral, hoisting his flag in the ship of the line *Indomptable.*

Of the 31 admirals on the French Navy's Active List in the year 1797, Bruix was senior only to one: the remarkable veteran Pléville le Pelley,[1] who succeeded Truguet as Navy Minister in July 1797 and was promoted rear-admiral in October. The List featured 12 future 'Admirals of the *Arc*', including Bruix. Its first revelation is that promotion to flag rank, never lavish in the pre-1789 Navy, certainly did not go by mere seniority on the Captains' List under the Republic. An astonishing total of 27 captains had been promoted rear-admiral under the Convention of 1792–95; 22 of them were still on the Active List in 1797. This compared with only three (Truguet, Thévenard, and Morard de Galles) of the ten promotions to rear-admiral made under the Constitutional Monarchy of 1789–92.

The Jacobin Terror of 1793–94 had taken the lives of only four admirals (Flottes lynched by a mob and the Comte d'Estaing, Grimouard and Kersaint guillotined). It had, however, cashiered as political suspects seven of the 31 rear-admirals active in 1797, including Bruix, and six of them (Truguet, Latouche-Tréville, Missiessy, Sercey, Thévenard, and Brueys) had suffered greater or lesser terms of imprisonment before their reinstatement. But the mass promotions to flag rank in 1793 certainly did not reflect any doctrinal prejudice against age, whereas the 14 similar promotions of the Directory (1795–99), half of them already active by the end of 1797, clearly favoured younger captains. With the exception of the honorary promotion of Pléville le Pelley, none was over 50, while Bruix, Lacrosse, Villeneuve, Decrès, and Dordelin were still in their 30s. (Of the two promotions to rear-admiral made by Bonaparte in Egypt in 1798, Ganteaume was 43 and Perrée 37.)

In his dual role as Major-General of the Navy and Rear-Admiral, Bruix threw himself into the task of building up the Brest naval base and its fleet, bound as the latter was to be the prime mover in any major enterprise against England. He earned the full approval of the regime for the speed in which he repaired the immense material and moral damage which the fleet had suffered during its foray to Ireland. On 28 April 1798, as the spotlight shifted from the Atlantic to the Mediterranean with Bonaparte's forthcoming expedition to Egypt, Bruix was appointed Navy Minister on the retirement of Pléville le Pelley.

Despite his unhappy memories of the last Irish expedition of 1796–97, Bruix's first task as Navy Minister was to support the rising of the 'United Irishmen' which had broken out on 26 May. The hopes of his political masters of exploiting this opportunity were as wild as their intelligence was lamentable. Unaware that the United Irishmen had been crushed at Vinegar Hill on 21 June, Commodore Savary's Rochefort squadron sailed on 6 August to land General Humbert's troops at Killala, hopefully to reinforce the Irish rebels. This time the Navy performed its mission perfectly, landing the troops on 22 August and returning safely to France. But by the time that Humbert's isolated force was compelled to surrender at Ballinamuck (3 September 1798), the battered ship of the line *Généreux* had arrived at Toulon with appalling news. On 1 August 1798, at the far end of the Mediterranean, the destruction of Brueys's battle fleet by Nelson in Aboukir Bay had isolated both the French garrison of Malta and Bonaparte's army in Egypt.

Over the next four months the Mediterranean scene went from bad to worse. In September Russia and Turkey joined the Second Coalition against France; in October a Russo-Turkish naval force reconquered the Ionian Islands; and in December British troops landed on Malta to bring the French garrison in Valletta under land siege as well as naval blockade. By the New Year of 1799 only desperate measures could redress the situation in France's favour. Since the core of the Toulon fleet had been destroyed in Aboukir Bay, the only French naval force capable of a powerful intervention in the Mediterranean was the Atlantic fleet at Brest.

Bruix's planning for the relief of Malta and Egypt turned on the collaboration of France's last powerful naval ally: Spain. He was also confident (as proved to be the case) that a sortie by the entire Brest fleet would throw all the British fleet dispositions into at least temporary disarray which, given luck and determination, could be exploited. Unwilling, as Navy Minister, to entrust the venture to any other admiral (all of them his seniors on the List), he determined to lead it in person; and on 23 March 1799, ten days after his promotion to vice-admiral, he arrived at Brest to take command of the fleet. After a month of provisioning and overhauling, Bruix was only waiting for the right weather conditions to make his breakout.

He got them on 25 April, sailing from Brest with 25 of the line and ten frigates, and taking the first trick with the British believing that his destination, as in the previous year, would be Ireland. He headed south for Cadiz which he approached on 4 May, in a gale which prevented Admiral Mazzaredo from coming out to join the French fleet, which ran the Gibraltar Strait and entered the Mediterranean on the 5th. Deprived of his hoped-for Spanish reinforcements, unaware that he was in a position to crush any of the British naval detachments scattered the length of the Mediterranean (off Minorca, Naples, Palermo, Malta, and Acre in Syria), Bruix took the prudent course and headed north for Toulon, which he reached on 13 May. That was the day before Mazzaredo got out of Cadiz with 17 Spanish ships of the line, followed Bruix into the Mediterranean, and arrived at Cartagena with his force intact.

Bruix knew that every day he spent at Toulon would give the British time to concentrate against him, but after 18 days at sea he needed more than supplies and repair facilities. He badly needed information, not only about British naval movements but about the progress of the land war in Italy. Bruix learned that General Masséna was besieged in Genoa and that General Moreau had withdrawn to Savona to safeguard General Macdonald's retreat from southern Italy. Deciding that the most urgent requirement was to relieve Masséna, Bruix sailed from Toulon on 27 May but was driven back from Genoa by bad weather. He altered course to Vado Bay and there landed much-needed supplies for Moreau's army.

Considering future prospects at Vado, Bruix decided that his next imperative must be to try again for a rendezvous with the Spanish battle fleet. With the British wrong-footing themselves again by deciding that his destination must be Egypt, Bruix sailed on 6 June for Cartagena and arrived there, still unmolested, on the 22nd. There Mazzaredo's 17 battleships created the first Franco-Spanish combined fleet with a total strength of 40 ships of the line. With such a force at his disposal in the first week of May, Bruix could certainly have raised the siege of Malta and reopened France's sea communications with Egypt, but by the last week of June the British had the central Mediterranean safely locked. Bruix and Mazzaredo decided that it was more important to keep their force intact than have it ground down in a strategically pointless battle, and that there was no option but to retreat to the Atlantic. On 7 July the combined fleet passed the Gibraltar Strait, with the French contingent arriving at Brest on 8 August.

Bruix had handed the British Navy the biggest scare it was to know before the invasion crisis of 1805, and contributed to the safe return of Bonaparte from Egypt later in the year. But he had also taught the British Admiralty the paramount need to keep the Brest fleet tightly blockaded at all times and in all weathers, and this strategic imperative, destined to bring Napoleon's invasion plans to nothing in the year of Trafalgar, may be seen as the most fateful legacy of 'Bruix's Cruise'.

For Bruix the immediate aftermath of his return to Brest was, almost inevitably, anticlimactic. He had been replaced as Navy Minister by Talleyrand on 11 July, while still at sea, and was now moved to the Île d'Aix to build up the Rochefort squadron. Bruix commanded at Rochefort, resigning on 11 June 1802 on grounds of ill-health. He was already fighting his last battle, with tuberculosis, and his last appointments were nominal: Councillor of State in September 1802, and commander of the Boulogne flotilla in August 1803. Bruix's last command was the 13th Cohort of the Legion of Honour (24 September 1803). Napoleon created Bruix a Grand Officer of the Empire (6 July 1804) with the title of 'Inspector of the Ocean Coasts' and awarded him the Grand Eagle of the Legion of Honour on 2 February 1805. But a month later – 18 March 1805 – Bruix died at Paris at the age of 46.

Note

1   Remarkable for having had his right leg – the original and two wooden ones – shot off three times.

Vice-Admiral Pierre-Charles-Jean-Baptiste-Silvestre de Villeneuve (1763–1806)

Twenty years of impeccable service, rewarded with steady promotions which carried him to his admiral's flag – then an uncertain seven-year career plateau ending in catastrophic defeat, followed by a violent death (ostensibly suicide) still surrounded in mystery. That was the story of the man Napoleon always blamed for the failure of his master-plan to invade and conquer England in 1805, Nelson's doomed opponent at Trafalgar: Pierre-Charles-Jean-Baptiste-Silvestre de Villeneuve.

Villeneuve's family, of the lesser aristocracy (in 1792 he was to drop the 'de' from his name in deference to Republican ethos) came from Valensole, near Digne in the

Villeneuve. (Wikimedia Commons)

Basses-Alpes, where he was born on 31 January 1763. The date of Villeneuve's birth meant that his boyhood was spent in the years when the French Navy, under the hand of the Duc de Choiseul, was regaining its strength and confidence after the humiliations of the Seven Years War. By 1778, when France joined the American colonists in their struggle to free themselves from British rule, the time for a French war of revenge was ripe.

Just turned 14 years old, Villeneuve joined the Navy on 12 January 1778 as an *aspirant garde-marine* cadet. His first ship was the frigate *Flore* (January–March 1779), in which he served as Guard to the Colours. From June 1779 to March 1781 he served in the ships of the line *Montréal* and *Hardi,* transferring on 5 March 1781 to the ship of the line *Marseillais*[1] in the fleet of de Grasse. Still six months short of his 18th birthday, Villeneuve was commissioned lieutenant (*enseigne de vaisseau*) on 9 May 1781, already marked down as a young officer of above-average promise.

Villeneuve remained with *Marseillais* during the dramatic months when de Grasse's star was mounting to its zenith. He got his first taste of amphibious operations during the capture of Tobago on 30 May 1781, being rewarded for his efforts with a company lieutenancy. And he further distinguished himself during the greatest achievement of de Grasse: the Battle of Chesapeake Bay (5 September 1781) which sealed the fate of the British army on the Yorktown peninsula, and ensured final victory for the rebel Americans and their French allies.

Villeneuve's luck carried him through the British counterstroke: Rodney's defeat of de Grasse in the Battle of the Saints (12 April 1782). *Marseillais* escaped the scattering of the French fleet and the capture of de Grasse. Villeneuve ended the war in the ship of the line *Destin,* to which he transferred in November 1782, with a swansong of frigate service in the *Blonde* (July 1783).

Many officers experienced stagnating careers and delayed promotion with the coming of peace in 1783, but on 1 May 1786 Villeneuve was promoted commander (*lieutenant de vaisseau*). In the French Navy, this was the most junior qualifying rank for the command of a sloop, corvette, or small frigate. Many worthy and able lieutenants (in the British Navy as well as the French) grew old and died in the service without having achieved the vital promotion to commander. With his war record and the enthusiastic endorsements of his commanding officers, Villeneuve had achieved it in a mere eight years of service. But promotion to commander did not win Villeneuve an independent small-ship command. Instead he was posted to the frigate *Alceste* (October 1787–December 1788), after which he went on long leave.

The first three years of the Revolution were inactive ones for Villeneuve, who did not get his first seagoing command, the frigate *Badine,* until February 1792. But on 30 August 1792, three weeks after the fall of the monarchy, he was transferred to the ship of the line *Tonnant,* the fleet flagship at Toulon. He joined the staff of Truguet, commander of the Toulon fleet, which opened France's maritime war when the new Republic declared war on the neighbouring Kingdom of Sardinia in September 1792.

The Toulon fleet's task was to extend France's south-eastern frontier by bombarding and landing troops to capture the Sardinian coastal towns of Nice, Montalban, Villafranca and Oneglia. Both Truguet and Villeneuve had gained plenty of experience in such operations during the American war, and the Sardinian towns were easily captured. Truguet recommended Villeneuve for promotion to *capitaine de vaisseau,* but before this was confirmed in February 1793, the Central Defence Committee in Paris had set the Toulon fleet an objective beyond its capacity. This was the capture of Cagliari, Sardinia, which being amply protected by shore batteries was impervious to a purely naval assault.

Truguet had no intention of sacrificing his fleet in a forlorn venture, and withdrew after his senior squadron commander, Trogoff, was wounded during a tentative bombardment of the outer forts. For this failure at Cagliari, Truguet was replaced as commander of the Toulon fleet by Trogoff in May 1793. Villeneuve's promotion to *capitaine de vaisseau* had been confirmed in February 1793 but brought him no immediate command – and on 30 November 1793, under the Jacobin Terror, he was stripped of his rank on the charge of being a politically suspect 'aristo'.

In this supreme crisis Villeneuve was far luckier than most of his naval contemporaries. He escaped imprisonment but remained without employment until the Terror imploded with the arrest and execution of Robespierre in July 1794, and was not reinstated in rank until 24 May 1795. On 5 August 1795, he got his first battleship command: the *Peuple-Souverain*. This resumed advancement of Villeneuve's career accelerated in the following month when he was appointed Major-General of the Navy – port commander, responsible for all attached troops, marines, sailors, militia, and civilian workers – at Toulon.

The restoration of the port complex, shattered during Toulon's brief-lived revolt and declaration for Louis XVII in 1793, was well advanced by autumn 1795; but much remained to be done, and Villeneuve's work earned him the enthusiastic approval of Admiral Martin, commander of the Toulon fleet. On 21 March 1796, Martin promoted Villeneuve commodore (*chef de division*). Villeneuve's former commander, Truguet, was now Navy Minister and on 22 September he approved the promotion of Villeneuve – still three months short of his 33rd birthday – to rear-admiral.

Villeneuve was now one of the three squadron commanders of the Toulon fleet, but he did not stay there long. He was now called upon to provide support for the ill-fated Irish expedition ordered by France's new government, the Directory. This was the sailing of the Brest fleet with an invasion force to raise Ireland against the British. Morard de Galles, commanding the Brest fleet, protested that the bad weather required to permit an escape from Brest would be too much for his ill-prepared warships, crammed as they were with troops. Truguet therefore ordered Martin at Toulon to dispatch a battle squadron to support Morard's fleet, and this task was entrusted to Villeneuve.

On 30 November 1796, Villeneuve escaped from Toulon with the 80-gun *Formidable* and four fast 74s, and passed Gibraltar on 8 December – eight days before Morard's fleet broke out of Brest. But the storms that blew the British blockaders off station and let Morard's ships escape from Brest delayed Villeneuve on the last leg of his voyage north, and he approached Brest four days too late. On 23 December he led his intact force into Lorient, where it provided France's storm-battered Atlantic fleet, struggling back from Ireland in the first days of 1797, with an invaluable hard core on which to rebuild.

In the overall fiasco of the Irish venture Villeneuve had played the most effective part, and his achievement had a fateful legacy. It had proved that it was *possible* – given the right sequence of unlikely circumstances falling into place – for one battle fleet to reinforce another. From this possibility grew the strategic mirage of adding one battle fleet to another, and then to the next, finally assembling an armada of overwhelming strength that could sweep into the Dover Straits and make possible an invasion of England. Eight years later, driven by Napoleon, this mirage would lead the French Navy – and Villeneuve – into the disaster of the Trafalgar campaign.

Another fateful outcome of Villeneuve's sortie was the strengthening of his ties with Decrès, Villeneuve's second-in-command during the Toulon-Lorient foray, and Napoleon's future Navy Minister in the year of Trafalgar. Villeneuve's official praise of Decrès's performance in December 1796 helped secure the promotion of Decrès to rear-admiral in the spring of 1798, when the Toulon fleet was preparing for the expedition to Egypt. Its objective was not merely the conquest of Egypt, but the lodgement of a French power base in the Middle East from which to strike at the flow of Britain's wealth from India.

The supreme commander of the expedition was Bonaparte, conqueror of Austrian North Italy in the campaigns of 1796–97. A huge transport fleet, well over double the size of the 1588 Spanish Armada, was assembled to carry the French expeditionary force of 30,000 infantry, 2,800 cavalry and its field and siege artillery. It was shielded by a battle fleet of 13 ships of the line and seven frigates. Brueys, who had made his name by capturing the Ionian Islands in July 1797, commanded the battle fleet. Villeneuve was one of his squadron commanders, and the newly-promoted Rear-Admiral Decrès commanded the frigates.

At first, the French enjoyed amazing luck. The unwieldy fleet formed up at sea without any molestation from the British, who were well aware that a major French *coup* was under way somewhere in the Mediterranean. On 9 June, the French fleet arrived off Malta, which became the expedition's first prize. Leaving a garrison of 4,000 to hold Malta, the fleet sailed on to reach Egypt on 30 June, land the troops, and capture Alexandria on 2 July. While Bonaparte completed the land conquest of Egypt from its Mameluke rulers, Brueys took order for the British naval counterstroke which he knew must come.

He moved the battle fleet to the apparently secure shallows of Aboukir Bay and anchored it in a tight line-ahead, with his most powerful ships – the 80-gun *Tonnant* and *Franklin* and his flagship, the mighty 120-gun *Orient* – in the centre. His plan was to present any British attack with an overwhelming concentration of broadside fire. Villeneuve's squadron, his flagship *Guillaume-Tell*, *Généreux*, and *Timoléon*, brought up the rear of the line. But what Brueys had not foreseen was the enveloping attack developed by Nelson on the evening of 1 August 1798: rounding the head of the French line, and crushing its Van and Centre with attacks from both sides.

Brueys was killed before *Orient*, set ablaze by the British bombardment at point-blank range, blew up and sank. By daylight on the 2nd, Villeneuve was commanding the last three French ships of the line capable of making sail, and he signalled them to break out. *Timoléon* grounded and was burnt to prevent her capture, leaving

Villeneuve with *Guillaume-Tell* and *Généreux*, and Decrès with the frigates *Diane* and *Justice*, to escape the holocaust of Aboukir Bay.

With this phantom fleet, Villeneuve's first imperative was to head for Malta and do what he could to strengthen its garrison. He then detached *Généreux* to return to France with news of the Aboukir Bay disaster and urgent pleas for naval reinforcements. On 18 August, she fell in with the 50-gun British *Leander*, heading west with Nelson's victory dispatch, and after a 6-hour battering the outmatched *Leander* struck her colours. Although the French had taken 288 casualties against the British 92, *Généreux* had proved that the decimated French fleet could still bite.

But that was the only chance it got. *Généreux* won through to France but was captured on 18 February 1800, leading Perrée's ill-fated relief expedition to Malta. Decrès, trying to escape from Malta in *Guillaume-Tell*, was captured off Malta on 29 March 1800. On 24 August, with the end in sight for the French defenders of Malta, Villeneuve ordered the two frigates to break out. *Diane* was captured by the blockading fleet, but *Justice* escaped her pursuers and returned to France, the sole survivor of the Aboukir Bay battle fleet. When General Vaubois surrendered to the British on 5 September, Villeneuve became a prisoner of war.

Repatriated to France under the surrender terms, Villeneuve returned to the new *regime* of Bonaparte's Consulate. His next appointment (April 1801) took him back to the Mediterranean as naval commander at Taranto, supporting the French 'Army of Observation of the South'. Villeneuve owed his escape from this strategic backwater to Decrès who had become Bonaparte's Navy Minister in October 1801. During the Peace of Amiens (March 1802–May 1803), when many naval careers languished on both sides of the Channel, Villeneuve served in the Caribbean as naval C-in-C, Windward Islands (September 1802–June 1803). When in May 1804, following Napoleon's proclamation as Emperor of the French, 18 Army generals were promoted to the rank of Marshal, three Navy flag officers were promoted to vice-admiral: Villeneuve (20 May) and Ganteaume and Decrès (30 May). And in the following month, on 20 June, Villeneuve was given command of the Rochefort squadron, drawing him into the coils of Napoleon's master-plan for the invasion of England.

The inspiration of this plan came not only from the Brest fleet's foray to Ireland and Villeneuve's cruise from Toulon to Lorient in December 1796, the safe passage of the Mediterranean armada in 1798, and Bonaparte's own successful running of the British blockade during his return voyage to France in August–October 1799. There was the far more dramatic exploit of Bruix in April–August 1799. Like Morard de Galles in 1796, Bruix proved that it was possible for the Brest fleet to evade the British and escape to the high seas, but, unlike Morard, Bruix kept his fleet together. With 25 ships of the line he headed south, entered the Mediterranean, reached Toulon, landed supplies for General Moreau's army at Vado Bay, collected an additional 16 Spanish ships of the line at Cartagena, and returned safely to Brest. A superficial review of these five successive exploits helps explain Napoleon's impatience with the objections of his naval experts to his grand design.

By midsummer 1804, Bruix was *hors de combat* – he was dying of tuberculosis. The key French fleet commands were now held by Latouche-Tréville (Toulon), Ganteaume (Brest) and Villeneuve (Rochefort). The bulk of the French Army, already re-styled the 'Army of England', was massed around Boulogne. It could not sail for England until the French Navy provided a massive covering force in the Dover Straits. To this end, Napoleon ordered successive breakouts by the Rochefort, Toulon, and Brest fleets. Together they were to draw the British battle fleets off their covering stations by feigning a blow at the British West Indies, then recross the Atlantic and head for the Dover Straits to cover the invasion of England.

The most favourable weather months for the passage of a cross-Channel invasion fleet were from June to September. This 'window' was already half-closed for 1804 when the wholly unexpected death of Latouche-Tréville on 19 August made a prior reshuffle of the fleet commands essential, switched the spotlight from Brest to Toulon, and effectively postponed the invasion attempt until 1805. On 10 September 1804 Missiessy took over command of the Rochefort squadron, and two days later Villeneuve set off for Paris as commander-designate of the Toulon fleet. Over the following weeks, Villeneuve learned that he and Missiessy were to make the opening moves of the invasion master plan in the New Year of 1805.

For a few fleeting days in January 1805, it almost seemed that the grand design was going to become reality. Missiessy's Rochefort squadron escaped on the 11th, and by 20 February had reached the Caribbean; on 17 January, Villeneuve broke out from Toulon with 11 of the line. But he ran right into storms which inflicted so much damage to sails, spars and rigging that after two days there was nothing for it but to head back for repairs; by the 20th, Villeneuve's battered fleet was back in Toulon.

Napoleon raged at admirals who ran back to port without repairing storm damage at sea, ignoring the fact that this was impossible without enough sea time for French crews to acquire anything like the competence of the British. On 14 March, he revised his master plan yet again, issuing another volley of orders to his admirals:

- **Missiessy** to bring the Rochefort squadron home from the West Indies;
- **Ganteaume** to sail from Brest with 21 of the line, collect as many French and Spanish warships as he could from Rochefort and Ferrol, then cross the Atlantic to Martinique;
- **Villeneuve** to sail from Toulon with his repaired fleet, collect as many Spanish battleships as he could from Cadiz, cross the Atlantic and rendezvous with Ganteaume at Martinique;
- **Ganteaume** to lead the combined Franco-Spanish fleet (by now hopefully at least 40 of the line) back to France, sweep the opposing British out of the way, and arrive off Boulogne between 10 June and 10 July.

Apart from Missiessy's successful return to Rochefort on 20 May (to be sacked by Napoleon for having failed to recapture the Diamond Rock off Martinique), Villeneuve's cruise from Toulon to the West Indies was the only part of the grand design to be carried out according to plan. Unlike Ganteaume, who, because of the tight British blockade of Brest, could not escape to sea without a battle (which Napoleon expressly forbade), Villeneuve had never been closely blockaded in Toulon; Nelson *wanted* him to come out and be fought at sea. Villeneuve sailed from Toulon with 11 of the line on 30 March, four days after receiving Napoleon's revised order.

Because of Nelson's initial determination to cover Naples and Sicily, Villeneuve was able to arrive off Cartagena on 6 April, only to find no Spanish ships ready to join him. He pushed on, passing Gibraltar on the 8th. On the following day, the Spanish Vice-Admiral Gravina joined him from Cadiz with six more ships of the line, and what was now the Franco-Spanish Combined fleet headed into the Atlantic. On 14 May, Villeneuve reached Martinique.

Once arrived in the West Indies, Villeneuve was under orders to await Ganteaume for 40 days, doing all he could to reinforce the impression that his main objective was the conquest of the British-held islands. He began with the reduction of the Diamond Rock, accomplished between 31 May and 2 June (with the future admiral Cosmao-Kerjulien, commanding the ship of the line *Pluton,* distinguishing himself in the operation). But on the 3rd a frigate arrived from France bearing further orders, with the news that Ganteaume was still in Brest but that Rear-Admiral Magon's Rochefort squadron had reached Guadeloupe. Villeneuve was to spend the next 35 days in the West Indies, capturing Antigua, St Vincent and Grenada before re-crossing the Atlantic to Ferrol in Spain, there hopefully to rendezvous with Ganteaume.

On 8 June, Villeneuve and the Combined Fleet, now numbering 18 of the line after Magon's reinforcement, was approaching Antigua when an obliging American ship informed him that a homeward-bound British West India Company convoy was in the offing. After a brief chase the Combined Fleet fell on the convoy and scattered it, taking no less than 15 prizes in a few hours. It was Villeneuve's first great victory as a fleet commander, and fated to be his last; his satisfaction was dashed by the electrifying news that Nelson had chased him across the Atlantic, in a crossing ten days faster than that of the Combined Fleet, and had reached Barbados on 4 June.

Even if he had known that the Combined Fleet outnumbered Nelson's by 18 to 11, Villeneuve's decision to evade Nelson and return at once to Europe would still have been sound. A fleet action over 3,000 miles from the Channel, with the inevitable casualties, loss and damage even if victory had been won, would have done nothing to further the imperial master plan. He sailed for Europe on the 9th.

Villeneuve's luck held for the last time thanks to bad intelligence on the British side, which diverted Nelson south to Trinidad before he guessed Villeneuve's true destination and resumed the long pursuit. On 22 July, the Combined Fleet was 300 miles from Ferrol, when it was intercepted west of Finisterre by Admiral Calder with 15 of the line. Calder hesitantly engaged the Combined Fleet, but in a confused action in thick and misty weather was only able to capture two Spanish warships. Villeneuve was able to break away with the bulk of the Combined Fleet, making landfall first at Vigo Bay and finally (1 August) at Ferrol, where Spanish reinforcements raised the Combined Fleet's strength to 30 of the line. The news reached Napoleon at Boulogne ten days later, but he did not issue his final orders for the abandonment of the Channel camps until the 24th, unaware that Villeneuve had in fact sailed from Ferrol on the 13th. He had headed for Brest only to be driven back by strong north-easterly winds, and turned back to Spain – this time heading for Cadiz, where the Combined Fleet arrived on 21 August.

The Spanish warships in Cadiz raised the Combined Fleet to a strength of 33 ships of the line (18 French and 15 Spanish), but it was beyond Villeneuve's power to convert it into an integrated unit in the two months before the final showdown with the British off Cape Trafalgar. Relations between the two navies were strained; the Spanish commanders Gravina and Alava felt that Villeneuve had exposed their ships to the brunt of Calder's attack off Finisterre. Merely feeding the fleet caused constant problems, with the Cadiz port authorities objecting to being paid in French paper money.

Continued Spanish cooperation with Villeneuve was only maintained by direct orders from Madrid. It was vital, because the Spanish navy provided the Combined Fleet's most powerful units: the 130-gun *Santissima Trinidad,* the 112-gun *Principe de Asturias* and *Santa Ana,* and the 100-gun *Rayo.* In the British fleet of 27 of the line which Nelson joined on 28 September, waiting hungrily out at sea, there were only three 100-gun ships: *Victory, Royal Sovereign,* and *Britannia.* But Nelson's opinion of the Combined Fleet, expressed back in June in a letter to the Governor of Barbados, was sound: 'Powerful as their force may be, mine is compact, theirs must be unwieldy, and although a very pretty fiddle I don't believe that either Gravina or Villeneuve know how to play upon it.'[2]

The last act of the drama was dominated by the appalling state of land communications between Paris and Cadiz. On 14 September, Napoleon, on the eve of departure for his Austro-Russian campaign, dashed off an order for Villeneuve to sail for the Mediterranean and reinforce Naples before returning to Toulon. This order reached Villeneuve on the 29th. On 23 September, however, Napoleon had appointed Vice-Admiral Rosily-Mesros to replace Villeneuve as Combined Fleet commander. On 18 October, ten days after an acrimonious Council of War with the Spanish admirals and senior captains, Villeneuve heard that Rosily had arrived at Madrid on the 12th. He also heard that six ships of the line from Nelson's fleet had been sighted at Gibraltar. It was in the belief that his successor could arrive at Cadiz at any moment, and that the British fleet was at least momentarily significantly weakened, that Villeneuve ordered the Combined Fleet to sea on the morning of the 19th. Alerted by his screen of frigates, Nelson easily cut off the Combined Fleet's initial course to Gibraltar, and Villeneuve was unavailingly trying to return to Cadiz when Nelson finally brought him to battle off Cape Trafalgar on 21 October 1805.

No Republican French admiral had ever commanded so large a fleet in battle – the Combined Fleet had seven more ships of the line than Villaret at the First of June, and 20 more than Brueys at Aboukir Bay – and given its composition and weakness in binational communication Villeneuve's options were limited. The course change towards Cadiz had reversed the Combined Fleet's order of battle. Its former Rear Division – Rear-Admiral Dumanoir's five French and three Spanish ships of the line – was now the Van. The Centre, of four French and three Spanish ships of the line, included the mighty four-decked *Santissima Trinidad* and Villeneuve's flagship, the 80-gun *Bucentaure*. The former Van Division was now the Rear: nine French and nine Spanish ships of the line under Gravina, joined by the Scouting Squadron of Rear-Admiral Magon which had led the Combined Fleet out of Cadiz on the 19th.

With vivid memories of how Nelson had rounded the head of the French line in Aboukir Bay, Villeneuve knew very well that Nelson would not be forming the conventional parallel line of battle. It was for this reason that Villeneuve had made the original Van Division the Combined Fleet's strongest, including two of the huge Spanish 112-gun battleships, *Santa Ana* and Gravina's flagship *Principe de Asturias*. But Villeneuve was totally unprepared for the two-pronged lunge at the Combined Fleet's Centre and Rear, severing the Van, with which Nelson opened the Trafalgar battle. It was a calculated risk, because the foremost British ships were exposed to vicious raking fire from the Franco-Spanish line lying across their bows, those in Collingwood's division suffering the worst. It would have gone far harder with the British if the Combined Fleet, like Villaret's on the First of June in 1794, had been deployed in tight line-ahead with each ship's broadside given full play. But the course reversal had resulted in bunching, with the fire of many French and Spanish ships obscured by others to windward, reducing the ordeal of the oncoming British.

With his Centre and Rear pierced and his flagship *Bucentaure* battered defenceless by Nelson's *Victory* as she passed through the allied line, Villeneuve's last remaining option was to shift his flag to Dumanoir's unscathed Van Division and lead a counter-attack. When he found that not a boat had escaped *Bucentaure's* ruin he had no option but surrender, with his British captors deeply impressed by his dignity in defeat. At the moment that he struck his colours, Villeneuve did not know that he had at least destroyed France's greatest living enemy. Shot down by a musket ball fired from the mizzen top of the French *Redoutable,* which had done her utmost to support *Bucentaure,* Nelson lay dying among the *Victory's* many wounded.

Villeneuve might also have derived a crumb of comfort from the ruinous condition to which he had reduced Nelson's fleet at Trafalgar. This was so bad that the British Admiralty censored Collingwood's victory dispatch. The following words were deleted to prevent their publication in the *London Gazette* from informing the French that they had nothing to fear from the victorious British: 'I have 23 infirm ships, 18 of them hulks, without a stick standing, and scarce a boat in the fleet'.

Villeneuve spent six months as a captive in England before he was returned to France under cartel in April 1806. Napoleon's hostility to him had not abated: Villeneuve was ordered to remain at Rennes in Brittany and not return to Paris. There he wrote forlornly to his wife that he was glad not to have any children who would remember his 'horrible héritage' and the disgrace of his name. And it was in Rennes, on 22 April 1806, that Villeneuve was found dead with no less than six knife-wounds in his chest.

Bleakly regretting this ostensible suicide – which bears comparison with the royalist supporter General Pichegru 'strangling himself' in prison in April 1804 – Napoleon wrote 'He should not have acted that way. He was a gallant man, although he had no talent.' Thirty years after his burial without honours, kinder justice was done to Villeneuve's memory by the inclusion of his name on the *Arc de Triomphe*.

Notes

1 Renamed *Vengeur* in February 1794 and destined for a glorious end in the Battle of the First of June (pp. 36–37).
2 Letter from Nelson to the governor of Barbados.

Vice-Admiral François-Paul, *Comte de* Brueys d'Aigalliers (1753–1798)

In the bitter aftermath of Trafalgar, there must have been many times that the defeated Villeneuve desperately envied François-Paul Brueys d'Aigalliers, *Comte de* Brueys. For Brueys, Nelson's beaten opponent in the so-called 'Battle of the Nile' in Aboukir Bay on 1 August 1798, had been killed in battle, cut down on his quarterdeck by a British cannon ball.

Brueys was 45 when he died at Aboukir Bay, and 32 of those years had been spent on the long professional climb from boy volunteer to fleet commander. He had served aboard and commanded just about every class of French warship afloat: ships

Brueys. Lithograph by Maurin, c.1835. (Wikimedia Commons)

of the line, frigates, corvettes, sloops – even that agile, lateen-sailed Mediterranean oddity, the xebec – *flûtes* and store ships. In that powerful catalyst of so many French naval careers, the American Revolutionary War (1778-1783), Brueys had served in the key American/Caribbean war theatre, under one of the greatest French naval commanders of the age.

It took Brueys 18 years to get his first command, and another 12 before he could hoist his admiral's flag. And in all those years of service, from his first ship to his last, there was for Brueys a strangely recurring theme: the eastern Mediterranean, the Levant. Duty took Brueys to the eastern Mediterranean no less than seven times, raising him to the rank of vice-admiral. It was the eighth voyage east at the summit of his career, ending in Aboukir Bay in 1798, which proved fatal.

Brueys was a Provençal, born at Uzès (Gard) on 11 February 1753. His family, of the lesser aristocracy, had no active naval tradition but once a career in the Navy had been decided for François-Paul, sufficient enquiries had been made to enter him as a

13-year-old Volunteer in the ship of the line *Protecteur*. This gave the young Brueys two useful years of sea time – and his first cruise to the Levant – before he could be properly entered as a *garde de la marine* officer cadet in the Toulon Company (13 August 1768). His first taste of active service was in the frigate *Atalante* in an expedition against the Barbary Corsairs of Tunis (May–November 1770).

Over the next two years Brueys made his second cruise to the Levant, in the frigate *Chimère* (September 1771–May 1772), and to the Caribbean in the ship of the line *Actionnaire*, based on Saint-Domingue, in November 1772. At Saint-Domingue he fell gravely ill; the island was a hotbed of dangerous diseases, with yellow fever and malaria topping the list of potential killers. Brueys was sent ashore to recuperate on 19 March 1773, having to be invalided home. But by the autumn of 1773 he was back at sea, serving in the storeship *Manon* on the Brittany coast.

Brueys's next ship was the frigate *Flore*, in which no fewer than four future admirals (the other three being Missiessy, Villeneuve, and Flotte de Beuzidou) served during the 1770s. During his service in *Flore* (17 June 1774–22 January 1775) he experienced his third cruise to the Levant, returning to Toulon to be posted to the xebec *Singe* in the Golfe du Lion (May–September 1775). This widely varied accumulation of sea time and experience continued with a posting to the ship of the line *Provence* (April–October 1776), after which he obtained his lieutenant's commission as *enseigne de vaisseau* (4 April 1777).

A two-month posting to the ship of the line *César* (April–June 1777) was cut short by Brueys's transfer to the corvette *Flèche*. This was the prelude to two more prolonged cruises to the Levant, the first in *Flèche* (June 1777–December 1778) and the second in the frigate *Gracieuse* (April 1779–March 1780). Brueys's return to Toulon in *Gracieuse* was followed by his promotion to *lieutenant de vaisseau* (4 April 1780). In his new rank as commander he was appointed to the ship of the line *Terrible* (May 1780–March 1781), after which he was transferred to the Brest fleet and the ship of the line *Zélé*.

Zélé was part of the squadron of de Guichen in the fleet of the *Comte de* Grasse, which sailed for American waters in March 1781. During his 15 months in *Zélé*, Brueys experienced his first fleet action: the raising of Admiral Hood's blockade of Martinique on 29 April 1781, followed by an exhilarating pursuit of the retiring British. In August de Grasse sailed for America to support Washington's army in Virginia, and *Zélé* took part in the defeat of Admiral Graves off Chesapeake Bay (5 September 1781), which sealed the fate of the British army under Cornwallis on the Yorktown peninsula. This was arguably the most momentous victory of the French Navy in the eighteenth century, ensuring as it did the final victory against Britain of the rebel Americans, and it was followed by de Grasse's landing of 6,000 troops to capture St Kitts (27 January 1782).

De Grasse had planned to continue this run of victory by launching an invasion of Jamaica, but was foiled by the manoeuvres of Admiral Rodney's fleet. On the night before the decisive encounter between de Grasse and Rodney, *Zélé* lost her bowsprit and foremast in a collision and had to be towed into Guadeloupe by a frigate. This accident meant that Brueys took no part in the Battle of the Saints (12 April 1782), which ended in the defeat and surrender of de Grasse. Brueys stayed with *Zélé* until 1 July 1782, when he was transferred to the frigate *Vestale*. Her mission was to muster a large convoy and escort it to France, which was successfully accomplished on 16 October.

Back in France, Brueys was created *Chevalier de Saint-Louis* on 17 November 1783, but another year passed before he was finally given his first peacetime command. This was the sloop *Chien de Chasse* in which, over the next three years, he cruised the length of the West Indies archipelago, not returning to France until June 1787. When this commission ended, Brueys was sent out on a similar cruise to the coasts of Spanish America in command of the sloop *Coureur* (June 1787–April 1788). After his return to France from Martinique in command of the *flûte Barbeau* in June 1788, Brueys was granted a year's leave.

Returning to service in the summer of 1790, Brueys sailed on his next mission in the corvette *Poulette* with an unusual cargo: tricolour flags. His task was not only to show the new national flag but to see it installed at every French commercial and diplomatic outlet in the Adriatic Sea and the Levant (September 1790–July 1792). During this leisurely cruise his promotion to *capitaine de vaisseau* was announced in the New Year's list of 1 January 1792. After this mission, when Brueys returned to Toulon to take up his first battleship command, it was appropriate that it should be the ship of the line *Tricolore,* formerly named *Lys* – the national emblem of the *Ancien Régime* – under Truguet in the Toulon fleet.

When the new Republic declared war on the Kingdom of Sardinia (16 September 1792), Brueys sailed with Truguet's fleet to bombard and land troops to capture Nice, Montalban, Villafranca and Oneglia. But the attack on Cagliari in Sardinia ordered by the Convention failed in February 1793, and Brueys became one of the many captains of the Toulon fleet to attract the censure of the Republican authorities at Toulon. On 5 May 1793 he was jailed in Fort Lamalgue, deprived of his command, and finally stripped of his commission as an 'aristo' in September. Brueys was not reinstated in rank by the rump Committee of Public Safety until 4 June 1795.

Many officers, similarly mistreated by the Jacobin dictatorship, found their careers accelerated by the Republic's new regime, the Directory, and Brueys was one of them. On 19 July 1796, promoted commodore (*chef de division),* he was given command of the French naval forces in the Adriatic Sea, flying his broad pendant in the ship of the line *Guillaume-Tell,* and was promoted rear-admiral on 22 September 1796. In July 1797 he directed the troop landings which occupied Corfu and the other Ionian Islands. This virtually bloodless conquest earned him promotion to vice-admiral on 12 April 1798, appointed commander-in-chief not only of the Toulon fleet but of all French naval forces in the Mediterranean. On 5 May 1798, Brueys hoisted his flag in the 120-gun ship of the line *Orient*, charged with the greatest mission of his career: conveying the expeditionary army of Bonaparte, 30,000 in all – horse, foot, field guns and siege artillery – to Egypt.

The huge invasion fleet of 300 transports and store ships was drawn from all major ports on the French Mediterranean coast and French-controlled northern Italy. To ensure its safety, Brueys commanded a battle fleet of 13 ships of the line and seven frigates. His chief of staff in *Orient* was Ganteaume, his squadron commanders were Rear-Admirals Blanquet du Chayla and Villeneuve, and the frigates were commanded by Decrès. But this command structure was not determined in the usual way, by the Navy Minister or the commanding admiral. It was laid down by Bonaparte in a directive to Brueys from Paris on 22 April – four weeks before the fleet sailed from Toulon on 19 May – in which Bonaparte made it clear that he was not going to be a mere passenger during his army's passage to Egypt. He would give orders as commander-in-chief of the entire 'naval army', of which Brueys's battle fleet was only the protective element. Not content with telling Brueys how his fleet was to be organised, Bonaparte's directive of the 23rd continued:

> 'Admiral Decrès will command the convoy and will have under his orders two first rates, three frigates and a number of fast brigs which you will select. With these ships he will lead the movement and will be ready to command the light squadron which you may decide to form by detaching ships from the fleet.
>
> 'But once the enemy is in sight and the line of battle is formed, all Admiral Decrès's care, with his frigates, will be for the convoy, to attend to its safety and carry out the orders you may have given him.
>
> 'Thus it seems to me that this officer has a splendid role. He sails at the head of the column, verifies the reports of his patrol boats and sends back exact messages to you. This single function is so important that it ought to be, as on land, the commander himself who can be the first to observe the enemy; but at sea the admiral can never leave his fleet because he is never sure of being able to rejoin it once he has left it.
>
> 'Should you, as soon as the enemy is sighted, judge it proper to support the frigates with two or three ships of the line, then the light squadron will be organised in accordance with established custom and that officer will command it. Finally, if you fight in line, the responsibilities of that admiral will be no less important; whatever the issue of the battle, he will have to shelter from every accident a convoy that is very precious to the Republic and, having done that, he may still with his frigates be of service to the fleet.
>
> 'What I am laying down is perhaps contrary to normal usage, but the advantages I foresee in it are so great that I am certain we shall profit by it...'

Unfortunately, Brueys's reaction to being taught his business by a brash young general 16 years his junior has not survived. When he read the above, he can hardly have known whether to laugh or cry. Brueys may well have prayed that Bonaparte's stated fear of being incapacitated by seasickness all the way to Egypt would come true, but any such prayer was denied. Nine days out from Toulon (by which time Bonaparte and Brueys were clearly communicating mostly in writing) the last detachments from the Italian ports had not yet joined the main body. Brueys proposed to detach four of the line and three frigates to bring in the convoy from Civitavecchia, which had the longest voyage to make. Bonaparte would have none of it. 'If, twenty-four hours after this separation, ten English ships are signalled', he wrote to Brueys on 27 May, 'I shall have only nine instead of thirteen'. But no such encounter occurred, and the fleet sailed on unmolested to arrive off Malta on 9 June.

Three days sufficed for the Knights of St John to capitulate and yield Malta to Bonaparte, and another six for Bonaparte to draw up detailed regulations for the island's new future as a French dependency, while the fleet watered and embarked fresh provisions. The voyage resumed on 19 June and finally arrived off Alexandria on 1 July. While Bonaparte attacked and took the city on the following day, Brueys moved the fleet west to expedite the disembarkation of the army in the roadstead of Marabout.

While insisting that the troop landings must take top priority (not that Brueys needed reminding), Bonaparte nevertheless sent a tart message on the 3rd rebuking Brueys for not having simultaneously blockaded the port of Alexandria, permitting all the light Egyptian craft and four large cargo ships to escape. Complaining that the fleet's new anchorage was too far away for rapid communication, Bonaparte insisted that it should be based in Alexandria, heedless of the fact that the harbour entrance was too shallow for the big French battleships. In a final piece of gratuitous rudeness, Bonaparte demanded that Ganteaume should be sent to Alexandria at once to serve as his naval liaison officer, but Brueys refused to lose the services of his Chief of Staff and Ganteaume remained aboard *Orient*.

Once his ships were free of the Army's troops and equipment, Brueys's priority was to find a secure anchorage for his fleet. On 8 July he led it into the semi-circular embrace of Aboukir Bay, 15 miles east of Alexandria and close to the Rosetta mouth of the Nile (whence the ensuing battle got its more familiar name). The western approach to the Aboukir anchorage was shielded by a curving arc of rocks and shoals, and these Brueys decided to enlist as protection for the head of his line.

Here he made one fatal mistake. Knowing that his charts of the Bay were inaccurate, he should have taken soundings and warped his leading ship, the 74-gun *Guerrier*, even closer into the shallows. But he had convinced himself that any British attack would opt for the traditional line-ahead gunnery duel, and to this end he placed the ships with the heaviest firepower – Blanquet's flagship *Franklin* (80), *Orient* (120) and *Tonnant* (80) – in the centre of his line. Blanquet's squadron formed the Van, Brueys commanded the Centre, and Villeneuve's squadron the Rear. The four frigates commanded by Decrès were deployed inshore of the battle line. Had they been scouting out at sea, they would certainly have given Brueys ample notice of Nelson's approaching fleet on the afternoon of 1 August 1798.

During the frustrating weeks in which he had scoured the eastern Mediterranean in search of the French, Nelson had impressed on his captains his intention of attacking the French line on both sides, in order to envelop its van and centre. Urged on by Nelson, it was Captain Hood's *Zealous* which, constantly sounding, crept round the head of the French line shortly before 1800, to be followed by *Theseus* and *Orion*. By 1900 Nelson had five ships to port of Brueys' line and three to starboard, and the crushing of the French van and centre began.

Brueys did not live to see the full catastrophe unfold, with only two of his 13 ships of the line surviving to escape on the following day. *Orient* was still pouring a murderous fire into the outmatched *Bellerophon,* leaving her totally dismasted, when the end came. By 2000 Brueys had already been lightly wounded in the face and one hand when a shot from the 'Billy Ruffian' nearly cut him in two. Brueys died 15 agonising minutes later. His body was never recovered, destroyed with almost all his surviving crew, when at 2200 the blazing *Orient* blew up with a shattering explosion that was heard in Alexandria. In stark contrast to his dismissive comments on Villeneuve, Napoleon later wrote of Brueys 'If, in this disastrous event, he made mistakes, he expiated them by his glorious end'.

Vice-Admiral Honoré-Joseph Ganteaume (1755–1818)

Ganteaume (the usual spelling of the family name, that on the *Arc de Triomphe* being the rarer 'Gantheaume') was one of the only three French naval officers to be promoted rear-admiral by an Army general[1]. Because the general in Ganteaume's case was Napoleon Bonaparte, commander-in-chief of the Army of Egypt, shortly to become First Consul and Emperor, that made Ganteaume very much 'Napoleon's Admiral'. It was Ganteaume who, in the crisis year of 1799, ran the British blockade the length of the Mediterranean, from Egypt to France, landing Bonaparte at Fréjus to make his bid for supreme power. To the discredited Directors whom he planned to overthrow, Bonaparte wrote on 10 October 1799: 'I owe my safe arrival to the energy and sound manoeuvres of Rear-Admiral Ganteaume'.[2] It was one of the most generous (and one of the very few honest) admissions that Napoleon ever made.

Ganteaume. Lithograph by Maurin, c.1835. (Wikimedia Commons)

Honoré-Joseph Ganteaume was a Provençal, born at La Ciotat between Marseille and Toulon, on 13 April 1755. His father was a merchant skipper; it was in his father's ship that he first went to sea in July 1769; and it was in the merchant service that he spent the first nine years of his seagoing career. Many naval celebrities of the eighteenth century had similar origins.

For all major navies of the age of sail, the merchant service was an invaluable source of trained seamen and gunners (who in the case of the British Navy usually had to be forcibly impressed). Then as today, it was the practice for merchant ships to be 'taken up from trade' in time of war, to serve either as transports or as auxiliary warships under naval command. It usually suited both parties, state navy and civilian owners alike, for the ship's civilian officers and crew to continue serving after being thus requisitioned.

So it was with the 23-year-old Ganteaume in the spring of 1778 when his ship, *Fier Rodrigue,* was requisitioned for naval service on France's entry into the American Revolutionary War. He was given an auxiliary officer's commission and stayed in *Fier Rodrigue* when she joined la Motte-Picquet's squadron (24 March 1779) escorting a convoy to North America. Once in American waters *Fier Rodrigue* was attached to the fleet of d'Estaing, taking part in the repulse of the British off Grenada (6 July 1779) and the ill-fated French assault on Savannah (9 October 1779). Advanced to an auxiliary lieutenant's commission as *lieutenant de frégate,* Ganteaume got his first naval command, the *flûte Marlborough,* in April 1781.

Marlborough was part of the convoy attached to the battle squadron of Suffren, bound for the Indian Ocean, where Ganteaume served for the next three years. His first real taste of warship service (23 August–8 October 1783) was in the frigate *Surveillante,* which had come out from France bearing the news that the war was over. Just how much Ganteaume had attracted Suffren's favour was marked by the fact that after this brief apprenticeship in *Surveillante,* Ganteaume was immediately appointed to command the frigate *Apollon* (9 October 1783). To have gained a frigate command after a service career of only five and a half years was a notable achievement. It was also a timely one, given the inevitable service cutbacks of peacetime, and Ganteaume remained *Apollon's* captain until her commission ended on 30 May 1785.

After this runaway climb to a frigate command, favoured by the greatest fighting commander in the French Navy, Ganteaume was left 'on the beach' with the substantive rank of sub-commander or *sous-lieutenant de vaisseau* (1 May 1786). Having received no seagoing appointment before the summoning of the Estates General of France in May 1789, Ganteaume found no difficulty in obtaining a captain's command in the French East India Company, the *Compagnie des Indes.* He made two cruises to the Orient in 1791 and 1792 but his third, in 1793, was overtaken by the outbreak of war with Britain, and his ship was captured. Released and returned to France, Ganteaume was immediately promoted *lieutenant de vaisseau* and appointed to the 74-gun ship of the line *Jupiter* in the Brest fleet.

With the tumultuous background of the events of 1793, under the eye of two successive commanders of the Brest fleet who had served with Suffren (Morard de Galles and Villaret-Joyeuse), Ganteaume's career accelerated again. He was promoted *capitaine de vaisseau* on 27 February 1794 and in the following month was given command of the new 74-gun ship of the line *Mont-Blanc* which, with one dramatic interlude, he retained until October 1797.

The dramatic interlude was the national crisis of May–June 1794. In those tense weeks, the fate of the bankrupt and starving dictatorship of Robespierre turned on the safe arrival of Vanstabel's massive supply convoy from America. Villaret-Joyeuse was ordered to sea with the Brest fleet, his mission to lure the British Channel Fleet away from the convoy at all costs. But Ganteaume did not sail with Villaret's fleet when it left Brest on 16 May. He had been detached from *Mont-Blanc* to take temporary command of the 74-gun *Trente-et-Un Mai* with the Cancale Squadron at St Malo, and take her out to reinforce Villaret. Ganteaume joined the fleet on the evening of the 29th and Villaret, welcoming this unscathed addition to his strength after his clashes with Lord Howe's fleet on the 28th and 29th, chose to send *Mont-Blanc* back to France as escort to the crippled 80-gun *Indomptable*. It was therefore as captain of the *Trente-et-Un Mai* that Ganteaume took part in the showdown battle with Howe on 1 June 1794.

Lying 11th in the French battle line, Ganteaume manoeuvred his ship with skill during the First of June battle. Exploiting the preference of the British ships confronting his division to fight at longer range, he spared his crew and his ship from the heavier casualties and battle damage suffered by other units of Villaret's fleet. For all that, Ganteaume was wounded three times during the action, two of them badly injuring his feet, but he remained in command during Villaret's deliberate withdrawal, entering Brest in triumph with Vanstabel's intact convoy on 14 June.

Back in command of *Mont-Blanc*, Ganteaume was attached to the Brest fleet squadron commanded by the newly promoted Rear-Admiral Renaudin, hero of the last fight of the *Vengeur* in the First of June battle. In the late autumn of 1794 Renaudin gave two further proofs of the Brest fleet's ability to escape to the high seas: first with a cruise which entered Irish waters, and second in the transfer of his squadron to join Martin's fleet at Toulon. Under Martin, Ganteaume fought in the clash with Hotham's fleet off Fréjus (13 July 1795). He later led a squadron into the eastern Mediterranean which broke the British blockade of Smyrna, permitting Commodore Rondeau to escape and rejoin the fleet with the frigate *Sensible* and corvette *Sardine*.

In November 1796, Ganteaume sailed with Villeneuve in the squadron which broke out of Toulon and headed for the Atlantic to reinforce the Brest fleet in its forthcoming descent on Ireland. His seniority and experience qualified him for a squadron command with the Atlantic fleet, but he next came under the orders of Rear-Admiral Lacrosse, Inspector-General of the Coast from Cherbourg to Antwerp, to inspect the Channel ports in the frigate *Vengeance* (December 1797–March 1798). This mission was part of the preparations for the invasion of England entrusted to General Bonaparte, the conqueror of Austrian north Italy in 1796–97. It was abandoned on Bonaparte's urging (23 February 1798) that 'to carry out a descent on England without mastery of the seas would be the boldest and most difficult operation ever undertaken'. This message to the Directors ended with the potent suggestion that 'an expedition could be made into the Levant which would threaten the commerce of India'; and the result was Bonaparte's expedition to Malta and Egypt in 1798, which drew Ganteaume firmly into the Napoleonic orbit for the next 16 years.

It was Bonaparte who appointed Ganteaume Captain of the Fleet which, commanded by Brueys, sailed from Toulon on 19 May 1798. During the long voyage to Egypt via Malta, Bonaparte clearly developed a high regard for Ganteaume, and after the securing of Alexandria (2 July) he tried unsuccessfully to poach Ganteaume from Brueys's staff to serve as naval liaison officer ashore.

When Nelson's fleet fell upon Brueys's battle line in Aboukir Bay (1 August 1798), Ganteaume, wounded in the head, was one of the few officers to escape from the blazing flagship *Orient* before she blew up and sank. While he was recuperating at Alexandria, Ganteaume received two messages from Bonaparte at Cairo, both dated 15 August and addressing Ganteaume as 'Rear-Admiral' (although his substantive rank was still commodore). The first was a personal condolence:

> The picture of the situation in which you found yourself is horrible, Citizen Admiral. That, under the circumstances, you did not perish is because fate destines you one day to avenge our navy and our friends; accept my congratulations thereon. That is the sole pleasant thought I have had since the day before yesterday, when I received your report… I salute and embrace you.

The second appointed Ganteaume as Brueys's successor:

> Citizen Admiral, you will take command of all that remains of our navy in Egypt and… arm and provision the frigates *Alceste*, *Junon*, *Carrère*, and *Muiron*, the ships *Dubois* and *Causse* and any other frigates, brigs and dispatch boats we still have. You will appoint to all commands.
>
> You will do everything possible to salvage the wrecks remaining in the Aboukir roadstead.
>
> You will at once send to Corfu, and thence to Ancona, a dispatch boat with the letters carried by the courier I sent from Cairo a fortnight ago, which I am told are still at Rosetta. Send an exact account of the battle to the Minister of Marine.
>
> I much desire to confer with you, but I shall wait a few days before ordering you to come to Cairo, since I intend if possible to go myself to Alexandria … I salute and love you.

Taking command of this hotchpotch fleet with the armed merchantman *Causse* as his flagship, Ganteaume's first priority was the defence of Alexandria. He soon discovered that the flotilla of gunboats supporting the army's advance up the Nile, commanded by Commodore Perrée, remained very much under Bonaparte's direct control, resulting in the potential weakness of a split command. Bonaparte was so impressed by Perrée's work with the Nile flotilla that he promoted both Perrée and Ganteaume rear-admiral on the same day: 7 November 1798.

Bonaparte's march into Palestine to forestall a Turkish invasion of Egypt ended with his unsuccessful siege of Acre (March–May 1799). Ganteaume lacked the force to defeat the British seaborne support of the defenders of Acre under Sir

Sidney Smith. He could only spare one frigate to escort the flotilla of nine gunboats carrying the army's siege artillery, all of which were captured by Smith off Haifa on 18 March. After Bonaparte's army had struggled back to Egypt in June, Ganteaume was powerless to prevent the landing of a Turkish army at Aboukir, smashed by Bonaparte on 25 July. But all these failures were redressed by Bonaparte's abrupt decision in August 1799 to abandon his command and return to France, because after the departure of Perrée's squadron for France in May, Ganteaume was the only man who could get him there.

True to form, Bonaparte decided which ships – the Venetian-built frigates *Muiron* and *Carrère* – were to attempt the long home run to France. His chosen fellow-passengers were Generals Berthier, Murat, Lannes, Marmont, and Andréossy, with the Academicians Gaspard Monge and Claude Berthollet. Bonaparte also gave Ganteaume the general course to follow: hugging the North African coast as far as Cape Bon in Tunisia. If intercepted by the British, Ganteaume was to run for the beach and get his passengers ashore, there to fight their way overland to the Gibraltar Straits (this with the best fighting man in the party, Lannes, still on crutches with a leg wound taken at Aboukir). Ganteaume knew that for all his experience and seamanship, he would need a massive helping of luck. In the event, he got three.

The party was ready to sail by 22 August, but the cruiser detailed by Smith to watch Alexandria did not head north to re-provision and water until the 23rd, when Ganteaume seized the chance to put to sea. Patiently beating along the Libyan coast took the frigates three weeks to cover the 1500 miles to Cape Bon. Here Ganteaume's second stroke of luck was twofold: a timely shift of wind making possible a rapid northward passage to Corsica, and the prevailing allied naval concentration on Sicily and Italy after 'Bruix's Cruise', keeping Nelson at Palermo and Admiral Ushakov's Russian fleet at Naples. The result was an unmolested landfall at Ajaccio on 1 October. And luck intervened for the third time during the final home run from Ajaccio to France: an allied squadron, lying squarely across the course to Toulon, sighted at nightfall on 8 October. The luck was in the timing, enabling Ganteaume to turn north-west and disappear in the gathering darkness to make a safe landfall at St Raphael – avoiding the 40 days of enforced quarantine which they would have got at Toulon – on the following day. Including the party's four-day stopover on Corsica, Ganteaume had brought his charges from Egypt to France in 42 days – arguably the most momentous voyage in modern history.

Within a week of the *Brumaire coup* which carried Bonaparte to power as First Consul, Ganteaume was appointed to the Navy Commission (19 November 1799)[3] and in the following year was appointed a Councillor of State. These were gifts straight from Bonaparte's hand; as France's new Constitution (13 December 1799) announced, 'The First Consul promulgates the laws; he appoints and dismisses at will the members of the Council of State' – as well as all ministers, ambassadors, and Army and Navy commanders.

After the failure of Perrée's attempt to get through to Malta in February 1800, Ganteaume was given command of the Brest fleet on 12 March. He was now required to succeed where Bruix had failed in 1799, taking the Brest fleet through the Mediterranean and making good Bonaparte's pledge to relieve the Army of Egypt. Ganteaume was finally hounded to sea by Bonaparte when confirmation was received that the British were sending a powerful expeditionary force to the eastern Mediterranean. Flying his flag in the 80-gun *Indivisible,* he sailed from Brest on 7 January 1801 with six of the line and two frigates, with 5,000 troops embarked. Headed back into Brest by a watchful British squadron, he sailed again on the 23rd after gales had blown the British off their blockading station, and this time broke out to the south.

The first success of the cruise came on 29 January with the capture of the British fireship-sloop *Incendiary.* Ganteaume's squadron ran the Gibraltar Straits on 9 February and on the following day took the cutter *Sprightly.* A third capture followed on the 13th: the 32-gun frigate *Success,* which had been shadowing the French intruders. This was a considerable fillip to French morale because *Success* had been instrumental in the capture of the French frigate *Diane* and the ship of the line *Généreux,* both of them survivors of the Aboukir Bay disaster. Ganteaume then headed north to Toulon for water and fresh provisions, arriving there on 19 February.

The squadron sailed for Egypt on 20 March, but – an almost exact foreshadowing of the similar experience of Villeneuve's fleet in January 1805 – ran into violent storms which inflicted extensive damage on the ships. Ganteaume had no choice but to head back to Toulon for repairs, but on 27 April he sailed again. This time his luck held. Escaping to the south, he succeeded in passing the Messina Strait between Sicily and mainland Italy on 25 May. Once arrived off the Egyptian coast, Ganteaume sent the corvette *Héliopolis* ahead to reconnoitre Alexandria on 7 June, but she was chased into Alexandria and blockaded there.

Assuming that *Héliopolis* had fallen victim to a superior force, Ganteaume decided to obey Bonaparte's order of last resort and headed for the harbour of Benghazi in Libya to land his troops. Having seen the state of Bonaparte's army after its retreat from Acre in 1799, Ganteaume can have had few illusions about the ordeal awaiting the troops on what would have been a gruelling 700-mile desert march, relying solely on the sparse local water supplies of eastern Libya. Mercifully they were spared from it because the furious reception encountered from the Libyans of Benghazi on 8 June, seconded by the untimely arrival of a British squadron under Admiral Keith, forced Ganteaume's ships to cut their cables and run for the open sea.

Even then, Ganteaume refused to abandon his mission. Shadowed all the way by Keith's squadron, he headed eastward along the Libyan coast and, in an action off Derna on 24 June, managed to capture the 74-gun ship of the line *Swiftsure* which had been one of Brueys's assailants in the Aboukir Bay battle. But this was the final success of the cruise. With water and provisions running low after nine weeks at sea, accepting that he had no chance either of getting through to Alexandria or landing his troops unmolested, Ganteaume turned for home, reaching Toulon on 22 July.

After this remarkable exploit Ganteaume remained in command of the Toulon fleet, leading it to the Caribbean (February–April 1802) in the Navy's combined lifting of the French expeditionary force to Saint-Domingue. On 23 July 1802 he was appointed Maritime Prefect of Toulon. After the proclamation of the new Empire, Ganteaume was promoted vice-admiral on 30 May 1804, and in June he was brought back to command the Brest fleet. On 2 February 1805, Napoleon invested Ganteaume with the Grand Eagle of the Legion of Honour.

Napoleon had cast Ganteaume as key player in the multiple chess game he contrived to bring about the invasion of England, but no chess player ever handicapped himself by ruling that his Queen was only to move if unimpeded and to take no enemy pieces. If there was one lesson the French Navy had taught the British Admiralty between 1793 and 1805, it was that the blockade of Brest was the all-important strategic clamp, to be maintained at all times. Ganteaume was willing to fight his way out of Brest to join Villeneuve's Combined Fleet from Toulon, Cadiz, and Rochefort, but Napoleon expressly ordered him not to sail from Brest unless he could do so without fighting the British. Given Villeneuve's return from the West Indies with the intact Combined Fleet in July 1805, Napoleon's restriction of Ganteaume proved in 1805 as vital for England's survival as King Philip II's order to Medina Sidonia in 1588, that he was not to land his troops in England during the Spanish Armada's progress up the English Channel.

Reserving all his spite for Villeneuve, Napoleon exempted Ganteaume from any blame for the collapse of the 1805 invasion plan, and the stream of imperial favour continued to flow Ganteaume's way. Three times over the ensuing five years – in 1806, 1807, and 1810 – Ganteaume was appointed as temporary Navy Minister until Decrès recovered from illness to resume the portfolio.

On 1 February 1808, Ganteaume was appointed naval Commander-in-Chief in the Mediterranean theatre, his immediate objective being the reinforcement and re-supply of the Corfu garrison. The speed and effectiveness with which Ganteaume carried out his mission shows how widely stretched Britain's naval net around Napoleon's Empire had become by the third anniversary of Trafalgar. He reached Corfu on 23 February and by 10 April, after trailing his coat along the shores of Africa and Sicily, had returned to Toulon. For this exploit, proving that Ganteaume had lost none of his energy and enterprise as a seagoing fleet commander, he was rewarded with the additional appointment as Inspector-General of the Ocean Coasts (18 April 1808).

When Ganteaume stepped down from his Mediterranean command in June 1810, he had passed his 55th birthday and the fleet commands were going to younger men. Napoleon created him a Count of the Empire on 11 July 1810, and in the same month Ganteaume became a member of the Council of Admiralty. His third spell as acting Navy Minister in that year was followed by the appointment as Chamberlain to the Emperor, and on 1 August 1811 he was appointed Colonel Commandant of the battalion of *Marins* (Sailors) of the Imperial Guard.

This last run of honours came as Napoleon's Empire reached its brief zenith, overthrown by the disasters of the 1812 Russian campaign and the loss of Germany in the following year. With southern France facing invasion after Wellington's arrival at the Pyrenees, Ganteaume received his last imperial appointment in December 1813: command of the 8th Military Division as Commissar Extraordinary at Toulon. But if Napoleon reckoned that he had bought Ganteaume's unyielding loyalty with all the honours rendered to 'his' admiral since October 1799, he was mistaken. In April 1814, after Napoleon's refusal to accept reality had left Paris open to the Prussians and Russians, Ganteaume joined the group of Army Marshals who insisted on Napoleon's abdication.

Once Ganteaume had made his decision to endorse the restoration of the Bourbon monarchy, he did not waver. He received no appointment under the first restoration of 1814–15, although Louis XVIII created him a Chevalier of St Louis on 3 June 1814. During the brief-lived return of Napoleon in the 'Hundred Days' of March–June 1815, Ganteaume kept determinedly out of the limelight. On his second restoration, Louis XVIII created Ganteaume a Peer of France (17 August 1815). In this capacity Ganteaume cast his vote, in the small hours of 7 December 1815, for the death sentence on Marshal Ney, who had vowed to bring Napoleon back to Paris in an iron cage only to rejoin the Emperor on the eve of Waterloo. Ney was executed by firing squad that same morning.

Two days after Ney's execution, Ganteaume received his last appointment, as Inspector-General of Classes and his last honour – advancement to the rank of Commander of Saint-Louis – followed on 3 May 1816. On 28 September 1818, Ganteaume died at his estate at Pauligne (Bouches-du-Rhône).

Notes

1 The other two were Perrée, promoted by Bonaparte on the same day as Ganteaume, and Magon, promoted by General Leclerc in Saint-Domingue.

2 Letter from Bonaparte to the Executive Directory, 10 October 1799.

3 Dumanoir, who had commanded *Carrère*, was promoted rear-admiral on 27 November.

Rear-Admiral Jean-Baptiste-Emmanuel Perrée (1761–1800)

Jean-Baptiste-Emmanuel Perrée was one of the two naval officers promoted rear-admiral by General Bonaparte in Egypt (the other being Ganteaume) in 1798. Perrée's other distinction was that he was the second 'Admiral of the *Arc*' to die in battle. The first had been Brueys, killed in the Aboukir Bay holocaust of 1 August 1798; Perrée outlived him by a mere 20 months.

Perrée was a Norman, born at Saint-Valéry-sur-Somme on 19 December 1761 to a seagoing family. As with Ganteaume, Perrée's father was a merchant skipper, and it was in his father's ship *Glorieuse* that Perrée first went to sea in September 1773 as a 12-year-old ship's boy. Over the following ten years he was constantly at sea, learning his trade in the merchant service. He qualified first as able seaman, then quartermaster *(timonier)*.

Perrée. Lithograph by Maurin, c.1835. (Wikimedia Commons)

Perrée saw no action during France's participation in the American Revolutionary War (1778–83), but in 1785 he served in the Navy *flûte Boulonnaise* as assistant pilot. In the same year, aged 24, he received his merchant navy ticket as master's mate *(second capitaine)*. When Republican France declared war on Britain in February 1793, Perrée applied for a commission in the regular Navy and was immediately accepted as a probationary lieutenant *(enseigne non entretenu)*. On 17 May 1793 he was promoted to acting commander *(lieutenant de vaisseau provisoire)*.

Perrée's acceptance and rapid promotion showed the Republican Navy at its best. It had a crying need for seasoned officers with Perrée's experience. But it also had a wealth of equally experienced officers from the pre-Revolutionary Navy who – despite their patriotic refusal to emigrate – found themselves politically suspect as 'aristos' by accident of birth. Under the Jacobin Terror of 1793–94, 27 of these unfortunates were cashiered, dismissed the service, and, mostly, imprisoned. (Only three of the 27 were actually guillotined, which shows that Navy officers were relatively low on the Jacobin scale of political suspects.) By no means all of them were reinstated in rank after their release.

When the Terror ended with the fall of Robespierre in July 1794, Perrée was at sea in command of the 40-gun frigate *Proserpine,* waging a highly effective commerce-raiding campaign. His tally of 63 British merchantmen captured over his eight months with *Proserpine* won him promotion to *capitaine de vaisseau* on 8 November 1794.

Perrée was then transferred to the Toulon fleet where he did not receive the conventional advancement to battleship command, with an appointment to a ship of the line. While Martin pressed ahead with his rebuilding of the Toulon battle fleet from its near-total destruction in 1793, he made the most of Perrée's proven ability as a frigate commander.

Martin gave Perrée a four-ship squadron – frigates *Minerve, Alceste, Badine,* and the corvette *Brune* – and sent him out to Tunis (15 November 1794) on a mission which was part diplomatic, part commerce-raid. To maintain an effective naval presence in the western Mediterranean, both Britain and France needed the goodwill of the Muslim Beys of Tetuan, Oran, Algiers and Tunis. There was a constant coming and going to all four ports by British and French naval missions (often in sight of each other, when hostilities were briefly suspended) to buy provisions and fresh water for their ships. There were two diplomatic constants. The first consisted of bribes to deter attacks on European merchant ships by the Barbary Corsairs, who were based on all major North African ports. The second was to negotiate for the release of European prisoners taken by the Corsairs.

After concluding his business at Tunis, Perrée embarked on a commerce-raiding cruise which had netted 25 merchant ships and 600 prisoners by the time of his return to Toulon on 7 January 1795. This was followed with a brief cruise in *Minerve* to the waters off Algiers (4–24 February 1795). These forays confirmed Perrée as an active and highly able commander of the Toulon fleet's frigate squadron, commodore in all but gazetted rank. When on 3 March Martin sailed from Toulon with the fleet on his bid to reconquer Corsica (p. 33), he was preceded by Perrée's frigates in their classic role as the battle fleet's 'eyes'.

In February 1795 Admiral Hotham, commanding the British Mediteranean Fleet, decided to shift his base from San Fiorenzo Bay, Corsica, to Livorno on the Italian mainland. He did so before the 74-gun ship of the line *Berwick,* dismasted in a gale on 7 January, had been sufficiently jury-rigged to enable her to rejoin the fleet. When the lone *Berwick* finally sailed from San Fiorenzo on 6 March, she was discovered on the following day by Perrée's frigates *Alceste, Minerve,* and *Vestale.*

Intent on causing *Berwick* minimal damage to expedite her addition to the Toulon battle fleet after capture and refit, Perrée's captains fired bar shot – disabling missiles designed to shred sails and cut rigging. *Berwick's* inevitable surrender was hastened by one of these missiles decapitating her captain.

After their prestigious capture of *Berwick*, Perrée's frigates went on to distinguish themselves in both of the two indecisive fleet actions between Martin and Hotham in 1795. In the first (13–14 March), *Vestale* was the first to take *Ça Ira* in tow before relinquishing the crippled ship of the line to *Censeur*. In the second (13 July) *Alceste* earned unstinted praise (and professional admiration) from British observers, who marvelled at the courage and seamanship displayed during her attempt to save the crippled *Alcide*. 'She [*Alceste*] got off most beautifully,' wrote one British admirer, 'to the astonishment and wonder of all our fleet, and I pronounce this to be the best executed (although unsuccessful) and most daring manoeuvre I ever witnessed in the presence of so very superior a force'.

But Perrée was not there to see. He had been a prisoner of the British for a month.

On 24 June Perrée had again been scouting for Martin's battle fleet in the 40-gun *Minerve*, with the 36-gun *Artémise* in company. They fell in with two British frigates performing the identical task for Hotham's fleet: *Dido* (28) and *Lowestoffe* (32). *Minerve* and *Artémise* had more than enough combined firepower to overwhelm their opponents, and once Perrée had confirmed that the two British frigates were unsupported, he headed in to attack. His plan was to close and board *Dido*, then join forces with *Artémise* against *Lowestoffe* – a plan wrecked by the timidity of Captain Charbonnier of *Artémise*. *Minerve's* attack was countered by an evasive manoeuvre by *Dido's* captain which briefly locked the ships and broke off *Minerve's* bowsprit, bringing down her headsails. Instead of heading in to support *Minerve*, *Artémise* shied away. This gave *Lowestoffe* time to come to *Dido's* aid with a spirited fire which brought down *Minerve's* foremast and mizzenmast, leaving Perrée with no option but to strike his colours. *Minerve* was towed to Minorca where Perrée remained captive until his exchange and return to France could be negotiated.

After Perrée's return to Toulon in August 1795, Martin picked him to command the next demonstration of the Toulon fleet's striking potential. This was a raid (September–November 1795) down the West African coast, preying on British merchant shipping and destroying British shore establishments. An exploratory raid in the previous year by Captain Zacharie Allemand, with the ship of the line *Duquesne* (now with Martin's battle fleet) had proved that this was a profitable and virtually undefended hunting ground. So it proved for Perrée, whose four frigates and two corvettes gave him far more range and scope than Allemand had enjoyed. By the time Perrée returned to Toulon he had captured 54 merchant ships during his West African foray.

The next mission which Martin entrusted to Perrée gave him command of the new 40-gun frigate *Diane* on a prolonged cruise (April–November 1796) to the eastern

Mediterranean. This was no mere flag-showing exercise to impress the Turkish court at Constantinople, but a reinforcement of Republican France's diplomatic presence across the entire Levant. Apart from ferrying relief diplomats to their posts, *Diane* also carried supplies and ammunition for French warships in the theatre. It was during this extended cruise that Perrée's long-overdue promotion to commodore or *chef de division* was formally confirmed (10 June 1796).

By the spring of 1797 Bonaparte's run of conquests in North Italy, culminating in his invasion of southern Austria and the French occupation of Venice, had transformed French naval prospects in the central Mediterranean – especially after the British withdrawal from the western Mediterranean in December 1796. The urgent need was to make good the French hold on the Adriatic, whither Martin dispatched Perrée with *Diane,* the corvette *Brune,* and the brig *Jason.* Confirming the Adriatic as a French lake was the prelude to the conquest of the Ionian Islands by Brueys in July 1797, followed by the promotion of Brueys to vice-admiral and his appointment to command the fleet carrying Bonaparte's expeditionary army to Egypt in May 1798.

Perrée's impressive record as a frigate commander made him a prime candidate to command the Egyptian fleet's frigates, but that appointment went to the newly promoted Rear-Admiral Decrès with *Diane, Sérieuse, Artémise,* and *Justice.* Perrée was advanced to battleship command and given the 74-gun *Mercure.* She sailed in the Centre Squadron with Brueys's flagship *Orient* (120), *Tonnant* (80) and *Heureux* (74). The six-ship Van Squadron (*Guerrier, Conquérant, Spartiate, Aquilon* and *Peuple-Souverain,* all 74s, were commanded by Rear-Admiral Blanquet from his flag-ship *Franklin* (80). Rear-Admiral Villeneuve commanded the Rear Squadron from the *Guillaume-Tell* (80), with the 74s *Généreux* and *Timoléon.*

Perrée remained with *Mercure* during the fleet's long voyage east from Toulon, taking Malta *en passant* and reaching Egypt unmolested at the end of June 1798. After Bonaparte landed with his advance troops to take Alexandria on 2 July, the fleet unloaded the remaining troops, guns, and Army stores from its temporary anchorage at Marabout. With Alexandria secure, Bonaparte needed control of the lower Nile to secure his march on Cairo and encounter with the main Mameluke army. Brueys agreed to detach one of his senior commodores – Perrée – to command an improvised lower Nile flotilla.

After handing over *Mercure* to Lieutenant Cambon, Perrée was given precious little time to prepare for his new task, detailing crews and arming his hotchpotch force of xebecs, gunboats and light craft. Bonaparte marched from Alexandria on 7 July and six days later came up against a powerful Mameluke army at Chabreis (Chobra Kyt), which was supported in force on the Nile. The Army easily smashed the Mameluke land force, but there was desperate fighting for Perrée and his men on the river. Their achievement was given full credit by Bonaparte in his victory dispatch to the Directors in Paris:

> Commodore Perrée, with three gunboats, a sloop and a galley, attacked the enemy flotillas. The fighting was extremely stubborn. More than 1500 rounds were fired. Commodore Perrée was wounded in the arm, and by his courage and good dispositions he succeeded in recapturing three gunboats and the galley that the Mamelukes had taken, and in setting fire to their flagship.

Bonaparte subsequently awarded Perrée one of the famous 'Sabres of Honour' which he had first presented, in recognition of conspicuous gallantry, to officers and rankers of the Army of Italy in 1797. Gold-hilted, with engraved Damascene blades and double pay for all recipients, they were the forerunners of the Legion of Honour cross instituted by Bonaparte as First Consul in 1802. After Chabreis, Bonaparte also gave Perrée honorary promotion to rear-admiral (which he had no authority to do). Ten days after shattering the Mameluke army in the 'Battle of the Pyramids' (21 July), Bonaparte curtly informed Brueys on the 30th that 'Rear-Admiral Perrée will be needed for a long time on the Nile, which he is beginning to know'.[1]

Perrée was therefore still on the lower Nile, preparing to support General Desaix's invasion of Upper Egypt against the surviving Mameluke forces, when the news reached Cairo that the fleet had been wiped out and Brueys killed in Aboukir Bay (1 August 1798). If Commodore Ganteaume had died in the same battle instead of escaping with a head wound, Perrée would have become commander of the remaining French warships in Egyptian waters. As it was the command passed to Ganteaume (also promoted to rear-admiral by Bonaparte), and Perrée remained with the Nile flotilla. Desaix began his southward march from Cairo on 25 August, but even with the support of Perrée's flotilla his advance was slow and stoutly contested by the Mameluk remnants under Murad Bey. (It was briefly interrupted by a temporary blindness which required Desaix's return to Cairo for medical treatment.) It took Desaix until 25 January 1799 to reach Thebes and 1 February to arrive at Aswan, his 'furthest south'.

By this date Perrée had been recalled to Alexandria from the Nile flotilla (November 1798) to support Bonaparte's forthcoming march into Syria, aimed primarily at safeguarding Egypt's north-east flank. On 7 November Bonaparte formally confirmed the promotions of both Ganteaume and Perrée to the rank of rear-admiral. To support the Syrian venture, Ganteaume gave Perrée the three frigates which had been in Alexandria at the time of the Aboukir Bay disaster: *Alceste* (flag), *Junon* and *Courageuse,* with the brigs *Salamine* and *Alerte.*

Bonaparte marched from Cairo in mid-February 1799, took El Arish, Gaza, Jaffa, and Haifa, but by 19 March, at Acre, was forced to undertake the one operation which he had hoped to avoid: a siege. On the 18th an unescorted gunboat convoy, carrying the all-important siege guns for Bonaparte's army, was captured by the British and promptly used against the besiegers. Stiffened by Turkish and British naval support, Acre's garrison held out throughout April while the French losses mounted. But on 5 April Perrée escaped from Alexandria with all five ships of his command. Ten days later they landed seven replacement siege guns at Jaffa, including four long 18-pounders from *Junon,* and so much ammunition that his frigates were left with only 15 rounds per gun. This generosity enabled Bonaparte to persist with the siege after the costly repulse of his assault on 29 April, but it left Perrée's ships incapable of facing a prolonged battle at sea.

By the second week of May 1799 Bonaparte had accepted that he had no choice but to abandon the siege of Acre and retreat to Egypt. On 11 May he issued orders for Perrée to bring his ships to Cæsarea and embark 400 of the Army's wounded. Perrée attempted to obey, but on the 14th he was intercepted by the British ships of the line *Tigre* and *Theseus,* and forced to run for the open sea. On the following day Perrée called a conference with his captains, who all agreed that given the weakened state of their ships and the renewed British presence in the eastern Mediterranean, there was nothing for it but a return to France.

When Perrée turned for home in mid-May 1799, the odds were hopelessly stacked against him. The western Mediterranean was dominated by the British deployments against the massive Franco-Spanish combination created by the arrival of the Brest fleet under Bruix. In the central Mediterranean, the French garrison on Malta was already hemmed in by naval blockade and land siege. In the eastern basin, the French hold on Egypt was perilously weak until Bonaparte brought back his weakened army from its foray into Palestine; and there was nothing Ganteaume could do to prevent a seaborne invasion by Britain's new ally, Turkey.

Three months later the situation was very different. By mid-August, Bruix had withdrawn from the western Mediterranean with the Franco-Spanish combined fleet, and British naval attention was once again fixed on Sicily and the Neapolitan coast. In Egypt, Bonaparte had smashed a seaborne Turkish invasion at Aboukir (25 July) and was already planning his return to France in Ganteaume's ships. In short Perrée, in May–June 1799, was denied the fortune enjoyed by Ganteaume and Bonaparte during their 'home run' in August–October; and it was Perrée, not the future First Consul and Emperor of the French, who ended his voyage home as a prisoner of the British.

The pity of it was that Perrée and his men came so close to success. Opting for speed rather than Ganteaume's autumnal crawl along the Libyan coast, Perrée chose Lampedusa, midway between blockaded Malta and the Tunisian coast, as his essential landfall for taking on water. He then ran the Sicilian Narrows without difficulty and made a remarkably fast passage north. By first light on 18 June, 33 days out from the Palestinian coast, Perrée was only 60 miles south of Toulon when he was trapped by the leading division of Lord Keith's fleet hunting for Bruix – three ships of the line and two frigates with the wind entirely in their favour, making flight impossible for the French ships. Perrée had no option but surrender.

As in 1795 after his surrender of *Minerve,* Perrée was rapidly exchanged and sent back to Toulon. This time, however, he had to face a court-martial – not only for having surrendered his squadron, but for having abandoned his post of duty, in support of the Army of Egypt, without orders. Perrée's court-martial finally convened on 6 October. The President of the Court was the Military Commander of Toulon, Vice-Admiral Thévenard, whose son had been killed at Aboukir Bay when captain of the *Aquilon.*

Three days after Perrée's trial began, Ganteaume disembarked Bonaparte at Fréjus. Bonaparte had most certainly abandoned the Army of Egypt without orders, which made Perrée's case comparatively trivial. If Bonaparte had not overthrown the Directory in the Brumaire *coup d'état* of 9 November 1799, he might very well have ended in front of a court-martial himself. Perrée's trial was not concluded until two weeks after *Brumaire*, ending with his honourable acquittal on 25 November.

When he returned to France, Bonaparte was well aware that he was open to charges of having left his troops in Malta and Egypt to their fate. As soon as he had made himself Consul (First Consul from 13 December 1799) he ordered the preparation of relief expeditions for both Malta and Egypt. Three days after his acquittal, on 28 November, Perrée was tasked with supplying Malta. He was given the Aboukir Bay survivor *Généreux* (74), 20-gun corvettes *Badine* and *Fauvette,* the 16-gun brig *Sans Pareil,* and the store ship *flûte Ville-de-Marseille.* Between them they carried 3,000 troops and the food supplies for which the Malta garrison was clamouring.

Waiting off Valletta was Lord Keith's battle fleet: the 100-gun *Queen Charlotte,* the *Audacious, Northumberland* and *Alexander,* all 74s, the 64-gun *Lion,* and Nelson himself as second in command in the 80-gun *Foudroyant.* From the outset Perrée's relief attempt was a propaganda gesture, an apparent 'mission impossible' if ever there was one. And yet, as Bruix had proved with the Brest fleet back in April, the vagaries of wind, weather, and human error meant that no blockade could ever be completely watertight. In the first week of January 1800 an agile French sloop dashed into Valletta, cheering the garrison troops with the news that their general was now head of state and that help was on its way.

Perrée sailed on 26 January, but the old enemy – storm damage, to the upper masts of *Généreux* – forced him to return to Toulon for repairs. He sailed again on 10 February, and this time made a rapid voyage south to Malta's westward approaches. On the 15th Perrée's oncoming squadron was spotted by the British frigate 32-gun *Success,* cruising off south-east Sicily, giving Keith ample time to deploy his ships. By the morning of 18 February, the British battleships were closing in, and at 8 am the slower *Ville-de-Marseille* was caught by *Alexander.* Perrée gave his light warships freedom to scatter and stood on towards Malta in the fast-sailing *Généreux.*

His last hopes of slipping through the tightening British net were dashed at 1.30 pm by the diminutive *Success,* boldly pitting 32 guns against 74. Captain Peard of *Success* closed *Généreux* to win time for Nelson, by now driving *Foudroyant* downwind to add *Généreux* to his tally of 11 Aboukir Bay victims out of 13. Peard raked *Généreux* at least twice, with a flying splinter blinding Perrée's left eye. He remained on his feet, calling out *'Ce n'est rien, mes amis, continuons notre besogne!'* ('It's nothing, boys, let's get on with the job!') – but by 4.30 both *Foudroyant* and *Northumberland* were within range, and the last act began. When Perrée collapsed on his quarterdeck, his right leg torn off by a cannon-ball, *Généreux* struck her colours.

Perrée died of his wounds that evening. On Nelson's orders, *'l'intrépide Perrée'*, as Bonaparte called him, was buried in the church of Santa Lucia, Syracuse.

Note

1 Letter from Bonaparte to Brueys, 30 July 1798.

Vice-Admiral Denis, Duke Decrès
(1761–1820)

The French equivalent of Britain's 'First Lord of the Admiralty' was 'Minister of the Navy and Colonies', and although the post was sometimes entrusted to a politician it usually went to a distinguished admiral – Truguet and Bruix were famous examples. But Decrès was the only Navy Minister to hold the post for 14 consecutive years (1801–14), throughout Napoleon's Consulate and Empire. It was fitting reward for an active and hard-fighting career at sea.

Denis Decrès was born at Château-Vilain (Haute-Marne) on 18 June 1761. In his 18th year he entered the Navy as a cadet *garde de la marine* on 17 April 1779, the second year of France's engagement in the American Revolutionary War. Although 15 months passed before Decrès joined his first ship, the frigate *Diligente,* on 17 July 1780, frigate service was to dominate the first ten years of his career. On 17 December 1780 he was transferred to the frigate *Richemond,* bound

Decrès. Painting by René Théodore Berthon, 1806. (Wikimedia Commons)

for the Caribbean in the fleet of de Grasse. He served in all the major engagements of 1781–82, including de Grasse's historic victory in Chesapeake Bay (5 September 1781), which ensured victory for the rebel American colonies.

During Rodney's defeat of de Grasse in the Battle of the Saints (12 April 1782), Decrès attracted notice as the young officer commanding the boat party carrying the towline from *Richemond,* during the vain attempt to rescue the dismasted ship of the line *Glorieux.* In the fleet redeployment after the Saints, Decrès was transferred to the frigate *Nymphe* (20 June 1782), receiving promotion to probationary lieutenant (*enseigne de vaisseau hors rang*) on 1 August. On 9 March 1783 he was detached from *Nymphe* and given his first command: taking the cutter *Zombi* into Jamaica under flag of truce to exchange prisoners, rejoining *Nymphe* on 9 April.

The signing of peace in September 1783 brought no immediate respite for the French Navy's frigates and corvettes. For many months they continued to patrol the sea lanes, protecting merchant shipping from attack by privateers and raiders yet to hear of the coming of peace. Decrès served in this role with the *Cayennaise* (August–November 1783) and *Pluvier* (December 1783–August 1784). Posted to the *Ecluse*, he returned to the West Indies from May 1785 to March 1786, with his promotion to *lieutenant de vaisseau* announced on 1 May 1786.

For Decrès, this unbroken run of peacetime active service continued with his first commission as commander: the North American station in command of the *Alouette* (May 1786–February 1789), showing the flag in the main ports of France's new ally, the United States. During this commission, Decrès returned to the *Nymphe* on an unusual survey mission: to confirm the extent of the bitumen lakes in Spanish-held Trinidad.

He returned to France in February 1789, three months before the summoning of the Estates General ushered in France's uneasy three-year experiment with constitutional monarchy (May 1789–August 1792). Decrès was next appointed to the Brest fleet, which gave him his first experience of battleship service in the ships of the line *Victoire* (October–December 1790) and *Éole* (December 1790). It was during his time in *Éole* that the monarchy was overthrown (10 August 1792).

By the time that Decrès learned of his promotion to *capitaine de vaisseau* in the first Republican New Year's List of 1 January 1793, he had been sent out to Île-de-France (Mauritius) in the Indian Ocean. With the rank of 'Major-General of the Indies Division' he joined the staff of Vice-Admiral the Marquis of Saint-Félix, Governor of the Mascarene Islands, replacing Magon in command of the frigate *Cybèle*, the station flagship. In her he sailed for the Indian mainland and (6 February 1793) recaptured a French merchant ship which had been taken by Mahratta pirates near the French outpost of Fort Culabo.

In autumn 1793 Saint-Félix named Decrès as his emissary to return to France and plead for urgent reinforcements to the Indies station. Decrès sailed from Île-de-France in the frigate *Atalante* on 9 October, but during the voyage home he was stripped of his rank, as a scion of the minor aristocracy, by the Jacobin Committee of Public Safety. (The same fate befell Saint-Félix on the same day, 30 November.) The moment he landed at Lorient on 10 April 1794, Decrès was arrested and taken to Paris under guard. He had the luck to be released and allowed to return to his family home but shared the fate of many senior naval officers, being left in limbo until after the fall of Robespierre's dictatorship on 27 July 1794. Decrès was not reinstated in rank by France's new government, the Directory, until 12 June 1795, when he was posted to Martin's Toulon fleet. There Martin gave him command of the 80-gun ship of the line *Formidable* (27 October 1795).

In late November 1796 *Formidable,* leading four fast 74s, became the flagship of the battle squadron under Rear-Admiral Villeneuve, dispatched by Martin to reinforce the Brest fleet in its forthcoming assault on Ireland. Sailing from Toulon on 30 November, Villeneuve's ships were delayed by storms on their northward run from Gibraltar and approached Brest four days too late, entering Lorient on 23 December. There they provided a hard core for the rebuilding of the French Atlantic fleet, after its storm-battered ships straggled home from Ireland in the first days of 1797.

Although Decrès had proved himself an able battleship commander during this dramatic episode, he was replaced as *Formidable's* captain in the New Year of 1797 and he experienced a depressing career slump throughout the rest of the year. In early 1798 Decrès was briefly appointed adjutant to the Inspector-General of Coasts (Cherbourg-Antwerp), from which humdrum duty he was rescued by promotion to rear-admiral (12 April 1798). At the same time he was given command of the frigate squadron attached to the 13-strong battle fleet commanded by Brueys, tasked with carrying Bonaparte's 'Army of the East'. On 19 May 1798 the fleet sailed from Toulon for Malta and Egypt.

Flying his new flag in the 40-gun *Diane,* Decrès first came to Bonaparte's attention (p. 68) as commander of the fleet's flying squadron, and on 10 June his frigates covered the French troop landings at Valletta, Malta. After the fleet reached Egypt on the 30th, disembarked the Army and moved to its defensive anchorage in Aboukir Bay, the role of the frigates became crucial. If they had been at sea at first light on 1 August, fanned out to the westward of Aboukir Bay, they could have detected Nelson's oncoming 74s and given Brueys up to 12 more hours in which to prepare for action. Instead Brueys chose to keep his frigates inshore of his battle line, relying on the latter's superiority in firepower. He never dreamed that Nelson would risk a night attack amid the uncharted shallows of the Bay, let alone envelop and crush the French Van and Centre from both sides.

By first light on 2 August, Brueys was dead and ten of his 13 battleships had been captured or destroyed. Only Villeneuve's ships of the rearmost battle squadron – *Guillaume-Tell* (80), *Généreux* and *Timoléon* (74s) – and Decrès with the frigates *Artémise, Diane,* and *Justice,* were capable of making sail. In the event only *Guillaume-Tell. Généreux, Diane* and *Justice* escaped from Aboukir Bay and headed for Malta.

During the weary naval blockade and land siege of Valletta (August 1798–September 1800), sailors and gun crews from Villeneuve's shadow fleet gave invaluable aid to General Vaubois's garrison, with Decrès taking command of the siege perimeter outposts. By the New Year of 1800 the Malta garrison was still obstinately holding out, but its food stocks were dwindling and the lists of sick and wounded mounting.

After Perrée was killed and *Généreux* captured during the ill-fated relief attempt of February (pp. 85–86), desperate measures were needed. Vaubois and Villeneuve ordered Decrès to take *Guillaume-Tell* to sea and break through to France, evacuating sick and wounded but above all delivering the bleak message that without immediate relief, Malta would be unable to hold out until midsummer.

By the end of March, Decrès had *Guillaume-Tell* ready for sea and was waiting for the right weather conditions for the breakout. He got them late on the 30th, a strong southerly gale and a dark night after an early moonset, but was sighted by the 32-gun frigate *Penelope* before he had been at sea for an hour. Only 42 days before, *Généreux* had been brought to grief by an outmatched but determined frigate captain, attacking to win time for the battleships to get within range, and now history repeated itself. On this occasion Decrès's assailant was *Penelope's* Captain Blackwood (best known as Nelson's frigate commander at Trafalgar). Having sent off the brig *Minorca* to alert Commodore Berry in the 80-gun *Foudroyant*, Blackwood set off in pursuit of *Guillaume-Tell*, came up with her half an hour after midnight, and unleashed the first of a punishing series of raking broadsides.

With the sails of the pursuing battleships already in sight, Decrès had no time to turn and crush *Penelope* but stood on to the north-east in hopes of winning clear. He was foiled by the faster speed of *Penelope* and Blackwood's superb seamanship which kept *Guillaume-Tell* under sustained fire until daybreak on the 31st, by which time she had lost her main topmast, mizzen topmast and main yard, drastically slowing her. By 0500 the first British battleship was within range: the 64-gun *Lion*. She came in confidently and manoeuvred to rake with triple-shotted broadsides but received such a ferocious return fire from *Guillaume-Tell* that within 30 minutes *Lion* was drifting out of the battle with extensive damage to spars and rigging.

Next on the scene was Berry in *Foudroyant*, at 0600 racing into point-blank range under full sail and calling on Decrès to surrender. Decrès replied with two broadsides which brought down *Foudroyant's* foretopmast, main topsail-yard, jib-boom and spritsail yard, shredding her foresail, mainsail and staysails, and forcing *Foudroyant* to haul off and make running repairs. But her broadsides had taken a heavy toll aboard *Guillaume-Tell*, whose main- and mizzenmasts fell at 0630, and by 0700 *Foudroyant* had returned to the attack. When *Guillaume-Tell's* foremast came down at 0800, it was all over. She was now completely defenceless with a mass of tangled wreckage obscuring her entire portside battery, and rolling so heavily that she had to keep her lower deck gun ports shut. Accepting the inevitable, Decrès struck his colours at 0820.

Decrès had put up a fight which the French long remembered with pride, and the British with deep respect. 'A more heroic defence than that of the *Guillaume-Tell* is not to be found among the records of naval actions.' Such was the verdict of William James, the famous nineteenth century chronicler of the 1793–1814 naval war. (James cited *Leander's* hopeless fight against *Généreux* in August 1798 [p. 59] as the only comparable action.) Under Decrès's leadership *Guillaume-Tell* had given *Lion* and *Foudroyant* such a battering that neither was able to take formal possession of her; that honour, fittingly, went to Blackwood and *Penelope*. *Guillaume-Tell* was towed into Syracuse, and subsequently joined the British fleet as HMS *Malta*.[1] Decrès was taken with honour to Port Mahon, Minorca, where his exchange was negotiated; he was eventually returned to France in August of that year.

The honours which First Consul Bonaparte paid Decrès on his return to France equalled and soon surpassed those lavished on Ganteaume (p. 75). Within a month he had been granted membership of the Navy Organisation Committee, followed by his appointment as Maritime Prefect at Lorient (30 September 1800). On 2 March 1801 Bonaparte formally presented Decrès with a 'Sabre of Honour' (p. 83) for his defence of the *Guillaume-Tell,* together with an inscribed naval chronometer. Decrès's appointment as commander of the Rochefort squadron (23 June 1801) was not only brief-lived but marked the end of his seagoing career. On 1 October 1801, replacing Pierre-Alexandre Forfait, Decrès was appointed Bonaparte's Minister of the Navy.

With Bonaparte pouring all his energies and every available franc into the building of the *Grande Armée,* and preparing for the proclamation of his Empire, the Navy was not even left with the scraps.[2] Although the brief-lived Treaty of Amiens (1802–3) offered an ideal respite for Decrès to force through a programme of naval reform, reconstruction and training, above all in seamanship and the maintaining and repairing of ships at sea, the opportunity was let slip. Had it not been, the prospects for Napoleon's planned invasion of England in 1804–5 could have been very different.

Decrès did his best, but at no time during his 14-year tenure as Navy Minister did he ever come near to educating Napoleon in the realities of naval warfare or the true nature of sea power. To Napoleon, sailing a fleet to a given objective at a given time was the same as marching an army corps on land: order given, objective achieved, regardless of the problems posed by adverse tides and weather. Perhaps the Emperor's supreme absurdity was his attempt to impose a Europe-wide trade embargo on trade with Britain, with his 'Berlin Decrees' of 1806 – to 'conquer the sea by the land'. As France's experience since 1793 should have taught him, blockades are not made good by vainglorious decrees, but by efficient fleets able to keep the sea in all weathers.

Like Adolf Hitler 140 years later, Napoleon believed in his own infallibility, resulting – before his own downfall – in constant frustration for reliable officials like Decrès. A good example was the case of Captain Allemand, whose promotion to flag rank had been delayed 13 years by his brutal and explosive character. For all his professional ability, Allemand had become the most detested officer in the Navy – but Decrès tried in vain to block Allemand's promotion to rear-admiral and get him dismissed the service because Napoleon insisted that Allemand was a 'lucky admiral'. In 1809, in the court of enquiry into the savaging of Allemand's fleet in the Basque Roads, Decrès had to swallow the humiliation of having to stage-manage Allemand's acquittal – to the outrage of the Navy of which Decrès was the professional head.

Yet Decrès must be credited with the remarkable naval building programme sustained across French-controlled Europe after the massive warship losses of 1805. From January 1806 to December 1813, the five major French naval shipyards – Toulon, Lorient, Brest, Rochefort, and Cherbourg – launched 27 ships of the line, from 118 guns to 74. But over the same period no fewer than 29 others were launched at Genoa, Venice, Antwerp, Rotterdam, and Amsterdam. (The record was held by Antwerp, where ten new French 74s were launched in 1807 alone.) The opening of the Peninsular War in 1808 ended all hopes of re-creating a Franco-Spanish combined fleet. But the unabated building of embryonic French battle squadrons, from the Adriatic to the North Sea, kept the British Navy at full stretch until the collapse of the French Empire in 1813–14.

For the rest, the honours paid to Decrès were lavish enough: promotion to vice-admiral on 30 May 1804 (in the same month as the similar promotions of Ganteaume and Villeneuve); Grand Eagle of the Legion of Honour in February 1805; from Grand Officer of the Empire in 1806 to Count of the Empire in July 1808, and finally to Duke in April 1813.

After Napoleon's first abdication in April 1814, the returning Bourbons grudged Decrès none of these honours, but created him a *Chevalier de Saint-Louis* (3 June 1814) before he was placed on the Retired List on 27 December 1814, at the age of 53. When Napoleon returned in the 'Hundred Days' of March–June 1815 he once more appointed Decrès Navy Minister, and on 2 June created him a Peer of France – 16 days before Waterloo. On the second Bourbon restoration there were again no recriminations for Decrès, merely his return to the Retired List, this time for good (1 August 1815).

Decres's retirement was brutally cut short. On the night of 22 November 1820, aged 59, he was mortally injured by a bomb placed under his bed by his valet, who committed suicide by leaping from the window when he found his master still briefly alive. Decrès was buried in the Père Lachaise Cemetery, Paris, where his ornate tomb features a bas-relief of the last fight of the *Guillaume-Tell*.

Notes

1 For *Malta's* performance at Cape Finisterre in July 1805, see p. 134.
2 Fewer admirals were promoted during the five years of the Consulate (1799–1804) than in any other phase of the First Republic and Empire.

PART 4

The Consulate, 1799–1804

Vice-Admiral Carel Hendrik, Count Ver Huell (1764–1845)

Despite the huge extent of Napoleon's 'Grand Empire' at its height, with its polyglot array of puppet states, comparatively few non-French names are honoured on the *Arc de Triomphe,* and all but one are those of Army generals: the Italians Campana, Colli-Ricci, Ferino and Rusca; the Poles Chlopicki, Dombrowski, Kniazewicz, Lazowski, Poniatowski and Zayonchek; the Germans Luckner and Marulaz, and one Irishman: Kilmaine. Amid their number, Carel Hendrik Ver Huell is the only Dutchman – and the only Dutch admiral.

The career of Ver Huell (also known as 'Verhuell', which is how his name appears on the *Arc*) provides an interesting com-

Ver Huell. Lithograph by Maurin, c.1835. (Wikimedia Commons)

mentary on the interplay and shifting of personal loyalties in the era of Revolution, Republic, and Empire. By nature Ver Huell was a conservative patriot, holding to his allegiance to the Dutch Republic presided over with varied efficiency by the hereditary *Stadhouders* of the House of Orange, in which he grew to manhood. Ver Huell shared none of the Republican enthusiasm of his contemporaries De Winter (defeated at Camperdown in 1797) or Buyskes, who both served on in the post-1795 Republican Dutch Navy.

Once the old Dutch Republic had been swept away, Ver Huell came to believe in the new Europe which Napoleon was forging, and in Holland's future as a Bonapartist kingdom. His work in making this vision a reality won him Napoleon's respect, with lavish imperial honours and preferment, and entitles him to be regarded as one of the founding fathers of the modern Dutch nation. (Ver Huell's supporters also credited him as the lover of Napoleon's stepdaughter, Queen Hortense of Holland.

If true, this would have made Ver Huell not only the cuckolder of his generous patron King Louis Bonaparte, but the father of the future Emperor Napoleon III.)

Ver Huell was born at Doetinchem, Gelderland, on 4 February 1764. At the age of 14 he opted for a military career in the Dutch Republic's army. He joined an infantry regiment as an officer cadet, but transferred to the Dutch Navy in 1779 as a midshipman. It was a time of rising tension between the Dutch Republic and Britain, whose attempt to subdue her rebel American colonies had already escalated into war with France and Spain. The hard-pressed Royal Navy was committed to a policy of stopping and searching neutral shipping in search of war contraband, deserters, and renegades. It was this practice which resulted in the Fourth Anglo-Dutch War of 1780–84 (and, 32 years later, in the Anglo-American War of 1812), but in 1780 the Dutch Republic also hoped for a share of the spoils from the apparently imminent collapse of Britain's colonial empire.

The 'Fielding and Bylandt Affair' occurred on the day of Britain's declaration of war (30 December 1779). Ver Huell witnessed it from his first ship, the 40-gun frigate *Argo*. She was at sea with a squadron under Rear-Admiral Bylandt's command, escorting a convoy which a British squadron under Commodore Fielding attempted to stop and search. The British were seen off by spirited manoeuvring and a sequence of warning shots from Bylandt's warships.

There was only one major fleet encounter during the Anglo-Dutch War: the Battle of the Dogger Bank (5 August 1781), in which the British got an unpleasant reminder that the Dutch Navy had lost none of its fighting qualities since the great days of Tromp and de Ruyter in the previous century. By this date, Ver Huell had gained his lieutenant's commission and was serving in *Argo* as third lieutenant.

The Dogger Bank fight was a strange encounter, with each of the rival fleets handicapped by the sizeable merchant convoy it was escorting. When Admiral Sir Hyde Parker finally engaged the Dutch, his ships suffered extensive battle damage from the vigorous Dutch return fire. The British withdrew after a three-hour mutual battering, although the leading Dutch ship of the line, the 68-gun *Hollandia,* was so badly damaged that she afterwards sank. Unlike their British counterparts the Dutch frigates were hotly engaged, and *Argo* had a narrow escape when a stack of cartridges exploded. Ver Huell, wounded by the explosion, was promoted to second lieutenant after the battle.

The eight years which followed the Dogger Bank battle saw Ver Huell constantly employed at sea, on commissions which took him to the Mediterranean, Baltic and North Seas. In 1785 he was commended for the adroitness with which he quelled a mutiny on a warship in the Zuider Zee, and promoted to senior lieutenant. Further promotion to commander came in 1791, and with it Ver Huell's first command: a corvette in which he cruised to Batavia in the Dutch East Indies. On his return he was appointed adjutant to Admiral Van Kinsbergen, commander-in-chief of the Dutch Navy.

Ver Huell had no time for the Revolutionary sympathies which flooded from France into the politically stale Dutch Republic, across the territorial barrier of Austrian-held Belgium, in 1789–92. Staunchly loyal to *Stadhouder* Willem V, Ver Huell mustered a corps of armed sailors to serve as a security force ashore, for which Kinsbergen promoted him captain in 1793.

This was the year in which the French Republic, after the execution of King Louis XVI, declared war on Britain and the Dutch Republic and proceeded to overrun Belgium. There was no respite. The whirlwind invasion of the Dutch Republic followed in the winter of 1794–95, with an icebound Dutch battle squadron captured by French cavalry while trapped in the frozen Zuider Zee. Willem V fled to Britain; a new 'Batavian Republic' came into being, upheld by a French army of occupation; and Ver Huell, along with all other Dutch officers who refused enthusiastic support for the new regime, was summarily dismissed. Excluded from naval service because of his adherence to the exiled *Stadhouder* Willem V, Ver Huell spent the ensuing seven years in domestic retirement with his wife and three sons. He therefore played no part in the defeat of the Batavian Navy's main battle fleet off Camperdown in October 1797. In 1802, Ver Huell followed in his father's footsteps by being elected Mayor of Doetinchem.

By this date Ver Huell's political sympathies had undergone a significant change. He naturally approved of the order brought to France by First Consul Bonaparte since November 1799, which included rapprochement with exiled aristocrats and the Catholic Church. Ver Huell also supported the *Staatsbewind,* the conservative Dutch Republican regime established by the French General Augereau in 1801 when C-in-C of the 'Batavian Army'. But when the brief-lived Peace of Amiens ended with the resumption of war in May 1803, the Batavian Republic and its Navy became a major player in the French preparations for the invasion and conquest of England.

Recalled to service and promoted rear-admiral, Ver Huell was given charge of the hastily-mustered Dutch fleet of flat-bottomed troop transports and flotilla craft at Vlissingen, and of conveying it to the main embarkation ports around Boulogne. In the summer of 1804 Ver Huell, in his flagship *Heemskerk,* fended off an attack off Cape Gris-Nez by Admiral Keith's squadron and successfully delivered his charges to Ambleteuse. For this achievement he was promoted vice-admiral (1 June 1804) and was appointed by Napoleon, now Emperor of the French, to command the right wing of the invasion fleet at Boulogne. Ver Huell held this command until the invasion plan collapsed in ruin in the early autumn of 1805. He then took up the appointment, previously offered by the *Staatsbewind,* as Dutch Navy Minister.

By the summer of 1806 Ver Huell, from his post in the cabinet of Batavian President Rutger Jan Schimmelpenninck, was secretly working to win support for Napoleon's latest project. This was the creation of a new 'Kingdom of Holland' under the Emperor's brother, Louis Bonaparte. On 5 June 1806, Ver Huell headed the deputation of Dutch ministers which petitioned Louis to accept the throne.

Their somewhat predictable success earned Ver Huell the Grand Eagle of the Legion of Honour from Napoleon and the title 'Marshal of Holland' from King Louis. The King kept Ver Huell as his Navy Minister but dismissed him in 1807, suspecting – rightly – that Ver Huell was working more in the Emperor's interest than in the King's. Louis then appointed Ver Huell as his ambassador to Tsar Alexander of Russia, but Napoleon insisted on Ver Huell being made ambassador to the imperial court in Paris.

The King and his Marshal worked competently together during the bungled British landings on Walcheren in 1809, with Ver Huell contributing naval guns and crews to stiffen the forts defending Antwerp, and Louis taking command of the Dutch land forces. But the Kingdom of Holland lasted only four years (1806–1810) because Louis made the fundamental mistake of trying to rule in the interests of his subjects rather than of his imperial brother. (For this he is still remembered by the Dutch as *goede Koning Lodowijk*: 'good King Louis'.) The main bone of contention was Napoleon's 'Continental System' banning all trade with Britain, which was ruinous to traditional Dutch mercantile interests. Yet despite the unfailing generosity of Louis, Ver Huell had become a committed adherent of Napoleon's imperial ideal and worked in opposition to his King as the breach between Louis and Napoleon widened.

On 1 July 1810, Louis accepted the inevitable and abdicated his throne. Eight days later the brief-lived Dutch kingdom was directly annexed to France. Even the wiping from the map of the historic Dutch 'Seven Provinces' (replaced by the new *départements* of 'Ems Occidentale', 'Frise', 'Bouches de l'Yssel', 'Yssel supérieur', 'Bouches de la Meuse', 'Bouches du Rhin', and 'Roer') did not shake Ver Huell's support for Napoleon. Ver Huell headed the junta of acceptable Dutch ministers appointed after the annexation, and was created vice-admiral of the French Navy in November. On 18 February 1811 Ver Huell became Deputy for *Yssel supérieur* in the Empire's rubber-stamp *Corps Legislatif;* on 25 May he was created Count of Sevenaer by Napoleon, and appointed C-in-C of all French naval forces in the North Sea and Baltic, his new command stretching from the Ems to Danzig.

For Ver Huell 1812, the year of Napoleon's disastrous invasion of Russia, began with his proclamation as Grand Officer of the Empire. He was also appointed to supreme command of naval forces in the Dutch *départements,* with his headquarters at Den Helder. The ensuing campaign of 1813 destroyed Napoleon's last field army in Germany and swept the victorious Austrians, Prussians and Russians to the Rhine. It also began the liberation of Holland in the name of the exiled *Stadhouder,* Willem, Prince of Orange. Two imperial admirals defended the last imperial strongholds in Holland. These were Truguet, Maritime Prefect of the Dutch Coast, at Rotterdam (surrendered in December 1813) and Ver Huell at Den Helder. Under Ver Huell's leadership, Den Helder held out stubbornly until the news came of Napoleon's abdication on 6 April 1814.

Now 50 years old, Ver Huell never even considered trying for reconciliation with the restored House of Orange. When he left Holland in 1814 to live as an exile in France, the question, given his length of service to Napoleon, was how he would be received by the restored Bourbon King Louis XVIII. Louis extended to Ver Huell the same generosity as that offered to all French generals and admirals prepared to accept the restored *Ancien Régime*. He not only confirmed Ver Huell's rank of vice-admiral and title as Count of Sevenaer, but appointed him naval commander of the Channel coast and made him a Knight of the Order of Military Merit. In December 1814, Ver Huell applied for and was granted French nationality.

During Napoleon's return in the 'Hundred Days' of March–June 1815, Ver Huell stayed with the exiled Louis XVIII, but Napoleon had a final compliment to pay him. After Waterloo and his second abdication, Napoleon discussed his chances of escaping from France to America, and told his Navy Minister Decrès that he wanted Ver Huell to convey him. Decrès dismissed the idea on the grounds that this would be far too insignificant a command for a vice-admiral. When he finally heard the story, Ver Huell said that he would have been honoured to carry the Emperor on his last voyage.

Ver Huell retired from the French Navy in 1816, and was created a Peer of France on 5 March 1819. He kept his seat in the House of Peers for the rest of his life, with a final brief spell of service as French ambassador to Berlin in 1836. When he died in Paris on 25 October 1845, he was given the equivalent of a state funeral: burial among the great names in Père Lachaise cemetery. His headstone bears the inscription 'Conceded in perpetuity to the family of Admiral Count Ver Huell, Peer of France.'

Vice-Admiral Maxime-Julien Émeriau, *Comte de* Beauverger (1762–1845)

Also spelt as 'Emeriaud', Émeriau's full name was Maxime-Julien Émeriau, *Comte de* Beauverger. He was a Breton, born at Carhaix (Finisterre) on 20 October 1762. On the eve of France's entry into the American Revolutionary War, he joined the Navy as a 14-year-old Gentleman Volunteer on 26 September 1776; his first ship was the *flûte Sylphe,* in which he served until 27 October 1777.

By the time of his 20th birthday, the young Émeriau had experienced a wealth of action both afloat and ashore, from home waters to the Caribbean. Under d'Orvilliers, he served in the ship of the line *Intrépide* (April–December 1778), taking part in

Émeriau. Lithograph by Maurin, c.1835. (Wikimedia Commons)

the first major Franco-British fleet action off Ushant (27 July 1778). Transferred to the ship of the line *Diadème* (February 1779–January 1781), he sailed for the Caribbean to join the powerful fleet of the *Comte d'*Estaing, taking part in its first major success: the capture of Grenada (4 July 1779), and the fleet action two days later which foiled Admiral Byron's attempt to recapture the island.

On 9 October, Émeriau was wounded in the right eye during the bloody repulse of d'Estaing's attempt to storm Savannah, Georgia. One in five of the French attackers was wounded at Savannah (including d'Estaing), but although unsuccessful the assault extended the war to the southern colonies, a long-term guarantee of Franco-American victory. After command of the fleet had passed to la Motte-Picquet Émeriau was wounded again (a musket ball in his right foot) during the Battle of Martinique on 20 March 1780.

A battle-scarred veteran at age 19, Émeriau was promoted lieutenant-commander (*lieutenant de frégate*) on 13 May 1781 and posted to the ship of the line *Fendant*. He stayed with the battle fleet with two further transfers, to *Dauphin-Royal* (October 1781) and *Triomphant* (November), while command of the fleet passed first to Vaudreuil and then to the *Comte de* Grasse. Under the latter's command, Émeriau in *Triomphant* was present at the French capture of St Kitts (January–February 1782). When Admiral Rodney ended de Grasse's run of victories in the Battle of the Saints (12 April 1782), Émeriau escaped capture but suffered two more wounds, in the ribs and lower abdomen. By the last month of the war, formally ended with the Peace of Paris (3 September 1783), Émeriau was still at sea, serving in the ship of the line *Fantasque*.

With no naval appointments available due to peacetime armed forces cutbacks, Émeriau turned to the merchant service for employment. He served as a merchant skipper from October 1785 to June 1786, during which time his promotion to sub-commander (*sous-lieutenant de vaisseau*) was confirmed on 1 May 1786. Émeriau's return to Navy service began with a brief posting to the frigate *Astrée* (October–December 1786), followed by a supply voyage to Cayenne, French Guiana, in the *flûte Chameau* (March–May 1787). In the New Year of 1787, he was awarded the Order of Cincinnatus, the decoration for service in the war of American liberation. Émeriau's return from Cayenne was followed by a posting to the ship of the line *Patriote* (May–November 1787) and a year 'on the beach' without employment until he was returned to *flûte* service in the *Mulet* (March–June 1789).

By the time that Émeriau came ashore from *Mulet* King Louis XVI had summoned the Estates General to solve France's bankruptcy and the opening phase of the French Revolution – the quest for a political constitution – was under way. But there were no immediate dramatic changes to the French armed forces, or the careers of serving officers. Émeriau had to wait for his next posting, to the frigate *Fine,* until October 1790. This took him to the French Caribbean colonies, Martinique and Saint-Domingue, until April 1793. He was still overseas when his promotion to commander (*lieutenant de vaisseau*) was announced in the New Year's List of January 1792, when the monarchy was overthrown on 10 August and when the French Republic was proclaimed in the following month.

Émeriau therefore returned from the Caribbean in April 1793 to find his country not only a Republic but at war with Austria, Prussia, the Kingdom of Sardinia, Spain, the Dutch Republic, and Britain. Naval officers with Émeriau's service and combat experience were in massive demand and he got his first command at once: the corvette *Cerf.* She was attached to the squadron sent out to the Caribbean under Sercey (p. 40), which found itself caught up in the slave rebellion raging on Saint-Domingue. Émeriau's role was to embark the white survivors displaced by the burning of the Cap Français settlement and take them to safety in America.

From this commission Émeriau was advanced to command the frigate *Embuscade* (September 1793–August 1795). In her he returned to American waters to join the escort of the huge grain convoy which, under Rear-Admiral Vanstabel, sailed for France in April 1794. While Villaret-Joyeuse engaged Lord Howe's battle fleet in the First of June campaign (pp. 22–23), Vanstabel's grain convoy reached Brest safely on 14 June, staving off national famine and the collapse of the Republican regime. For the part he played in the First of June campaign, Émeriau was promoted to *capitaine de vaisseau* on 7 December 1794, advanced to battleship command and posted to Martin's Toulon fleet (10 August 1795).

Émeriau joined the Toulon fleet too late to participate in its two clashes with the British in 1795, being successively appointed to the ships of the line *Conquérant* (August 1795–May 1796), *Timoléon* (May–June 1796), and *Jemappes* (June 1796–October 1797). In *Jemappes,* Émeriau sailed with the five-ship battle squadron *(Formidable, Jemappes, Jean-Jacques Rousseau, Mont-Blanc,* and *Tyrannicide)* dispatched under Villeneuve (p. 57) to reinforce the Brest fleet on the eve of its descent on Ireland. They sailed from Toulon on 30 November 1796, passed Gibraltar on 8 December, and reached Lorient on the 23rd. For his role in this dramatic foray (in which future admirals Ganteaume and Decrès also took part) Émeriau was promoted to commodore *(chef de division)* on 12 January 1797.

After *Jemappes,* Émeriau's next ship of the line was the 74-gun *Spartiate* which, in the spring of 1798, sailed with Brueys's battle fleet to convey Bonaparte's 'Army of the East' to the conquest of Malta and Egypt. They sailed from Toulon on 19 May and arrived off Malta on 9 June, with Émeriau leading the first French warships to enter the port of Valletta. After the capitulation of the Knights of St John, the voyage to Egypt was resumed on 19 June, with Alexandria falling on 2 July. Once the army and its equipment had been disembarked, Brueys led his 13 battleships to a defensive anchorage in Aboukir Bay, where they were discovered and immediately attacked by Nelson's battle fleet on 1 August 1798.

Brueys and his captains were completely unprepared for Nelson's enveloping attack, rounding the head of the French line to attack it from both sides and crush the French Van and Centre. Third in line after *Guerrier* and *Conquérant*, Émeriau's immobile *Spartiate* was exposed to a merciless battering from Captain Miller's *Theseus* to port and Nelson's own *Vanguard,* backed by Captain Louis's *Minotaur,* to starboard. After a stout but hopeless 3-hour resistance, with all three masts lost and himself twice wounded, Émeriau was forced to strike his colours at 2100. Early in the battle, however, *Spartiate's* gunners came close to killing Nelson, which would have had incalculable effects on the Anglo-French naval conflict. A fragment of langridge (anti-personnel scrap iron) from one of *Spartiate's* guns slashed open Nelson's forehead, leaving an ugly flap of bleeding flesh hanging and momentarily blinding him. ('I am killed! Remember me to my wife', was his first reaction.)

The after-effects of this head wound dramatically affected Nelson's behaviour over the next 18 months, leading him into acts of outright insubordination working greatly to the advantage of the French in the Mediterranean. If he had not won a victory without precedent in Aboukir Bay – *Spartiate* was one of the 11 out of 13 French battleships captured or destroyed – and become a national hero, these delinquencies would probably have ended Nelson's career with court-martial and disgrace.

After receiving emergency treatment from his British captors, Émeriau was landed at Alexandria under flag of truce three days after the battle, and was immediately hospitalised. He was not fit to be invalided home until late October, eventually sailing in the *tartane* (a fast, lateen-rigged coastal craft) *Nativité* on 7 November. She successfully ran the British blockade and landed Émeriau at Ancona, Italy, on 4 December. After his return to France, Émeriau went on home leave to undergo a prolonged convalescence.

During the lull in hostilities imparted by the Peace of Amiens of March 1802–May 1803, Émeriau was promoted to rear-admiral (23 July 1802). Flying his flag in the ship of the line *Indomptable,* he sailed on 5 November 1802 with a division of warships and transports reinforcing the garrison of Saint-Domingue (pp. 13–14). On his return from the disease-ridden island, Émeriau briefly commanded the naval reserve division before being appointed to a command in the right wing of the invasion flotilla mustering at Ostend (10 June 1803).

Given the action-studded progress of Émeriau's first 20 years of service, from Ushant to Aboukir Bay, the last ten years of his active career were depressingly disjointed. After brief spells of command at Lorient and Rochefort he was appointed Maritime Prefect at Toulon, a post which he retained until March 1811. In that month, Émeriau took over command of the Toulon fleet from Vice-Admiral Allemand, and was created Count of the Empire by Napoleon. Promotion to vice-admiral followed on 16 August 1811.

A final appointment was that of Inspector-General of the Ligurian Coasts (7 April 1813), but Émeriau saw little of them save by land. By late autumn 1813 the new 74-gun *Agamemnon,* launched at Genoa in February 1812, was ready to join the fleet. Flying Émeriau's flag and escorted by two frigates as she sailed from Genoa she was pounced on by a superior British force, and only reached Toulon thanks to the timely intervention of Rear-Admiral Cosmao-Kerjulien with five of the line. The iron British blockade was still clamped tightly on Toulon when Napoleon abdicated in April 1814.

The restored King Louis XVIII created Émeriau *Chevalier de Saint-Louis* on 3 June 1814, and on 24 August of that year awarded him the Grand Cordon of the Legion of Honour (the Bourbon substitution for Napoleon's Grand Eagle). During the 'Hundred Days' of March–June 1815 Napoleon created Émeriau a Peer of France, but Waterloo and the Emperor's second abdication prevented him from taking his seat. Émeriau received no further honours after the second Bourbon restoration and was placed on the Retired List on 8 July 1816.

During his long retirement at Toulon, Émeriau devoted much of his time to Freemasonry, of which he was an enthusiastic member. (He belonged to four lodges, his favourite being the Toulon-based '*Paix et Parfaite Union*'.) Fifteen years after his retirement, Émeriau was again created a Peer of France by France's last King, Louis-Philippe (19 November 1831). At the age of 83, Émeriau died at Toulon on 2 February 1845.

Rear-Admiral Charles-René Magon de Médine (1763–1805)

Magon. Portrait by Olivier Pichat, 1847. (Wikimedia Commons)

When candidates are proposed for the French admiral who might have changed the course of the 1805 Trafalgar campaign, Magon's name comes high on the list. He had all the fire and willingness to take risks which Villeneuve conspicuously lacked as commander of the Franco-Spanish Combined Fleet. Had Magon commanded during the Combined Fleet's return from the Caribbean in July 1805, he might well have battered aside Calder's blocking force and arrived off Brest to bring out Ganteaume's fleet. But neither Magon nor any other French admiral had the vital quality which alone could have welded the Combined Fleet into an integrated fighting force: the ability to work effectively with his half-hearted Spanish opposite numbers. As it was, Magon was the French commander who came closest to capturing a British ship at Trafalgar. After Brueys and Perrée, Magon was the third French admiral to die in battle, and he is justly numbered among the French heroes of Trafalgar.

Born in Paris on 12 November 1763, Charles-René Magon was a sprig of the French *Ancien Régime*'s provincial nobility. His family came from Saint-Malo and his father was Governor of the Mascarene Islands and Île-de-France (Mauritius) in the Indian Ocean. When his father died in 1778, Charles-René inherited the family estate of Médine on Île-de-France, entitling him to sign himself 'Magon de Médine'.

Two months before his 14th birthday, on 12 September 1777, Magon joined the Navy as a cadet mid-shipman (*aspirant garde de la marine*). When he qualified as a full midshipman on 12 March 1778, France was on the brink of war with

Britain in support of the rebel American colonies. Magon joined his first ship of the line, *Bretagne,* on 1 May 1778; she was attached to the battle squadron of the *Comte d'*Orvilliers and in her he took part in his first naval action: the Battle of Ushant on 27 July 1778. In the following year he was posted to two more ships of the line: *Annibal* (March–April 1779) and *Saint-Esprit* (April–December). In January 1780 Magon was transferred to the ship of the line *Solitaire* in de Guichen's battle squadron, and on 16 February was commissioned lieutenant (*enseigne de vaisseau*).

During Magon's time in *Solitaire* (January 1780–August 1781), he served through the three actions fought off Dominica between de Guichen and Rodney, on 17 April, 15 May and 19 May 1780. His transfer to the ship of the line *Caton* (2 August 1781) brought him under the command of the *Comte de* Grasse. In *Caton* Magon served in the greatest French victory of the war: de Grasse's defeat of Graves's fleet in Chesapeake Bay (5 September 1781), which sealed the fate of Lord Cornwallis's army at Yorktown and clinched American victory. *Caton* escaped from Rodney's subsequent defeat and capture of de Grasse in the Battle of the Saints (12 April 1782), but six days later was overtaken and captured in the Mona Passage by the pursuing battle squadron of Hood.

Magon spent five months as a prisoner of the British before his exchange and release was arranged. He went straight back to sea in the ship of the line *Marseillais*[1] (November 1782–February 1783) before receiving his first posting to a frigate: *Sémillante,* bound for the East Indies station. When Magon joined her on 5 April 1783, he could not know that 15 years were to pass before he saw France again.

Based on Île-de-France and the Mascarene Islands in the southern Indian Ocean, the French East Indies station was vast. It existed to provide safe passage for the rich cargoes carried by the *Compagnie des Indes,* the French East India Company. Its beat extended from the Cape of Good Hope and Madagascar, where there was a French outpost at Foul Point, to the Coromandel Coast of southern India with its French bases at Mahé and Pondichéry, and eastward to the Dutch East Indies, the Spanish Philippines, and the South China Sea.

After the Peace of Paris ended the American war in September 1783, Britain and France remained officially at peace for the next ten years. But India was another matter. There the willingness of the French to help Indian warlords in arms against the British East India Company (most notably, from 1782, Tipu Sultan of Mysore) provoked British efforts to search French shipping in Indian waters for war contraband. India and its seaborne approaches remained a constant potential Anglo-French flashpoint until the outbreak of war in February 1793.

After the outward voyage to Île-de-France (April–August 1783), Magon remained with *Sémillante* until November 1784. In the following year he served in two *flûtes, Marquis-de-Castries* and *Nécessaire,* before his promotion to commander (*lieutenant de vaisseau*) was confirmed on 1 May 1786. Magon's first command was the *flûte Amphitrite* (October 1786–April 1787), after which he transferred to the frigate

Dryade and served in her as first lieutenant *(commandant en second)* from April 1788 to April 1789. His first warship command was the corvette *Pandour* (April–August 1789). This brief commission was followed by the longest of his career in peace or war: 17 months with the corvette *Minerve,* delivering the new Tricolour national flag to every French station in the East Indies theatre (June 1791–November 1792). Rosily-Mesros, senior naval officer of the East Indies station in the frigate *Méduse,* was tasked with a similar mission (as was Brueys in the eastern Mediterranean).

Rosily's successor as East Indies naval C-in-C was Rear-Admiral Saint-Félix. When Magon brought *Minerve* back to Île-de-France (20 November 1792), Saint-Félix gave him command of the station flagship, the frigate *Cybèle.* In the New Year of 1793, the newly promoted Captain Decrès came out to Île-de-France to join Saint-Félix's staff, and as Magon's senior took over command of *Cybèle.*

Throughout 1793 it seemed that every packet arriving at Île-de-France brought yet more bewildering news from France. The colonists barely had time to accept that they were now subject to the orders of a Republic, transmitted through 'People's Representatives' with dictatorial powers, than they were confronted by the new regime's anti-slavery policy. The Mascarene planters flatly refused to ruin themselves by abolishing slavery and were supported by their Governor, General the *Comte de* Malartic.

Magon found himself with split loyalties. Although himself an Île-de-France estate owner, he was also bound to obey the orders of the Republican Navy Ministry in Paris. But the prevailing situation at Île-de-France worked to his distinct advantage in the autumn of 1793, when orders arrived from France that all officers with aristocratic connections were to be arrested and tried as suspect anti-Republicans. When Decrès sailed with despatches for France on 9 October 1793 Magon was reappointed to command *Cybèle,* but on the 14th he was placed under arrest as an 'aristo'. Saint-Félix was powerless to intervene but Magon was immediately released on the orders of Malartic, who refused to have one of his planters pilloried in the interests of Republican dogma, and proclaimed his support for Magon by appointing him his naval *aide-de-camp.*

Ever jealous of his own authority – as Sercey was to find in 1796–98 – Malartic had felt outranked and threatened when Saint-Félix was promoted vice-admiral in January 1793. He was only too pleased when Saint-Félix himself was arrested on 30 November and kept him imprisoned for 16 months. With Saint-Félix deposed, the East Indies naval command passed to its senior commodore, Captain Jean-Marie Renaud.

By this date the war had spread from Europe and the Caribbean to Indian waters. When news of the outbreak of war with France reached British-held Bengal in June 1793, the East India Company moved rapidly to occupy France's trading posts on the Indian mainland, culminating in the siege of Pondichéry (July–August). During the siege Renaud sent a small supply convoy, escorted by *Cybèle,* to run supplies into Pondichéry, but she was chased off by the British frigate *Minerva* and three East Indiamen. (This was not to be the last time that a French commander mistook British East Indiamen for ships of the line – see pp. 43, 122).

After the surrender of Pondichéry (23 August 1793), the obvious next objective for the British was the blockade and invasion of the French Mascarenes, but it took time before a sufficient naval squadron could be spared from home waters. By the time that the first British ships of force reached India in autumn 1794 the French on Île-de-France had advance notice of their coming: two 5th-rates, the *Centurion* (50) and *Diomede* (44). Renaud had also received reinforcements and in late October sailed to fight the new arrivals.

Flying his broad pendant in the 36-gun frigate *Prudente* commanded by Magon, Renaud had with him *Cybèle,* the 20-gun corvette *Jean-Bart,* and the brig *Courier.* Late in the morning of 22 October he sighted *Centurion* and *Diomede* approaching 30 miles north-east of Île-de-France, and coolly hove-to to let them come on. Co-operation between the two British ships was lamentable throughout the ensuing action; *Diomede's* captain was subsequently court-martialled and cashiered for his failure to support *Centurion.* There was extensive damage to spars and rigging on both sides but the British had the worst of it, and were unable to prevent the French ships from disengaging and returning to Île-de-France in good order. (When the news reached France, Republican propaganda inflated the battle into a resounding victory by an outmatched frigate squadron, breaking the blockade of Île-de-France by defeating two British 'ships of the line'.)

Renaud was wounded in the action, leaving Magon as acting commander of the East Indies station in *Prudente*; Magon's promotion to *capitaine de vaisseau* was confirmed on 23 January 1795. Magon remained in this caretaker role until, in the summer of 1796, the role of the East Indies squadron was transformed by the arrival of Rear-Admiral Sercey's frigate squadron from France.

As Sercey's second-in-command, Magon remained in command of *Prudente* until the New Year of 1798. He took part in the extraordinary action of 8 September 1796, when Sercey's six frigates attacked the British ships of the line *Arrogant* and *Victorious* north of Sumatra. Sercey kept together his four heavy frigates – *Forte, Vertu, Cybèle,* and *Seine* – with Magon in *Prudente* and Willaumez in *Régénérée* acting as a light flying squadron to bring the two British 74s under fire from both sides. The wind died away as the action began, rendering manoeuvring and signalling difficult for both sides, but the heavy French frigates gave *Arrogant* and *Victorious* such a battering that they were incapable of pursuit when Sercey broke off the action. Magon had handled his ship intelligently, keeping *Prudente* out of range of the British 74s' broadsides; she emerged from the action as the least damaged ship in the French squadron.

The fight with *Arrogant* and *Victorious* was Magon's only experience of action during his remaining time with Sercey's squadron, which ended in January 1798.

He was transferred to *Vertu* which, with *Régénérée*, was tasked with escorting two richly-laden merchantmen from the Philippines home to Spain; they sailed from Île-de-France on 23 January. It was a slow but largely uneventful voyage, with the frigates tied to the leisurely sailing pace of their charges. On two occasions a patrolling British frigate – HMS *Pearl* off Sierra Leone on 24 April and HMS *Brilliant* at Santa Cruz in the Canaries on 26 July – blundered into their anchorage but was driven off with ease. The safe delivery of the Spanish merchantmen in August gave a much-needed boost to the Franco-Spanish alliance; the Spanish Philippine Company registered its gratitude by presenting Magon with a magnificent suit of armour.

After returning *Vertu* and *Régénérée* safely to Rochefort, Magon's welcome home to France was less than cordial. Summoned to Paris, he was dismissed the service by the Directory on the unjust charge of having been party to the expulsion of government agents Baco and Burnel (p. 41) from Île-de-France in 1796. This act of naked political spite was annulled by Navy Minister Bruix, who not only exonerated and reinstated Magon but promoted him to commodore (*chef de division*) on 3 September 1799.

Magon was briefly appointed to command a division of the Saint-Malo squadron before being recalled to Paris for a year of administrative duty in the Navy Ministry. His seagoing career only recommenced in March 1801 when Villaret-Joyeuse assumed command of the Brest fleet with Magon as his flag captain in the flagship *Jemappes*. From June to August 1801 Magon commanded the ship of the line *Océan* before taking over *Mont-Blanc* on the eve of the Saint-Domingue expedition (August 1801–July 1802).

It was in the crucial first six months of the Saint-Domingue campaign, culminating in the capture of rebel leader Toussaint l'Ouverture, that Magon made his name and won his flag. When Army C-in-C General Leclerc landed at Cap Haïtien on 6 February 1802 he called on the Navy to reduce the key objective of Fort Dauphin[2] with its seaward approaches. Magon undertook this combined operation with the guns and crews of four of the line and two frigates. The speed with which they took the fort, sparing the Army from a prolonged and difficult siege, so delighted Leclerc that he promoted Magon rear-admiral on the spot (an echo of Bonaparte's similar promotions of Ganteaume and Perrée in Egypt). Leclerc claimed in his report that Magon's promotion 'was the Army's unanimous wish', adding that 'I do not doubt that the Government' [the Government being Leclerc's brother-in-law, First Consul Bonaparte] 'will confirm it.' And confirmed it duly was, on 16 March 1802.

Back in France after his Saint-Domingue triumph, Magon was given command of the Rochefort squadron (June 1803) before Bruix brought him north in August to command the right wing of the Boulogne invasion flotilla. His success in beating off a British attack on 28 September won him the award of Officer of the Legion of Honour from Napoleon, rising to Commander of the Legion of Honour in June 1804.

After Missiessy sailed for the Caribbean with the bulk of the Rochefort squadron in January 1805, Magon was sent to take command of the two 74s remaining at Rochefort, *Algésiras* and *Achille*, hoisting his flag in *Algésiras* on 14 March. In April he sailed with his division to join Villeneuve in the Caribbean, carrying 800 troops to reinforce the planned diversionary strikes at the British-held West Indies islands. When *Algésiras* and *Achille* joined Villeneuve off Martinique in the first week of June 1805, they raised the strength of the Franco-Spanish Combined Fleet to 18 ships of the line.

Magon's division took part in the Combined Fleet's last victory: the capture of the West India convoy on 8 June 1805, in the course of which Villeneuve learned that Nelson had crossed the Atlantic on his track, and headed back to Europe. In the indecisive clash with Calder's fleet off Finisterre on 22 July, Magon commanded the Combined Fleet's Rear squadron as it disengaged and headed into Ferrol. There followed the sortie from Ferrol of 13 August and Villeneuve's halting attempt to get through to Brest, discouraged by malignant north-easterly winds and the mistaken identity of French warships from Rochefort – Allemand's squadron, trying to join Villeneuve – as British. Turning back for Spain, the Combined Fleet reached its last base, Cadiz, on 21 August.

In the two ensuing months which culminated in the disaster off Cape Trafalgar on 21 October 1805, the Combined Fleet's leadership displayed all the classic weaknesses bedevilling every coalition. The ten-year Franco-Spanish alliance had failed to produce a joint naval signalling code, let alone any effective joint command structure. The Spanish Admirals Gravina and Alava chafed at being under Villeneuve's orders when the Spanish Navy was providing the Combined Fleet's most powerful warships: the 130-gun *Santissima Trinidad,* the 112-gun *Principe de Asturias* and *Santa Ana,* and the 100-gun *Rayo.* They felt that with better support from the French, two Spanish ships would not have been lost in the Finisterre battle. And they were opposed to any premature action which would send the Combined Fleet into action on any but the most favourable terms. On the French side there was a conviction that the attitude of the Spanish commanders fell far short of half-hearted. All these resentments surfaced in the famous conference aboard Villeneuve's flagship *Bucentaure* on 8 October, at which Magon was present.

By October 1805, 11 years of seagoing experience had given Magon a contempt for cautious and half-hearted command and counsels. He had commanded *Cybèle* when Renaud had attacked and bested *Centurion* and *Diomede.* He had supported Sercey's unprecedented frigate attack on two ships of the line and agonised over Sercey's retreat from an undefended convoy. He had chased off two interloping British frigates with vigorous pursuit, and had won his own flag with his all-out attack on Fort Dauphin in 1802. Villeneuve's failure to press on for Brest and the Channel after the Finisterre action had been the last straw. At the *Bucentaure* conference Magon was enraged when Villeneuve's own Chief of Staff, Captain Mathieu Prigny, endorsed the Spanish admirals' advice for caution. A furious comment brought Magon close to being challenged to a duel by the Spanish Commodore Galiano. Magon was only mollified by the Spanish agreement that the fleet would sail at the first favourable opportunity.

Magon must have relished his attachment to Gravina's powerful squadron, with *Principe de Asturias* as its flagship, which Villeneuve had intended to cover the Van of the Combined Fleet in battle and frustrate any attempt by Nelson to round the head of the Franco-Spanish line. But the course reversal hastily ordered by Villeneuve to bring the Combined Fleet safely back to Cadiz threw the fleet into confusion. The best it could do on 21 October was to form a long, loose line of battle, sagging off to leeward, which left Gravina and Magon at the Rear rather than the Van of the Combined Fleet. They became the objective of Collingwood's southern or 'lee' division of the British fleet, heading downwind to engage the Combined Fleet's centre and rear.

Like Captain Jean-Jacques Lucas of the *Redoutable* (one of whose marksmen mortally wounded Nelson on *Victory's* quarterdeck), Magon had insisted on *Algésiras* being prepared for offensive rather than defensive action, ready to close her assailants and carry them by boarding. Magon's flag, flying atop *Algésiras*, was an obvious lure for Captain Tyler of the oncoming 80-gun *Tonnant*. As *Tonnant* had been captured from the French at Aboukir Bay in 1798, her recapture was no less of a lure for Magon, who steered to close and board. With the marksmen in her tops scourging *Tonnant's* upper decks – Captain Tyler was shot through the thigh and had to be carried below – *Algésiras* locked her bowsprit into *Tonnant's* starboard main shrouds and prepared to board.

The two ships closed to the accompaniment of a furious gunnery duel, the intensity of which impressed the British. One of *Tonnant's* midshipmen commented that

> [Algésiras] was one of the very few, perhaps one of the four or five' [out of the Combined Fleet's 33 of the line] 'that had been constantly exercised at her guns. Had we not been well exercised, I think the Frenchman would have got the advantage of us. We had actually our fire-engine playing on her broadside to put out the fire caused by the flame of our guns.

There had been few if any fights like this since the brutal mutual battering of *Brunswick* and *Vengeur* in the First of June battle, 11 years before (pp. 36–37).

In the end, superior British gunnery carried the day. With her boarding party swept by blasts of grape from *Tonnant's* forecastle guns, *Algésiras* lost all three masts, shot through below the deck and taking her marksmen with them. When *Tonnant's* crew carried *Algésiras* by boarding, they found Magon's body at the foot of the poop ladder. Although twice hit by musket balls he had continued cheering on his men until killed instantly by a third shot to his head.

In her last battle *Algésiras* lost 77 killed and 142 wounded, against *Tonnant's* tally of 26 killed and 50 wounded. (More French survivors would certainly have been rescued from the sea if *Tonnant* had not lost all her boats to *Algésiras's* gunfire.) And on the day after Trafalgar, the surviving crewmen of *Algésiras* recaptured their ship from her British prize crew, got jury rig on her and brought her back to Cadiz. It was a final tribute to the fighting spirit which Magon had inspired in his men.

Notes

1 See p. 55 & fn.
2 Where Bruix had been born in 1759.

Vice-Admiral Charles-Alexandre Léon Durand, *Comte de* Linois (1761–1848)

Algésiras, the flagship in which Magon was killed at Trafalgar, had a unique distinction. She was the only Napoleonic battleship named after a French naval victory, which in turn confers distinction on the admiral who won it. At Algeciras in 1801 he also became the only Napoleonic admiral apart from Ganteaume and Perrée to capture a British ship of the line: Charles-Alexandre Léon Durand-Linois.

Linois was born at Brest on 27 January 1761. At the age of 15 he joined the Navy in 1776, two years before France went to war in support of Britain's rebel American colonies. His first ships were the Brest-based ships of the line *César* and *Protée* (April–November 1776). Linois's war began in the ship of the

Linois. Lithograph by Maurin, 1837. (Wikimedia Commons)

line *Bien-Aimé* which he joined in August 1778, serving with the fleet of d'Orvilliers in the Caribbean. In his first eight months of active service he showed such promise that on 27 February 1779 he received the highly unusual probationary – 'hostilities only', in modern parlance – promotion as lieutenant-commander *(lieutenant de frégate pour la campagne)*. In this capacity Linois remained under d'Orvilliers's command, in the ship of the line *Scipion,* from May 1779 to January 1781. His two-year probation ended on 1 July 1781 with his commission as lieutenant *(enseigne de vaisseau)*.

The ending of hostilities in the American Revolutionary War found Linois in the ship of the line *Diadème* (October 1782–April 1783). His first peacetime commission took him to Far Eastern waters for the first time: a supply-and-despatches voyage to Île-de-France (Mauritius) in the storeship *Barbeau* (March 1784–January 1785). This was followed by a posting to the ship of the line *Réfléchi* (March 1785) and a return to the Caribbean, where Linois served for the next two years.

On arrival at Saint-Domingue, he was transferred for service in the frigate *Danaé* (23 April), returning to *Réfléchi* on 23 December 1785. Then came a spell of shore duty as *sous-lieutenant de port* at Port-au-Prince (May–December 1786), before returning to sea for two months in the frigate *Proserpine*. He finally sailed for France (again in *Barbeau*) on 1 March 1787.

For Linois the last two years before the coming of the Revolution were unemployed months 'on the beach', not ended until his appointment as *lieutenant de port* at Brest (1 May 1789). He did not get his next warship posting, to the ship of the line *Victoire* with the Brest fleet, until 12 October 1790. On 25 January 1791, he joined the frigate *Atalante,* bound on a three-year commission to the East Indies station.

As with scores of similarly affected officers, so far the Revolution had done absolutely nothing to accelerate Linois's painful 14-year service climb to the rank of lieutenant. All that changed in 1791 when the reforming politicians turned their attention from carving France into *départements* and bestowing on her such varied gifts as the metric system and the guillotine, to the armed forces. In the overhaul of the naval officers' list published on 15 May 1791, Linois was promoted commander *(lieutenant de vaisseau)* with seniority backdated to 1 May 1789.

Commanded by Decrès with Linois as his second officer, *Atalante* sailed from Île-de-France for home on 9 October 1793. Their homecoming coincided with the greatest crisis faced by the French Republic since the invading Prussians had been halted at Valmy in September 1792. This time the danger was not enemy armies but imminent famine. The fate of Robespierre's dictatorship was hanging on the safe arrival from America of a massive grain convoy led by Rear-Admiral Vanstabel. Every warship and able commander which the French Atlantic fleet could muster was needed at sea to guarantee the convoy's safe arrival.

Yet even in this supreme crisis the illogical, random impact of Revolutionary dogma intervened. As soon as he set foot ashore at Lorient, Decrès was arrested as a suspect counter-Revolutionary. As for Linois, no less tinged with minor aristocratic lineage, orders were waiting for him from Brest fleet C-in-C Villaret-Joyeuse (9 April 1794). He was to take command of *Atalante* – for which there was to be no prolonged overhaul and refit after her long voyage home from Île-de-France – and take her back to sea at the earliest opportunity, with the corvettes *Levrette* and *Epervier*. Sailing from Lorient, Linois's lightweight squadron was to act as a decoy on the northern flank of Vanstabel's convoy for which Rear-Admiral Nielly, with five of the line from Rochefort, was to provide a fighting spearhead. Finally, Villaret-Joyeuse would sail from Brest with 25 of the line to lure Lord Howe's British Channel Fleet into action instead of locating and destroying Vanstabel's convoy (p. 22–23).

The French defence plan of 1794 succeeded, as the British defence plan of 1805 was to succeed. Vanstabel, Nielly and Villaret came through and the Republic was saved, ensuring Europe 20 more years of war. But Linois was not so lucky. On 5 May, off south-western Ireland, his squadron was sighted by the British 74-gun *Swiftsure* and the 64-gun *St Albans*. The two corvettes broke away, unavailingly pursued by *St Albans*, but after a two-night chase *Atalante* was overhauled and brought to action by *Swiftsure* in the small hours of the 7th. The scratch crew with which *Atalante* had been manned and rushed back to sea proved no match for the professionals in the British 74. Out manoeuvred by superior seamanship and overwhelmed by gunnery which cut *Atalante's* rigging to pieces, Linois was forced to strike his colours.

The British prize crew had barely completed repairs to *Atalante's* rigging when three 74s from Nielly's squadron hove into view and it was the turn of the British to run for it. The superiority of British seamanship was rubbed home by the ease with which *Atalante's* prize crew not only outsailed their pursuers with ease but bent a new main topsail while doing so. (*Swiftsure* also escaped, if only after a 12-hour chase.[1]) Because of his comparative juniority Linois remained a prisoner of the British for the next eight months. His exchange was finally negotiated in January 1795, but he was not returned to French soil under cartel until 27 March.

On 4 May 1795 Linois was promoted *capitaine de vaisseau* with seniority backdated to January 1794, his first command as captain being the ship of the line *Formidable* in Villaret's Brest fleet. He was soon in action, in the scrambling battle off the Île de Groix on 23 June when Villaret, withdrawing with his 12 of the line from Lord Bridport's 14, lost his three rearmost ships. Two of them were the *Alexandre* and *Tigre;* the third was Linois's *Formidable*. With his left eye blinded, his ship battered and set on fire aft by gunfire from *Queen Charlotte* and *Sans Pareil,* Linois was forced to strike his colours for the second time in 13 months. This time, however, he was rapidly exchanged and returned to France on 29 August.

After taking much-needed convalescent leave, Linois returned to the Brest fleet and was given command of the 74-gun ship of the line *Nestor* (14 December 1795). Villaret promoted him to commodore (*chef de division*) on 22 March 1796 and in December he sailed with the ill-fated expedition, commanded by Villaret's successor Morard de Galles, to carry General Hoche's army to Bantry Bay and raise Ireland against the British. Most of the fleet made the Bantry Bay rendezvous but appalling weather made any troop landings impossible. By New Year's Day of 1797 there was no option but a straggling retreat to France, mercifully unmolested by the equally scattered British, with Linois bringing *Nestor,* in company with *Tourville, Éole* and *Cassard,* into Brest on 13 January.

Linois remained with *Nestor* until October 1797, his next flagship being the 74-gun *Jean-Jacques Rousseau* (22 April 1798). By now he had become accepted as one of the ablest senior captains in the Brest fleet, to which he was appointed Chief of Staff on 27 February 1799. Six weeks later (8 April) Linois received promotion to acting rear-admiral from Navy Minister Bruix, who was preparing to lead the Brest fleet on its dramatic bid to join forces with the Spanish battle fleet and regain command of the Mediterranean from the British. As Chief of Staff, Linois sailed in the 120-gun flagship *Océan* on 'Bruix's Cruise' (pp. 52–53). After the fleet's return to Brest on 8 August, Linois served on as Chief of Staff until October 1800, his promotion to rear-admiral confirmed by decree of First Consul Bonaparte on 25 January 1800.

For Linois, seven years of uninterrupted service with the Brest fleet ended with his posting to Toulon as second-in-command to Ganteaume (28 October 1800). When Ganteaume sailed on his dramatic but unsuccessful bid to reinforce the Army of Egypt (April–July 1801 (pp. 76–77), Linois remained in command at Toulon. In May 1801 he took the rump of the Toulon fleet to reinforce the siege of Porto-Ferraio on Elba, and won the respect of his fleet by personally extricating three cholera-ridden ships from Livorno on the Italian mainland, and bringing them home to France.

All this high-profile activity by the Toulon fleet was part of Bonaparte's strategy of intensifying pressure on a war-weary Britain, alone again since Austria's defeat in the 1800 Marengo campaign. So was the ostentatious mustering of an 'invasion flotilla' at Boulogne; the latter prompted Nelson's ill-prepared assault of 15–16 August, decisively repulsed by Latouche-Tréville (p. 13). In June 1801, with Ganteaume still at large in the central Mediterranean, Linois was ordered to repeat Bruix's feat of 1799 and create a new combined Franco-Spanish battle squadron in the Western Mediterranean. He was to sail from Toulon with three of the line and head for Cadiz, where Rear-Admiral Dumanoir was negotiating for the transfer of six Spanish battleships to the French Navy, and additional help from the Spanish battle fleet had been promised.

Flying his flag in *Formidable*, Linois sailed from Toulon on 13 June with *Desaix*, *Indomptable* and the frigate *Muiron* (the latter famed for having conveyed Bonaparte back to France from Egypt in 1799). The squadron made an unopposed passage down the Spanish coast and passed Gibraltar on 3 July. On the following day it captured the British brig *Speedy*, heading eastward to Gibraltar with Captain Lord Cochrane on board. Cochrane informed Linois that Rear-Admiral Saumarez was blockading Cadiz with seven of the line, but if he hoped that this news would make Linois turn back into the Mediterranean he had misjudged his man.

Displaying the same tenacity currently being shown by Ganteaume in his efforts to break through to Alexandria, Linois chose instead to seek shelter at Algeciras, 6 miles west of Gibraltar and in sight of the British base, where the outnumbered French squadron would enjoy the cover of powerful Spanish shore batteries.

When Saumarez received word of the French arrival he immediately headed for Algeciras with six of the line, but was delayed by headwinds and did not arrive off Algeciras until the morning of the 6th. This gave Linois and his Spanish allies a clear day in which to prepare their defences. They made full use of their advantages, the first of which were the tricky rocks and shoals imperilling navigation in the bay of Algeciras. Apart from their heavy shore batteries the Spaniards contributed two groups of gunboats north and south of the French anchorage: from north to south

Formidable, Desaix, Indomptable and *Muiron,* anchored in line 500 yards apart. Linois also had his captains alerted to warp their ships closer into the shallows as soon as the topsails of Saumarez's leading ships were sighted.

The ensuing battle at Algeciras inevitably prompts comparison with Nelson's 1798 assault on Brueys's fleet in Aboukir Bay. Although both British commanders attacked as soon as they came in sight of the French, the two outcomes could not have been more different. Brueys had lacked the powerful land battery and gunboat support which Linois enjoyed at Algeciras, while at Aboukir the sea breeze had held steady, enabling Nelson's ships to create the deadly vice which crushed the French Van and Centre from both sides – a manoeuvre which was impossible at Algeciras. Saumarez had been one of Nelson's captains at Aboukir. In his attempt to repeat Nelson's attack plan he clearly underestimated the strength of the Spanish shore defences at Algeciras – every battery of which, in plain view of Gibraltar across the bay, should have been completely familiar to the British.

A concerted swoop by the entire British squadron might have suppressed the defences with concerted broadsides but Saumarez's ships straggled piecemeal into the bay, with two hours passing before his rearmost ships came into action. But what undid Saumarez at Algeciras was the repeated dying of the sea breeze, preventing his ships from moving swiftly into their attack positions and leaving them drifting, exposed to heavy fire from the shore batteries (including red-hot shot), gunboats and Linois's warships. The boats which should have landed assault parties to silence the shore batteries had to be used to tow the becalmed British warships instead.

The battle began shortly after 0730 when *Venerable* nosed into the bay and was promptly becalmed by the dying of the breeze. *Pompée* and *Audacious,* following some 20 minutes later, managed to close the French line under heavy fire, with *Pompée* anchoring alongside *Formidable* at 0845 – but a freak current swung *Pompée* bows-on to *Formidable,* exposing her to a raking broadside from Linois's flagship. Another half hour passed before the rearmost British ships – *Cæsar, Hannibal,* and *Spencer* – began to enter the fray, and when *Hannibal* tried to support *Pompée* against *Formidable* she ran aground. Exposed to a ferocious bombardment from *Formidable* and the shore batteries, *Hannibal* lost her main- and mizzenmasts. Frantic work with the boats succeeded in bringing out *Pompée* but there was no shifting *Hannibal,* which had to be left to her fate when Saumarez ordered a withdrawal to Gibraltar at 1335. With his ship totally defenceless, dismasted and on fire, Captain Ferris of the *Hannibal* struck his colours at 1400.

Linois had not only beaten off an attack by twice his force but captured a British ship of the line, yet there was no time for complacency. Although both sides had suffered extensive battle damage, and Saumarez believed that he had left Linois's squadron incapable of putting to sea, all three French battleships were rendered fit for sea after five days of non-stop repair work. Meanwhile, powerful Spanish reinforcements arrived from Cadiz, only a day's sail from Algeciras: the three-deckers

Real Carlos and *San Hermenegildo* (112), *San Fernando* (98), *Argonauta* (80), and *San Agustin* (74), all of which, commanded by Vice-Admiral Moreno, reached Algeciras by the late afternoon of 9 July. A late arrival on the following morning was the *Saint Antoine* (74), formerly *San Antonio*: the first French purchase from the Spanish Navy, hastily manned with a Franco-Spanish crew.

Across the bay at Gibraltar, the arrival of Moreno's ships made it Saumarez's turn to contemplate hostile odds of 2 to 1, although he clung to his belief that the three French battleships were incapable of sailing. Frantic repair-work restored four of the five ships which had retired from Algeciras on the 6th. (*Pompée* could not be repaired in time; her crew was distributed through the other ships in the squadron.) Saumarez had also been joined by *Superb*, by 12 July his only undamaged battleship. He planned to harry the Spanish squadron when it put out from Algeciras, heading – as he initially believed – for Cartagena. In fact Moreno was under orders to escort Linois and his squadron to Cadiz, taking with them the captured *Hannibal*, jury-rigged and towed by the French frigate *Indienne*. Before they sailed on 12 July, Moreno shifted his flag to the frigate *Sabina* and persuaded Linois to do the same, entrusting *Formidable* to Captain Troude, formerly commander of *Desaix*.

The first Spanish ships got under way at dawn on the 12th, heading for the agreed rendezvous-point with the French, but *Hannibal* proved such an encumbrance that it was not until 1945 that Moreno ordered *Indienne* to tow her back to Algeciras. At the same time he ordered the entire force to make sail for Cadiz, heading west into the 'Gut of Gibraltar'. Saumarez, flying his flag in *Cæsar* with *Superb, Spencer, Venerable* and *Audacious* in company, set off in pursuit but as night came down most of the French and Spanish ships were already out of sight. At 2040 Saumarez therefore ordered his ships to take independent action against the ships of the Franco-Spanish rear-guard: the two Spanish 112s, *Real Carlos* and *San Hermenegildo*, and *Saint Antoine*.

The ensuing night action of 12–13 July 1801 was one of the most extraordinary ever fought, notorious for the most horrific loss of life ever suffered in an episode of so-called 'friendly fire'. By 2330 Saumarez's leading ship, *Superb* (Captain Keats) was engaging *Real Carlos,* whose foretopmast was brought down by the third British broadside. The wreckage fell across the wildly-firing gun muzzles of *Real Carlos* and set her on fire. As *Superb* moved on to engage *Saint Antoine*, battering her defenceless after 30 minutes, *San Hermenegildo* mistakenly opened fire on the blazing *Real Carlos.* The two ships then collided, the fire leaped across to *San Hermenegildo*, and both subsequently blew up with the loss of some 1,700 men out of 2,000.

First light at 0400 on the 13th saw most of the Franco-Spanish squadron already becalmed off Cadiz, *Superb* remaining with the beaten *Saint Antoine,* and *Venerable,* now the leading British pursuer with the frigate *Thames* in company, closing on the rearmost French warship. This was Troude's *Formidable,* limping along under the jury topmasts rigged after the battle of 6 July. Hood of the *Venerable* opened fire on *Formidable* at 0520, but soon found that he had caught a Tartar. In an epic 90-minute duel, Troude's gunners brought down first *Venerable's* mizzen topmast and finally her mainmast. While *Venerable* drifted helplessly ashore, *Formidable* slowly drew away to reach Cadiz in safety.

Linois came well out of the 'Battle of the Gut of Gibraltar'. As Moreno's subordinate he bore no responsibility for the disasters of the night, and although the lost *Saint Antoine* had been commanded by a French officer her Franco-Spanish crew had never had the chance to 'shake down' as an efficient ship's company, let alone reach battle readiness. Troude's defeat of *Venerable* was a genuine source of French pride. It added to the laurels won at Algeciras on 6 July, for which First Consul Bonaparte presented Linois with a 'Sabre of Honour' (p. 83) on 28 July 1801. Yet none of the predictable French trumpeting of the Algeciras victory and the capture of *Hannibal* could change the hard fact that the latest Franco-Spanish bid to win control of the western Mediterranean had failed. Linois and his ships remained under blockade in Cadiz until the signing of peace preliminaries with Britain on 22 October 1801.

In January 1802 Linois contributed to the French bid to reconquer Saint-Domingue. Flying his flag in *Intrépide,* he led a troop-carrying squadron of three of the line and three frigates to Saint-Domingue, returning to Brest with Villaret-Joyeuse on 31 May.

Eight months later, as the fragile Peace of Amiens entered its final weeks, Linois was appointed French naval commander-in-chief for the Indian Ocean (31 January 1803). He was thus commissioned to undertake the first display of the Tricolour in Far Eastern waters since Sercey's cruise ended in 1799. With the bulk of the French fleet still committed to supporting the wretched troops in the pesthole of Saint-Domingue, Linois was left with the scrapings. He sailed from Brest on 6 March 1803 with the 74-gun *Marengo* as his flagship and three frigates – half the force of the powerful frigate squadron which Sercey had commanded. With Linois sailed the new French 'Captain-General of French India', General Charles Decaen. Their first setback was the refusal of the British Governor-General of Bengal, Lord Wellesley, to hand back Pondichéry to Decaen, who found himself obliged to base himself on Île-de-France where Linois arrived on 16 August 1803. There was an inevitable time-lag before the French and British East Indian outposts knew for certain that war had been resumed. For the French on Île-de-France the news was brought out at the end of September by the corvette *Berceau*, a welcome reinforcement to Linois's squadron.

On the outward voyage he had detached the 40-gun frigate *Atalante* on a mission to the Portuguese settlement at Muscat in the Persian Gulf. By the beginning of October, when his first East Indies cruise began, Linois had at his disposal *Marengo* (74,) the frigates *Belle-Poule* (40) and *Sémillante* (36), and *Berceau* (22), with *Atalante* under orders to rejoin him at Batavia in December. Having landed the troops brought out to reinforce Île-de-France and its satellite garrisons, Linois sailed on 8 October to deliver the remainder to Batavia. The cruise began promisingly with an attack on the British trading outpost at Sellabar, Sumatra. This destroyed eight trading vessels, captured three others, and burned three warehouses filled with rice, spices, and opium. The squadron then headed east to arrive at Batavia on 10 December.

The Dutch authorities at Batavia provided the French squadron with six months' provisions, contributed the 16-gun brig-corvette *Aventurier*, and advised Linois that a rich British homeward-bound convoy from China was due to pass through East Indies waters. With *Atalante* yet to rejoin, Linois sailed from Batavia on 28 December 1803 with *Marengo, Belle-Poule, Sémillante, Berceau*, and *Aventurier*. Patient patrolling north of Sumatra was rewarded on the morning of 14 February 1804 when the China convoy – 39 ships with the East India Company armed brig *Ganges* as sole escort – was sighted north-east of Pulo Auro.

Linois found himself in the same position as Sercey, seven years before in the Bali Strait (p. 43): presented with a rich prize ripe for the taking. Yet, unaccountably, history repeated itself. Linois's cautious reconnaissance of the China convoy on the 14th gave Commodore Nathaniel Dance all the time he needed to repeat Lennox's tactic against Sercey in January 1797. He marshalled his charges into close formation and deployed the heavy East Indiamen, with their imposing rows of painted 'gunports', to simulate a threatening line of battle from which Linois retreated on the 15th. He withdrew to Batavia from where, reprovisioned and with *Atalante* finally back under his command, he headed back to Île-de-France where he arrived on 2 April. Governor-General Decaen was furious to hear of the retreat from the China convoy, denouncing it in a stinging dispatch which he sent back to France in *Berceau*.

In late June 1804, after dispatching *Belle-Poule* on a separate raiding cruise, Linois sailed with *Marengo, Atalante,* and *Sémillante* on his second foray from Île-de-France. This time he headed south-west, choosing the Mozambique Channel as his initial hunting-ground before turning in his tracks and re-crossing the Indian Ocean to raid Ceylon and the Coromandel Coast. Encouraged by the capture of several rich prizes south of Ceylon he headed for Vizagapatam, having heard that British East Indiamen were heading there with only a single frigate for escort, and on the morning of 15 September the French warships entered Vizagapatam roads. There they sighted the Indiamen *Barnaby* and *Princess-Charlotte*, loading cargo before being escorted to Madras by the 50-gun *Centurion*.

The British ships should have fallen as easy prey to the French squadron; but they were supported by a 3-gun shore battery and Linois was clearly determined not to court the fate of the British at Algeciras by risking an immediate attack in unknown shoal waters. He was disconcerted, too, by the determination shown by *Centurion*, which drove off *Atalante* with a full broadside and then settled to a prolonged long-range gunnery duel with *Marengo*. This exchange prevented *Centurion* from averting *Princess-Charlotte's* capture by *Sémillante; Barnaby,* the other Indiaman, ran ashore and was lost.

When Linois withdrew with his prize at sunset, *Centurion* had earned full battle honours; she had inflicted considerable superficial damage to *Marengo,* including at least one shot-hole below the waterline. On his return voyage to Île-de-France he took another prize, and when he arrived on 1 November he found that *Belle-Poule* had returned from her raid with a third. If Linois had been denied a smashing victory on this second cruise, at least his squadron had not returned from it empty-handed.

Before *Marengo* was fit for a third cruise in the spring of 1805, *Atalante* was sent off to sweep the Cape of Good Hope sea lane and *Sémillante* was dispatched to the Philippines with news of the renewed war between Britain and Spain. It was therefore only with *Belle-Poule* in company that Linois embarked on his third cruise from Île-de-France on 22 May 1805. By this date he had decided to shift his area of operations from the Indian Ocean to the South Atlantic, with *Atalante* under orders to rejoin him at Simon's Bay near the Dutch outpost of Cape Town. After a final unproductive sweep north-west to the Red Sea approaches, Linois turned back to work the Cape Town-Ceylon sea lane. Off the coast of Ceylon, on 11 July, he fell in with the unescorted East Indiaman *Brunswick*, sailing in company with the merchantman *Sarah*. While *Belle-Poule* chased the *Sarah* ashore, Linois in *Marengo* captured *Brunswick* after a token resistance.

With *Brunswick* in company under a French prize crew, Linois now headed south-west for the Cape of Good Hope. He found himself on a collision course with an outward-bound East India convoy, ten strong, escorted by the 74-gun *Blenheim.* (Aboard the latter was the commander designate of the British East Indies station, Rear-Admiral Troubridge.) The French squadron sighted the convoy at 1600 on 6 August 1805 and this time – despite the lateness of the day, thick haze and a heavy sea running – Linois headed straight in. Having dispatched *Brunswick* to make her way to Île-de-France, *Marengo* and *Belle-Poule* closed the rear of the convoy and overhauled it, firing on the nearest Indiamen as they passed.

If Linois had hoped to make the convoy scatter or to lure *Blenheim* away from her charges, he was frustrated on both counts. His passage of the convoy's flank included a 30-minute exchange of fire with *Blenheim* which put two shot-holes into *Belle-Poule's* hull and damaged *Marengo's* mainmast and foreyard. The Indiamen maintained formation as the French warships passed ahead of the convoy at 1800, crossing its bows during the night to lie off its weather flank by daybreak. Two more tentative passes on the 7th, and his ever-dwindling ammunition reserves with no possibility of replenishment, convinced Linois that he had no chance of a successful attack, and as darkness fell he broke away to the southward. Leaving the convoy to sail on and reach Madras intact on 23 August, Linois headed for the Cape of Good Hope.

By 13 September *Marengo* and *Belle-Poule* had rounded the Cape and anchored in Simon's Bay, having spent 17 weeks at sea since leaving Île-de-France in May. There they remained for the next eight weeks, repairing, overhauling, and waiting for *Atalante* to rejoin – but shortly after doing so she was lost by accidental stranding, her divided crew providing much-needed reinforcements to the complements of *Marengo* and *Belle-Poule*. After this invaluable interlude Linois left Simon's Bay on 11 November 1805 on his penultimate cruise. This took *Marengo* and *Belle-Poule* the length of the west African coast as far as Cape Lopez (Gabon) with only meagre pickings: a ship and a brig.

By December 1805 Linois was aware that his only remaining hope of material success lay in chance encounters with lone sailings and stragglers from convoys. His tiny force was left with only one strategic purpose: to maintain the nuisance value represented by its continued existence for as long as possible. After watering his ships at the Portuguese island of Principe he therefore headed south-west, planning to hover around the British convoy landfall of St Helena. But on 29 January 1806 he spoke an American ship who gave him the dramatic news that Cape Town had fallen to the British on the 10th. With Simon's Bay now closed to him as a South African anchorage of refuge, Linois knew that only one option was left to him: return to France.

Marengo and *Belle-Poule* made a good northward passage, on 17 February crossing the Equator for the 12th time since sailing from Brest three years before; but at 0300 on the night of 12–13 March, north of the Cape Verdes, their luck ran out. They headed into the arms of the British battle squadron of Vice-Admiral Borlase Warren: his flagship *Foudroyant* (80), *London* (98), and the frigate *Amazon* (38), which promptly gave chase. By 0500 on the 13th *London* was within range of *Marengo* and a five-hour running fight began. While *Amazon* engaged *Belle-Poule*, *Marengo* endured the heavier fire of the British three-decker until 1025, when *Foudroyant* entered the fray and both French ships struck their colours.

For the third time Linois was a prisoner of the British, but after the defeated Villeneuve's return to France in April 1806 Napoleon ordered that no future similar concessions were to be made. Although Napoleon created his captive admiral a Count of the Empire on 15 August 1810, Linois remained in British captivity until Napoleon's abdication (6 April 1814). On 22 April he landed in France for the first time in 11 years. The restored Louis XVIII rewarded Linois by appointing him France's first peacetime Governor of Guadeloupe (13 June 1814), and in the following month created him *Chevalier de Saint-Louis*.

When the news reached the West Indies that Napoleon had returned to France and was Emperor again, Linois finally declared for him but his timing was bad: 19 June 1815, the day after Waterloo. For the fourth and last time Linois surrendered to the British (10 August). On his return to France Linois escaped the fate of Marshal Ney (condemned to death by the Council of Peers and shot in December 1815) but was hauled before the Council of War and accused of insubordination, fomenting revolt and abusing his office as Governor of Guadeloupe.

From these charges Linois was acquitted on all counts (11 March 1816) but his active career was over, and in the following month he was placed on the Retired List

(18 April). Two further honours awaited him: promotion to Honorary Vice-Admiral (22 May 1825), and the appointment as Grand Officer of the Legion of Honour (1 March 1831). After a long and peaceful retirement, Linois died at Versailles on 2 December 1848 at the age of 87.

Note

1 To be captured by Ganteaume seven years later off the Libyan coast (p. 76, 150).

PART 5

The Empire, 1804–1814/15

Rear-Admiral Julien-Marie Cosmao-Kerjulien (1761–1825)

Magon of the *Algésiras* and Lucas of the *Redoutable* were two of the best-remembered French naval heroes of Trafalgar; Cosmao of the *Pluton* arguably outstripped both of them. He was already a man of note for his capture of the Diamond Rock during Villeneuve's Caribbean cruise. At Trafalgar, with his superior line of command wiped out by Villeneuve's surrender and the departure of the surviving French Van warships under Dumanoir, it was Cosmao who not only rallied the French and Spanish survivors of the Trafalgar disaster but, two days later, led them back to sea to recapture as many prizes taken by the British as he could. It was this exploit, crowning 27 years of action-packed

Cosmao. Lithograph by Maurin, c.1835. (Wikimedia Commons)

service from the age of 15, which justly earned Cosmao his promotion to rear-admiral.

Julien-Marie Cosmao-Kerjulien was a Breton, born at Châteaulin (Finisterre) on 27 November 1761. At the age of 14 he joined the Navy as a Boy Volunteer on 1 June 1776, two years before France's entry into the American Revolutionary War. Cosmao began his seagoing career with a year-long cruise to the Caribbean (June 1776–June 1777) in the frigate *Aigrette*. In 1778 he served in two more frigates (*Oiseau* and *Nymphe*) before being posted to the brig *Hirondelle* in January 1779. Cosmao served in *Hirondelle* until September 1781, getting his first taste of action against privateers off the coast of Guiana (November–December 1780). By his 20th birthday he had developed and demonstrated enough seamanship, watchkeeping and navigating skills to be granted a probationary commission as *lieutenant de frégate auxiliaire* (8 September 1781).

Cosmao's first posting as an officer was to the newly launched 74-gun ship of the line *Pégase* (21 October 1781). He therefore participated in the rigging, arming, and fitting-out of a major new addition to the battle fleet. To this invaluable experience, unusual for a young officer, was now added a genuine slice of luck. On 18 March 1782 Cosmao was transferred to the ship of the line *Protecteur* – only a month before *Pégase* was captured by the British in the Bay of Biscay.

After a year in *Protecteur* Cosmao was transferred to the frigate *Fidèle* (13 May 1783), during which commission the American Revolutionary War ended with the Peace of Paris (3 September). When *Fidèle* paid off in April 1784, Cosmao spent eight months unemployed before joining *Lourde* on 25 January 1785. There followed 22 months of service in a succession of *flûtes* – *Lourde, Vigilante, Dorade* – during the second of which he was promoted sub-commander or *sous-lieutenant de vaisseau* (1 March 1786).

The coming of the Revolution in May 1789 found Cosmao serving in the longest commission of his career to date: in the *flûte Boulonnaise* (29 November 1787–8 March 1790). The troubled months of France's failed experiment with constitutional monarchy (July 1789–August 1792) brought Cosmao no rapid promotion but a sequence of appointments: to the frigates *Fine* (July–October 1790) and *Précieuse* (October 1790–January 1791), and from February 1791 to the ship of the line *Orion* with the Brest fleet.

Cosmao's promotion to commander or *lieutenant de vaisseau* was confirmed in the New Year's List of January 1792. His first command was the frigate *Sincère* (4 May 1792) in which he was serving when the monarchy was overthrown on 10 August 1792. In *Sincère* Cosmao supported the Toulon fleet's first wartime operations under Truguet against the Kingdom of Sardinia (September–October 1792), including the failed attack on Cagliari, Sardinia, in February 1793. Three days before he left *Sincère,* Cosmao was promoted to *capitaine de vaisseau* (1 April 1793). His first commands as captain were the ships of the line *Centaure* and *Duguay-Trouin* under Trogoff, Truguet's successor at Toulon.

By midsummer 1793 Cosmao had made the successful transition from King's officer to Republican captain. But his career was thrown into the balance by the pro-royalist revolt of Toulon (August 1793) and its brutal reconquest by the Republican army in December. Cosmao succeeded in confirming his loyalty to the Jacobin regime in Paris; he also managed to escape imprisonment under the Terror of 1793–94, but he remained without employment until February 1795. He was posted back to the Toulon fleet, by that date, under Rear-Admiral Martin, fast recovering from its near-annihilation in 1793.

On 8 February 1795 Cosmao took command of one of the heavyweights of the Toulon fleet, the 80-gun *Tonnant.* He took part in both fleet actions between Martin and Hotham in 1795 (pp. 33–34), most notably in the Cape Noli battle of 14 March. In the desperate fighting of 14 March around the crippled *Ça Ira* and *Censeur, Tonnant's* gunfire played a key role in disabling the British 74 *Illustrious,* subsequently driven ashore and lost. This was Cosmao's first demonstration of his readiness to sail to the aid of stricken comrades in a fleet mêlée.

After Martin's second inconclusive clash with Hotham off Fréjus (13 July 1795) the Navy Ministry decided that, to create any serious prospect of an invasion of England, the Brest fleet needed reinforcement from the Mediterranean. On 14 September Martin dispatched Commodore Richery from Toulon with six of the line and three frigates, and two days later Cosmao came ashore from *Tonnant*. He had the right to expect another ship at Toulon or a posting to Brest and a new command there. What he actually got was two and a half years without active employment, sweetened only by promotion to commodore *(chef de division)* on 21 June 1797. (This casual willingness to squander its best talent remained a characteristic of the French Navy Ministry under both the Republic and the Empire. Latouche-Tréville remained unemployed from 1795 to 1800, while Rosily-Mesros languished for nine years in the Department of Naval Charts and Maps before receiving his abrupt appointment as Villeneuve's successor in 1805.)

Cosmao finally got his next command on 13 May 1798: the 80-gun ship of the line *Jemappes,* in the Brest fleet. Under Navy Minister and Brest fleet commander Bruix, Cosmao took part in 'Bruix's Cruise' of April–August 1799, during which the first Franco-Spanish combined fleet was formed (pp. 52–53). He remained with the Brest fleet for the next two years, from February 1800 under Villaret-Joyeuse, until peace preliminaries with Britain were signed on 1 October 1801.

In the following month, as the Brest fleet prepared to join the massive joint expedition ordered by Bonaparte to reconquer Saint-Domingue, Cosmao became flag captain to Rear-Admiral Alain-Joseph Dordelin, flying his flag in *Jemappes.* During the expedition Dordelin shifted his flag to the 118-gun *Océan,* in which Cosmao returned to Brest with Dordelin on 3 April 1802.

From August 1802, Cosmao's last ship during his seven-year stint with the Brest fleet was *Mont-Blanc,* but in the spring of 1805, he returned to Toulon for the first time in ten years. On 16 March 1805 he was appointed to command the new 74-gun *Pluton,* launched at Toulon in January 1805 and assigned to the squadron of Villeneuve. Cosmao thus found himself bound for the Caribbean for the first time in 21 years, part of Napoleon's grand deception plan to lure the blockading British fleets off station and make possible the invasion of England.

Cosmao's *Pluton* was an invaluable addition to Villeneuve's fleet, which had staggered back to Toulon with extensive storm damage after its first sortie in January. Cosmao had a bare fortnight in which to ready *Pluton* to sail with the repaired fleet. They were 14 days of hectic activity, embarking water, provisions, ammunition, and finding accommodation for *Pluton's* share of the 5100 troops with which Villeneuve was ordered to *'faire tout le mal possible à l'ennemi'*: do all the damage he could to the British in the West Indies while waiting for Ganteaume to join him with the Brest fleet.

On 30 March 1805, *Pluton* sailed from Toulon with Villeneuve's other ten ships of the line. Their first objective was Cartagena, where the French fleet discovered on

6 April that no Spanish battleships were ready to come out and join it. Undeterred, Villeneuve stood on for the Straits, passing Gibraltar on the 8th and being joined on the following day by Vice-Admiral Gravina's six Spanish ships of the line from Cadiz. As it headed out into the Atlantic, having gained a ten-day start over the pursuing Nelson, the Franco-Spanish Combined Fleet was back in being for the first time since Linois and Moreno (p. 120) had sailed from Algeciras in July 1801.

When the Combined Fleet reached Martinique on 14 May, its larger French contingent had been continually at sea for more than six weeks. Once the troop reinforcements for Martinique had been landed, taking on fresh water and provisions was an inevitable priority. While this work was in progress Villeneuve, Gravina and Villaret-Joyeuse, Governor-General of Martinique, conferred over what the expedition's first objective should be. The obvious choice was the capture of the precipitous Diamond Rock, at its closest less than a mile off the coast of Martinique and manned, since January 1804, by a tiny British garrison armed with heavy naval guns.

'HMS *Diamond Rock*', as it was rated by the British, dominated the deep-water channel into Fort Royal, Martinique and compelled French shipping to make a wide detour round the islet to evade the reach of its guns. Although the sheer impudence of its retention by the British was known to infuriate Napoleon, Rear-Admiral Missiessy, arriving at Martinique with the Rochefort squadron in February 1805, had failed to persuade Villaret to take the Diamond Rock (p. 17). With his fleet more than three times the size of Missiessy's squadron, Villeneuve had no such difficulty and in the last week of May gave Cosmao the mission of opening the campaign by reducing the *'Diamant'* without further ado.

Cosmao had all the resources he needed for the job: two 74s, his own *Pluton* and the *Berwick* (captured by Perrée's frigates back in February 1795), the 40-gun frigate *Sirène,* the 16-gun brig-corvette *Argus,* the armed schooner *Fine,* 11 gunboats, and a landing force of 300-plus troops. To defend the Diamond Rock, Captain Maurice had a garrison of 107 officers and men, two long 24-pounders at sea level, another 24-pounder emplaced halfway up the cliff, and two long 18-pounders emplaced in 'Fort Diamond' on the summit. (All five guns had been landed from the 74-gun HMS *Centaur* and mounted, overcoming incredible difficulties, in January 1804 – the British seaman at his versatile best.) As soon as he sighted Cosmao's powerful flotilla emerge from Fort Royal on 29 May, Captain Maurice abandoned his sea-level battery, spiking the two 24-pounders and throwing into the sea all shot and powder that could not be hauled up the cliffs. With no hope of relief, reinforcement or re-supply, he knew that he would have no option but surrender after putting up a decent defence and firing off his ammunition.

Fully aware that he held all the cards, Cosmao had no intention of exposing his ships and men to needless battle damage and casualties before the British saw sense. As the guns on the Rock had been sited not for defence but to bombard

French shipping heading in and out of Fort Royal, their traverse was limited and Cosmao took his time in deploying his ships out of their reach. The French 74s finally opened fire at 0800 on 31 May, with Maurice's guns stoutly replying. The artillery exchange continued throughout the daylight hours of the 31st and 1 June until, by the late afternoon of the 2nd, the British gunners were down to their last few cartridges. French troops were already on the Rock, having lost three gunboats and two launches during their approach and casualties of about 30 dead and 40 wounded. To avoid further pointless loss of life, Maurice flew a flag of truce at 1630 which was acknowledged by *Fine*. A surrender with the full honours of war was negotiated that evening, and Cosmao entered French Navy records as the man who reconquered the Diamond Rock.

Events now moved fast for the Combined Fleet. On 1 June, while Villaret, Villeneuve and Gravina were watching the Diamond Rock bombardment through their telescopes, the frigate *Didon* arrived from Guadeloupe. She brought the news that Rear-Admiral Magon had arrived at Guadeloupe from Rochefort, bringing the Combined Fleet two more ships of the line and new orders from Napoleon. Ganteaume had not escaped from Brest by the time *Didon* had sailed on 2 May. Villeneuve was therefore ordered to wait for him in the Caribbean no longer than 35 days, using the troops from Martinique and Guadeloupe to capture St Vincent, Antigua and Grenada from the British. He was then to re-cross the Atlantic, looking for a rendezvous with Ganteaume between Ferrol and Brest.

The speed with which Cosmao reduced the Diamond Rock was therefore all the more welcome and the embarkation of the bulk of Martinique's garrison began at once. On the fourth the Combined Fleet sailed for Guadeloupe, collecting Magon's *Algésiras* and *Achille* on the brief voyage and raising its strength to 18 (the Spanish *Santa Madalena* and three frigates had been left at Fort Royal.) When Guadeloupe was reached on the 6th, further troops were embarked before the Combined Fleet sailed to begin its task of conquest and plunder amid the British-held islands.

By 8 June Villeneuve was within striking distance of Antigua, one of the prime objectives designated by Napoleon, when news came from a passing American schooner. A homeward-bound convoy of British merchantmen, 15 strong, had sailed from Antigua on the 7th, steering north-north-east. The Combined Fleet promptly set off in pursuit and within 24 hours had overhauled and captured the entire convoy – a rich windfall valued at 5 million francs. But even as the captured merchantmen were readied for passage to Guadeloupe with the frigate *Sirène* as escort, interrogation of the merchant skippers yielded electrifying news. Nelson had followed the Combined Fleet across the Atlantic, reaching Barbados on 4 June.

As a pointless battle in the West Indies would do nothing to further Napoleon's plans to invade England, Villeneuve and Gravina agreed that the Combined Fleet must return to Europe at once. Two days of frantic activity saw the hapless French troops crammed aboard the frigates *Hortense*, *Didon*, *Hermione* and *Thémise* to be returned to Guadeloupe. By 11 June the battleships of the Combined Fleet were on their way across the Atlantic to the Azores, where the five French frigates rejoined company on the 30th.

Before he resumed his long chase of Villeneuve by re-crossing the Atlantic, Nelson sent ahead the fast-sailing brig *Curieux* to overhaul the Combined Fleet and report its course to England. She reached Plymouth on 7 July with the news that Villeneuve was clearly heading for the Bay of Biscay rather than the Gibraltar Straits. This vital intelligence enabled the 80-year-old Lord Barham, First Lord of the Admiralty, to order Vice-Admiral Calder to raise his blockade of Ferrol and intercept Villeneuve 100 miles west of Cape Finisterre.

Barham had delivered the nearest fleet to the right place at the right time – but not under the right admiral. Villeneuve was lucky in the opponent he faced when the fleets sighted each other at 1100 on 22 July 1805. Calder's ideal was the sacredness of the line of battle, to break which was blasphemy; he had no idea of how to tackle a stronger force (the Combined Fleet outnumbered him by 20 to 15) by concentrating his entire force against a portion of the enemy. Calder was also perplexed by the prevailing weather: light winds and persistent mist which only got worse as the day wore on and evening approached. Six hours passed before he tentatively ordered an attack at 1715, with worsening visibility intensified by gun smoke (as at Jutland in 1916).

The resulting confused mêlée was nothing like the 'pell-mell battle' for which Nelson yearned. In the centre Captain Buller of the 80-gun *Malta* (none other than the former *Guillaume-Tell* which Decrès had defended so tenaciously in 1800 – pp. 90–91) extricated himself from a group of five Spanish ships of the line by simultaneously battering the 80-gun *San Rafael* and 74-gun *Firme* with devastating broadsides. At 2025, half an hour after both *San Rafael* and *Firme* surrendered to *Malta,* Calder signalled his ships to break off the action. Although the fleets remained in contact until the 24th, Calder followed the example of Lord Howe after the First of June in 1794 (p. 23), making sure of his prizes and declining to renew the action (for which Calder was court-martialled and severely reprimanded).

Cape Finisterre did nothing to improve Franco-Spanish relations within the Combined Fleet, the prevailing Spanish view being that Villeneuve had sacrificed his allies. In fact, two French 74s had done their utmost to support *San Rafael* and *Firme.* One was *Atlas,* which suffered 14 dead (including her captain) and 52 wounded. The other was Cosmao's *Pluton* (14 dead and 24 wounded). If Commodore Villavicencio had not been demoralised into surrender by the extensive battle damage and casualties inflicted by *Malta,* Cosmao might well have succeeded in extricating *Firme.* When he broke the line a second time, supported by *Atlas* and *Mont-Blanc,* Cosmao did succeed in rescuing the *España.* His efforts were warmly appreciated by Gravina and his captains as the Combined Fleet headed for Vigo and Ferrol (1 August) to land its sick (a list of well over 800) and wounded.

The Spanish warships in Ferrol raised the Combined Fleet's strength to 30 of the line. Villeneuve hoped to raise it still further by incorporating Commodore Allemand's Rochefort squadron when he sailed from Ferrol on 13 August – his last bid to free Ganteaume's fleet from Brest and enter the Channel in overwhelming strength. Villeneuve and Allemand did briefly sight each other on the 14th, but each mistook the other for British and broke away. Baulked by persistent north-easterlies, Villeneuve finally abandoned the Channel venture and headed back to Spain, leading the Combined Fleet into Cadiz on 21 August. When it next sailed, its destination would be the Mediterranean.

Villeneuve knew that he was not likely to reach the Gibraltar Straits without a battle with the British fleet blockading Cadiz, from 28 September commanded by Nelson. With vivid memories of how Nelson had engulfed the French Van and Centre seven years before in Aboukir Bay, Villeneuve planned an order of sailing which placed his most aggressive captains – Baudoin in *Fougueux,* Magon in *Algésiras,* Cosmao in *Pluton* – in a powerful Van squadron. But when he made his break for the Mediterranean on 19 October Villeneuve was disconcerted by the speed with which Nelson moved to intercept and ordered a return to Cadiz. The clumsiness with which the Combined Fleet executed its course reversal left it by noon on 21 October strung out in a sagging arc, with the original Van division now lying in the Rear. The Franco-Spanish line was also bunched in places, with many ships obscuring the field of fire of others to leeward.

A classic tight line-ahead could well have defeated Nelson's two-pronged assault, with Nelson's division aimed at severing the Combined Fleet's Van and Centre and Collingwood's at the Centre and Rear. Both British divisions suffered extensively as they came within range of the Franco-Spanish line, with Collingwood's bearing the brunt. Vice-Admiral d'Alava's 112-gun flagship *Santa Ana,* Collingwood's initial target, was energetically supported by Baudoin's *Fougueux,* Cosmao's *Pluton,* and Magon's *Algésiras,* the next ships in the allied line. Between them *Fougueux* and *Pluton* comprehensively wrecked *Belleisle* and *Mars* as they followed Collingwood into action. But although they managed to blunt Collingwood's spearhead, they could not halt the relentless advance of the remainder of his division. By 1430 the ruin of the Combined Fleet's Centre and Rear was all but complete; aboard his devastated flagship *Bucentaure,* Villeneuve had struck his colours at 1345. With his immediate superior, Magon, lying dead in the captured *Algésiras,* Cosmao could only head for Cadiz with the survivors of the allied Centre and Rear.

As the Trafalgar battle petered out, the greatest danger facing the two battered fleets was the rising wind, escalating into the storm of 22–23 October and threatening disabled and badly damaged ships with foundering or being driven ashore. Captured French officers marvelled at the professionalism which roused exhausted British crews to save their ships after the battle, while their own surviving crewmen remained prostrate – or drunk. In many captured ships, French and Spanish seamen joined forces with the British prize crews to save the floating wrecks which the battle had left them. But only Cosmao saw the mounting crisis off Cadiz as an opportunity to recoup some credit after the disaster of the battle. As the gale from the south increased on the 22nd, preventing the British from towing their prizes to Gibraltar, Cosmao received the mortally wounded Gravina's approval to lead a sortie with the fittest ships which had taken refuge in Cadiz.

In the late morning of 23 October, Cosmao headed out into the gale with the French *Pluton, Indomptable,* and *Neptune,* and the Spanish *Rayo* and *San Francisco de Asis.* With them sailed the squadron of French frigates which had played no part in the battle: *Cornélie, Hermione, Hortense, Rhin* and *Thémis,* with the brigs *Argus* and *Furet.* The frigates succeeded in recapturing *Santa Ana* and *Neptuno,* and brought both back into Cadiz. But in the ever-worsening weather *San Francisco de Asis, Rayo,* and *Indomptable* failed to get back into Cadiz and all three were wrecked on the 24th. The loss of life in *Indomptable,* which had nearly 500 survivors from *Bucentaure* on board, came to over 1,000 men. The tragic ending of the Cadiz sortie did nothing to diminish Cosmao's standing after Trafalgar, both in France and Spain. After he left *Pluton* in Cadiz and returned to France, the Spanish Crown created Cosmao a Grandee of Spain, First Class, although his thoroughly deserved promotion to rear-admiral was not confirmed until 29 May 1806.

Cosmao was appointed to the Toulon fleet, where he hoisted his flag as one of Ganteaume's squadron commanders. In this capacity he shared in the rebuilding of the Toulon fleet, which at the time of Cosmao's promotion to flag rank numbered barely five of the line. In February 1808 he sailed with Ganteaume on the Toulon fleet's first major operation since the 1805 Trafalgar campaign. This was the reinforcement and resupply of the French garrison on Corfu, carried out by ten ships of the line, three frigates, two corvettes, and seven armed *flûtes.* The fleet sailed from Toulon on 7 February and reached Corfu, unmolested by Collingwood's Mediterranean Fleet, on the 23rd. On 16 March, the return voyage to Toulon began, during which Ganteaume deliberately trailed his coat along the coasts of Tunisia, Sicily and Sardinia before reaching Toulon safely on 10 April.

One month later, Spain exploded in revolt against Napoleon's attempt to make his brother Joseph King of Spain backed by French military force. The unfolding of the subsequent Peninsular War, with ragged Spanish forces fighting on despite repeated defeats, aided by British expeditionary forces, gave the Toulon fleet a new strategic role: supporting the French Army in eastern Spain. In the spring of 1809 Ganteaume tasked Cosmao with taking a large supply convoy down to Barcelona. His force consisted of his 80-gun flagship *Robuste,* the 74s *Donauwerth* (the newest addition to the fleet, launched at Toulon in July 1808), *Génois, Borée,* and *Lion,* and two frigates, escorting 12 transports. Cosmao carried out his mission with textbook efficiency, sailing from Toulon on 24 April and returning to base on 1 May.

These two operations, serving notice that the Toulon fleet was very much back in business, help explain why the British Admiralty kept Collingwood in command of the Mediterranean Fleet until he died of exhaustion in March 1810. Cosmao served on with the Toulon fleet, with Napoleon creating him a Baron of the Empire on 18 December 1810. In October 1811 he was transferred from Toulon for seven months' duty with the Scheldt squadron under Missiessy, flying his flag in the 80-gun, Antwerp-built *Tilsitt*. On 4 April 1812, Cosmao was proclaimed Commander of the Legion of Honour and in the following month returned to the Toulon fleet, now commanded by Émeriau.

Cosmao's last two battles both involved sorties to bring in Genoa-built additions to the Toulon battle fleet. They took place right at the end of the 21-year naval war with Britain, during the collapse of the Empire and the invasion of France. Both were successful, both foiled determined British attempts to intervene, and both were demonstrations of the classic value of a 'fleet in being' to frustrate a more powerful naval enemy. The first occurred on 5 November 1813 when Cosmao at sea with five of the line, ensured the safe arrival at Toulon of Émeriau with the 74-gun *Agamemnon* and two frigates. The second came on 10 February 1814 – barely two months before Napoleon's abdication. With Austrian forces closing in on Genoa, Cosmao had sortied from Toulon to bring out the 74-gun *Scipion,* launched at Genoa in September 1813. He returned in triumph with *Scipion* after a spirited action in which he saved his rearmost ship, *Romulus,* from encirclement and capture.

On the first Bourbon restoration Cosmao was immediately given command of the Toulon fleet (29 April 1814) and was created *Chevalier de Saint-Louis* on 5 July. During the 'Hundred Days' of March–June 1815, Napoleon appointed Cosmao Maritime Prefect at Brest and created him a Peer of France on 2 June. These were Cosma's last appointments and honours. He was finally pensioned off on the Retired List on 12 March 1817, with back-dated effect to 1 January 1816, and died at Brest on 17 February 1825, aged 64.

To Napoleon, Cosmao was 'the best sailor of his time; none was ever braver and more generous'. It was a just tribute to the most striking recurrent theme of Cosmao's fighting career: his urge in battle to sail at once to the aid of any endangered comrade in arms.

Rear-Admiral Jacques-Félix-Emmanuel Hamelin (1768–1839)

Born at Honfleur (Calvados) on 13 October 1768, Jacques-Félix-Emmanuel Hamelin was one of the four 'Admirals of the *Arc*' who hailed from Normandy (the other three being Lhermitte, Perrée, and Troude.) He was 15 when the American Revolutionary War ended in 1783, and with an uncle who was a merchant shipowner the choice in peacetime France of a career in the merchant navy was both obvious and easy. It was in one of his uncle's ships, *Asie,* that Hamelin first went to sea as a merchant apprentice (*pilotin*), on an 18-month trading voyage to Portuguese-held Angola (April 1786–September 1787).

Hamelin. Lithograph by Maurin, c.1835. (Wikimedia Commons)

In consecutive voyages over the next five years Hamelin worked hard at his chosen career, qualifying as a watchkeeping officer and, by January 1790, as a merchant navy lieutenant. He sailed to Angola for the second time (July 1788–September 1789) as a probationary officer in the *Jeune-Minna,* followed by a voyage to the Gold Coast and Saint-Domingue (January–November 1790) in the *Aimable-Dorothée.* By the time that Hamelin returned from a third Angola voyage in *Eléonore* (April 1791–July 1792) France was at war, and Hamelin applied for a transfer to the Navy. On 27 August 1792 he became quartermaster of the 74-gun ship of the line *Entreprenant* in Truguet's Toulon fleet, with Latouche-Tréville as his squadron commander.

The time and place of Hamelin's first Navy posting meant that he took part in the Republican Navy's first wartime operation. This was directed at the latest enemy of the fledgling Republic: the Kingdom of Sardinia, on which France declared war on 16 September 1792. In the following month the Toulon fleet sailed to bombard and land troops to capture the Sardinian mainland ports of Nice, Montalban, Villafranca, and Oneglia. Hamelin next experienced the Toulon fleet's failure to capture Cagliari, capital of Sardinia, in February 1793. He remained in *Entreprenant* throughout 1793, receiving his lieutenant's commission as *enseigne de vaisseau* on 15 August.

In April 1794, Hamelin was posted to the 40-gun frigate *Proserpine*, commanded by Perrée and serving with Villaret-Joyeuse's Brest fleet. This commission, extending through the dramatic weeks of May–June 1794, gave Hamelin his first experience of action with the British Channel Fleet of Lord Howe, reaching its climax with the First of June battle in which Villaret and his crews saved the Republic (pp. 22–23). Hamelin shared in the ensuing spate of naval promotions, being promoted to commander (*lieutenant de vaisseau*) on 12 August 1794.

Hamelin's first posting as commander took him back to the Toulon fleet, now under Martin's command. His new ship was the frigate *Minerve,* flagship of Perrée's frigate squadron. During the capture of the British ship of the line *Berwick* by Perrée's frigates on 7 March 1795 (pp. 80–81), Hamelin was wounded in the left leg. He nevertheless served in the scrambling fleet action off Cape Noli between Martin and Hotham on 13–14 March, in which the British captured *Ça Ira* and *Censeur* (pp. 33). Repaired and refitted at Toulon, *Berwick* joined the French battle fleet (and served with it for the next ten years, until Trafalgar in 1805). With Dumanoir as captain and Hamelin serving as one of her first complement of French officers, *Berwick* sailed with the battle squadron – six of the line and two frigates, commanded by Commodore Richery – which sailed from Toulon on 14 September 1795 to reach the Atlantic and reinforce the Brest fleet.

Richery's escape from the western Mediterranean was made all the easier by Hotham's failure to blockade Toulon. By the first week of October the French squadron had passed Gibraltar and was heading up the Spanish coast. On the morning of the 7th it fell in with a convoy of 31 richly laden British merchantmen, homeward bound from the eastern Mediterranean. The modest British escort included the captured *Censeur* under jury rig, intended for repair and re-rigging before being added to the British fleet. While Richery's frigates rounded up the merchantmen and took them into Cadiz – one of the richest captures ever achieved by the French Revolutionary Navy – Hamelin shared the unique kudos of recovering a captured French battleship (*Censeur*) with a battleship which had been captured from the British (*Berwick*).

Hamelin remained in *Berwick* during the no less dramatic sequel to this spectacular *coup*. This was Navy Minister Truguet's order to Richery not to proceed to Brest as originally planned. In 1796, Year IV of the Republic, France would carry the war to its coalition of enemies: against the Austrians in southern Germany and Italy, and against the British at sea. While Sercey's frigate squadron sailed east to challenge the British in the Indian Ocean, Richery was to replenish his squadron in Cadiz for a transatlantic strike at Newfoundland and the coasts of British Canada. With these twin ventures by the French Navy, the war would become global.

After a thorough refit and re-provisioning at Cadiz, Richery finally sailed for Canada in August 1796 and on the 28th arrived like a thunderbolt off the Grand Banks of Newfoundland. Over the next 15 days his ships wiped out the British Grand Banks fishing fleet and comprehensively wrecked its shore facilities, packing centres and storage depots, followed by those of St Pierre and Miquelon – a total of more than 80 craft captured or sunk, and several hundred prisoners taken.

There was no respite for Hamelin when Richery's triumphant squadron returned to Rochefort in November 1796. Hamelin found himself promoted *capitaine de frégate* and appointed 2nd Captain of the 74-gun *Révolution,* serving again under Captain Dumanoir. *Révolution* and *Pégase,* the only two ships of the line in Richery's squadron fit to return at once to sea, were transferred to Brest. The Brest fleet, commanded now by Morard de Galles, was preparing for the latest French blow at Britain. It was under orders to sail for Bantry Bay, where it would land General Hoche's army, 18,000 strong, to raise Ireland against the British. The fleet consisted of 17 of the line, 14 frigates (one of them serving as a powder-vessel), six corvettes, and seven transports. Every warship in the fleet, including the corvettes, was doubling as a troop transport, with the ships of the line carrying an average of 600 troops each and the frigates 250.

The Irish expedition was ruined by the same bad weather which blew the British off station and enabled the Brest fleet to escape to sea (16–17 December). It speaks volumes for the determination of the French captains that by the 24th the bulk of the fleet had fought its way into Bantry Bay. In the teeth of blizzards and screaming gales of unprecedented severity, landing the hapless troops was out of the question. Not only did the ships repeatedly find themselves dragging their anchors, but rapidly mounting storm damage threatened disaster which, in the case of *Scévola,* was only narrowly averted.

Scévola was a cut-down *(razée)* ship of the line with 400 troops on board, and by the 29th had been battered to the point of sinking. A major tragedy was only averted by the promptness and seamanship of Dumanoir and Hamelin, who laid *Révolution* alongside the sinking *Scévola* and took off every man. This forced Dumanoir to signal that with 1,200 men now on board and nothing like enough provisions for them, he had no option but to return at once to Brest. With food and water stocks rapidly dwindling in every ship of the fleet, the result was a straggling retreat to the Biscay ports. *Révolution,* forced to make a southerly detour to evade a belated appearance by the British fleet, did not reach Rochefort until 14 January 1797.

Hamelin remained with *Révolution* until the summer of 1797, when he was given his first command (22 August–14 November): the frigate *Fraternité,* which had served as Morard's flagship during the Irish fiasco. From *Fraternité* Hamelin was transferred to the frigate *Précieuse,* which he commanded from 19 November 1797 until 29 June 1798. But after this promising step upwards, Hamelin's career marked time for the next 18 months. He was transferred from the Brest fleet to the comparative backwater of the Gulf of Saint-Malo on the north Breton coast, his next ship (July 1798) being the *flûte Cormoran*. From October 1799 to January 1800 he commanded a division of the St Brieuc-Granville flotilla before being posted back to Brest and the ship of the line *Formidable,* in which he dutifully served from February to August 1800. But Hamelin's next command – wholly unconnected with his previous naval career – gave him a key role in one of the most extraordinary events of the Revolutionary and Napoleonic Wars.

The Baudin expedition of 1801–3 was unique: a geographical and scientific voyage of exploration, sent out by one of the leading protagonists in the midst of a world war. By 1798, former merchant navy captain Nicolas Baudin had led two successful tropical expeditions to collect previously unknown specimens of flora and fauna and bring them back for study in France. In that year he approached the French Directory with the proposal for a comprehensive survey and collecting cruise to the coasts of Pacific South America and the virtually unexplored continent of Australia.

Baudin's project had received provisional approval by November 1799, when the Directory was overthrown and replaced by Bonaparte's Consulate, but it was in the summer of 1800 that Bonaparte ordered Baudin's expedition to go ahead. The scientific team which had accompanied Bonaparte to Egypt in 1798 had brought back priceless information about that country (the most important leading to the deciphering of the Rosetta Stone), and Bonaparte was anxious to expand his reputation as an enlightened patron of scientific knowledge. Any intelligence about the British settlements in Australia would have obvious future value to France, but was of secondary importance to the geographical and scientific motive for the expedition. Two ships were provided for the voyage. The corvette *Géographe* served as Baudin's headquarters ship. Hamelin was appointed to the large *flûte Naturaliste,* taking command on 1 October 1800; they sailed from Le Havre on the 19th.

Baudin had assembled the largest group of scientists and *savants* ever to set sail for the tropics: 24 in all, including two astronomers, six zoologists, four gardeners, three botanists, and four artist-illustrators. But it was a far from harmonious team; Baudin proved to be a dictatorial leader, adept at creating friction. To make matters worse, the course he chose on the first stage of the voyage to the Indian Ocean kept the ships at sea for far too long, resulting in rampant scurvy and other diseases. When *Géographe* and *Naturaliste* finally reached Île-de-France on 20 April 1801, ten of the scientific team abandoned the expedition, seven suffering from illness, the other three from disenchantment with Baudin's leadership. (Over the next two years another six were to die, including Baudin himself; only four of the original 24 returned to France in 1803–4.)

After landing their sick and taking on fresh water and provisions at Île-de-France, the two ships headed south-east for Australian waters. With Baudin opting for the more northerly latitude of 35° South than the traditional route to Tasmania and New South Wales, they arrived off Cape Leeuwin at Australia's south-western tip on 27 May 1801. Over the next two months, Baudin and Hamelin completed the first mapping of Australia's west coast. On the island off Shark Bay first discovered and named for the Dutchman Dirk Hartog in 1616, one of Hamelin's shore parties discovered the memorial plate left there by Willem de Vlaminck in 1697; on Hamelin's orders, it was left *in situ*. When the opening stage of the expedition ended at Timor in the Dutch East Indies in August 1801, Baudin's reduced team of researchers was already replete with specimens and data. (By the time they returned to France, they would have identified some 2500 previously unknown species.)

From Timor, *Géographe* and *Naturaliste* sailed south-east to reach Van Diemen's Land (Tasmania) in January 1802, mapping the New Guinea coast (and fortunately escaping any close encounters with the Great Barrier Reef) *en route*. While the team from Hamelin's *Naturaliste* carried out an extensive exploration of Tasmania, Baudin in *Géographe* headed north to explore the Australian mainland's south-eastern coast. In April 1802, Baudin met and consulted with the British explorer Matthew Flinders in Encounter Bay. It was with pooled information that Baudin pushed on to his 'furthest west' – Cape Adieu on the Great Australian Bight – before turning back to the east and heading for Botany Bay and the British settlement at Port Jackson (Sydney).

As arranged, Hamelin's *Naturaliste* had already crossed to Port Jackson from Tasmania. After wintering at Port Jackson Baudin and Hamelin finally parted company in April 1803 when Hamelin was charged with returning to France, carrying the bulk of the expedition's specimens and records in *Naturaliste*. After a final exploration of the south-eastern Australian coast Baudin also headed for France via Tasmania and Timor, but died of tuberculosis at Île-de-France on 16 September 1803; *Géographe* did not return to France until the New Year of 1804.

When Hamelin brought *Naturaliste* into Le Havre on 23 June 1803, the brief-lived Peace of Amiens (1802–3) had already come and gone. Work was already well advanced on reforming the French Army into seven corps and massing three of them between Dunkirk and Boulogne for the invasion and conquest of England. Boulogne was the concentration-point for the invasion fleet of troop transports and supply ships. Promoted *capitaine de vaisseau* on 15 September 1803, Hamelin was tasked with conveying one of the invasion fleet's four divisions from Le Havre to Boulogne.

In October, Hamelin was given command of the 7th *Équipage* of the new Guards battalion of picked 'Sailors of the Guard' – the *Marins de la Garde*. (Another future admiral, Baste, was appointed at the same date to command the 3rd *Équipage*.) In May 1804, following Napoleon's proclamation as Emperor of the French, the vastly expanded Guard corps became the Imperial Guard. The prime task laid down for the *Marins de la Garde* was to ensure the safety of the Emperor and his staff during the cross-Channel passage of the 'Army of England'. As the invasion preparations reached their peak in 1804–5, Hamelin was posted to a command with the right wing of the invasion flotilla. He was also responsible for controlling the flow of signals directing the invasion force once it put to sea.

By the end of August 1805, it was all over. Villeneuve's Franco-Spanish Combined Fleet had failed to join forces with Ganteaume's Brest fleet, enter the Channel in overwhelming force and ensure the safe passage of the 'Army of England'. Abandoning his invasion plans, Napoleon had turned his back on the Channel, where the embarkation camps lay empty; his re-styled *Grande Armée* was on the march for southern Germany. The *Marins* marched with the Imperial Guard during the ensuing Austerlitz campaign, but unlike Baste Hamelin did not go with them. He was helping direct the cumbersome dispersal of the invasion flotilla, with hundreds of much-needed freight barges being returned to canal duty and seagoing freighters to the coasting trade.

After the Combined Fleet's destruction at Trafalgar in October 1805, the most urgent priority for the French Navy Ministry was the rebuilding of the Toulon fleet, but while this vital two-year programme was pursued, Navy Minister Decrès never lost sight of the wider picture. As long as France retained her colonial base of Île-de-France in the southern Indian Ocean, Decrès was determined to keep the Tricolour flying in eastern seas. This would be an ideal task for the tough new frigates of the Imperial French Navy's building programme. Compared with the massive losses in ships of the line during the year of Trafalgar, the Navy's frigate arm was not only comparatively untouched but the best option for keeping the British Navy on the stretch in distant waters.

The Revolution, and the subsequent turmoil of the Republican experiment and its replacement with Empire, had done nothing to reduce the traditional excellence of French naval shipbuilding. A good example was the 'Gloire' class frigate *Vénus*, launched at Le Havre on 5 April 1806. The 40-gun broadside of *Vénus* and her sister-ships consisted of 28 18-pounders and 12 8-pounders, making these ships formidable commerce-raiders. Other examples were the 'Hortense' class *Manche* (launched at Cherbourg on the same day as *Vénus*) and *Caroline,* launched at Antwerp on 15 August 1806; and the 'Consolante' class *Bellone*, launched two years later at the Saint Servan yard, Saint-Malo.

In 1796 Sercey had commanded a squadron of four frigates and two corvettes. In 1803, Linois had had the ship of the line *Marengo* and three frigates. But when *Manche, Caroline, Bellone,* and *Vénus* sailed for the Indian Ocean in the last weeks of 1808, they did so independently, not in the form of a united squadron. Hamelin, who had been captain of *Vénus* since 18 July 1806, sailed from Cherbourg on 12 November 1808, but only as a *capitaine de vaisseau* of five years' seniority, with the status but without the rank of commodore. The most junior of the four frigate captains was future admiral Duperré of the *Bellone,* who had only been promoted *capitaine de vaisseau* in July 1808. Still more junior was *lieutenant de vaisseau* Le

Feretier, who took command of *Caroline* in the Indian Ocean after her captain died on the outward voyage to Île-de-France.

Following their separate courses, all four frigates reached Île-de-France, unmolested and undetected, between February and April 1809, and after replenishing wasted no time in sailing on individual raiding cruises. *Caroline* was the first to make her mark, surprising an unescorted convoy of four homeward-bound British East Indiamen on 31 May. The British captains repeated the tactic of forming a simulated line of battle which had worked against both Sercey and Linois (pp. 43, 122), but this time it failed to work. Although all four Indiamen were armed with 30-gun broadsides, *Caroline* closed successively with the rearmost pair, *Streatham* and *Europe,* captured them both, and after completing extensive repairs on both prizes brought them triumphantly into St Paul's Bay, Île Bourbon (Réunion) on 22 July.

Hamelin's cruise did not enjoy any such dramatic debut. After bringing *Vénus* to Île-de-France in March and completing her replenishment, he sailed again on 26 April with *Manche* and the 14-gun schooner-corvette *Créole* in company. Two and a half months' cruising the Bay of Bengal only yielded the capture by *Vénus* of the East India Company brig *Orient,* outward bound from Madras with despatches, on 26 July. The three French ships then proceeded to the Nicobar Islands to take on water, after which Hamelin decided on a change of strategy. He headed south to strike at the British trading outposts off the west coast of Sumatra. Between 12–23 October 1809, after evacuating the women civilians to Padang on the Sumatran mainland, Hamelin's ships comprehensively destroyed the East India Company's offshore settlement of Tappanouti in the Mentawai Islands before returning to the Bay of Bengal.

Vénus, Manche, and *Créole* were still in company when at first light on 18 November, they fell in with the unescorted British East Indiamen *Windham, United Kingdom,* and *Charlton.* The latter two ships were rapidly captured by *Manche* and *Créole,* but *Windham* broke away, with Hamelin giving chase in *Vénus.* Over the next three days Captain Stewart of *Windham* made every effort to win free by jettisoning cargo and otherwise lightening ship, but was finally overtaken and forced to strike his colours to *Vénus* on the morning of the 22nd.

With their prizes secured, the French captains now began the 2,000-mile voyage south-west from the Bay of Bengal to Île-de-France. Their glow of victory was muted by the knowledge that the voyage – even given fair weather – was bound to push French food and water supplies to the limit. By 19 December *Vénus,* separated from *Manche* and *Créole,* was fighting ever-worsening weather, which over the following week degenerated to cyclone conditions.

On the 27th, not only crammed with *Windham's* captured officers and crew, but with her own complement depleted by the French prize crew aboard *Windham, Vénus* lost all three topmasts and was left with more than 7 feet of water in the hold. To

146 • NAPOLEON'S ADMIRALS

avoid the otherwise certain loss of his ship, Hamelin was forced to conclude a truce with the senior British officer, Captain Stewart, to enlist the seamanship skills of his captives. Thanks to their joint efforts, reminiscent of similar truces aboard the storm-battered prizes after Trafalgar (pp. 135–36), *Vénus* limped into Rivière-Noire, Île-de-France, on 31 December 1809. Another day at sea would have left her without a drop of water or crumb of food.

Several months passed before, drawing on the meagre shipyard resources of Île-de-France, Hamelin had *Vénus* fit for sea again. From January to April 1810 he lay at Port-Louis with *Vénus, Manche,* and the brig-corvette *Entreprenant.* Grand-Port, in the south-east of the island, was the base of Duperré with *Bellone, Minerve* (a Portuguese frigate captured in November), and the corvette *Victor.* In the last week of April another frigate, *Astrée,* arrived from France and anchored at the mouth of Rivière-Noire on Île-de-France's west coast before joining Hamelin at Port-Louis.

From its advanced base at the Cape of Good Hope, encouraged by a successful landing and cutting-out expedition on Île-de-France (1–2 May), Commodore Rowley's British frigate squadron was meanwhile preparing for the piecemeal conquest of the Mascarenes. They began resoundingly with the *coup de main* which captured Île Bourbon on 6–8 August, moving east to take the Île de Passe, 4 miles off Grand-Port, Île-de-France, on 14 August. From this offshore base they confidently prepared for their assault on Grand-Port which Duperré smashed on 23–26 August. Hamelin, entering the fray on the 27th with *Vénus, Manche,* and *Astrée* from Port-Louis, completed the destruction of the British force which lost no less than four frigates – one of them, *Néréide,* with appalling loss of life.[1]

The crushing defeat inflicted on the British at Grand-Port in August 1810 marked the zenith of success for the frigates sent out from France in 1808–9, but one more victory remained. On 17 September 1810, Hamelin in Port-Louis was alerted by signal chain that a lone British frigate had been sighted on passage westward towards Île Bourbon. Putting to sea with *Vénus* and *Victor,* he overhauled the 32-gun frigate *Ceylon* and captured her in a night action (17–18 September), with *Vénus* losing her topmasts and mizzenmast in the fight.

Seldom has a hard-won victory been more swiftly reversed. Within two hours of *Vénus* taking possession of *Ceylon,* Commodore Rowley's squadron hove into sight. With the sloop *Otter* and brig *Staunch* in support, Rowley gave chase in his flagship, the frigate *Boadicea,* and wasted no time in recapturing *Ceylon.* He then set off in pursuit of the damaged *Vénus* as Hamelin tried to return to Île-de-France, and after a running fight forced Hamelin to strike his colours.

Returning to France in February 1811, Hamelin was rewarded for his exploits by being created a Baron of the Empire (19 July) and promoted rear-admiral on 15 September. He was then posted to the Scheldt command, where he commanded a squadron under Missiessy (23 September 1811–28 June 1812). Hamelin's last command under the Empire was that of the 1st Squadron of the Brest fleet, which he held from 13 May 1813 to 28 July 1814, with the restored King Louis XVIII creating him *Chevalier de Saint-Louis* on 28 June 1814.

After the second Bourbon restoration in 1815, Hamelin served as Major-General of the Navy at Toulon from April 1818 to July 1822, being created Grand Officer of the Legion of Honour on 23 August 1820. In 1822–23 he commanded the French naval forces operating off the Italian and Barbary coasts. When the French Army invaded Spain to restore the Spanish Bourbons in 1823, Hamelin was commanding a division of the Brest fleet (April–September 1823), which he led south to blockade Cadiz until his relief by Duperré.

This was Hamelin's last seagoing command. With his health failing, he resigned his command (14 September 1823) and retired to the country to convalesce. His last senior administrative posts, under King Louis-Philippe, were as Inspector-General of Personnel and Equipment for the 1st, 3rd, and 4th maritime *arrondissements* (November 1832), and Director-General of Naval Charts and Maps (July 1833). On 23 April 1839, at the age of 71, Hamelin died in Paris.

Note

1 For a detailed account of the Grand-Port battle *see* Duperré, pp. 189–93.

Jérôme Bonaparte (1784–1860)

Apart from the obvious fact that he was Napoleon's brother, the inclusion of Jérôme Bonaparte's name amid the French Revolutionary and Imperial heroes honoured on the *Arc de Triomphe* is uniquely hard to explain. If nothing else, Jérôme's career illustrates one of Napoleon's greatest weaknesses: his tendency not only to ignore but to reward consistent failure on the grounds of family sentiment.

Jérôme was born at Ajaccio, Corsica on 9 November 1784, three months before his father Carlo died at the age of 39. Although the baby of the Bonaparte clan, Jérôme outlived all his future imperial and royal siblings – in order of appearance, Joseph, Napoleon, Lucien, Elisa, Louis, Pauline, and Caroline – with his descendants extending the Bonaparte dynasty into the twentieth

Jérôme Bonaparte. Collection: Musee de la Legion d'Honneur. (Wikimedia Commons)

century. He is best remembered for his brief reign as King of Westphalia, for his service at Waterloo – and probably least remembered for having received his rear-admiral's flag 44 years before his baton as Marshal of France: the only Bonaparte to have begun his career in the French Navy.

When brother 'Nabulio' made himself First Consul of the Republic in December 1799, Jérôme was 15 years old. In the following year he joined the Navy on 29 November 1800, in classic eighteenth century mode: as a midshipman *aspirant de marine,* second class. His first ship was the ship of the line *Indivisible,* in Ganteaume's Toulon fleet, and his career at sea opened in dramatic style: sailing with the fleet on Ganteaume's bid to reinforce the trapped Army of Egypt (pp. 76–77). This took

Jérôme as far east as Derna in Libya, and he witnessed the capture of the British ship of the line *Swiftsure* on 24 June before the fleet returned to Toulon on 22 July.

A month after peace preliminaries were signed with Britain, Jérôme was posted as *aspirant* 1st class to the Rochefort squadron, joining the ship of the line *Foudroyant* under Latouche-Tréville's command (29 November 1801). With the coming of peace, the first order of First Consul Bonaparte to the fleet was for every squadron to participate in the lifting of General Leclerc's army to Saint-Domingue, there to reconquer the island from the rebel black slaves. The Rochefort squadron sailed with its contingent of troops on 14 December 1801, and on 4 February 1802 Jérôme took part in the capture of the capital, Port-au-Prince. In the following month, naval C-in-C Villaret-Joyeuse gave Jérôme his commission as lieutenant (*enseigne de vaisseau*) and charged him with carrying fleet despatches back to France; he landed at Brest on 11 April.

Jérôme's next appointment made it clear that although certainly marked down for what would nowadays be called 'fast-track promotion', he would still have to climb the conventional promotions ladder. It was a posting to the brig *Epervier*, bound for the Caribbean on a voyage with little other purpose than to groom Jérôme for his next promotion, to commander. Five days after *Epervier* reached Martinique on 28 October, Jérôme's promotion to *lieutenant de vaisseau* was duly confirmed, along with his first command: to *Epervier* (the feelings of whose displaced captain may be imagined). All Jérôme had to do was to turn in a model performance with *Epervier* (the Peace of Amiens was still holding) and his promotion to *capitaine de vaisseau* must have followed within a couple of years at most. Instead, in the high summer of 1803 (since May of that year, with France at war again) the wild unpredictability of Jérôme's character boiled to the surface. Abandoning his command at Martinique in June 1803, he took passage in an American ship and fled to the United States.

Letizia Bonaparte, 'Madame Mère', was a strict disciplinarian with the rest of her brood (she once famously slapped Napoleon for what she took to be disrespect from him); but if she did not set out to spoil her youngest son she certainly failed to instil any steadiness of character in him. The level-headed scientist Jean Chaptal, Napoleon's Minister of the Interior at this time, did not mince his words when describing Jérôme. 'It would be difficult to find a vainer, worse brought up, more ignorant and ambitious young man,' was Chaptal's icy verdict on Jérôme, who may have been considered professionally fit to command a ship and take the lives of her men into his hand, but was only an arrested adolescent with no clear notion of what he wanted, only a panic refusal to have his life governed at every turn by his family. He was still only 19 years old.

All Jérôme brought with him when he landed at Norfolk, Virginia on 20 July 1803 was his undoubted celebrity value as the brother of France's overlord. (Napoleon was now Consul for life with the power to name his successor – monarch in all but name.) After moving to Baltimore Jérôme caught the eye of Elizabeth Patterson, daughter of a wealthy merchant who can hardly have been oblivious to the business prospects of having such a son-in-law. For Jérôme, his marriage to Elizabeth Patterson (24 December 1803) – regardless of the fact that he was still a minor by French law – was an act of defiance against the family whose approval he did not even try to obtain.

What Jérôme could not know was that the timing of his marriage could hardly have been worse. Only two months before, his brother Lucien had married his mistress, a loose-living young widow who had already borne Lucien a son. Napoleon, who regarded his siblings as pawns in the political and diplomatic marriage markets and as the potential rulers of puppet states, was outraged. Lucien, nine years older than Jérôme, had far more backbone than his younger brother, and bluntly told Napoleon that he had no right to dictate his brothers' marriages. But Jérôme's marriage was altogether different, and as soon as the news reached France in the New Year of 1804 massive pressure was unleashed across the Atlantic.

In 1804 the French Ambassador to the United States was forbidden to advance any funds to Jérôme, and the skippers of all French merchant ships were told on no account to embark as a passenger 'the young woman with whom Citizen Jérôme is involved'. 'Madame Mère' put her name to a legal annulment of the marriage – a document dictated by Napoleon, who wrote brutally to Jérôme that:

> Your union with Miss Patterson is null and void in the eyes of both religion and the law. Write to Miss Patterson to return to the United States. I will allow her 60,000 francs annuity for life, on condition that she will in no circumstances use my [not 'our'] name. You must make her understand that you could not and will not be able to change the situation. When your marriage is thus annulled by your own wish, I will restore my friendship, and return to the feelings I have had for you since childhood.

This ultimatum from Napoleon – Emperor of the French since May 1804 – was delivered after Jérôme's pathetic attempt to retrieve the situation by sailing to Europe with his wife, in an American ship; they landed at Lisbon on 8 April 1805. Any hopes Jérôme had of winning over Napoleon and 'Madame Mère' by presenting his 'beloved wife' were soon shattered: they never met. Instead Jérôme was summoned to Alessandria to make his formal inevitable submission to Napoleon, which took place on 6 May. Napoleon was as good as his word. A week after Jérôme agreed to put away his wife, he was given command of the frigate *Pomone* and a light squadron in the Mediterranean (18 May), with his promotion to *capitaine de frégate* following on 2 June.

Rapid though it was, Jérôme was far from satisfied with (let alone grateful for) his new promotion. He impertinently demanded the right not only to advance himself to *capitaine de vaisseau* but to promote his own junior officers. This was angrily vetoed by Napoleon, who in a letter to Navy Minister Decrès wrote on 16 June:

M. Jérôme Bonaparte cannot be a *capitaine de vaisseau;* it would be a fatal innovation to suffer him to give himself rank… Not only has Jérôme no right to make an *enseigne* a lieutenant, but I annul the appointment: this conduct is altogether ridiculous. Even if he were to fight and capture an English battleship, he would not have the right of giving rank, but only of recommending those who may have distinguished themselves.

Sent to command the French naval forces at Genoa (7 July), Jérôme was given his first mission since his restoration to imperial favour. This was a cruise to Algiers to negotiate with the Barbary Corsairs for the release of European captives (July–August 1805). Jérôme's promotion to *capitaine de vaisseau* was confirmed on 1 November 1805 and he was advanced to battleship command: the 74-gun *Vétéran,* in the light squadron of Willaumez in Ganteaume's Brest fleet.

Given the passive role played by the Brest fleet during the momentous naval campaign of 1804–5, its sudden eruption onto the high seas in December 1805, two months after Trafalgar, was all the more astonishing. On 13 December the cream of the Brest Fleet, 11 of the line and four frigates, broke out of Brest in wild weather. On the following day they separated into two separate squadrons, one commanded by Leissegues, the other by Willaumez. Both were provisioned for six months and both were under orders to stay at sea until their provisions ran out – *'manger à son dernier biscuit'.*

This was no mere two-pronged temporary raid, but a deliberate attempt to challenge the British and keep them guessing across the length and breadth of the North and South Atlantic, from Newfoundland to the Cape of Good Hope. Willaumez's squadron – his flagship the 80-gun *Foudroyant* and the 74s *Cassard, Impétueux, Patriote, Éole,* and Jérôme's *Vétéran,* with the frigates *Valeureuse* and *Volontaire* – was assigned to the South Atlantic. He was to head for St Helena or the Cape of Good Hope, at his discretion, then return to the Caribbean and re-provision his ships at either Martinique or Guadeloupe. After calling at Cayenne for local information, he was to make a brief cruise off Barbados, then make a final foray to the waters round St Helena before returning to France.

Although given no explicit orders on the subject, Willaumez knew very well that he dared not risk any action which would expose the Emperor's brother to danger, especially of capture – probably a greater incubus than Villaret-Joyeuse had suffered during the 1794 First of June campaign, having the notorious commissar Jeanbon Saint-André as a passenger in his flagship (p. 22). The timeframe envisaged for Willaumez's cruise was in the region of 14 months.

On 15 January 1806, Willaumez's squadron fell in with a homeward bound convoy from Gibraltar, escorted by the 64-gun *Polyphemus* and the frigate *Sirius.* Two transports from the convoy were captured while *Vétéran* helped chase off the *Sirius.* While the frigate *Volontaire* took the first prizes of the cruise into Tenerife, Willaumez resumed his southerly course. Ten days after this auspicious start,

Willaumez's force was sighted north of the Cape Verdes by a powerful British battle squadron commanded by Vice-Admiral Duckworth. After a day and a night's chase which left the British force considerably dispersed, Duckworth cautiously called off the pursuit on the afternoon of the 26th.

After this extremely welcome escape, Willaumez stood on to the south. He had planned to refit and reprovision at the Cape of Good Hope before hunting for the next homeward-bound British China convoy, but the first prize captured in southern waters informed him that the British had captured the Cape on 10 January. Thus deprived of a South African *pied à terre*, Willaumez headed west for a South American landfall, with March 1806 passing in a profitless zig-zag traverse of the South Atlantic. At the beginning of April, the squadron put into San Salvador (Bahia) for much-needed supplies and a 16-day make-and-mend stopover. From San Salvador Willaumez continued northward, re-crossing the Equator to return to French soil at Cayenne, Guiana, at the end of the month. At Cayenne Willaumez divided his force into three divisions, each under orders to spend May cruising between Barbados and Latitude 9° South before reuniting at Martinique in the second half of June 1806.

Jérôme was the first of Willaumez's captains to head for the rendezvous, bringing *Vétéran* into Fort-Royal, Martinique, on 9 June. He was successively joined by *Impétueux* and *Éole* (15 June), Willaumez in *Foudroyant* with *Valeureuse* in company (20 June), and finally by *Patriote* and *Cassard* (24 June). With his squadron reunited and replenished at Martinique, Willaumez sailed on 1 July for neighbouring Montserrat, arriving on the 2nd and snapping up three unprotected merchantmen at anchor in the main harbour. His main objective was a homeward-bound British convoy, 54 strong, but it escaped to sea without being detected. When Willaumez tried to take nine latecomers which had failed to join the convoy before it sailed, they sheltered under shore batteries whose fire drove off the French ships in short order.

Quitting Montserrat on the 4th, Willaumez now headed for the known convoy departure-point of Tortola, but at daybreak on 6 July he sighted the British West Indies squadron of Rear-Admiral Cochrane. Although markedly superior in force, Willaumez declined battle and withdrew in the direction of the Great Bahama bank. His new objective was the next homeward-bound merchant fleet from Jamaica; but more than three weeks passed in fruitless cruising, which finally exhausted the always fragile patience of Jérôme Bonaparte.

In the darkness of night on 31 July, Jérôme parted company with the rest of the squadron and headed back to France. He seems to have gambled correctly on the probability of Willaumez anxiously quartering the area for the missing *Vétéran*, as he in fact did, thus giving the absconding Jérôme a useful start. And then, ten days into his homeward voyage, Jérôme was handed an altogether undeserved piece of luck. He fell in with a homeward-bound British Canada convoy, 16 strong, with only a single 22-gun sloop as escort, powerless to prevent the lone *Vétéran* from capturing and burning six of its ships.

By 26 August, *Vétéran,* on course for Lorient, was closing the French coast when she was sighted and chased by the 80-gun *Gibraltar* and two frigates. This time Jérôme was saved by the expertise of his officers (most notably Commander Duperré) who, knowing the coast as Jérôme could not, brought *Vétéran* with great skill through a narrow passage into the minor port of Concarneau.

On Napoleon's orders the French press went into overdrive, praising Jérôme's victory over the Canada convoy to the skies. Less than three weeks after leaving *Vétéran,* Jérôme was promoted rear-admiral – 19 September 1806 – but with this last token advancement his highly-chequered six years with the Navy came to an abrupt end. Proclaimed Prince of France on 24 September, Jérôme was immediately ordered to join the *Grande Armée* on its campaign against Prussia. Jérôme played no part in the double battle of Jena-Auerstädt which pulverised the main Prussian army on 14 October 1806, but was active in overrunning the isolated Prussian fortress-towns over the ensuing six months.

Promoted *général de division* on 14 March 1807, Jérôme now entered the imperial galaxy of client kings. Brothers Joseph and Louis were already kings respectively of Naples and Holland; on 16 August 1807, before the French Senate, Jérôme was proclaimed King of Westphalia, the territorial lynchpin of Napoleon's restructured Germany. Six days later he married Princess Catherine of Württemberg, the queen chosen for him by Napoleon, taking possession of his new kingdom on 7 December 1807 with his capital at Cassel.

To Jérôme, Napoleon wrote: 'I want your subjects to enjoy a degree of liberty, equality and prosperity hitherto unknown to the German people', and the Emperor provided Jérôme with two capable French ministers, Joseph Siméon and Jacques Beugnot, to draw up much-needed reforms. These included vaccination, civic and political equality for Jews, and a drastic reduction of excise taxes from 1682 articles to 10. Yet, unlike Joseph and Louis, Jérôme never really tried to take his royal role seriously and rule as an enlightened monarch. The trappings were what interested Jérôme most and he proved to be the most spendthrift of all the client kings, with his daily expenses devouring one fifth of the Kingdom of Westphalia's annual revenues.

With no illusions about Jérôme's weaknesses, Napoleon nevertheless continued to groom him for ever higher Army commands. As the Emperor prepared for his fourth campaign against Austria, he appointed Jérôme commander of the new 10th Corps of the *Grande Armée* in Germany (9 April 1809). As in the 1806 Prussian campaign, Jérôme was not involved in the desperate battles of Aspern-Essling and Wagram which forced Austria to sue for peace. But the next command which Napoleon gave Jérôme was nothing short of mind-boggling. Not yet 28 years old, completely untried in any senior military capacity – he had never commanded so much as a brigade in action – Jérôme was entrusted with the centre right wing of the multi-national *Grande Armée* on the eve of the invasion of Russia in June 1812.

Leaving Cassel on 3 April, he took command of his 79200 Westphalians, Saxons and Poles on the 22nd.

When his vast host (more than half a million strong) lumbered across the River Niemen on 24 June, Napoleon's first aim was to drive a wedge between the two Russian armies in eastern Poland and Lithuania commanded by Barclay and Bagration. The immediate need was to prevent them from joining forces. While Napoleon moved against Barclay with the French main body, Jérôme's polyglot corps was assigned to the isolation and, hopefully, encirclement of Bagration: a task which should properly have been entrusted to Davout, the most able of the French marshals. By the time Jérôme reached Grodno on 30 June, Bagration had evaded his clumsy advance with ease and was continuing his retreat. The fact that Napoleon had also failed to catch Barclay west of Vilna did not stop him from blaming Jérôme for Bagration's escape – 'You compromise the success of the campaign on the right wing. It is impossible to make war in this way' – and placing him under Davout's orders on 14 July. Considering himself replaced (doubtless to Davout's enormous relief), Jérôme promptly handed over his command and headed back to Germany to play the king again, reaching Cassel on 26 August.

Any mistakes Napoleon chose to lay at Jérôme's door during his three-week participation in the 1812 Russian campaign were nothing to those made by the Emperor over the ensuing four months, culminating in the disastrous retreat from Moscow. Jérôme spent the last 14 months of his reign – August 1812–October 1813 – at Cassel, while the Russian catastrophe was followed by the loss of Germany and final collapse of Napoleon's 'Grand Empire'. Finally chased out of Cassel a week after Napoleon's shattering defeat at Leipzig (16–18 October 1813), Jérôme retreated to Paris. He was followed by the exhausted survivors of Leipzig with the triumphant Russian, Prussian and Austrian armies on their heels, and the Allied invasion of France in the New Year of 1814.

From February to April 1814, despite fleeting victories, Napoleon failed to split the invading Allies and throw back their advance on Paris with his untrained, ill-equipped 'army' of teenagers outnumbered by 4 to 1. During this hopeless campaign, Jérôme performed his last act of service to the dying First Empire: escorting Napoleon's Empress Marie-Louise from Paris on March 29, on her journey to Blois via Rambouillet and Troyes. Before the next fortnight was over Paris had surrendered, Napoleon had abdicated on the insistence of the Army marshals, the return of the exiled Bourbons to head a constitutional French monarchy had been agreed, and the leaders of the Bonaparte family had been effectively proscribed.

During the ten months of Bourbon royal mismanagement which paved the way for Napoleon's return from Elba in March 1815, Jérôme lived in obscurity at Trieste. As soon as he heard that Napoleon was back in Paris, Jérôme set off to join him – a circuitous route from Trieste via Ancona, Florence and Naples, where he took ship for France. Grateful for all the support he could get, Napoleon proclaimed Jérôme a Peer of France on 2 June – and once again chose to ignore Jérôme's long record of failure in command. On 10 June Jérôme was given command of the 6th Division in General Reille's II Corps, as the 'Army of Belgium' prepared for its all-or-nothing campaign against Wellington and Blücher.

Reille therefore found himself in the same situation as Willaumez nine years earlier: nominally Jérôme's commanding officer, but in practice saddled with the unwelcome responsibility for the Emperor's wayward and totally inexperienced brother. On 16 June, Marshal Ney's failure to drive Wellington from the vital crossroads of Quatre Bras prevented Napoleon from destroying Blücher's Prussians at Ligny, which would have left Wellington's multinational patchwork of an army fatally isolated. Reille and Jérôme had been under Ney's command at Quatre Bras. On the 17th, under torrential rain, they followed up Wellington's retreat to form the left-wing corps of Napoleon's army on the morning of Waterloo – 18 June 1815.

While Napoleon impatiently waited for the rain sodden ground to dry out and give the French artillery full play, his HQ was the scene of considerable doubt and dissension. All French generals present who had fought Wellington in Spain – Reille foremost among them – warned Napoleon of the one phenomenon he had never experienced: the deadly firepower of British troops deployed against frontal attack. Others were not convinced that the Prussians had been swept from the board after Ligny, as Napoleon insisted, and here Jérôme, of all people, had some important evidence to offer. On the previous evening he had dined at an inn where the retreating British had lunched, and an obliging waiter told Jérôme that he had overheard British officers stating that Blücher was still in touch with Wellington and was less than a day's march away. But Napoleon sarcastically rejected all these warnings, insisting that Wellington was a bad general whose army could not survive a central assault, that the surviving Prussians could not reach this battlefield for at least two days, and that the coming battle would be no more serious than eating breakfast.

Having failed to persuade Napoleon of the Prussian threat which would ensure his final defeat, Jérôme proceeded to ruin the Emperor's plan for the destruction of Wellington's army deployed along the Mont St Jean ridge.

Intent on winning the battle with a crushing central breakthrough, Napoleon intended to weaken Wellington's centre first. He ordered Reille's corps to threaten the outpost garrison in the small château of Hougoumont in front of Wellington's right flank, thus hopefully drawing off troops from the British centre. What he actually got during the opening two hours of the battle, was a series of bloody but fruitless assaults on Hougoumont led by Jérôme's division, which Reille felt obliged to support and reinforce. With Wellington dribbling in just enough reinforcements to enable Hougoumont to hold out, it was the French centre which found itself deprived of more and more support troops. Worse still, the Hougoumont sideshow robbed Napoleon of two vital hours before the arrival of the Prussians tipped the balance. When Napoleon finally hurled the Imperial Guard against the British centre at 1930, an unavailing last throw, it was too late.

From the streaming rout and retreat from the field of Waterloo on the night of the 18th, Jérôme rallied a handful of troops and led them south to rejoin Marshal Soult at Laon on the 22nd. It was his last military service to France before he left the Army for ever and set off to join Napoleon in Paris, which he reached on the 23rd – the day of Napoleon's second abdication. In the Chamber of Peers, Lucien Bonaparte made a gallant attempt to preserve the Empire in the person of the former Emperor's son, 'Napoleon II, Emperor of the French'. This was rejected out of hand by the Peers, who voted for a provisional government headed by turncoat minister Joseph Fouché. His first act was to urge Napoleon, who had been proclaimed an international outlaw by the Allies on 13 March (Blücher had vowed to shoot or hang Napoleon if he caught him), to leave Paris at once. Three days later, Fouché gave the same advice to Jérôme. With the cause of the Bonapartes in total eclipse, Napoleon bound for lifelong exile on the island of St Helena and his entire family banished from France, Jérôme, still five months short of his 31st birthday, became a rootless political outcast. He was not to see France again for 32 years.

Jérôme's first host was his former Queen, Catherine of Württemberg, in whose palaces of Göppingen and Ellwangen he lodged from August 1815 to August 1816. With his marriage over in all but name, he then took the alias of 'Prince de Montfort' and migrated to Austrian territory, finally settling at Trieste in December 1819. During this sojourn Napoleon died on St Helena (5 May 1821). Such future hopes still entertained by the Bonapartes now reposed with his son. The one-time boy King of Rome and son of Napoleon was being reared as an Austrian princeling in Vienna, required to speak only German and answer to the name of 'Franz'. Formally created 'Duke of Reichstadt' in 1817, neglected by his mother Marie-Louise, he was firmly isolated from any contact with his Bonaparte blood relatives.

Insofar as the Bonapartes had a family leader it was unquestionably the indomitable 'Madame Mère', since August 1815 residing with unshakeable dignity at the Falconieri Palace in Rome. It was to Rome that Jérôme next moved, in March 1823. When the Empire was still at its brief peak of glory, 'Madame Mère' had drily told her children 'When all this is over you will be glad of my savings'. Now her prophecy had come to pass, with Jérôme and Lucien as foremost applicants for handouts.

Such compensations as she had were fleeting. Her contempt for the Bourbons was partially requited by the expulsion of the last Bourbon King of France, Charles X, in July 1830. At the end of 1831 it fell to Jérôme to delight his mother with the news that the new French King, the Orleanist Louis-Philippe, had approved the restoration of Napoleon's statue to his column in the Place Vendôme in Paris. But in the following summer 'Madame Mère' was crushed by the news that her grandson Reichstadt had died of tuberculosis in Vienna (22 July 1832), extinguishing her hopes for her family's future. Both Lucien and Jérôme were able to make their farewells at her bedside before 'Madame Mère' died in Rome on 2 February 1836 – four years before the body of Napoleon was brought home from St Helena to lie in the Invalides in Paris.

Forced by an outburst of Italian revolutionary activity in 1831 to decamp hurriedly from Rome to Florence, Jérôme moved on to Quarto in 1836. From 1840, the year of Lucien's death, Jérôme lived on a pension granted by his daughter, Princess Mathilde of Württemberg. After the deaths of Joseph in 1844 and Louis in 1846 left him the last surviving brother of Napoleon, Jérôme petitioned the French government for permission to return to France. His first attempt (April 1847) failed, but he persisted – and on 22 September 1847 received a three-month permit to reside in France.

Before the year was out, Jérôme's life had been transformed. More than three decades of obscurity and humiliation were ended by the second French Revolution of 1848 and the establishment of a Second Republic, with Jérôme's nephew Louis-Napoleon, Louis's son, as President. Under the new President's ægis Jérôme was restored to his Army rank of *général de division* (11 October), and appointed Governor of the Invalides (23 December). On 1 January 1850, Jérôme was proclaimed a Marshal of France. Two years later (28 January 1852) he was appointed President of the Senate.

The declaration of the French Second Empire on 1 December 1852, with President Louis-Napoleon as Emperor Napoleon III, was followed within 24 hours by the proclamation of Jérôme as First Prince of the Blood in the new dynasty. When he finally died of chronic bronchitis on 24 June 1860, he was laid to rest in the Invalides.

Vice-Admiral Jean-Baptiste-Philibert, *Comte* Willaumez (1763–1845)

Jean-Baptiste-Philibert Willaumez was a Breton, born at Belle-Isle-en-Terre (Morbihan) on 7 August 1763: the last year of the Seven Years War. His family antecedents were military rather than maritime or naval – his father was a captain of artillery – but on 3 February 1777 he joined the Navy as a 13-year-old apprentice seaman (*pilotin*).

Willaumez's first ship was the 74-gun ship of the line *Bien-Aimé* and his first captain was France's most famous maritime explorer: Louis-Antoine de Bougainville, renowned for having completed the first French circumnavigation of the world in

Willaumez. Lithograph by Maurin, c.1835. (Wikimedia Commons)

1766–69. (Best remembered for having given his name to a flowering plant and to the biggest of the Solomon Islands, Bougainville was also a fighting officer with a fine record both ashore and afloat.) Willaumez served in *Bien-Aimé* from February to November 1777, qualifying as quartermaster (*timonier*).

In the first two years of France's participation in the American Revolutionary War (1778–83), Willaumez's service began in the 58-gun *Flamand* (January 1778). A posting to the Indian Ocean station in the schooner *Fourmi* ended dramatically in shipwreck on 28 October 1778, with the 15-year-old Willaumez forced to swim for his life. He came home from the Mascarene Islands as a volunteer pilot in the merchantman *Les Amis,* which landed him at Lorient in the spring of 1780. At an unusually early age Willaumez, in his first three years of Navy service, had made his mark as a young non-commissioned officer of mark, ripe for promotion.

His next posting (April–December 1780) was as assistant pilot in the 110-gun *Ville de Paris* at Brest. This was followed (1 January 1781) by his appointment as second pilot in the new 32-gun frigate *Amazone,* under orders to join the fleet in the American theatre. For Willaumez this proved to be an action-packed commission. In its opening weeks, when barely out of French waters, *Amazone* captured the British privateer lugger *Pitt* (21 March 1781). Still five months short of his 18th birthday, Willaumez was given command of the prize crew which sailed *Pitt* to Lorient. Back in *Amazone,* Willaumez was present at the summer 1781 actions off St Eustachius, St Kitts and St Barthélemy before the run of de Grasse's victories was cut short by Admiral Rodney in the Battle of the Saints (12 April 1782). For Willaumez the war ended with a hard-fought action off Cape Henry on 29 July 1782 which ended with Willaumez wounded in the face and left leg, and captured when *Amazone* was forced to strike her colours. He was a prisoner of war for less than 24 hours, for *Amazone* was recaptured on the following day.

Even senior French naval officers found themselves without employment after the Peace of Paris was signed in September 1783, and Willaumez was no exception. In the merchant service he made two voyages to Saint-Domingue between January 1784 and July 1785 in the merchantman *Tharon,* employed as first officer. He was first pilot in the sloop *Sylphe* (August–November 1785) and the transports *Lionne* and *Forte* (November 1785–November 1786). By December 1786 Willaumez was back in Navy service in the frigate *Astrée,* posted to the East Indies from December 1786 to March 1790.

Willaumez now had a solid service record of 13 years in the Navy, yet without achieving an officer's commission. His prospects began to improve after *Astrée's* return to France, when he was posted to the new 74-gun ship of the line *Patriote* at Brest, commanded by Captain the Chevalier d'Entrecasteaux (9 July 1790). In September 1791, d'Entrecasteaux, newly promoted rear-admiral, was given the *flûtes Recherche* and *Espérance* and the mission of discovering the fate of missing ocean explorer La Pérouse. The latter had sailed in 1785 to find the Pacific entrance to the elusive North-West Passage. Neither he nor his ships, the corvettes *Boussole* and *Astrolabe,* had been heard of since his last dispatch to the Navy Ministry, from the British settlement at Botany Bay, in February 1788.

During his time in *Patriote,* Willaumez's performance had sufficiently impressed d'Entrecasteaux not only to recommend Willaumez for an officer's commission and recognition for his service in the American war, but to pick Willaumez as one of his officers in *Recherche* for the new expedition. Willaumez was created *Chevalier de Saint-Louis* on 15 May 1791 and *on* 3 September, three weeks before *Recherche* and *Espérance* sailed from Brest, he received his commission as lieutenant (*enseigne de vaisseau*).

D'Entrecasteaux's plan was to follow La Pérouse's track to his last-known landfall in Australasia, and follow up whatever clues could be gleaned from there. He passed the Cape of Good Hope in January 1792 and on 9 June reached the Moluccan island of Amboina in the Dutch East Indies, having touched at Tasmania, New Caledonia, the New Hebrides and the Admiralty Islands. From Amboina he headed south again to explore the south-east coast of Australia and southern Tasmania before sweeping east as far as Tonga, then returning to New Caledonia.

In May 1793 d'Entrecasteaux sailed again, heading westward from New Caledonia to the Santa Cruz Archipelago. There he visited the island of Vanikoro where, unknown to him, the wrecks of the *Boussole* and *Astrolabe* lay (the site of La Pérouse's shipwreck would not be confirmed until 1827).

From Vanikoro he sailed on past the Louisiade Archipelago before heading north up New Guinea's eastern coast. By the time he reached New Britain and the Admiralty Islands d'Entrecasteaux was mortally ill with dysentery and scurvy. He died at sea on 20 July 1793 and his second-in-command, d'Auribeau, took command of the expedition, steering north-west to replenish at the Dutch East Indies.

When *Recherche* and *Espérance* had left France in 1791, the French Navy was still a King's service and the only visible effect of the Revolution on its ships was the flying of the new national flag, the Tricolour. But while d'Entrecasteaux was threading the islands of the South-West Pacific on his vain quest, France had changed out of all recognition. France had still been at peace with the Dutch Republic, the United Provinces, when *Recherche* and *Espérance* first visited the Dutch East Indies in June 1792. When they reached Java at the end of 1793, they got their first news that the new French Republic had been at war with the Dutch since February.

The Dutch authorities at Batavia accepted that the French ships were on a humanitarian rather than a war cruise, but they still ordered d'Auribeau and his officers to haul down the Tricolour or be treated as prisoners of war. As one of the French officers who refused to comply, Willaumez – who had still to learn that he had been promoted commander (*lieutenant de vaisseau*) on 17 November 1792 – became a prisoner of the Dutch (23 February 1794). It was not until five months later that he was released and sent under cartel in a Dutch ship to the French Mascarenes, landing at Île-de-France on 8 August.

Once arrived at Île-de-France, Willaumez promptly offered his services to Commodore Jean-Marie Renaud, commanding the French naval squadron in the Mascarenes. As a supernumerary officer he joined the squadron flagship, the 36-gun frigate *Prudente*, commanded by Captain Magon, and on 22 October 1794 took part in the spirited action with the British 5th rates *Centurion* and *Diomede* (pp. 110). Wounded in the left hand during the battle, Willaumez was next charged with carrying the news of the victory and the records and papers of the d'Entrecasteaux expedition back to France. He sailed from Île-de-France in the corvette *Léger* on 4 November and was promoted *capitaine de vaisseau* on 14 March 1795, a month after his return to France on 3 February. (Willaumez's promotion was both due and richly deserved, but in the French Navy as in the British, promotion for any officer bearing a victory dispatch was commonplace.)

Willaumez's stay in France lasted barely ten months. After briefly commanding the ship of the line *Pluton* in Villaret-Joyeuse's Brest fleet (12 May–3 November 1795) and the corvette *Bergère* (4 November–15 December), he was given command of the 36-gun frigate *Régénérée* attached to Sercey's frigate squadron, bound for the Indian Ocean (pp. 41–44).

Sercey's cruise got off to a loose-footed start when one of his four frigates, *Cocarde*, was heavily damaged by accidental grounding and he was left with three: *Forte* (flag), *Seine*, and *Régénérée*. Lhermitte would follow as soon as the only other available frigate, *Vertu*, was ready for sea.

The squadron eventually sailed from La Rochelle on 4 March 1796 but its two attendant corvettes, *Mutine* and *Bonne-Citoyenne,* were separated from the frigates by a storm, and both were captured by a British squadron (7–8 March). The squadron reached the Canary Islands on 17 March, waited for Lhermitte to join with *Vertu*, rounded the Cape of Good Hope in the last week of May and arrived at Île-de-France on 18 June. There the two frigates on the Indies station, *Cybèle* and *Prudente*, came under Sercey's command. Thus, reinforced to a strength of six frigates, the squadron embarked on its war cruise from Île-de-France on 14 July 1796.

Fought in light airs with recurring periods of flat calm, the extraordinary battle between Sercey's frigates and the British 74s *Arrogant* and *Victorious* (p. 42) took place on 9 September 1796. Manoeuvering *Régénérée* in the centre of Sercey's line of battle, Willaumez avoided any serious damage to his ship while making a full contribution to the discomfiture of the British battleships. A week after the battle the squadron was anchored at Île-du-Roi in the Mergui Archipelago, replenishing with water and repairing battle damage.

Given the hostility offered to him by Governor Malartic and the Île-de-France planters (pp. 41, 44), Sercey then headed south for the Dutch East Indies – now allied territory, since the 'Batavian Republic' imposed on the conquered Dutch in 1795. At Batavia, Java, Sercey revictualled his ships and negotiated a supply treaty between Batavia and Île-de-France, sailing for the latter destination in the New Year of 1797.

On 28 January 1797, in the Bali Strait, Sercey's lookouts sighted every frigate commander's dream: an unescorted convoy of six richly-laden British East Indiamen. But Sercey was decisively out-bluffed by the British convoy Commodore, Charles Lennox, who hoisted a rear-admiral's flag and manoeuvred his ships like an aggressive battle squadron eager for action, chasing off *Cybèle* which had been sent forward to reconnoitre. *Cybèle's* captain reported a superior force of two of the line and four frigates, and Willaumez shared the frustration of his fellow captains when Sercey hastily withdrew.

After the crestfallen return of his squadron to Île-de-France in February 1797, Sercey's ships spent most of the rest of the year in implementing the new trade treaty with Batavia. This came down to a series of troop-carrying voyages from Île-de-France to Batavia, transferring most of the 800 troops which the squadron had brought out from France. In return for these military reinforcements, the Dutch authorities at Batavia undertook to supply Île-de-France with shipments of rice, cordage and canvas.

The New Year of 1798 saw the arrival at Île-de-France of two Spanish East Indiamen from the Philippines, whose joint cargoes were valued at a staggering 4 million *piastres*. Always with an eye to the main chance, Malartic agreed to see the ships safely home to Spain in return for a fee of 60,000 *piastres* from the Spanish Philippine Company. He then ordered Sercey to provide two of his frigates as escorts and Sercey gave the job to Magon in *Vertu,* with Willaumez's *Régénérée* as consort. They sailed from Île-de-France on 23 January 1798.

During the long voyage home (January–August 1798), Willaumez played a key role in two separate actions with interloping British frigates. The first occurred on the afternoon of 24 April when the 32-gun HMS *Pearl* discovered *Vertu, Régénérée* and their charges at anchor amid the 'Isles of Loss' off the coast of Sierra Leone. Both of the French ships opened a heavy fire on *Pearl* as she raced for the nearest exit passage from the narrow anchorage. *Vertu* had her topmasts and yards lowered for overhaul but Willaumez promptly sailed in pursuit. He chased *Pearl* throughout the night and the following day, only abandoning pursuit at nightfall on the 25th.

The next encounter took place on 26 July, by which time the dogged little convoy had reached the Canary Islands. The last leg of the long home run to Spain and France was about to begin, but Magon and Willaumez knew that the closer they got to Europe, the greater would be the chance of falling in with a superior British force, and both French frigates had been raised to a full state of readiness. When Captain Henry Blackwood of the 28-gun frigate *Brilliant* looked into Santa Cruz on the morning of the 26th, both *Vertu* and *Régénérée* slipped their cables and set off in immediate pursuit, determined to capture the British intruder before she could raise the alarm.

It was a thrilling day-long chase in which *Brilliant* was steadily overhauled, with *Régénérée* taking the lead. Unfortunately for the two French captains, their opponent was one of the best seamen in the Royal Navy. (In March 1800 Blackwood's outstanding seamanship would be instrumental in the capture of *Guillaume-Tell,* p. 90). At 1930, with *Régénérée* coming in for the kill, Blackwood swung *Brilliant* across Willaumez's bow and let fly with a devastating broadside at point-blank range, disabling *Régénérée's* bowsprit, foremast, and main topmast. Willaumez's crewmen deserve full marks for the speed with which they jury-rigged their ship to stay in the chase. It continued until after midnight, when Blackwood finally managed to shake off his pursuers in the dark. But Magon and Willaumez had done their full duty. The Spanish treasure ships were safely delivered to Cadiz and, after being given full repair facilities by their grateful hosts, *Vertu* and *Régénérée* arrived at La Rochelle on 24 September.

The first task which the Navy Ministry gave Willaumez after his return to France in autumn 1798 was a literary one: seeing through the publication of the official history of d'Entrecasteaux's expedition. Willaumez was then promoted commodore (*chef de division*) on 5 January 1799, but although he had proved himself an aggressive and capable frigate commander he was given a strangely desultory series of appointments. From September 1799 to March 1800 Willaumez commanded a division of three frigates and a corvette at Saint-Malo, but was then left without employment for the whole of the following year. April 1801 saw Willaumez recalled to sea, commanding the ship of the line *Duguay-Trouin* in Latouche-Tréville's Rochefort squadron during the Saint-Domingue expedition (April 1801–September 1802).

Bonaparte's objective in sending General Leclerc's army to Saint-Domingue was to overturn all previous agreements between the French Republic and Toussaint l'Ouverture, leader of the rebel blacks in the island. Leclerc was to crush the rebels and restore Saint-Domingue to direct French colonial rule, including the reimposition of slavery. It was a total failure. The treacherous abduction of Toussaint in June 1802 (to die a year later as a prisoner in France) solved nothing: Toussaint was replaced by the equally determined black leaders, Jean-Jacques Dessalines and Henri Christophe. Leclerc died of yellow fever in November 1802, as did most of the hapless French troops over the next 18 months. The spring of 1803 saw the resumption of war with Britain and the prompt reimposition of a British blockade of Saint Domingue.

In the early stages of the doomed venture, most of the French admirals and senior naval officers assigned to the Saint-Domingue expedition were fortunate to be recalled for duties elsewhere. Willaumez was not so lucky. On 2 September 1802 he was transferred from *Duguay-Trouin* to the 20-gun light frigate *Poursuivante* and charged with blockading the rebels. From May 1803 and the arrival of the British Navy, Willaumez also had the impossible job of covering the western and southern approaches to Saint-Domingue. By this time the surviving French forces on Saint-Domingue had been forced westward to the naval anchorages of Cap-Français and Saint Nicolas Mole.

On 28 June 1803, Willaumez in *Poursuivante* with the corvette *Mignonne* in company were surprised off Saint Nicholas Mole by a British battle squadron. This consisted of three 74s: *Cumberland* (flag), *Goliath*, and *Hercule*. The British commodore signalled *Goliath* to tackle *Mignonne* – which was becalmed and easily captured – and ordered *Hercule* to catch Willaumez, who was making for the shelter of Saint Nicolas Mole.

In the ensuing action Willaumez showed all the energy and seamanship he had displayed in the two actions during the return voyage from Île-de-France. He had two advantages, one known, one shrewdly guessed. The first advantage, after ten months' experience in these tricky inshore waters, was personal knowledge of the approaches to Saint Nicolas Mole. His second advantage was that *Hercule* was under the temporary command of her first lieutenant. Willaumez therefore deliberately courted a smart exchange of gunfire to disconcert his obviously hesitant pursuer. This left both ships considerably cut up in their sails and rigging, but enabled *Poursivante* to escape to the temporary haven of Saint Nicolas Mole. Willaumez then goaded his men into a spell of furious repair work and broke out from Saint Nicolas Mole before he could be blockaded there. He headed north for American waters, and after being granted extensive repair facilities in the Chesapeake headed for France, bringing *Poursuivante* safely into Rochefort on 28 May 1804.

Against the disastrous finale of the Saint-Domingue expedition – General Rochambeau, Leclerc's successor, had capitulated on 28 November 1803 – the achievement of Willaumez stood out in high relief. On 26 August 1804 he was appointed to be the first captain of the new 74-gun ship of the line *Algésiras,* launched at Lorient on 8 July. As a captain of ten years' seniority, Willaumez was promoted rear-admiral on 1 March 1805 and left *Algésiras* (to become Magon's flagship at Trafalgar) on the 7th, when he was posted to Ganteaume's Brest fleet.

Ganteaume appointed Willaumez to command the Brest fleet's 'light' or Van Squadron, flying his new flag in the 80-gun *Alexandre.* When Willaumez took up his new command, Napoleon's grand design to bring about French command of the Channel and the invasion of England was already under way. Missiessy had sailed for the Caribbean with the Rochefort squadron in January and Villeneuve, after his false start with the Toulon fleet in that month, was preparing to follow. Villeneuve's delayed sailing had obliged Napoleon to redraft the master plan, which would have had Ganteaume crossing the Atlantic with the Brest fleet, joining forces with Missiessy and Villeneuve in the Caribbean, and returning to sweep into the Channel in overwhelming force. On 14 March Napoleon ordered the recall of Missiessy, assigning Ganteaume the impossible task – given the tautness of the British blockade – of escaping from Brest without fighting, then collecting all the French and Spanish battleships he could from Rochefort and Ferrol before joining Villeneuve.

The impossibility of the task imposed on Ganteaume was brought home on two occasions, with Willaumez to the forefront in each of them. By the second week of April, the semaphore telegraph had reported Villeneuve's successful escape from Toulon on 30 March. By 9 April, the day after Villeneuve's passage of the Gibraltar Straits, Ganteaume had the 21 ships on the line of the Brest fleet ready to sail, provisioned for six months with 2,000 troops on board. On the evening of 14 April, HMS *Warrior* reported that the Brest fleet was getting under way. Thus alerted, Admiral Lord Gardner moved close inshore with his 24 of the line and on the morning of the 15th sighted the French Van squadron, led by Willaumez in *Alexandre,* leading Ganteaume's main body into Berthaume Bay. Faced with an unavoidable battle in restricted waters against superior odds, Ganteaume reluctantly ordered his fleet to withdraw to Brest roads.

An uneasy two-month lull ensued – May–July 1805 – during which Ganteaume and his squadron commanders concentrated on keeping the Brest fleet at an instant pitch of readiness for sea. But by 9 July the fast-sailing brig *Curieux* had overtaken Villeneuve and reached Britain, telling the Admiralty that the Combined Fleet was heading for the Bay of Biscay rather than the Mediterranean. The immediate reaction of the British First Lord, Barham, was to dispatch the battle fleets of Admirals Calder and Cornwallis to block the approaches to the Channel between Finisterre and Ushant. Calder was placed to deny Villeneuve a clear run north to Brest.

On 22 July came the confused battle off Finisterre (p. 134) in which Calder took two Spanish prizes but left the bulk of the Combined Fleet intact. To Napoleon's fury, Villeneuve headed first for Vigo and then Ferrol, which he remained until 12 August. Thus, by 20 August, when Ganteaume was finally ordered to sea for his anticipated rendezvous with Villeneuve off Brest, Villeneuve was in fact already approaching Cadiz – and Cornwallis had resumed the British watch on Brest, outnumbered by 17 of the line to Ganteaume's 21. The advance sailing of Willaumez's Van squadron was spotted by the British on the 20th, and by 2030 on the 21st – the day of Villeneuve's arrival at Cadiz – Ganteaume's whole fleet had reached its new defended anchorage between Bertheaume and Camaret.

On the morning of 22 August 1805, Ganteame made his formal demonstration of the impossibility of a fleet escape from Brest without fighting a battle, which the outnumbered Cornwallis was only too anxious to bring on. A two-hour exchange of long-range gunfire, with Willaumez in *Alexandre* foremost in the action, ended with Ganteaume ordering his line of battle to reverse course and retire to the shelter of its shore batteries. The Brest fleet's necessarily impotent role in the pre-Trafalgar naval campaign was over.

Trafalgar left the intact Brest fleet as the only available instrument of bringing serious pressure to bear on the British Navy. The story of the dramatic breakout from Brest in December 1805, and the initial cruise of Willaumez's battle squadron, may be followed on pp. 152–53.

Throughout the opening seven months of this cruise, Willaumez laboured under an incubus imposed on no other French admiral: care for the safety of Napoleon's youngest brother, Captain Jérôme Bonaparte of the *Vétéran*. This burden was only lifted by Jérôme's deliberate desertion from the squadron on the night of 31 July 1806. Days of anxious search, boxing the compass in a vain quest to locate the missing *Vétéran*, cost Willaumez the chance of striking at a rich Jamaica convoy, 109 merchantmen with a weak escort, which had sailed for England on 28 July.

Only after an encounter with a neutral ship confirmed that the Jamaica convoy was long gone, Willaumez decided that it was time to proceed with the second stage of his mission. This was a North Atlantic foray to destroy the British fisheries off Newfoundland and Labrador, and harass the British sea lanes from Canada to Britain. In mid-August Willaumez in his flagship *Foudroyant*, with *Impetueux, Éole, Cassard* and *Patriote* in company, headed north from the Caribbean only to encounter immediate disaster. On 18 August, the squadron was shattered by a gale, mounting to hurricane strength, which scattered its ships and inflicted severe damage to all of them. It was never to reassemble.

When the storm blew itself out *Foudroyant*, partially dismasted and her rudder lost, was alone.

With his ship under jury rig and with a makeshift rudder, Willaumez set a course for the nearest friendly port: Havana, Cuba. (Of the other four ships, *Cassard* headed for France and reached Rochefort safely; *Impétueux* was attacked and beached in American waters; *Éole* and *Patriote* reached the Chesapeake where *Éole* was subsequently broken up, with only *Patriote* escaping to return to France.)

At first light on 15 September, *Foudroyant* was approaching Havana in a virtual calm when she sighted the British 44-gun frigate *Anson,* and Willaumez sent a boat into Havana to apprise the Spanish authorities of his coming. This was prudent, for as soon as a light breeze sprang up Captain Lydiard of *Anson,* having noted *Foudroyant's* makeshift sail plan, headed in to engage. A 45-minute exchange of fire convinced the British captain that there was nothing amiss with *Foudroyant's* 80 guns and he broke off the action – by which time the Spanish 74 *San Lorenzo,* with gunboats in company, was coming out to support *Foudroyant.* By evening Willaumez's flagship was safely anchored under the guns of Havana's Morro Castle.

After a thorough five-month refit at Havana, Willaumez sailed for France and reached Brest without incident in February 1807. So far from being scapegoated for Jérôme Bonaparte's defection, the virtual destruction of his squadron and a thoroughly abortive cruise, Willaumez was appointed to command the reduced Brest fleet – nine of the line, three frigates and three corvettes – from May 1808 to February 1809.

By the New Year of 1809 the fate of Martinique, in the face of British naval blockade and troop landings, was hanging in the balance. It was now that Napoleon proved that he had learned precisely nothing from the collapse of his naval master plan against England in 1805. He ordered Willaumez to sail with the Brest Fleet's eight of the line; collect Commodore Troude's three at Lorient; proceed to Rochefort and collect the three there; then cross the Atlantic to save France's last Caribbean colony. Both familiar ingredients of the project's inevitable failure were there: the impossibility of precisely coordinating the French squadrons in the teeth of weather, wind, and tide; the relentless British blockading grip on the French Atlantic coast. Above all there was the transatlantic communications gap. Three days after Willaumez finally succeeded in escaping from Brest, Villaret-Joyeuse's garrison on Martinique capitulated, rendering the objective of the whole venture null and void.

Willaumez's breakout from Brest on 21 February 1809 was achievement enough, but its timing meant that when he arrived off Lorient the set of the tide made it impossible for Troude to come out and join him. There was nothing for it but to press on to Rochefort, where Willaumez arrived on the 24th and was promptly blockaded. To the British, now committed to supporting their army in the Spanish Peninsula, Willaumez's creation of a powerful new battle fleet on the Biscay flank of the England-Lisbon sea lane caused serious alarm. But Napoleon never saw the

Peninsular potential of this latest French 'fleet in being'. Instead he blamed Willaumez for the failure of the Martinique relief plan. On 18 March Willaumez was relieved of his command at Rochefort and replaced by Rear-Admiral Zacharie Allemand.

For Willaumez this humiliation soon proved a blessing in disguise. It relieved him of any responsibility for the devastating British fireship attacks on the Rochefort fleet (11–12 April 1809), which grounded all warships apart from the flagship *Océan*, destroyed two of them by fire and another two by scuttling. Yet Willaumez was left without further employment for the next two years. Only on 1 August 1811 was he given command of a division of the Zuider Zee flotilla – a commodore's command, and a trumpery one at that – which he held until 20 July 1812. His 35-year sea-going career was over.

The restored Bourbons granted Willaumez the honours which Napoleon had withheld. Under Louis XVIII he was promoted vice-admiral (18 August 1819), and made Commander of Saint-Louis in the following year. Willaumez received his last honours from the hand of France's last King, Louis-Philippe (1830–48): President of the Navy's Committee of Works (14 January 1834), Grand Officer of the Legion of Honour (30 May 1837), and Peer of France, with the title of *Comte* (3 October 1837). In the following month (17 November 1837) Willaumez was finally placed on the Retired List. He lived on at his estate at Suresnes (Seine) until 17 May 1845, when he died at the age of 82.

Rear-Admiral Count Pierre Baste (1768–1814)

Before the Revolution, French officers who blended a naval career with one or more spells of military service were not uncommon. In the late 1760s the young Latouche-Tréville had suspended his naval career for four years, serving as a captain of dragoons before transferring back to the Navy. But this practice was swept away during the Revolutionary Wars and Pierre Baste was a true echo of the *Ancien Régime:* a rear-admiral of the Napoleonic Navy who died on the battlefield in 1814 at the age of 46, as a brigadier-general of the Imperial Guard, fighting desperately to halt the Prussian invasion of France.

Born at Bordeaux on 21 November 1768, Baste was also one of the relatively

Baste. (Wikimedia Commons)

few Napoleonic commanders who left detailed memoirs (his personal account *[see below]* is a key document of the 1808 French surrender at Bailén in Spain). These memoirs describe how Baste's father, a timber merchant, was 'employed variously in the armaments industry during the war in America' (1778–83), which gave him 'a comfortable living'. It was Baste's father who 'steered me in the direction of a naval career at an early age'.

Baste first went to sea at the age of 13 as an apprentice in the armed merchantman *Pactole*, on a voyage to Saint-Domingue (July 1781–May 1782). He spent the next five years ashore, completing his education (concentrating on the mathematics required for navigation, essential for a watch-keeping officer). Baste resumed his seagoing merchant service apprenticeship with a second Saint-Domingue voyage in the *Galathée* (July 1787–January 6 1788). This was followed by what was still a legitimate venture for the pre-Revolutionary French merchant navy, a voyage in the slave-ship *Zizette* – the full round-trip from the crammed barracoons of the West African coast across the 'Middle Passage' to the slave markets of the Caribbean (October 1788–September 1790).

All this sea time qualified Baste for a merchant navy commission as lieutenant in the *David*, in which he put in a third cruise to Saint-Domingue (April–October 1791). By September 1792 he had been promoted to 2nd Captain in his former ship *Galathée* on yet another voyage to Saint-Domingue (16 September 1792–13 April 1793). It was at Saint-Domingue that Baste transferred to what was now the French Republican Navy, accepting a reduction in rank to auxiliary lieutenant, commanding the schooner *Hirondelle* in action against the rebel slaves (14 April–15 May 1793).

On 15 May, at Cap-Français, Baste rejoined *Galathée* yet again as Rear-Admiral Sercey assembled a homeward-bound convoy of French West Indies merchant shipping. This was routed via the United States to embark cargoes of American grain for the famine-racked French Republic. At Baltimore, Baste transferred to the brig *Petit-Jacobin* (28 September 1793). With preparations already under way for the sailing of a second huge grain convoy from America, Baste was appointed 2nd Captain of the merchantman *La Pucelle* at Baltimore (6 February 1794). Commanded by Rear-Admiral Vanstabel, the convoy sailed on 11 April and, thanks to the manoeuvring of Villaret-Joyeuse's fleet and the Battle of the First of June, reached Brest safely on 14 June; Baste came ashore from *La Pucelle* at Bordeaux on the 25th.

When Baste returned to France in midsummer 1794 he applied for a regular Navy commission. Although he had sufficient seagoing and indeed command experience, he had to wait until 8 December before he was granted a probationary lieutenancy in the corvette *Résolue* at Toulon. Nine months later (21 September 1795) Baste transferred to the brig *Infante*, detached by Toulon fleet commander Martin to provide inshore support for the right wing of the Army of Italy, then confronting the Piedmontese and Austrian armies in the Ligurian Alps. In November 1795 *Infante* covered the 20-mile advance of Massena's corps along the coast road from Loano to Savona (22–26 November). Baste's 18-month association with the Army of Italy, destined to bring him to the attention of his future hero and patron, Bonaparte, had begun.

A month after taking command of the Army of Italy at Nice on 27 March 1796, Bonaparte had knocked Piedmont out of the war and was preparing to tackle the Austrian armies defending the North Italian plain and the Po valley. He crossed the Po at Piacenza on 7 May, forced the River Adda crossing at Lodi on the 10th, and entered Milan on the 14th. To achieve his goal of an eastward advance through Lombardy and Venetia into southern Austria, Bonaparte now had to overrun the Austrian-held 'Quadrilateral' between the fortresses of Peschiera, Verona, Mantua, and Legnago. The key fortress was Mantua, plugging the gap between Lake Garda and the Po.

Bonaparte's advance into the Quadrilateral began on 30 May with the crossing of the Mincio, flowing from Lake Garda to the Po, and the occupation of Peschiera. Verona was occupied on 1 June. But to isolate Mantua and place it under close siege, the French needed light naval forces to deny the Austrians unlimited use of Lake Garda and exploit the lakes, waterways and marshes surrounding Mantua itself. To this end Baste, now confirmed in the rank of lieutenant (*enseigne de vaisseau*), was ordered to Peschiera on the fourth day of the siege of Mantua (12 June 1796).

Baste's first appointment was to the flotilla hastily improvised from captured light craft on Lake Garda where, on 18 June, he took command of the oared gunboat *Voltigeante*. By 9 July the French control of Lake Garda was sufficient for Baste to be transferred to the flotilla reinforcing the siege of Mantua. But the French Republic's failure to launch a simultaneous offensive north of the Alps enabled Austria to throw in a series of powerful counter-attacks aimed at relieving Mantua and destroying Bonaparte in Lombardy.

The first of these materialised in the last week of July, forcing Bonaparte to raise the siege of Mantua in order to concentrate the outnumbered Army of Italy. Speed was vital: General Sérurier, commanding at Mantua, was ordered to bury his siege guns, destroy their carriages and blow up his ammunition; Baste won Sérurier's approval for his efficiency in destroying the siege flotilla. The Austrian Marshal Wurmser, obsessed with relieving Mantua, divided his forces and enabled Bonaparte to defeat them piecemeal at Lonato (3 August) and Castiglione (5 August). Withdrawing only to regroup before resuming his offensive, Wurmser was beaten again at Roveredo (5 September) Primarolo (7 September) and Bassano (8 September), before being driven into Mantua and closely blockaded.

The relief of Mantua was the objective of the last two Austrian offensives of the campaign, both of which forced Bonaparte's outnumbered Army of Italy to fight for its life: at Arcola (14–15 November 1796) and Rivoli (14–15 January 1797). Despite these two mortal crises the French maintained their grip on Mantua, where Baste served as commander of the blockading flotilla from 12 October. His performance prompted General Sérurier to write enthusiastically that

> I could not be more satisfied with the conduct that *enseigne de vaisseau* Baste has displayed during the blockade of Mantua, on the lake where he commands a squadron. I sent a report at the time to General Bonaparte who undertook to solicit his well-deserved advancement.

Well-deserved it certainly was, but no such advancement came Baste's way. The Austrian defeat at Rivoli sealed the fate of Mantua, which capitulated on 3 February 1797. At last Bonaparte was free to carry out his long-planned invasion of the Austrian Tyrol, which culminated in the Austrian request for an armistice on 7 April 1797 and the preliminary peace treaty signed at Leoben on the 18th. After a brief spell in command of the felucca *Joséphine* with the Lake Garda flotilla, Baste's next appointment was to the commandeered transport *Laharpe* in the Adriatic. In one of the most unorthodox missions ever entrusted to the French Navy, Baste was sent to Venice to embark the famous quartet of bronze horses, removed from the portico of San Marco's cathedral, on the first leg of their journey to Paris. This was arguably the most flagrant example of the mass spoliation of northern Italy's artworks, destined for the adornment of Paris, which dishonoured the Italian campaign of 1796–97.

After a month in command of the 18-gun brig *Mérope* in the northern Adriatic, Baste was posted to the 40-gun frigate *Diane* at Ancona (21 January 1798), already under orders to return to Toulon. There *Diane* became flagship of the frigate squadron attached to the battle fleet and transport armada which – under Vice-Admiral Brueys but with Bonaparte in supreme command – sailed for Malta and Egypt on 19 May 1798.

After cruising the length of the Mediterranean unmolested, capturing Malta *en passant* on 10 June, the fleet reached Egypt safely and landed Bonaparte's army, which captured Alexandria on 2 July. But the luck of the French ran out on 1 August, when Nelson's battle fleet caught Brueys at anchor in Aboukir Bay. By the morning of the 2nd, Brueys was dead and 11 of his 13 battleships had been captured or destroyed. Only *Guillaume-Tell* and *Généreux*, with the frigates *Diane* and *Justice*, escaped from the holocaust under Rear-Admiral Villeneuve.

Detaching *Généreux* to carry the news of the disaster back to France, Villeneuve headed west to reinforce the French garrison on Malta, now a vital link in the imperilled sea lane between France, Malta, and Bonaparte's marooned Army of Egypt. The British naval blockade and siege of Malta lasted two years, from late August 1798 to September 1800. One of Villeneuve's first priorities after his arrival was to improvise a gunboat flotilla, not only to make the British cruisers keep their distance but to support the outlying French garrison on Gozo, and in this Baste's experience from the Mantua campaign proved invaluable. Baste spent the first 18 months of the siege with the Malta defence flotilla, commanding Gunboat No. 1, but in the spring of 1800, he was called upon to succeed where the fleet heavyweights had failed.

On 18 February, Rear-Admiral Perrée was killed and *Généreux* was captured off Lampedusa, along with the convoy which Perrée had led from Toulon for the relief of Malta. On 29 March Decrès, ordered to break out in *Guillaume-Tell*, was captured off Malta by the blockading squadron. Desperate to update the French government of the plight of Malta and Egypt, Villeneuve was reluctant to risk his only two frigates, his last two warships of force. He asked Baste to see what could be done with one of the elusive, fast-sailing feluccas, and Baste rose magnificently to the challenge. On 21 April, he slipped out of Valletta in the felucca *Légère*, ran the British blockade and reached Toulon on the 30th. Baste personally delivered Villeneuve's despatches to the Navy Ministry in Paris, his exploit earning him not only promotion to *lieutenant de vaisseau* (17 May) but full compensation for the personal kit ruined during his voyage from Malta (*Légère* lacking a deck, let alone a cabin). He then volunteered to run the blockade a second time with a return voyage to Malta, where Villeneuve gave him command of the armed merchantman *Athénien* (15 July).

Baste brought nothing but cold comfort for Villeneuve and General Vaubois when he returned to Malta in July 1800. Bonaparte, First Consul since November 1799, had no resources to spare for the relief of Malta. The Toulon fleet was committed to Ganteaume's desperate bid to reinforce the Army of Egypt; this had failed, and Ganteaume was already heading back to Toulon. A month after Baste's return to Malta, Villeneuve ordered the two frigates to break out; *Diane* was captured on 24 August, but *Justice* won clear and returned safely to France. In the weeks before the inevitable French capitulation, Villeneuve placed Baste in command of the seaman garrisons of the Malta defences, commending him for his energetic support of the garrisons of Forts Chambray and Ricasoli. Baste earned further praise for his execution of the terms of surrender (5 September 1800), and care for the seamen under his command. He and his charges were returned to Toulon on 2 October.

Baste now returned to his hometown of Bordeaux for an 18-month leave, which he spent working on a survey aimed at improving navigability on the lower River Isle; his subsequent report earned him the thanks of the Transport Ministry (*Ponts et Chaussées*). He returned to sea with a posting to the frigate *Atalante* (21 April 1802). In her he took part in the ill-fated expedition to Saint-Domingue, 'whose outcome' (drawing on the experience of his four previous voyages to the island) 'I foresaw'. During his involvement in this dismal venture, Baste says in his memoirs that 'I should have died twice': first during a fire at Cap Haïtien, then by sickness; one of the mortal diseases ravaging the island, yellow fever, carried off the Army C-in-C, General Leclerc.

Thankfully recalled from the pest-hole of Saint-Domingue, Baste returned to France in August 1803, and on 18 September was posted to the La Rochelle division of the Rochefort squadron. But the days of Baste's career as a conventional naval officer were numbered. He was promoted to *capitaine de frégate* on 24 September and in the following month (8 October) came the 'enormous piece of good fortune that decided my military career. I was appointed commander of the 3rd *Équipage* of the battalion of *Marins de la Garde*'.

In his overhaul of the French Army which produced the glittering *Grande Armée* of 1805, Bonaparte had always envisaged a *corps d'élite* pledged to the protection of his person, to which every French soldier would yearn to belong and strive, through merit, to do so. The core of Bonaparte's new guard division was the company of 'Guides' which had served him as a personal bodyguard in Italy; and the guards battalions of the former Directory, the 'Guards of the Legislature' and 'Guards of the Directors'. On 3 January 1800 these were amalgamated into the new 'Consular Guard', with its own complements of horse, foot, and guns. Its expansion continued unabated for the next four years, culminating, in the proclamation of the Empire in March 1804, with its renaming as the 'Imperial Guard'.

The *Marins* ('Sailors') *de la Garde* were ordered into being during the period of the Guard's expansion, in September 1803: a battalion of 737 picked officers and sailors (the latter selected by the Maritime Prefects), organised into five *équipages* ('crews'), each of five squads, and awarded the same rate of pay as the Guard cavalry. *Capitaine de vaisseau* Daugier was the unit's first commander, and Baste was soon recognised as one of the most energetic of the five *équipage* commanders (Hamelin among them).

The main duty envisaged for the *Marins de la Garde* was to ensure the safety of Bonaparte and his staff during the cross-Channel passage of the 'Army of England', and on 11 January 1804 Baste was appointed to command a division of the invasion flotilla at the main embarkation port: Boulogne.

On 22 March he was given command of the flotilla's 3rd Division of Gunners, covering the embarkation coast between Ostend and Le Havre. He seized his first chance of action on 1 August, when a British squadron backed by two ships of the line stood in to bombard Le Havre and the flotilla craft sheltering under the guns of the fortress. In the gunboat *Bolonaise* Baste led his division out to counterattack. He closed with a cutter and a brig, bringing down the brig's main topmast and forcing the British to withdraw. Baste's feat earned him a glowing report in the press and in an order of the day to the French fleet. It also earned him the praise of Napoleon (Emperor since 18 May) and, on 19 August, promotion to command the 1st Division of Gunners of the Invasion Flotilla.

Over the following 12 months, as the failure of fleet commanders Villeneuve, Missiessy, and Ganteaume to join forces spelled the eventual ruin of Napoleon's invasion plan, Baste was active along the entire length of the embarkation coast. In his own words,

> I was detached to Ostend, where I served under Rear-Admiral Magon, to reinforce the port's defences. I distinguished myself again at Calais and at Dunkirk; there I was praised by Marshal Soult [commanding the IV Corps at Boulogne] for my bravery and conduct during the various combats I was involved in round the ports of Calais and Boulogne.

But by the last week of August 1805 the invasion plan had been scrapped and Napoleon and his army – no longer the 'Army of England' but the *Grande Armée* – was marching east to confront the formidable new coalition of Austria and Russia.

Serving as an amphibious service arm, the *Marins de la Garde* marched with the Imperial Guard during the *Grande Armée*'s Ulm-Austerlitz campaign of August–December 1805. Baste's most useful service was in covering the river crossings of the Danube east of Vienna, which Napoleon entered on 14 November. (The discovery of the vital importance of the island of Lobau in ensuring this crossing-point was to prove of prime importance in the Aspern/Wagram campaign of 1809.) The battle of Austerlitz (2 December 1805) knocked Austria out of the allied coalition; Prussia's belated entry into the war was crushed in the Jena/Auerstädt campaign of October 1806. But Russia remained in the field, and Napoleon's determination to batter Russia into a subservient peace resulted in the dismal winter campaign of 1806–7.

The East Prussian capital of Königsberg was the main Russian base, and the key to Königsberg was the heavily fortified Baltic port of Pillau, together with the long inland waterway of the Frisches Haff along which Pillau could be supplied from the west. After Danzig fell on 24 May 1807 Baste, with his customary energy, assembled a makeshift gunboat flotilla there which succeeded in cutting off Pillau by sea. His masterstroke was the capture of a convoy of 42 coastal craft carrying provisions to Pillau – provisions desperately needed by the over-stretched *Grande Armée* in its wretched Polish bivouacs. He had no way of knowing that this was to be the last purely naval action of his career.

By the time that the decisive French victory at Friedland (14 June 1807) forced Tsar Alexander to seek an accord with Napoleon, the Emperor had already decided on direct intervention in the Iberian peninsula. Apart from adding Portugal and Spain to his Empire as tribute-paying dependencies, Napoleon also had his eye on the battle fleets of both countries, based respectively at Lisbon and Cadiz, which under French command would go far towards making good the massive battle fleet losses suffered by Villeneuve at Trafalgar.

Napoleon's first objective was Portugal, England's oldest Continental ally, targeted by browbeating Spain into allowing free passage for a French 'corps of observation' commanded by General Andoche Junot. With the veteran corps of the *Grande Armée* still in Poland, Junot's force was a scraped-together hotchpotch of 24,000 untrained conscripts, completely unfit for the forced marches required for a rapid pounce on Portugal. Luckily for them they met no resistance on their chaotic six-week march into Portugal. When Junot's leading units staggered exhausted into Lisbon on 30 November 1807, he found that the Portuguese government, court, treasury and fleet had quit the country to join the British.

Meanwhile a second French 'corps of observation', ostensibly to reinforce Junot in Portugal, had crossed the Spanish frontier under General Pierre Dupont. It advanced from Irun at the end of November 1807 via Burgos and Valladolid, which Dupont entered on 20 January 1808. His force was of much the same composition as Junot's hapless troops in Portugal and badly needed basic training, but it now got an important reinforcement.

> It was at Valladolid', writes Baste, 'that I rejoined the Army with the battalion of *Marins de la Garde Impériale*, commanded by Capitaine de vaisseau Daugier, and of which I was the second in command. The fact that the *Marins de la Garde* were joined with an army corps began to make us suspect that our destination was to be Cadiz, where we knew a naval force lay at anchor.

The occupation of Andalusia, Spain's southern province, was indeed the designated objective for Dupont's corps; Cadiz, home since October 1805 to Rosily-Mesros and the five French ships of the line to have survived Trafalgar, was the ultimate goal. But before Dupont could head south the French hold on northern and central Spain had to be made good, and he put the waiting time to good use in training his raw troops. As Baste admitted:

> The weather was so good in February [1808] that it resembled early May in France; we thus occupied the troops in large-scale exercises. They had great need of training since, with the exception of several battalions of the *Garde de Paris* and a Swiss regiment, the troops consisted almost entirely of conscripts raised during the winter of 1807, scarcely broken in at the depots of the regiments to which they had been attached and badly dressed and equipped. As for the officers, the greater part of them had been recalled to duty after a long period of inactivity, or had come direct from military colleges. They were all brave and of good will; but they lacked the necessary experience.

The stealthy French build-up of force in northern Spain continued while Dupont's troops route-marched and drilled at their Valladolid base. By the second week of March 1808, Baste claimed, 'the conscripts were already manoeuvring as well as the more seasoned troops'. But their musketry drill was another matter, and cost Dupont's corps its first senior casualty.

> On 13 March, during a firing exercise, Général de Division Malher was killed by a ramrod that penetrated his skull – his loss was greatly regretted. The same evening the entire corps received orders to march for Madrid in three divisions by three different routes.

On their march south, Dupont's men were following the powerful force of regulars with which Marshal Murat, Napoleon's 'Lieutenant-General in Spain', entered Madrid on 23 March.

Dupont's corps reached the outskirts of Madrid two days later and remained encamped there for the next two months. These were the fatal weeks in which the high-handedness of Napoleon and Murat goaded the Spanish people into outright revolt. In the last week of April 1808 the *Madrileños* heard that Napoleon was holding the entire Spanish royal family captive at Bayonne. The mass rioting against the French in Madrid on 1 May 1808 was savagely punished by Murat's firing squads on the following day, the *Dos de Mayo*. In the wholly misguided belief that Spanish resistance had been crushed and that the country was reconciled to French rule, Murat ordered Dupont – three weeks after the *Dos de Mayo* – to proceed with the conquest of Andalusia. Dupont's designated route was southward through the Sierra Morena to Andujar on the Guadalquivir, then down river through Cordoba and Seville to Cadiz.

'Everywhere en route', noted Baste, 'we found evidence – in the general demeanour of the Spanish people – of the unfortunate perceptions that had led to the fatal confrontation of 2 May. Individually, our security was compromised; to avoid ambush and assassination we had to march closed up in column. Stragglers and thieves were inevitably massacred.' In its 9-day march from Madrid to Andujar (22–31 May) Dupont's corps met no outright opposition but suffered a steady rise in the sick list, with 120 sick troops left behind at La Carolina and Bailén. At Andujar, Baste noted, 'the fact that practically all the inhabitants of this large town had left confirmed my appreciation of the situation we were in, that we were certainly on the verge of an event that would lead – in one way or another – to a declaration of war.'

Baste was right. The march south had coincided with the extraordinary, uncoordinated Spanish national uprising led by the provincial *juntas:* Valencia on 23 May, Galicia and Asturias on the 24th and – fatefully for Dupont – the Andalusian *junta* at Seville on the 27th.

> The commanding general [Dupont] soon learned that the whole of Andalusia had risen up; that bodies of rebels were forming in every part of the province, combining with regular troops... The militia regiments of the southern provinces were also being combined with regular troops, and a *levée en masse* was in effect.

Despite this knowledge, Dupont reported to Murat that he intended to press ahead with the march on Cadiz.

The road to Cordoba was blocked by the Alcolea bridge which the local Spanish commander, Echavarri, had screened with earthworks and protected with an artillery battery. On 7 June, Baste was the man who smashed this bottleneck and placed Cordoba in Dupont's hand. After personally leading a reconnaissance to ensure that the bridge was not mined, Baste led a storming party of *Gardes de Paris* and *Marins de la Garde* which swept the Spanish defenders off the bridge, overran the defences and captured the guns. Elated by winning their first fight, Dupont's men surged forward to take Cordoba on the same day. Completely out of control, they treated the city to a brutal sack: looting, burning and raping, a chain reaction of atrocities inflamed by drunkenness on captured wine. Baste himself had to use his sword on three French soldiers, intent on gang-raping the daughter of a Spanish family which frantically begged him for help.

Dupont cannot be blamed for letting his troops off the leash; exactly the same horrors were to be inflicted by British troops during the sack of Badajoz in 1812, when Wellington only restored order after three days by erecting gallows. But the sack of Cordoba had a fatal consequence apart from providing a lasting grievance for enduring Spanish resistance. The loot of Cordoba – not only gold and silver plate stolen from churches and private houses, but more than 2 million francs from the Andalusian treasury – distracted Dupont from pushing on to Seville and ousting the Andalusian *junta*. He remained at Cordoba for ten days, waiting in vain for the promised reinforcement of General Vedel's division from Madrid. This gave the Seville *junta* time to reorganise its regular forces and armed peasantry under General

Castaños. At Cadiz, General Morla emplaced heavy batteries and demanded the surrender of Vice-Admiral Rosily-Mesros's five French ships of the line, blockaded there since escaping from Trafalgar in October 1805. After making a decent show of resistance, Rosily-Mesros hauled down his flag on 14 June.

On the night of 15–16 June Dupont finally accepted that Castaños was clearly preparing to advance in overwhelming strength, and that the French had no chance of conquering Andalusia. He decided to withdraw to the Sierra Morena via Andujar and Bailén. Disbelieving, Baste watched his commanding officer on the morning of 16 June: 'Sat on a drum he watched the baggage train pass for five consecutive hours without taking any action to reduce its numbers or its encumbrance.' By now the French had no illusions about the horrific fate awaiting their sick, stragglers, or any party without a powerful escort.

> One had his arms cut off, another his legs; several had their ears, eyes, nails and genitals removed. I myself saw one whom these tigers had crucified on a tree. He was horribly disfigured and presented such a hideous spectacle that I can still see this horrible scene today... we saw a sergeant of the 4th Légion on the side of the road with his feet and legs burned off up to the knee.

Baste was also critical of the decision to withdraw no further than Andujar, where Dupont halted on 18 June. 'The position was in no way a military one and could not be considered as such by any definition... it was dominated by significant heights and, having no more than a single road by which we could march to the Sierra Morena, left us vulnerable to having our retreat cut off.' Andujar was also bare of supplies and the sick list continued to soar, with Baste reporting 600 chronic dysentery cases in 14 days. On 20 June Dupont sent Baste with 600 troops to raid the town of Jaen, between Andujar and Granada to the south: a combined forage for supplies and punitive strike at a notorious concentration-point for Spanish guerrilleros. Baste carried out the raid with clinical efficiency, plundering Jaen 'from doorstep to eaves', forming a supply convoy and leading it back to Andujar without losing a man.

Baste's return to Andujar from his Jaen raid was followed by welcome news from the north: Vedel's division was on its way at last. Dupont sent Baste north with a powerful force, 1,000 strong, to clear the route and make contact with Vedel, which he did on 27 June. With Vedel solidly established at Bailén, Dupont now had a secure line of withdrawal all the way north to the passes of the Sierra Morena. Although his main body at Andujar was swamped with sick and starved of supplies while Jaen was once more swarming with insurgents, Dupont shrank from concentrating his forces for a fighting retreat. Instead he ordered Vedel to send a brigade to Jaen, with Baste serving as guide and adviser. This second foray to Jaen (1–3 July) ran into massively superior forces and had to fight its way empty-handed back to Bailén, with, in Baste's deadpan phrase, 'greater glory than any real advantage'.

When Baste returned to Andujar on 6 July he was aghast at Dupont's continued indecision; 'whether for continuing the withdrawal or for a renewed advance… a decision – any decision – made and implemented firmly, is the only way to save armies in critical circumstances'. Dupont's irresolution played into the hands of his Spanish opponent, Castaños, whose forces outnumbered those of Dupont and Vedel by nearly 3 to 1. By 17 July, when Dupont finally made up his mind to abandon Andujar and join forces with Vedel at Bailén, it was too late. Castaños had more than enough regular troops and irregular forces pushed forward, including another advantage – heavier guns massed in bigger batteries – to complete Dupont's demoralisation.

When Dupont did begin to move on the 18th it was obvious that his main objective was not effecting a rapid concentration and turning the tables on Castaños, but securing his lumbering baggage train crammed with the loot of Cordoba. Baste named this as one of the major causes of the unfolding disaster.

> It cannot be doubted that, had [Dupont] left the baggage train at the end of the column of march, instead of placing the bulk of his forces behind the train, and that, instead of allowing the gradual arrival of units, 7,000 bayonets could have marched against the enemy as one, in battalion columns, then the passage would have been forced and our own troops would have been masters of the field of Bailén.

The confused clash at Bailén on 19–20 July saw Dupont's conscripts give their all in repelling the Spanish attacks, but the intense heat, hunger and thirst pushed them to their limit. Baste noted with pride that 'only the intrepid *Marins de la Garde* demonstrated a resolution none could overcome'. But Castaños succeeded in keeping Vedel and Dupont separated. The brigade of Swiss troops, formerly in Spanish service before Dupont enlisted them in January, deserted *en masse* to the Spaniards, a defection which reduced Dupont, wounded in the ribs on the 19th, to opening negotiations for a cease-fire.

Not surprisingly, Dupont failed to persuade Castaños to sign an armistice permitting the French to withdraw to Madrid with their booty. Castaños agreed that the French, after surrender, would be repatriated to France by sea, but insisted that Vedel's division, still outside the Spanish ring round Bailén, must be included in the capitulation. This took place on the 24th, the French parading with full military honours before laying down their arms. Once the French were safely disarmed the Seville *junta* predictably reneged on the terms agreed by Castaños, permitting only Dupont, Vedel and their staff officers, including Baste, to embark for France. Baste sailed from Cadiz in the *Minerve* on 24 October, landing at Marseille on 12 November.

Baste had feared that he would share in the disgrace meted out by Napoleon to Dupont and Vedel after their return to France, but the Emperor accepted that the *Marins de la Garde* had done their duty with full credit and that Baste bore no responsibility whatever for the capitulation at Bailén. Napoleon had also ordered Baste's promotion to *capitaine de vaisseau* (23 July) in recognition of Baste's successes at Alcolea and Jaen. Further imperial promotion followed on 11 April 1809, when Baste was named as Colonel of the *Marins de la Garde*. This was two days after Austria's declaration of war opened the Danube campaign of April–July 1809.

Baste led the *Marins de la Garde* in the *Grande Armée's* latest Austrian campaign, in which the Archduke Charles proved the most formidable enemy commander yet faced by Napoleon. Worsted on the Danube at Abensburg, Landshut, and Eckmühl (20–24 April), the Archduke was forced to abandon Vienna, which Napoleon entered for the second time on 12 May, and withdrew to the east bank of the Danube. Baste and his *Marins* got their first chance to shine in assisting Napoleon's leapfrog across the Danube via the island of Lobau, in which defence of the *Grand Armée's* bridges was vital. By floating loaded barges downstream the Austrians managed to smash the key bridge from Lobau to the east bank, resulting in a costly defeat for Napoleon – his first – in the battle of Aspern/Essling (21–22 May). But over the next six weeks Napoleon converted Lobau into a vast armed camp, with reinforcements called in from Italy and Croatia, and with new pontoon bridges protected by the flotilla manned by Baste's *Marins*.

On the night of 4–5 July, under cover of a dramatic thunderstorm, the *Grande Armée* streamed across the new bridges to the east bank, wheeling east and north to confront the Archduke's army. The result was the two-day pounding-match of Wagram (5–6 July), in which the *Grande Armée* got the hardest fighting it had known since Eylau in February 1807. The Archduke withdrew in good order but was obliged to ask for an armistice on the 11th. With no support from Prussia, Russia or Britain, Austria was eventually forced to swallow the humiliating Peace of Schönbrunn (14 October 1809). Baste's immediate reward for his contribution to this latest imperial triumph was his elevation to the dignity of Count of the Empire, announced on 15 August 1809. He was created Commander of the Legion of Honour on 28 February 1810.

On 25 March 1810 Baste was granted his Letters Patent as Count with an endowment of 20,000 francs, and on 25 April he received his next military appointment. He was to lead the *Marins de la Garde* back to Spain under General Count Jean-Marie Dorsenne, on the same day appointed Imperial Guards commander in Spain and Governor of the province of Burgos. Baste's second experience of Peninsular campaigning proved mercifully short. Dorsenne set him to clearing *guerrillero* resistance from the province, but the day after taking Almazan on 10 July Baste was recalled to Paris. He was promoted rear-admiral on 19 July, and on the 25th his six-year association with the *Marins de la Garde* ended with his appointment to command the Boulogne flotilla.

The importance of Baste's latest command, which he held for the following 29 months, was dwarfed by the two successive campaigns which destroyed both the *Grande Armée* and Napoleon's European Empire: the invasion of Russia and retreat from Moscow in 1812, and the loss of Germany in the Leipzig campaign of 1813. By December 1813 Napoleon, in that year alone, had seen an improvised army of 375,000 men melt away like snow, with the survivors driven west to the Rhine.

He now proposed to defend France from the invasion of the victorious Prussian, Austrian and Russian armies with a ghost force, virtually unserved by cavalry or artillery, of less than 42,000 ill-equipped youths far less prepared for battle than Dupont's conscripts back in 1808. In the scraping-together of this spectral 'army' the frantic recall of Rear-Admiral Baste and his appointment as an Imperial Guard brigadier-general (21 December 1813) was entirely symptomatic. Baste was given command of a light infantry (*voltigeur*) brigade in the 2nd Division of the Young Guard commanded by General Pierre Decouz. There was no time to familiarise himself with his new command, or even provide the most basic rudimentary training for its raw troops.

On the night of 29 January 1814, Decouz's division was hurled into the chaotic battle for Brienne, in which Napoleon was trying to separate Blücher's Prussians from their allies. Decouz, shot twice in the chest, died of his wounds; Baste died as he had lived, still yelling *'En avant!'* ('Forward!') to his men when he was shot in the head and killed instantly. They buried Baste where he fell, at Brienne-le-Château.

Vice-Admiral Guy-Victor, Baron Duperré (1775–1846)

A *receveur des tailles,* one of Louis XV's tax-farmers, Jean-Agustin Duperré believed in frequent marriages and large families. Guy-Victor Duperré was his 22nd child, born at La Rochelle on 20 February 1775. One of Napoleon's youngest admirals – Duperré was only 36 when he hoisted his flag in 1811 – he enjoyed a long naval career, neatly bisected by the defeat of the First Empire in 1814. After the restoration of the Bourbon monarchy Duperré went on to play a key part in the foundation of France's North African Empire, commanding the fleet which invaded Algiers in 1830.

Guy-Victor's father may have envisaged a civil service or even clerical career for his son, who was a pupil at the Oratory of St Philippe Néry at the Collège de Juilly until

Duperré. Portrait by Georges Rouget, c.1835. (Wikimedia Commons)

the age of 12. But over the next four years the appeal of a career at sea proved the stronger, and on 24 May 1791 the 16-year-old Duperré joined the East Indiaman *Henri IV* as a merchant navy apprentice (*pilotin*). When *Henri IV* sailed for the East Indies France was still a monarchy; when she came home in November 1792, France was not only a Republic but at war with a widening array of counter-revolutionary enemies.

Back in France with a useful 18 months of sea time to his credit, Duperré applied for a transfer to the Republican Navy. In July 1793 he was posted to the corvette *Maire-Guiton* as second helmsman, cruising the Gulf of Gascony from 23 July 1793 to 25 January 1794. He was then transferred in the same capacity to the frigate *Tartu* (1 February 27 March 1795). By his 20th year Duperré had clearly made enough of a mark to be recommended for a probationary lieutenant's commission (*enseigne de vaisseau auxiliaire*) which he received on 1 August 1795, with a simultaneous posting to one of the newest and hardest-hitting frigates in the French fleet: the 40-gun *Virginie*, launched at Brest in 1794 with 28 18-pounders and 12-pounders.

Virginie's Captain, Jacques Bergeret, was one of the most able and energetic of the French frigate commanders, and with a weapon like *Virginie* to his hand could have caused the British untold damage. He also kept a sharp eye on his most promising junior officers, and on 21 March 1796 Duperré received his substantive lieutenant's commission as *enseigne de vaisseau titulaire,* as *Virginie* was preparing for an aggressive cruise to the mouth of the English Channel.

But on the morning of 20 April 1796, off the Lizard, it was Bergeret's bad luck to fall in with the British Navy's crack frigate squadron: Captain Sir Edward Pellew, flying his pennant in the no less remarkable *Indefatigable,* with frigates *Concorde* and *Amazon* in company. *Indefatigable* was a prodigy: a cut-down 64 with her upper gundeck removed to leave her with a main deck battery of 26 24-pounders, and extensively re-rigged to give her superior sailing qualities over all frigates of similar size. Faced with this overwhelming force, Bergeret promptly turned and ran for France; Pellew ordered a general chase, with *Indefatigable* out in the lead under every stitch of sail. Denied a fair wind to take her round Ushant and straight into Brest, *Virginie* was steadily overhauled in a tenacious pursuit covering 168 miles in 15 hours.

By midnight *Indefatigable* was within range and Bergeret was forced to give battle. In a hectic action lasting 1 hour 45 minutes, *Virginie* lost her mizzen-mast and main topmast, while bringing down *Indefatigable's* gaff, mizzen topmast and maintop-sail, and allowing Bergeret to come within an ace of raking his opponent. But as Pellew drew off to make running repairs, the other two British frigates were entering the fray. When *Concorde* crossed *Virginie's* stern and prepared to rake, Bergeret accepted the inevitable and surrendered.

Such was Duperré's first battle, which left him a prisoner of war in England for the best part of the next three years before his exchange could be negotiated. He did not return to France until 24 December 1798 and spent the next year in port service ashore. Duperré's next ship gave him his first experience of battleship service: the 74-gun *Wattignies*, in which he served from 6 November 1799 to 20 July 1800. This was followed – at the notably early age of 25 – by his first command: the corvette *Pélagie,* which he was to retain until the breakdown of the Peace of Amiens and the resumption of war with Britain in 1803.

Duperré's first 20 months with *Pélagie* were spent in French waters, escorting coastal convoys. In March 1802, the month of the formal peace-treaty signing at Amiens, Duperré received orders to take *Pélagie* on an extended peacetime cruise to the Caribbean via Senegal on the West African coast. In the first month of the cruise, on 24 April 1802, Duperré's promotion to commander (*lieutenant de vaisseau*) was confirmed.

Duperré's Caribbean cruise lasted from 27 March 1802 to 19 August 1803, when he received orders to leave *Pélagie* at Saint-Domingue and return to France. War with Britain had been resumed three months before and it took him until 24 December to get back to France. He was immediately posted to the main invasion flotilla base at Boulogne, where he served as adjutant on the flotilla staff until 3 October 1805. Duperré was then posted to the Brest fleet and an appointment as senior officer of the 74-gun ship of the line *Vétéran,* in the squadron of Willaumez.

It must have been with a sense of outrage that Duperré and his fellow-officers saluted their new captain on 23 November 1805: the 21-year-old Jérôme Bonaparte, youngest brother of the Emperor. Most of them would have been disgusted by what they had heard of Jérôme's highly chequered four-year career in the French Navy (pp. 149–52). Jérôme was manifestly unfit to command a cutter, let alone a ship of the line, and his appointment to *Vétéran* was imperial nepotism at its most shameless. His officers would have to carry Jérôme throughout his time in command, fully responsible for sailing and fighting the ship, in the certain knowledge that any credit due from *Vétéran's* performance would go exclusively to this pampered incompetent.

The French losses at Trafalgar (21 December 1805) left the Brest fleet as the only naval force capable of taking offensive action against Britain. This Navy Minister Decrès was determined to do. He put fleet commander Ganteaume under orders for a two-pronged simultaneous offensive, at the earliest opportunity, in the North and South Atlantic. Two months before Trafalgar, no unopposed breakout by the Brest fleet had been possible. Fewer than two months later, with the British blockade dislocated by wild weather, 11 of the line and four frigates escaped from Brest on 13 December 1805. Once at sea they separated into two squadrons, that of Leissegues assigned to the North Atlantic, that of Willaumez, including *Vétéran*, to the South.

The story of *Vétéran's* seven-month cruise with Willaumez's squadron is told on pp. 152–53. It ended on 31 July 1806 when Jérôme, abandoning his role in the cruise, parted company under cover of darkness and headed back to France. Ten days into his homeward voyage, the imperial delinquent had an easy and totally undeserved victory dumped in his lap. On 10 August *Vétéran* fell in with a 16-strong homeward-bound British convoy from Canada, escorted by a single 22-gun sloop, whose captain bravely tried to lure *Vétéran* away from his defenceless charges. Even the feckless Jérôme needed little urging from Duperré to ignore the bait and go for the ships of the scattering convoy, of which *Vétéran* burned and captured six. Then she resumed her course for France, making for Lorient as the nearest port.

Vétéran's homeward voyage would surely have ended in disaster without Duperré's detailed knowledge of the Brittany coast and its anchorages, amassed during his convoy duties in *Pélagie* five years before. On 26 August *Vétéran* was within a day's sail of Lorient when she was sighted by a patrolling British squadron: the 80-gun *Gibraltar* and two 36-gun frigates. After an unrelenting four-day chase *Vétéran's* interception seemed inevitable, until Duperré picked an unerring course through the rock-studded approaches to the tiny harbour of Concarneau. This anchorage was so confined that no ship of the line had ever dared use it, but on 1 September Duperré brought *Vétéran* to anchor in Concarneau, safe from all British pursuit.

While Napoleon's *Moniteur* trumpeted Jérôme's 'destruction' of the Canada convoy and proclaimed his promotion to rear-admiral on 19 September, the Navy Ministry was fully aware of how much Jérôme had depended on the professional skills of his officers. Four days after Jérôme's advancement to flag rank, Duperré was promoted from commander to junior captain (*capitaine de frégate*) on 23 September 1806. After seven weeks of port service ashore, he was appointed to command the 40-gun frigate *Sirène* on 12 November 1806.

Launched at Bayonne as *Fidèle* but renamed *Sirène* in May 1795, Duperré's new ship had had a more incident-studded career than most French frigates. She had taken part in the ill-fated Irish expedition of December 1796, and nine years later had sailed for the Caribbean with Villeneuve's Franco-Spanish Combined Fleet. There she had supported Cosmao-Kerjulien's recapture of the Diamond Rock off Martinique, and after the Combined Fleet's capture of the West Indies convoy (p. 61) had been entrusted with escorting the captured merchantmen to Guadeloupe. Rejoining the Combined Fleet as it re-crossed the Atlantic, *Sirène* had then taken part in its clash with Calder's battle fleet off Cape Finisterre (22 July 1805) but had been detached from the Combined Fleet before Trafalgar.

Under Duperré's command, *Sirène* was assigned no major mission before the New Year of 1808. This was a much-needed troop-carrying run to the Caribbean, in partnership with the 40-gun frigate *Italienne,* to reinforce Villaret-Joyeuse's garrison on Martinique. They delivered their troops successfully and were returning to France when history chose to repeat itself. By 22 March 1808 *Sirène* and *Italienne* were shaping their course for their home run into Lorient when they were sighted by a British battle squadron: the 74s *Impetueux* and *Saturn,* and the frigates *Aigle* and *Narcissus.*

To split the British pursuit the French frigates parted company. *Italienne* made Lorient safely but Duperré's *Sirène* was not so lucky. The wind died away, forcing him to lower boats and tow *Sirène* towards the shelter of the powerful shore batteries on the Île de Groix. The fluky wind favoured her British pursuers, and by 2030 *Impetueux* and *Aigle* had edged close enough to take *Sirène* in flank. After a bruising gun action lasting 1 hour 20 minutes the British drew off after bringing down *Sirène's* mizzenmast. In no doubt that the attack would be resumed at first light, Duperrè refused to expose his ship to certain capture or destruction and beached her under the guns of the Pointe des Chats coastal battery. Four days later, after the frustrated British ships had retired, Duperré managed to refloat *Sirène* and rejoin *Italienne* in Lorient.

Sirène proved too damaged to repair, and Duperré served ashore from April to June 1808. He was then picked (1 July) to be the first commander of the new 40-gun frigate *Bellone,* launched at Saint Servan in February 1808. This timely appointment enabled Duperré to oversee every crucial detail of *Bellone's* rigging and armament during the final stages of her fitting-out and completion. His promotion to *capitaine de vaisseau* was confirmed on 12 July.

Duperré was now chosen as one of the frigate captains entrusted with the new French attempt to strike at the British in the East Indies. As before, this venture would be based on France's colonial outposts of Île-de-France (Mauritius) and Île Bourbon (Réunion) in the southern Indian Ocean, but it was a very different affair to the previous forays led by Sercey (pp. 41–44) and Linois (pp. 121–24). Both had sailed for the Indian Ocean with compact squadrons but this time, to reduce the chances of alerting the British Admiralty, single frigate captains were ordered to make individual passages to the Indian Ocean, only joining forces when they had arrived at Île-de-France. Four of them – *Manche, Caroline,* Hamelin's *Vénus* and Duperré's *Bellone* – sailed from France in the last weeks of 1808, all successfully reaching Île-de-France between February and April 1809. Their arrival failed to prevent the eventual British conquest of Île Bourbon and Île-de-France in 1810 – but before the islands fell the French frigates would inflict the most shattering defeat suffered by the British fleet in the entire naval war of 1793–1814.

The struggle for the Mascarenes opened promisingly for the French. On 31 May 1809, Acting Captain Le Feretier of the *Caroline,* cruising the Bay of Bengal, captured the British East Indiamen *Streatham* and *Europe.* After repairing his prizes – *Europe* had hit back stoutly and suffered extensive damage before she struck – Le Feretier nursed them through the 2,000-mile voyage south-west to the Mascarenes, bringing them triumphantly into St Paul, Île Bourbon, on 22 July.

This early warning that French raiders were again at large in Indian waters naturally imposed caution on British mercantile sailings, denying similar easy pickings to the other French frigates. It took Hamelin, cruising the empty waters of the Bay of Bengal, until 26 July to score his first victim: the diminutive 18-gun Company brig *Orient.* Momentarily abandoning commerce-raiding, Hamelin then turned south-east to strike at British shore installations in the East Indies (p. 145).

Caroline's early success did far more than impose defensive measures on British trade sailings in the Indies. It prompted a dramatic counterstroke by Commodore Rowley's British East Indies naval squadron, with its advanced base on Rodriguez Island within easy striking distance of Île-de-France and Île Bourbon. On 21 September, a landing force of 600 British seamen and Marines landed on the north coast of Île Bourbon. After a 7-mile forced march on St Paul, they captured its coastal batteries from the landward and turned their guns on the shipping in the harbour. These were *Caroline* and her two captured East Indiamen, from which their valuable cargoes had been landed. When the British squadron warships entered the bay, their victory was complete. The upshot was the capture of *Caroline* and the recovery not only of *Streatham* and *Europe* but their crews and most of their cargoes as well. The

British re-embarked on the 28th after remaining in unchallenged possession of St Paul for a week and destroying all five batteries of its harbour defences.

But before two months had passed, the French frigates based on Île-de-France had struck back. On 2 November 1809 Duperré, cruising the Bay of Bengal, opened *Bellone's* score by capturing the 18-gun sloop *Victor,* which he promptly took into service. On 22 November, in the same waters with *Victor* in company, Duperré struck again, winning an even more useful prize: the Portuguese heavy frigate *Minerva.* Given a halfway competent crew and standard of gunnery, *Minerva* with her 52-gun broadside should have been more than a match for the out-gunned *Bellone,* but she struck to Duperré after only a feeble show of resistance. He then headed south for Île-de-France with his two captures, *Victor* and *Minerva* (rechristened *Minerve* in French service).

On 2 January 1810, Duperré safely arrived at Port Napoleon (as Port-Louis was now styled), with two invaluable reinforcements for the French squadron at Île-de-France. By the New Year of 1810 this now consisted of two divisions, led by Hamelin and Duperré as acting commodores. At Port Napoleon on the north-west side of the island was Hamelin with *Vénus, Manche,* and the brig-corvette *Entreprenant.* At Grand-Port, on the eastern coast, was Duperré with *Bellone, Minerve,* and *Victor.* Yet another frigate, *Astrée,* was on her way out from France.

On 24 March 1810, a month before *Astrée* reached Île-de-France, Duperré sailed again for the Bay of Bengal with *Bellone, Minerve,* and *Victor.* After sending off two early prizes to Île-de-France, he abandoned what had become a barren hunting-ground on 1 June and headed for St Agustin, Madagascar, to water and overhaul his ships. At the end of the month Duperré sailed again to sweep up the Mozambique Channel, a well-worn sea lane for outward-bound British sailings to India.

On 3 July, off Mayotte Island in the Comores Archipelago, the French squadron sighted the outward-bound East Indiamen *Ceylon, Windham,* and *Astell.* After a dramatic day-long running action *Astell* managed to escape *Victor's* pursuit, but *Ceylon* was obliged to strike to *Minerve* and *Windham* to *Bellone. Windham* and *Ceylon,* both 800-ton ships with useful broadsides of 26 guns, were taken into French service, with *Ceylon* renamed as *Ceylan.* It took nearly a month of repairs before the ships were fit for the voyage to Île-de-France, but by 20 August Duperré and his prizes were preparing to enter Grand-Port.

While Duperré was still at sea, the British opened their bid to conquer the French Mascarenes. Encouraged by their virtually unopposed raid of September 1809, they planned a full-scale invasion of Île Bourbon from their base on Rodriguez Island.

Transported and covered by the frigates *Néréide, Sirius, Boadicea, Iphigenia* and *Magicienne,* 3650 British and native Indian troops landed on 7 August 1810. Able to call on no more than 576 French regulars and a shaky militia of 2717, the French commander on Île Bourbon capitulated on the 8th, for the total cost to the British of 22 killed and wounded.

Determined to give the French no respite, the British planned an immediate invasion of Île-de-France. Rather than attempting a direct strike at Port Napoleon, the principal town and naval base, they selected Grand-Port, on the far side of the island, as their initial objective. After months of coastal reconnaissance the British naval commanders knew that Grand-Port, with its convoluted and rock-strewn harbour entrance, would be no easy nut to crack. They marked down the small island of Île de la Passe, commanding all approaches to Grand-Port, for their first lodgement.

The British began with the storming of the fort on Île de la Passe on the night of 13–14 August. After a tough fight they captured not only the fort's batteries but the French signal code, which the defenders had failed to destroy. This gave a protected anchorage to the only British frigate in support, *Néréide*. Two nights later (16–17 August) the British crossed the channel to destroy the fort at Pointe du Diable, freeing the north-eastern passage into Grand-Port.

From the 17th to the 20th the British reverted to propaganda warfare ashore, distributing leaflets promising the French colonists a rosy future under British rule, and winning their goodwill by refraining from any acts of pillage. But this promising interlude was cut short on the morning of 20 August, when the shore party was recalled by an urgent signal from Île de la Passe that five French ships were approaching from the east-south-east. Over-confidence, born of earlier easy successes, had caused the British to fall between two stools. They had lacked the force both to impose a tight blockade of the French warships in Port Napoleon, and to provide support in strength for the attack on Grand-Port. Now, with only *Néréide* to oppose them and the bulk of the British shore party still to re-embark, the oncoming warships were Duperré's *Bellone* with *Minerve, Victor, Windham,* and *Ceylan,* returning from the Comores.

Captain Willoughby, the British commander off Grand-Port, was determined to hold on at Île de la Passe until the rest of the British squadron could join him. Hoping to lure the oncoming Frenchmen into the anchorage and engage them with *Néréide* and the guns of the Île de la Passe fort, Willoughby boldly played the best card in his hand: the captured French signal codebook. French colours were hoisted on *Néréide* and Île de la Passe, with an accompanying signal that 'the [*British*] enemy' was cruising off the north of Île-de-France.

Willoughby was delighted when the French ships not only acknowledged the fake signal but proceeded to identify themselves with their private signal numbers. Fairly deceived by this classic *ruse de guerre*, Duperré ordered his ships to enter the anchorage inshore of Île de la Passe with *Victor* leading, followed by *Minerve, Ceylan,* and *Bellone.* By 1330 *Victor* had passed the Île de la Passe fort and arrived within pistol-shot of *Néréide*, which hoisted British colours and opened a devastating fire on the unsuspecting corvette at point-blank range. Overwhelmed, Captain Morice of *Victor* struck his colours. The dramatic opening round of the Battle of Grand-Port had passed to the British.

In less than an hour, however, the battle had been stood on its head. On Île de la Passe the abandoned French flag, rapidly lowered when the garrison hoisted British colours, was blown onto a lighted brazier, blazed up and detonated a stack of 100 cartridges. A shattering explosion killed three of the British garrison, inflicted hideous burns on 12 others and dismounted six guns, both from the seaward and landward batteries. Meanwhile the British had been denied the chance to take possession of the surrendered *Victor*. Opening fire on *Néréide*, Captain Bouvet of *Minerve* furiously hailed *Victor*, ordering Morice to re-hoist French colours, cut his cable and follow *Minerve* and *Ceylan* into the anchorage.

With three of his ships safely inshore of Île de la Passe, Duperré first detached *Windham* to make for Grande Rivière, then prepared to join the rest of his squadron. His telescope revealed the blast damage and dismounted guns on Île de la Passe but he could not know that *Néréide* was not only isolated but grossly undermanned, desperately awaiting the return of the boats from the shore with over 160 officers and men of her crew. Unaccountably, *Minerve*, *Ceylan* and *Victor* failed to sink any of the boats which passed – within touching distance of the French ships – to make a safe return to *Néréide*. It was in the nick of time for at 1440, after firing at Île de la Passe, Duperré took *Bellone* in to savage the out-gunned *Néréide* with a passing broadside.

A freak gust of wind, heeling *Bellone* as she fired, limited *Néréide's* damage to her spars, foremast and upper rigging, but by 1600 Duperré had his squadron concentrated inshore, protecting Grand-Port from further British attacks and out of range from the guns on Île de la Passe. He sent a situation report overland to Governor Decaen at Port Napoleon, 25 miles away, requesting support troops and guns to restore the batteries destroyed by the British. By nightfall on the 20th, Willoughby had sent off *Néréide's* launch to find the nearest British frigate – Captain Pym's *Sirius* – report the arrival of the French squadron and request immediate support. It was clear that the French ships could only endanger *Néréide* as long as the nightly land breeze blew, but Duperré had no intention of weakening his hand by trying a risky night attack.

The second day of the Battle of Grand-Port – 21 August – opened with both Willoughby and Duperré playing for time. Willoughby sent a flag-of-truce message to Duperré, arguing that as *Victor* had struck her colours to *Néréide* the day before, she should be immediately handed over. Duperré replied that only Decaen at Port Napoleon had the authority to rule on the matter, and asked the British to return on the morning of the 22nd.

Meanwhile Pym in *Sirius*, still unaware of the situation at Grand-Port, had chased but failed to prevent *Windham* from reaching the shelter of the batteries at Grande Rivière. But an extraordinarily bold cutting-out foray from *Sirius* – by a lieutenant, a midshipman, and nine seamen armed with makeshift wooden clubs – boarded *Windham* and brought her out in the teeth of fire from the shore. Prisoner interrogation finally acquainted Pym of the situation at Grand-Port. Issuing orders for *Magicienne* and *Iphigenia* to follow at their best speed, Pym immediately headed for Île de la Passe in *Sirius*, collecting *Néréide's* launch on the way.

Sirius arrived off Île de la Passe at 1100 on the morning of the 22nd, two hours after Willoughby had received the predictable rejection by Decaen and Duperré of the '*extraordinary*' British demand to hand over *Victor*. Decaen had also advised Duperré that the British frigates had quit the approaches to Port Napoleon (thereby opening the door for a sortie by Hamelin's squadron), presumably heading for Grand-Port. Duperré responded by withdrawing even further inside the shoals and coral outcrops constricting the seaborne approach to Grand-Port, and anchoring them in a defensive crescent.

Willoughby's greeting signals to *Sirius* showed no signs of appreciating the strength of the new French position, nor of the difficulties of coming to grips with Duperré's ships: 'READY FOR ACTION' followed, perplexingly, by 'ENEMY OF INFERIOR FORCE'. The latter assertion would have been questionable even if all four British frigates – only *Sirius* and *Iphigenia* had broadsides to match the French 18-pounders – had been present instead of only two; but Pym took Willoughby at his word. After signalling for *Néréide's* sailing master to come out and guide *Sirius* past Île de la Passe into the entry channel, Pym headed straight for the French squadron under full sail at 1440 with *Néréide*, more prudently under staysails only, following. At 1600 *Sirius* ran aground on a shoal, grounding so firmly that it took until 0830 on the following morning, 23 August, for *Néréide* to help haul her off.

The fourth day of the Grand-Port encounter – 23 August 1810 – was when the bill for British over-confidence in the innate superiority of the Royal Navy was forcefully presented. *Iphigenia* and *Magicienne* hove into view at 1000, but by the time they joined company at 1410 *Néréide* and *Sirius* were still sorting themselves out after the refloating operation. Before the squadron finally got under way at 1640, Pym and Willoughby drew up an attack plan: *Néréide*, leading, to anchor between the furthest French ships, *Victor* and *Bellone*; *Sirius* opposite *Bellone*; *Magicienne* between *Ceylan* and *Minerve*; *Iphigenia* opposite *Minerve*. It was a plan loosely based on Nelson's famous approach to the Danish line at Copenhagen in 1801, but it was ruined at the outset by *Sirius* running aground again, 15 minutes after getting under way, with *Magicienne* following suit 20 minutes later.

The chaotic following sequence of events saw *Ceylan* strike her colours and run herself ashore, in the process fouling *Bellone* which also went aground – but with her full broadside still bearing on the hapless *Néréide*. The latter was exposed to a merciless five-hour bombardment by Duperré's gunners which left *Néréide* a shattered wreck with her decks heaped with killed and wounded. At about 2300 a piece of langridge from one of the last of *Néréide's* guns still able to fire laid open Duperré's cheek and knocked him unconscious, but Bouvet of the *Minerve* – which had also run aground while pursuing *Ceylan* – crossed to *Bellone* and took command.

At about the same time that Duperré was rendered *hors de combat,* Willoughby of the *Néréide* – who had amazingly remained in command despite having had his left eye gouged out by a splinter – accepted the inevitable and struck. But the impossibility of notifying *Bellone* of *Néréide's* surrender meant that her agony continued, with Bouvet not ordering a cease-fire until about 0150 on the 24th. When daylight revealed a Union flag, which none of her surviving crewmen could reach to lower, still flying from *Néréide's* mizzen, *Bellone* reopened fire, continuing until *Néréide's* last survivors frantically cut down both mast and flag. By this time an appalling total of 230 of *Néréide's* 281 officers and crew had been killed and wounded. (The first French officer to board *Néréide* dazedly reported that she was, to quote from Duperré's subsequent despatch, 'in a condition impossible to describe'.)

The morning of the fifth day, 24 August, found *Bellone* and *Minerve* still aground, as were *Sirius* and *Magicienne. Iphigenia* was afloat but drawing heavy fire from the French ships and shore batteries; she was also dangerously low on 18-pound shot, and Pym ordered her Captain Lambert to warp her out of range. But *Iphigenia's* withdrawal left *Magicienne* exposed, as *Néréide* had been, to intensive fire with little chance to reply. By mid-afternoon Duperré had sufficiently recovered from his concussion to resume command at Grand-Port. He sent off a party to take formal possession of the charnel-house that was *Néréide,* intensified the bombardment of the helpless *Magicienne,* and pushed forward efforts to refloat *Bellone.*

By late afternoon on the 24th it was obvious that nothing was going to refloat *Magicienne,* and to avoid a second fruitless bloodbath Pym ordered her crew to transfer to *Iphigenia,* with all ammunition and stores which could be moved by boat. The last two officers to leave *Magicienne* were Captain Curtis and Lieutenant Smith, who set her on fire at 1930. Three and a half hours later, with her colours still flying, the fire reached *Magicienne's* magazines and she blew up.

The turn of *Sirius* followed next morning: 25 August, the sixth day of this extraordinary battle. *Sirius* was now under fire from Duperré's ships and a newly-mounted shore battery and at 0730, after a light shore breeze had wafted *Iphigenia* completely out of range of all French guns, Pym ordered work to begin on transferring the crew, ammunition, and stores of *Sirius* to *Iphigenia.* At 0800 he sent off a pinnace to carry his disaster-laden despatches to the British commander on Île Bourbon. She was spotted and unavailingly chased by a new arrival: the French brig *Entreprenant* from Hamelin's frigate squadron, which had sailed from Port-Napoleon at midnight on the 21st. At 0900 *Entreprenant's* look-outs sighted the eruption of smoke and flame as *Sirius* was set on fire, followed at 1100 by the explosion which destroyed her.

With his own ship and three-quarters of his squadron lost, Pym ceded command to Captain Lambert of *Iphigenia,* urging him to position her where he could support the garrison on Île de la Passe. Meanwhile Duperré, with total victory now in his grasp, hounded his crews to refloat their ships. Preceded by *Bellone,* all had succeeded in doing so by noon on the 27th, by which time Hamelin's frigates from Port Napoleon – *Vénus, Astrée* and *Manche* – were lying off Île de la Passe.

It was Hamelin, as Duperré's superior, who handled the initial negotiations for the inevitable surrender of *Iphigenia* – now facing odds of 5 to 1 with dangerously low reserves of ammunition, water, and stores – and the Île de la Passe garrison. After a bleak ultimatum from Governor Decaen – immediate surrender or resumption of hostilities with annihilation guaranteed – Lambert surrendered on the afternoon of 28 August. *Iphigenia,* the only one of the four British frigates fit for sea after the battle, was promptly renamed *Iphigénie* and taken over by the triumphant French squadron defending Île-de-France.

Fought five years after Trafalgar, Grand-Port was the French Navy's greatest victory, and the deepest humiliation inflicted on the Royal Navy, in the entire naval war of 1793–1814. The British reaction might well be called typically British. When the four British captains were eventually court-martialled for the loss of their ships at Grand-Port they were honourably acquitted, and the heroism displayed by the officers and men slaughtered in *Néréide* was selectively praised to the skies as exemplifying the best traditions of the Service. (Even Willoughby's fatal signal 'ENEMY OF INFERIOR FORCE', catalyst of the British defeat, got off with being described only as *'injudicious'.*)

Grand-Port bears close comparison with Saumarez's ill-prepared assault on Linois at Algeciras in 1801 (pp. 119–20): inadequate British reconnaissance before a piecemeal attack on an enemy well deployed in treacherous shoal waters, backed by powerful shore defences. Instead of being lured to destruction after being deceived by Willoughby's opening *ruse de guerre,* Duperré reacted by making excellent use of the natural and artificial defences of the Grand-Port anchorage and thoroughly deserved his victory, even when the substantial help he got from his second-in-command, Bouvet, is taken into account.

On paper, the Grand-Port victory achieved by Duperré and Hamelin in August 1810 raised the French frigate strength at Île-de-France to six: *Vénus, Manche, Astrée, Bellone, Minerve,* and *Iphigénie.* Again, on paper, this was the strongest French naval force in the Mascarenes since that of Sercey in the summer of 1796. But only three of the six – Hamelin's squadron, unscathed by the Grand-Port battle – were fully battle-worthy, and by autumn 1810 the British were preparing for a full-blooded invasion of Île-de-France. This was preceded by the capture of Hamelin's *Vénus* by Commodore Rowley's *Boadicea* on 18 September (p. 146). By 20 October the remaining French frigates, under Duperré's command as senior French naval officer since Hamelin's capture, were closely blockaded in Port Napoleon.

Profiting from the traumatic lesson of Grand-Port, the British invasion of Île-de-France was not launched until Commodore Rowley had conducted a thorough survey of the island's west coast. This time there was no mistake. An invasion force of nearly 70 ships carrying 10,000 troops – including a covering fleet of the 74-gun

Illustrious and 11 frigates – anchored off the chosen landing site of Grande-Baie, 12 miles north-east of Port Napoleon, on the morning of 29 November 1810. By nightfall all the troops had been safely landed, and after a token clash with the totally outnumbered French defenders on 1 and 2 December, Governor Decaen surrendered the island on the following day.

Released under the capitulation terms, Duperré sailed for home on 5 December and had been proclaimed a Baron of the Empire (16 December 1810) before he set foot in France. He and Hamelin were both promoted rear-admiral on the same day: 15 September 1811. Hoisting his flag in the new 80-gun *Sceptre* on 1 October 1811, Duperré commanded the Toulon fleet's light squadron until February 1812. His last service to the Empire was as commander of the French and Italian naval forces at Venice (23 February 1812–27 April 1814. When Napoleon abdicated on 6 April 1814, Duperré was defending Venice for his Emperor, only relinquishing his naval charges to the Austrians after the Convention of Schiarino-Rizzino was signed on 23 April.

The first Bourbon restoration of 1814 ended Duperré's 21 years of service to the French First Republic and Empire, but another 25 years of service to the restored French monarchy lay before him. They began inauspiciously. Louis XVIII created Duperré *Chevalier de Saint-Louis* on 5 July 1814, but after serving Napoleon as Maritime Prefect at Toulon during the 'Hundred Days' of March–June 1815, Duperré was pointedly left without active employment for the next three and a half years. Finally restored to favour, he served as naval C-in-C in the French Antilles, based on Fort-de-France, Martinique, from January 1819 to September 1821.

When France sent land and naval forces to restore Ferdinand VII to the Spanish throne, Duperré replaced his former superior Hamelin in command of the French naval blockade of Cadiz in September 1823. For this service he was promoted vice-admiral (4 October 1823) and was awarded the Spanish Grand Cross of the Order of Charles III of Spain. After a month in command of the French Atlantic flying squadron (July 1824) he was created Commander of the Order of Saint-Louis by King Charles X. For conveying a Danish diplomatic mission to the West Indies in the summer of 1826, Duperré added the Grand Cross of the Royal Order of the Dannebrog (21 September 1826) to his impressive array of decorations. On 8 January 1827 he replaced Vice-Admiral Gourdon as Maritime Prefect at Brest.

By far the most historic command held by Duperré in his later career was that of the invasion fleet carrying General de Bourmont's expeditionary force – 38,000 troops, 4,500 horses and 91 heavy guns – to the conquest of Algiers (11 April–2 September 1830). The naval contribution was huge: 103 warships escorting a transport fleet of 469, dwarfing Bonaparte's expedition to Egypt in 1798 (p. 68). Apart from establishing the core of a huge new French empire in North Africa, the expedition finally ended centuries of Mediterranean piracy by the notorious 'Barbary Corsairs' of Algiers. (The Corsairs' loot seized when Algiers fell on 5 July was so vast that it repaid the cost of the whole expedition.) For their joint achievement, de Bourmont was promoted Marshal and Duperré was created a Peer of France (15 July 1830).

These were the last honours bestowed by Charles X, who before three weeks were out had been driven into exile by the 'July Revolution'. The new King, Louis-Philippe d'Orleans (1830–48) confirmed Duperré's peerage (momentarily abolished by the revolutionaries), and presented Duperré with the Grand Cross of the Legion of Honour when he was appointed President of the Council of Admiralty on 1 March 1831.

Before he was finally placed on the Retired List (6 February 1843), Duperré served three terms as Navy Minister: November 1834–September 1836, May 1839–March 1840, and from October 1840 to his retirement. He died in Paris on 2 November 1846 at the age of 71. Apart from the imposing statue erected in his native city, La Rochelle, the final honour paid to Duperré was a state funeral in the Invalides.

Rear-Admiral Jean-Mathieu-Adrien Lhermitte (1766–1826)

No relation to his fellow-admiral and quasi-namesake Pierre-Louis L'Hermite (a Dunkirker by birth, and five years older), Jean-Mathieu-Adrien Lhermitte was a Cotentin Norman, born at Coutances (Manche) on 29 September 1766. His father was a pillar of the local establishment, a councillor to the Cotentin Bailiwick, but the young Lhermitte opted for a naval career. Two years into France's war with Britain in support of the rebel American colonies, he joined the French Navy as a 14-year-old Boy Volunteer on 1 January 1780.

Lhermitte. Lithograph by Maurin, c.1835. (Wikimedia Commons)

Lhermitte's first ship was the patrol sloop *Pilote des Indes* (1 January–6 September 1780) in home waters, where he saw his first action: the capture of a British privateer off the Chauseys, the French Channel Islands. He was then transferred (14 October) to the ship of the line *Northumberland,* bound for the American theatre with the battle fleet of the *Comte de* Grasse. In *Northumberland* Lhermitte took part in de Grasse's great victory in Chesapeake Bay (5 September 1781), which ensured the capitulation of Cornwallis's army at Yorktown and sealed the independence of the American colonies.

On 23 March 1782 Lhermitte was transferred from *Northumberland* to the frigate *Medée,* which spared him from sharing in the defeat of de Grasse's fleet by Rodney in the Battle of the Saints (12 April 1782). During his time in *Medée,* Lhermitte sufficiently impressed his superior officers to be posted with an auxiliary officer's commission to the lugger *Oiseau* (January–March 1783). He then transferred as a volunteer to the *flûte Pintarde,* leaving the fleet on a voyage to the newly-fledged United States of America (April–November 1783). During this commission the Peace of Paris (3 September 1783) brought the American war to its formal end.

Peacetime Navy cutbacks left Lhermitte without service employment and he followed the customary route into merchant service. From 1784 to 1787 he served as first officer with the merchantman *Modeste* on the Newfoundland fisheries trade route, followed by three months (July–October 1787) in French waters with the coaster *Surveillante*. By the New Year of 1788 he was back in Navy service, commissioned as a sub-commander (*sous-lieutenant de vaisseau*) in the ship of the line *Achille* on a goodwill cruise to America (January–November 1788).

The coming of the Revolution in 1789 ushered in the three-year experiment (May 1789–August 1792) of trying to give France a constitutional monarchy. This ended with the Girondin Party's desperate bid to seal the King's commitment to the Revolution by declaring war on Austria (April 1792). For Lhermitte the last months of peace gave him a rapid series of brief seagoing appointments: to the corvette *Goëland* (June 1790–May 1791, with another voyage to Newfoundland), the *flûte Dromedaire* (May–June 1791), the *Duc-de-Bourgogne* (July–September 1791), and a return to *Goëland* as second captain on a cruise to Saint-Domingue (September 1791–April 1792). From Saint-Domingue Lhermitte sailed for France in *Rodolphe* on 10 April 1792, and when he landed at Bordeaux on 22 May he found that his country and its Navy were again at war.

Lhermitte's first seven months of war service in 1792 saw him given such a bewildering sequence of postings that he can hardly have had time to unpack his kit in one ship before being moved on to the next. All were with the French Atlantic fleet, based on Brest and Lorient: the ships of the line *Superbe* (17 June–23 July) and *Patriote* (24 July–9 September); the frigate *Fidelité* (23 September–4 October); his former ship of the line *Achille* (5–20 October); the frigate *Engageante* (7 November–18 December); and finally the frigate *Résolue* (19 January 1793).

It was in *Résolue,* attached to Allemand's frigate squadron, that Lhermitte took part in the capture of the first British warship taken in European waters since the outbreak of war. This was the frigate *Thames* (24 October 1793), by which time Lhermitte had been promoted to acting commander (*lieutenant de vaisseau provisoire*) on 15 August. Even before the badly-damaged *Thames,* renamed *Tamise,* had been repaired and rendered fit for service in the French fleet, Lhermitte had been appointed her first captain (27 October 1793).

The New Year's List of 1794 saw Lhermitte confirmed as commander (2nd class). On 16 May he sortied with Villaret-Joyeuse's Brest fleet in the French Navy's supreme bid to save the tottering Republic (pp. 22–23). In the First of June battle Lhermitte's *Tamise* played a highly important role as 'repeating frigate': duplicating the signals from Villaret's flagship *Montagne* to make them visible to as many ships in the fleet as possible.

After the fleet's triumphant return to Brest, having ensured the arrival of the all-important grain convoy from America, Lhermitte was appointed captain of the new 38-gun frigate *Seine* (14 June 1794). His 20 months with *Seine* (June

1794–February 1796) saw Lhermitte involved in no dramatic actions, but they did reveal a talent for scoring and surviving deep in enemy waters. A cruise to Irish waters in spring 1795 captured several small coasters and the 16-gun Royal Navy sloop *Hound.* A second cruise in autumn 1795, with the 32-gun frigate *Galathée* in company, crossed the North Sea, entered the Skagerrak and raided the southern Norwegian coast. After a harrowing winter in Norwegian waters with sick lists soaring, Lhermitte came home with three prizes in January 1796, but *Galathée* was wrecked off the Brittany coast.

In February 1796 Lhermitte left *Seine* for the 36-gun frigate *Cocarde,* which was attached to the frigate squadron bound for the East Indies under Rear-Admiral Sercey (p. 41). Lhermitte had barely taken command when *Cocarde* was damaged by accidental grounding. The only available replacement was the 40-gun frigate *Vertu,* then repairing at Rochefort. Lhermitte was transferred to *Vertu* with orders to ready her for sea without delay. With Sercey putting to sea from Rochefort on 4 March, Lhermitte was ordered to sail in pursuit as soon as possible and join the rest of the squadron at Santa Cruz in the Canaries. It was no mean achievement that Lhermitte was able to sail only 11 days after Sercey's departure, with his hasty promotion to *capitaine de vaisseau* confirmed on 21 March. He made an equally rapid voyage to the Santa Cruz rendezvous which he reached on 29 March, and Sercey's united squadron promptly sailed for the Cape of Good Hope and the Indian Ocean.

The three years of Sercey's operations in the Indies, with all the difficulties confronting him from the moment of his squadron's arrival at Île-de-France (Mauritius) on 18 June 1796, are covered on pp. 41–44. Lhermitte distinguished himself throughout. In the attack on the British 74s *Arrogant* and *Victorious* (9 September 1796), Lhermitte led Sercey's battle line into action. *Vertu* brought down *Arrogant's* ensign with her first broadside, although the British return fire did the same to *Vertu's* foretopsail yard. The attack left the British warships in no case to pursue when Sercey withdrew his squadron, to repair battle damage and refit at Île-du-Roi in the Mergui Archipelago.

When in the New Year of 1798 Sercey had to give up a pair of frigates to escort two treasure ships from the Philippines home to Spain (p. 43), he chose *Vertu* and *Régénérée.* Magon, who had served on the Indies station without a break since 1783, was sent home in *Vertu,* while Lhermitte took command of the 40-gun *Preneuse.*

Lhermitte's first mission in *Preneuse* was to return two envoys from Tipu Sultan of Mysore, who had requested French reinforcements for his wars with the British East India Company. Lhermitte sailed from Île-de-France on 8 March 1798, heading for Mangalore, and hoisting British colours as he approached the Indian west coast in the third week of April. Thus disguised, he was preparing to pounce on two unescorted British East Indiamen in the roadstead of Tellicherry when, on the afternoon of 21 April, a violent thunderstorm intervened. *Preneuse* was lucky to survive a lightning strike on her mainmast which killed one man and injured 15 others. Unperturbed by this narrow escape, Lhermitte moved in to hoist French colours and capture both Indiamen, *Woodcot* and *Raymond*. He then landed 600-odd prisoners (obtaining a receipt for them from the Tellicherry commandant), sent the captured Indiamen off to Île-de-France under prize crews, and proceeded to Mangalore which he reached on the 24th.

At Mangalore Lhermitte disembarked Tipu's envoys with due ceremony, along with the pitiful 'reinforcement' of 150 French colonial volunteers which was all that the depleted Île-de-France garrison could spare. He then sailed on 26 May to rejoin Sercey at their pre-arranged rendezvous: Batavia, Java, capital and main naval base of the Dutch East Indies.

The sequence of woes which had withered Sercey's frigate squadron and obliged him to transfer from Île-de-France to Batavia is described on p. 44.

By the time Lhermitte joined him at Batavia in late June 1798, Sercey's force had been reduced, from a peak strength of six frigates two years before, to his own corvette *Brûle-Gueule* and Lhermitte's *Preneuse*. The latter was the last strong card in the depleted hand which Sercey nevertheless attempted to play out to the end. Months of refit and replenishment at Batavia came to an end in the early summer of 1799, when Lhermitte undertook the most ambitious lone cruise of his career to date. He would take *Preneuse* westward across the widest extent of the southern Indian Ocean, and seek what he might devour along the British sea lane round the Cape of Good Hope.

By mid-September 1799, *Preneuse* was approaching the South African coast. After a voyage of more than 5500 sea miles, Lhermitte's most urgent need was a secure anchorage where he could embark fresh water and provisions and overhaul his ship. He chose Algoa Bay, site of the future Port Elizabeth, which he reached on the late afternoon of 20 September only to find that the British Navy was there before him. Lying at anchor, with their topmasts and yards down and both their captains ashore, were the 44-gun store ship *Camel*, armed *en flûte*, and the 16-gun sloop *Rattlesnake*. They were delivering stores for a minor land campaign against insurgent Kaffirs, and were completely unprepared for the apparition of a powerful enemy from the far side of the Indian Ocean.

As at Mangalore in May 1798, Lhermitte took the time to make a careful assessment of the opposition. The last thing he wanted, after the interminable voyage from Batavia, was a premature battle. He approached obliquely as the daylight failed, again under false (Danish) colours, and only decided on a night attack when he was satisfied that both British ships were incapable of making sail or manoeuvring. But the first lieutenants of *Camel* and *Rattlesnake* were thus given the time to attach springs to their anchor cables, enabling both ships to swing and present their broadsides to their attacker, and between them they gave *Preneuse* a hot reception. Lhermitte's gunners silenced *Camel's* fire by holing her at the waterline and forcing her gunners to rush to the pumps, but *Rattlesnake* was not then blown out of the water as that diminutive sloop might well have been. Instead the British watched in disbelief as *Preneuse* broke off the battle and limped away under lower sails only, her upper masts left tottering from high-aimed disabling fire.

At daylight on 21 September the British lookouts sighted *Preneuse* at anchor at the far end of Algoa Bay, her men hard at work fishing (splinting) her damaged upper masts and spars. Apprehension of a British counterattack before his ship was fit for action caused Lhermitte to slip his cable and run for the open sea, with no option but a return to Île-de-France. Alerted by a message rushed overland from Algoa Bay, the British 50-gun *Jupiter* sailed from Table Bay on 1 October, reaching Algoa Bay on the 8th. Learning from the officers of *Camel* and *Rattlesnake* of *Preneuse's* damaged state, *Jupiter's* Captain Granger sailed at once in pursuit.

On the afternoon of 10 October, in a rising gale, *Jupiter* sighted *Preneuse* away to the north-east and a long chase began, lasting through the night until the afternoon of the 11th, when a close action began. Battle damage had made it impossible for *Preneuse* to outrun *Jupiter*, but when the ships closed the height of the gale-driven waves made it impossible for *Jupiter* to open her lower-deck gun ports. This enabled Lhermitte's gunners to reverse the experience of Algoa Bay, reducing *Jupiter's* upper rigging to shreds and badly damaging her mainmast and foremast. Immediate running repairs were essential and *Jupiter* sheered off to make them, leaving *Preneuse* to continue her retreat.

Île-de-France proved no safe haven. On the morning of 11 December 1799 – two months to the day after his escape from *Jupiter* – Lhermitte had just sortied from Port-Louis in *Preneuse* when he was caught on a lee shore by the British 74-gun *Tremendous* and 50-gun *Adamant*. Lhermitte's response was to run *Preneuse* ashore under the guns of coastal batteries at the mouth of the Tombeau River. When these failed to drive off *Adamant*, Lhermitte struck his colours to avoid a pointless sacrifice of lives, sent off the bulk of his crew in boats to safety ashore, and remained on board to make the formal surrender of *Preneuse*, which the British burned where she lay. After his release on parole, Lhermitte remained on Île-de-France until the British conquest of the island in December 1800, when he was exchanged and freed to take ship for France.

Lhermitte's return to France in 1801 coincided with the suspension of Anglo-French hostilities briefly sealed with the Peace of Amiens (1802–3). He was now earmarked for battleship command and his first was the 74-gun *Brutus* at Lorient. This was followed in 1803 with a posting to the 80-gun *Alexandre*, Truguet's flagship at Brest, to whom Lhermitte was appointed Flag Captain (*capitaine de pavillon*). After Ganteaume replaced Truguet as Brest fleet commander in May 1804 Lhermitte returned to Lorient, briefly commanding the 110-gun first rate *Républicain* before transferring to the 74-gun *Régulus*, destined to be his last seagoing command.

From August 1805, the British blockade of Villeneuve's Combined Fleet in Cadiz left Ganteaume's as the only French fleet capable of independent action in Atlantic waters. It fell to Lhermitte to lead the first of several 'nuisance cruises' ordered by Ganteaume in the autumn and winter of 1805. On 23 September Lhermitte received his orders for the foray. With *Régulus,* the 40-gun frigates *Présidente* and *Cybèle* and the brig-corvette *Surveillante,* he was to raid the British sea lane and trade settlements along the West African coast before crossing the Atlantic. The squadron was to make its presence felt on both sides of the Atlantic, remaining at sea for a year.

Without formal promotion to *chef de division* but with a classic commodore's command, Lhermitte led his squadron out of Lorient on 31 October 1805 – ten days after the destruction of the Combined Fleet at Trafalgar. By the New Year of 1806 he had taken and destroyed over 50 merchant ships – including slave ships outward bound to embark their lucrative human cargoes from the West African Slave Coast – and inflicted considerable damage on trading posts ashore. The highlight of the cruise came on 6 January 1806, with the capture of the *Favourite,* an 18-gun British sloop. Lhermitte took this valuable prize into service as an extra cruiser, sending *Surveillante* back to France with his prisoners, but she never got there. (The French press subsequently admitted to her capture and sinking by a large British privateer which she had 'attacked' – unlikely, given the skeleton crew which she would have been carrying.)

After crossing the Atlantic to refit and replenish his ships on the Brazilian coast, Lhermitte headed north in hopes of a second run of success in the West Indies, but it was not to be. On 20 August 1806 his squadron was battered and dispersed by the same hurricane which terminated the cruise of Willaumez (pp. 116–17). Nothing more was heard of *Favourite; Cybèle* lost her topmasts but struggled north to reach Hampton Roads, Virginia, on 1 September; *Présidente,* sailing independently, headed for France but was captured by a British battle squadron on 27 September. Lhermitte was luckier, bringing *Régulus* safely home to Brest on 5 October. (After refitting in America, *Cybèle* also made a successful home run, to Rochefort, in summer 1807.)

It was the end of Lhermitte's long and varied seagoing career. He was promoted rear-admiral on 6 January 1807 and created Baron of the Empire in October 1810, but his only other appointment was as Maritime Prefect at Toulon (4 June 1811). He held this without interruption through Napoleon's first abdication, the first Bourbon restoration and the 'Hundred Days', until 19 April 1815.

The last time Lhermitte hoisted his admiral's flag at sea was in June 1814, on a voyage to bring the Duchess of Orleans home to France from Messina. For this service the restored Bourbons honoured him with a double creation as *Chevalier de Saint-Louis* and Commander of the Legion of Honour (14 August 1814). Placed on the Retired List with the rank and pension of vice-admiral in January 1816, Lhermitte enjoyed a ten-year retirement before dying at Plessis-Picquet (Seine) on 28 August 1826.

Rear-Admiral Amable-Gilles Troude (1762–1824)

Born early enough to see a wealth of service in the American Revolutionary War (1778–83), Amable-Gilles Troude went on to complete an action-packed service career under the First Republic and Empire. But arguably his most historic seagoing mission for the French Navy was his last: carrying the restored King Louis XVIII home to France from England in April 1814, after the downfall of Napoleon's ten-year Empire.

Troude was born on 1 June 1762, the last year of the Seven Years War of 1756–63, at Cherbourg. Though never a great shipbuilding centre like Brest, Lorient, Rochefort or Toulon, Cherbourg was a notable hub of the French merchant navy, both coastal and

Troude. Lithograph by Maurin, c.1835. (Wikimedia Commons)

ocean-going, and was an equally valued source of experienced seamen for the regular French Navy, the *marine d'État,* in time of war. For the first 16 years of his seagoing career, before being chosen as officer material by the Navy of the First Republic, Troude learned his trade both as a seasoned merchant seaman and as a fighting sailor.

Troude first went to sea at Cherbourg as a 14-year-old merchant navy apprentice (*pilotin*); his first ship (March 1776–March 1777) was the coaster *Sainte-Catherine.* From May to December 1777 he made his first Atlantic crossing (from Cherbourg to Martinique) in the *Aimable-Victor,* repeating the voyage in January–August 1778. By the time *Aimable-Victor* returned to Cherbourg France had gone to war (6 February 1778) in support of Britain's rebel American colonies, and on 11 May 1779 Troude embarked at Rochefort as an ordinary seaman (*matelot*) in the newly completed 74-gun ship of the line *Pluton.*

Troude's war began in earnest in January 1780 when he was posted to the 74-gun *Hercule,* bound for the Caribbean with de Guichen's squadron. *Hercule* took part in the three fleet actions between de Guichen and Rodney off Martinique and Dominica on 17 April, 15 May and 19 May 1780. Passing to de Grasse's command, *Hercule* went on to support the successive captures of St Kitts, St Lucia and Tobago (January–May 1781). But Troude was not present at the decisive Battles of Chesapeake Bay (2 September 1781) and the Saints (12 April 1782). He was landed from *Hercule* at Saint-Domingue on 30 July 1781, and in September joined a draft of battle-hardened seamen shipped back to France. The day after his return to France (28 January 1782) Troude was posted to the frigate *Crescent,* dispatched to join the Franco-Spanish armada pressing the 'Great Siege' of Gibraltar (1778–83).

Paid off from *Crescent* on 7 April 1783, Troude was left with no peacetime Navy appointment in the foreseeable future, but he did not follow the usual peacetime resumption of a merchant navy career. After one three-month voyage in the merchantman *Union* of Bordeaux (December 1783–February 1784), Troude went home to Cherbourg. There, from April 1784 to August 1789, he joined the army of workers expanding Cherbourg into a major fleet base and warship building yard (inaugurated by King Louis XVI in June 1786 – p. 11.)

Apart from providing him with a living, these years gave Troude the time to study navigation and earn his certificates as ship's mate and master. With these in his pocket, Troude returned to sea in September 1789 on the first of three voyages to Saint-Domingue, in the merchantmen *Europe* and *Asie.* On the third of these voyages (June–August 1792) Troude sailed as *Asie's* captain: his first command. On 15 August 1792, Troude brought *Asie* home to Le Havre to find that the monarchy had fallen five days earlier. France had been at war with Austria since 20 April, and the Navy was avid to recruit and offer rapid promotion to experienced merchant skippers with battle experience (*see also* Perrée, pp. 79–80).

Commissioned as lieutenant (*enseigne de vaisseau*), Troude joined the 74-gun ship of the line *Achille,* in which he served with the Brest fleet from 16 January 1793 to 3 March 1794. Only six months into his first Navy commission, Troude was promoted commander (*lieutenant de vaisseau*) on 2 July 1793. On 4 March 1794 he was posted to the 74-gun *Éole* in which, under Villaret-Joyeuse's command, Troude served in the campaign and battle of the First of June which saved the French Republic.

Troude's 18-month service in *Éole* earned him his first Navy command. This was the corvette *Bergère* which he took from Rochefort on a prolonged cruise (18 December 1795–16 August 1798) to Cayenne, Brazil, the Azores and Guadeloupe. During this odyssey Troude was promoted (21 March 1796) to junior captain (*capitaine de frégate*). He returned to service in the Brest fleet under Bruix and was advanced to battleship command, the 74-gun *Tyrannicide,* on 3 September 1799. By the end of the month Troude was at sea, bound for the Mediterranean to join the command of Linois at Toulon. In August 1800 Troude's command of *Tyrannicide* came to an unusual end when his ship was re-named. *Tyrannicide* became *Desaix*, in honour of the hero-general who had won the Battle of Marengo (14 June 1800) for Bonaparte, only to be killed in the moment of victory.

After Marengo knocked Austria out of the Second Coalition, French pressure was intensified on an isolated and war-weary Britain. In summer 1801 First Consul Bonaparte ordered Linois to sail with a battle squadron from Toulon to Cadiz, there to reform a Franco-Spanish combined fleet. With Ganteaume at sea with the bulk of the Toulon fleet, vainly trying to relieve the trapped Army of Egypt (p. 76), the force left available to Linois was small but far from negligible: his own 80-gun flagship *Formidable*, the 80-gun *Indomptable*, Troude's *Desaix* (74), and the 38-gun Venetian-built frigate *Muiron* which had returned Bonaparte from Egypt to France in 1799. They sailed from Toulon on 13 June 1801.

With the British Mediterranean Fleet deployed to contain Ganteaume in the central Mediterranean, Linois and his ships enjoyed an unmolested passage south-west down the Spanish coast. They passed Gibraltar on 3 July and on the 4th had the luck to capture the British brig *Speedy*, heading for Gibraltar with Captain Lord Cochrane aboard. Instead of maintaining a stoical silence when interrogated by his captors, Cochrane – hoping to persuade these French interlopers to return to the Mediterranean – told Linois that Rear-Admiral Saumarez was blockading Cadiz in force, with seven of the line. This had the unexpected effect of inducing Linois not to retreat but to press on and seek momentary shelter in Spanish Algeciras, across the bay from Gibraltar. There – as with Duperré at Grand-Port nine years later (p. 191) – the French squadron would be protected from the seaward by shoals and supported from the landward by powerful shore batteries.

Linois led his ships into Algeciras Bay on 5 July on 5 July and anchored them in a north-south line inshore of the shoals. Meanwhile Saumarez, alerted from Gibraltar of the French arrival, left one of his ships to watch Cadiz, sailed for Algeciras with the remaining six and issued orders for an attack on the morning of 6 July.

The ensuing Battle of Algeciras is described in detail on p. 119. It ended with the repulse of Saumarez, who had blundered piecemeal into an attempt to repeat Nelson's attack (in which Saumarez had served) on the French battle line in Aboukir Bay three years before. Saumarez's retreat to Gibraltar abandoned the 74-gun *Hannibal*, hard aground and dismasted, as the second British ship of the line captured by the French in a month; *Swiftsure* had fallen to Ganteaume off Derna, Libya, on 24 June.

Although the lion's share had been taken by the British, both sides had suffered considerable battle damage; all three French ships of the line, especially *Formidable* (which had lost her topmasts), needed extensive jury-rigging to their upper masts and spars. But they had not been rendered helpless cripples, as Saumarez hopefully believed. All three had been rendered fit to sail by the afternoon of 9 July, when Linois was massively reinforced by the arrival of Vice-Admiral Moreno's battle squadron from Cadiz: *Real Carlos* and *San Hermenegildo* (112s), *San Fernando* (96), *Argonauta* (80) and *San Agustin* (74). A late arrival from Cadiz was flying the Tricolour: *Saint Antoine,* formerly *San Antonio,* purchased from the Spanish Navy and rushed to sea with a scratch Franco-Spanish crew. Two years after 'Bruix's Cruise' from Brest to the Mediterranean, a Franco-Spanish combined fleet was again in being.

The allies wasted most of 12 July in discovering that the shattered *Hannibal* was too badly damaged to be towed to Cadiz as a trophy. Before the fleet finally shaped its course for Cadiz, Moreno shifted his flag from *Real Carlos* to the frigate *Sabina* and persuaded Linois to join him, with Linois ordering Troude to take command of *Formidable.* As the Franco-Spanish fleet got under way, Saumarez sailed in pursuit from Gibraltar with his hastily repaired five of the line.

There followed the extraordinary night action of 12–13 July 1801, the chaotic 'Battle of the Gut of Gibraltar' (p. 120). It saw the Spanish heavy-weights, *Real Carlos* and *San Hermenegildo,* successively open fire on each other and set each other on fire, both blowing up around midnight with horrendous loss of life (an estimated 1,700 out of 2,000 officers and men). Meanwhile the leading British pursuers, *Superb, Cæsar,* and *Venerable,* overhauled *Saint Antoine* and battered her into surrender in 30 minutes.

First light on 13 July revealed only one French ship in sight: Troude's *Formidable,* labouring under her jury topmasts in the wake of the Franco-Spanish main body. By 0515 the leading British ships, the 74-gun *Venerable* and the 32-gun frigate *Thames*, were closing rapidly on *Formidable.* Holding doggedly to his course, Troude opened fire with his stern-chaser guns, but *Venerable* kept coming until she was close alongside.

In the ensuing duel Troude made full use of his best asset: the formidable weight advantage of the heaviest French shot (some 8 lbs heavier than the biggest British equivalent, the 32-pounder), increased by firing triple-shotted loads at point-blank range. These brought down *Venerable's* mizzen-topmast at 0530 and her mainmast at 0645. Now totally unmanageable, the stricken 74 fell away from *Formidable* – still under fire from the French stern-chasers – to be gripped by the inshore current and cast ashore at 0750, losing her foremast in the process and her mizzenmast ten minutes later. Continuing to fire until out of range, Troude drew away as the foremost British leaders abandoned the chase and went to *Venerable's* aid.

By the afternoon of the 13th *Formidable* had rejoined the fleet, to an ecstatic reception, in Cadiz roads.

In both France and Britain, government propaganda clutched every possible rag of credit from the two battles: praise to Linois for his capture of *Hannibal,* praise to Saumarez (who was made a Knight of the Bath) for having chased the Franco-Spanish fleet back to Cadiz with his outnumbered squadron. After the night-time disasters in the Gut of Gibraltar, Troude's bulldog rear-guard action naturally stood out. His feat earned him the nickname of '*l'Horace français*' – the 'French Horatius' – from

Bonaparte, and immediate promotion to *capitaine de vaisseau,* with effect from 14 July 1801.

After his promotion to Post Captain, Troude remained in command of *Formidable* until 30 April 1802, by which time the Peace of Amiens (1802–3) was in force. Commanding the frigate *Indefatigable,* he sailed on the Saint-Domingue expedition (March–November1803), after which he was posted to the 74-gun *Suffren* in Missiessy's Rochefort squadron.

Troude commanded *Suffren* in both major ocean-going forays made by the Rochefort squadron in 1805. The first was to the Caribbean under Missiessy, from January to May (pp. 17–18); the second was under Commodore Zacharie Allemand, Missiessy's successor in command. This lasted from July to December 1805 and ranks as one of the most remarkable achievements of the French Navy in the entire naval war of 1793–1814.

When Allemand broke out of Rochefort on 16 July with five of the line, three frigates and two brigs, he was under orders to join Ganteaume's Brest fleet at sea. If the latter had failed to escape from Brest, Allemand was to join forces with Villeneuve's Combined Fleet, returning from the Caribbean. But Admiral Calder's outnumbered fleet found Villeneuve first, off Cape Finisterre on 22 July, after which confused encounter Villeneuve headed first for Vigo and then for Ferrol in Spain. Allemand meanwhile was heading north to his secondary rendezvous point: Penmarch Point on the Brittany coast, south of Brest. He persisted with his vain quest for Villeneuve for 40 days after the Finisterre battle. Not until 6 September did Allemand accept that the grand invasion plan had failed and that Villeneuve must have headed south to Cadiz.

Allemand arrived off Cadiz on 11 September, to find the Combined Fleet under close British blockade. Eight weeks since he had sailed from Rochefort, left to his own devices with his original mission wrecked, he decided that the best help he could give Villeneuve was to raid the British sea lane down the Portuguese and Spanish coasts. One of the least-remembered chapters in the history of commerce warfare, Allemand's ten-week war cruise with his 'invisible squadron' began.

The first blow was struck on 15 September when Allemand attacked a West Indies convoy, capturing ten merchantmen and the 64-gun *Calcutta.*[1] He spent the last six days of the month off the mouth of the Channel before returning to Finisterre (9 October) on the track of a Lisbon-bound convoy. Captain Strachan's squadron, tasked with denying Allemand a clear home run to Rochefort, was still sweeping the seas for him when the Combined Fleet was defeated at Trafalgar on 21 October.

When Strachan destroyed Dumanoir's four Trafalgar survivors on 4 November, he originally thought that he had caught Allemand at last. But Allemand was at Tenerife in the Canary Islands, landing his sick, re-provisioning and watering his ships and selling his prizes, and he remained off the Canaries until 16 November. He only turned for home in mid-December, when he received confirmation of the magnitude of the Trafalgar disaster, and his luck held to the last. On 24 December 1805 Allemand led his intact force home to Rochefort. He had been at large for 161 days (only 13 of them spent in port), captured 52 British merchantmen and taken 1200 prisoners. It was a feat unmatched by any other French naval commander of 1793–1814, and Allemand could not have done it without solid professionals like Troude under his command. (Troude apart, two other future admirals of the Empire sailed with Allemand in July–December 1805: Pierre-François Violette, Captain of the *Magnanime,* and Jean-Nicolas Petit of the *Jemappes.*)

For three weeks in March–April 1806 Troude at Rochefort took command of the 40-gun frigate *Armide,* taking her to sea to drive off a British probe at the coastal defences at Sables d'Olonne. He was then given the 74-gun *Courageux* at Lorient (5 April 1806), a command he was destined to retain for the next 5½ years, and which would give him his last experience of battle.

By the close of 1808 it was clear that France's hold on her last Caribbean colonies would not last long. From Martinique, Governor-General Villaret-Joyeuse had sent urgent requests for a supply convoy in strength without which the island would fall in months. Napoleon's response was to order another impossible combination of battle squadrons – Willaumez at Brest plus Troude at Lorient plus Allemand at Rochefort – creating an armada which would sweep zcross the Atlantic to the relief of Martinique.

Troude, at Lorient, commanded the main supply complement: his own *Courageux* with the 74s *Polonais* and *d'Hautpoult,* escorting the frigates *Félicité* and *Furieuse.* The two frigates were armed (or more accurately, half-disarmed) *en flûte* and crammed with flour, military stores, and troops. Napoleon's admirals did their best, but it was all for nothing. By the time the ships began to move, the British were already ashore on Martinique in force.

It was not until 21 February 1809 that Willaumez, escaping from Brest with eight of the line, chased Commodore Beresford's blockaders off Lorient, only to find that the tide was too low for Troude's 74s to get to sea. Willaumez stood on for Rochefort, followed on the 22nd by three frigates from Lorient, *Cybèle, Calypso,* and *Italienne.* On the following day all three were beached and battered to wrecks at Sables d'Olonne by Admiral Stopford's three of the line – but they had done their work. With the tide now in his favour and British attention fixed on Rochefort, Troude escaped unseen from Lorient and headed straight for the Caribbean.

By the time he sighted the islands on 29 March, Troude had learned from a captured merchantman that Villaret-Joyeuse had surrendered Martinique on 24 February. To take stock of the transformed situation he headed for Guadeloupe and found a momentarily secure anchorage amid the little archipelago of the Îles des Saintes[2], across the channel from Vieux-Port, Guadeloupe. There he could not escape detection from the British at Martinique, but there were too many channels between the islets of his refuge for them either to get at him in force, or for them to impose a watertight blockade.

After a tense two weeks of waiting-game it was Admiral Cochrane at Martinique who forced the pace, landing troops on the main islet on 14 April. They promptly emplaced two howitzers which threatened Troude's ships with certain destruction by shellfire unless he escaped. He planned a night breakout through the western inlet with his ships of the line, luring away Cochrane's ships of force to give *Félicité* and *Furieuse* the chance to dash into Vieux-Port and land their cargoes. By 2130 on the night of 14 April, they reached the open sea; but an unusually dark night had not screened them from the British inshore flotilla of sloops and brigs and a night action engaged Troude's rearmost ship, *d'Hautpoult.*

A running fight ensued throughout the daylight hours of the 15th. Troude had the chance of concentrating against the only ship of force engaging *d'Hautpoult,* the *Pompée,* but rejected the idea. The time it would take to beat *Pompée* would only give the rest of Cochrane's ships time to arrive on the scene, and it would be better to win clear with two ships rather than none. As night fell, he ordered his force to separate, standing on to the west-south-west with *Courageux* and *Polonais* while *d'Hautpoult* headed west-north-west. The upshot was the capture of *d'Hautpoult* after a gallant fight on the morning of the 17th, while Troude shook off his pursuers to return safely to Cherbourg on 29 May.

Troude had made the best of an impossible situation, saving two-thirds of his force while achieving his mission. By drawing Cochrane's hunters off to the west, he had enabled *Félicité* and *Furieuse* to make their successful dash across to Vieux-Port on the morning of 15 April. (Both were subsequently captured during their attempted home runs to France, *Félicité* on 18 June, *Furieuse* on 6 July.)

Troude's dramatic Caribbean foray in the spring of 1809 marked the end of his active seagoing career. He remained in command of the Cherbourg naval base and flotilla until Napoleon's abdication in April 1814, retaining command of the faithful *Courageux* until November 1811. This was six months after Troude's well-earned promotion to rear-admiral on 27 May 1811.

Troude's last official voyage was as historic as it was appropriate. In April 1814 the *Polonais,* which he had brought home from Guadeloupe in 1809, was renamed *Lys* in honour of the restored Bourbon monarchy. On 15 April, Troude was tasked with taking *Lys* to England to bring King Louis XVIII home to France. After disembarking the King at Calais, he returned to Cherbourg, and was rewarded by being created *Chevalier de Saint-Louis.* Placed on the Retired List on 1 January 1816, Troude died at Brest on 1 February 1824.

Notes

1 *Calcutta,* formerly the East Indiaman *Warley,* had been converted into a light ship of the line by the indefatigable labours of Captain William ('Bounty') Bligh in 1795.

2 Scene of de Grasse's defeat by Rodney on 12 April 1782.

Appendix 1

Admirals of the Tricolour

The Constitutional Monarchy

July 1789–August 1792

d'Entrecasteaux – d'Estaing – Flottes – Grimouard – Lavilléon – Le Gardeur de Tilly – Morard de Galles Rivière – Saint-Félix – Thévenard – <u>Truguet</u>

The Convention

September 1792–November 1795

Bouvet – Cambis – Coeuret de Secquville – Cornic – Dalbarade – Delmotte – Flotte de Beuzidou – Kerguelen – Kersaint – Landais – <u>Latouche-Tréville</u> – Le Dall de Kéreon – Le Dall de Tromelin – Leissegues – Lelarge – Martel – <u>Martin</u> – <u>Missiessy</u> – Nielly – <u>Renaudin</u> – Rochegude – <u>Rosily-Mesros</u> – Rosily-Vieuxbourg – Saint-Julien – <u>Sercey</u> – Thirat de Chailly – Trogoff – Vanstabel – Vaultier – Vence – <u>Villaret-Joyeuse</u>

The Directory

November 1795–November 1799

Bedout – Blanquet – <u>Brueys</u> – <u>Bruix</u> – Courand – <u>Decrès</u> – Dordelin – <u>Ganteaume</u> – Lacrosse – <u>Perrée</u> – Pléville le Pelley – Richery – Terrasson – <u>Villeneuve</u>

The Consulate

November 1799–May 1804

Dumanoir – <u>Émeriau</u> – <u>Linois</u> – <u>Magon</u> – Savary – <u>Ver Huell</u>

The Empire

May 1804–April 1814/March–June 1815

Allemand – <u>Baste</u> – Baudin – <u>Bonaparte, Jérôme</u> – Buyskes – <u>Cosmao-Kerjulien</u> – <u>Duperré</u> – Gourdon – <u>Hamelin</u> – Jacob – L'Hermite – <u>Lhermitte</u> – Petit – <u>Troude</u> – Violette – <u>Willaumez</u>

Underlining indicates names inscribed on *Arc de Triomphe*

Appendix 2

Admirals of the *Arc*

On the 40 tabular columns listing the names chosen to honour the marshals, generals and admirals of the First Republic and Empire on the *Arc de Triomphe,* the 26 admirals' names are located as follows:

NORTH PILLAR (Avenue de la Grande Armée/Avenue de Wagram), from left to right:

Ver Huell – Missiessy – Hamelin – Truguet – Latouche-Tréville
Villaret-Joyeuse – Jérôme Bonaparte – Cosmao-Kerjulien

EAST PILLAR (Avenue de Wagram/Avenue des Champs-Elysées), from left to right:

Bruix – Rosily – Villeneuve

SOUTH PILLAR (Avenue des Champs-Elysées/Avenue Kléber), from left to right:

Perrée – Magon – Émeriau – Willaumez – Brueys – Ganteaume

WEST PILLAR (Avenue Kléber/Avenue de la Grande Armée), from left to right:

Martin – Decrès – Linois – Duperré – Baste
Troude – Sercey – Renaudin – Lhermitte

Appendix 3

Absentees from the *Arc*

The committee of historians appointed to select the names to be honoured on the *Arc* completed its work in the opening months of the French Second Empire proclaimed by Prince Louis-Napoleon, the new Emperor Napoleon III, on 2 December 1852. This made one name virtually inevitable for selection: the Emperor's uncle, Jérôme Bonaparte, already a Marshal of France and proclaimed First Prince of the Blood on the first day of the Second Empire. (Only one other brother of Napoleon I is honoured on the *Arc*: Louis Bonaparte, one-time King and military commander-in-chief of the brief-lived Kingdom of Holland.)

In Bonapartist legend, Napoleon I had been the mastermind who brought the work of the French Revolution to its triumphant conclusion. The selection committee therefore had to do justice to the great names both of the Revolutionary Wars and of the First Empire. Thus, they included General Dumouriez, victor of the 'Miracle of Valmy' in 1792, overlooking his desertion to the enemy in the following year; and General Custine, unjustly cashiered and executed in the same year as Dumouriez's defection. Justice was also done to Villeneuve, disgraced by Napoleon and (ostensibly) driven to suicide after his defeat at Trafalgar in 1805.

Although the Army marshals and generals inevitably claimed the lion's share, the Navy was not overlooked. It was the Navy which, by ensuring the safe arrival of a massive grain convoy from America in May–June 1794, saved the Republic from famine and collapse. This feat was acknowledged by the selection of Villaret-Joyeuse, Lord Howe's adversary in the Battle of the First of June 1794; and of Renaudin, hero of the last fight of the *Vengeur* in that battle.

Inevitably, more than one equally worthy name was overlooked in the selection process. It was only the 11th-hour reinforcement by the squadron of Nielly which enabled Villaret to accept battle with Howe on the First of June; and it was Vanstabel whose skill and judgement brought that vital grain convoy safely through to Brest. Two months before, famine had also been averted in southern France by the timely delivery of relief convoys to Marseille and Toulon by Vence. And Vence was only saved from the tender mercies of the Committee of Public Safety by the testimony of the French Navy's most respected hero, the redoubtable one-legged Pléville le

Pelley. It is therefore in belated homage that condensed biographies of all four[1] are included in this Appendix.

Nielly (1751–1833)

Born at Brest on 2 September 1751, son of a Navy captain. Entered by his father as a ship's boy (*mousse*) on 2 May 1758, in ship of the line *Formidable,* two years after the outbreak of the Seven Years War.

Still not 9 years old, serving in *Formidable* as apprentice seaman (*pilotin*), wounded in thigh in Battle of Quiberon Bay (20 November 1759). Transferred to ship of the line *Royal-Louis*, remained in home waters, seeing no further action, until coming of peace in 1763.

At sea for all but one of the next 15 years, rising from apprentice seaman to master mariner under the constant guidance (and three times direct command) of his father. Granted his ticket as master mariner (*capitaine au long cours*) with special age-limit waiver on 23 July 1774. First merchant command (*Charlotte*) June 1775. Appointed to command merchantman *Adelaïde on* 6 March 1778, a month after France's entry into American Revolutionary War (6 February).

Two months after outbreak of shooting war at sea (Battle of Ushant, 27 July 1778), transferred to regular Navy with rank of lieutenant-commander (*lieutenant de frégate*), commanding armed transport *Guyane*. Spent entire American War on convoy escort duty, seeing none of the major fleet actions.

Survived peacetime service cutbacks after 1783, commanding a series of *flûtes* and corvettes interspersed with port duty ashore at Brest. His posting to the 74-gun *América* (June 1790–May 1791), during which he was created *Chevalier de Saint-Louis* (9 March 1791), gave him his first experience of service in a ship of the line since boyhood.

Completing his third spell of port duty at Brest when France declared war on Austria (20 April 1792). Promoted commander (*lieutenant de vaisseau*) on 29 May 1792, commanded transport *Lourde* on supply voyage to Saint-Domingue. On returning to now-French Republic (30 December 1792), promoted *capitaine de vaisseau* (1 January 1793); commanded frigate *Résolue* in Allemand's frigate squadron, assisting in capture of British frigate *Thames* (24 October 1793). Appointed to command 80-gun ship of the line *Sans-Pareil* (27 October). At age 42, promoted Rear-Admiral in Atlantic Fleet (16 November 1793).

On 6 May 1794, Nielly sailed from Rochefort with *Sans-Pareil* and the 74s *Trajan, Audacieux, Patriote,* and *Téméraire.* His mission: to reinforce the escort of Vanstabel, bringing a vital grain convoy, 117 strong, from America. On the 11th, detached *Patriote* to advise Villaret that Vanstabel and the convoy had not yet been located. On the 25th, deciding that Vanstabel was clearly still out of immediate danger, Nielly decided that his best course was to turn back and reinforce Villaret. On 30 May rejoined Villaret, who transferred Nielly to command the Rear Squadron in the 110-gun *Républicain.* Put up stout defence against converging attacks in Battle of the First of June, which ensured safe arrival of the Vanstabel convoy.

Retained as fleet Rear Squadron commander by Villaret after First of June. On 6 November 1794, captured the 74-gun *Alexander,* first British ship of the line taken since the outbreak of war; publicly thanked by National Convention.

December 1794–February 1795: sailed under Villaret in the Brest fleet's dramatic *Croisière du Grand Hiver,* capturing nearly 100 British merchantmen but losing four French 74s wrecked in storms.

December 1796: Nielly's last seagoing command – the abortive attempt by the Brest fleet to land General Hoche's army in Ireland, frustrated by wild storms in Bantry Bay. Nielly flew his flag in the frigate *Résolue,* dismasted in collision and towed back to Brest.

April–September 1797: military commander at Brest; interim commander of Atlantic fleet at Brest, March–May 1798; military commander at Lorient from May 1798 to September 1800, when First Consul Bonaparte appointed him Maritime Prefect at Dunkirk. Finally placed on the Retired List, 17 September 1803.

Commander of the Legion of Honour, 14 June 1804; created Baron by Louis XVIII August 1804; promoted honorary vice-admiral, May 1821. Nielly died at his birthplace, Brest, on 13 September, 1833, aged 82.

Vanstabel (1744–1797)

Born at Dunkirk on 8 November 1744 into a family with a long sea-faring tradition. First went to sea at age 14 as a merchant seaman apprentice. By 1778 had risen via quartermaster and mate to qualify as ship's master.

Commanded Dunkirk privateers in American Revolutionary War. As captain of corvette *Rohan Soubise,* captured British privateer *Admiral Rodney* (May 1781); presented with silver-hilted sword by King Louis XVI and promoted lieutenant-commander (*lieutenant de frégate*). Ended American war on convoy escort duties along French Channel coast. Between 1783–89, took part in French Navy's programme of surveying cruises, charting French Channel coast from Dunkirk to Cherbourg (1788).

January 1792, promoted commander (*lieutenant de vaisseau*). One-year cruise to Saint-Domingue, Martinique and Guadeloupe commanding frigate *Proserpine* (1792–93). On the coming of war with Britain (February 1793) promoted *capitaine de vaisseau* in command of frigate *Thétis.* Unleashed on commerce-raiding in the Channel, in a four-month cruise captured or destroyed some 40 British merchant ships. November 1793, recommended by Republican 'People's Representatives' for promotion to rear-admiral. In a two-week cruise (16–30 November) captured 17 ships from a homeward-bound Newfound-land convoy.

December 1793, sailed for Virginia with two of the line to take command of the emergency grain convoy for France forming at Norfolk to save the Republic from famine. Drew on his convoy experience in the American war, using the time needed to assemble and load the 117 ships of the convoy to drill its captains in the paramount need to keep formation and avoid straggling.

Departed Chesapeake Bay on 2 April 1794, proceeding at pace of the slowest ship and reducing sail at nightfall. Thanks to the manoeuvres of Nielly and Villaret-Joyeuse, unmolested during entire crossing. On 3 June sighted floating wreckage from First of June battle between Villaret and Howe. Decided both battle fleets were returning to base and held on for Brest, arriving in triumph on 11 June. Publicly thanked by decree of the National Convention.

Appointed commander of Brest fleet's Van Squadron by Villaret, leading it safely through the crisis-wrecked midwinter cruise (*Croisière du Grand Hiver*) of January–February 1795. Left with chronic bronchial trouble by rigours of the *Croisière*; on sick leave until summer 1796.

July 1796, accepted last seagoing command, escorting a convoy to Antwerp before taking command of the new French Scheldt Flotilla based at Vlissingen, Walcheren. Forced by ill-health to resign his command and retire to Dunkirk, dying there of pneumonia on 30 March 1797, aged 53.

Vence (1747–1808)

Born at Marseille on 6 April 1747 with a silver spoon in his mouth: son of a provincial governor (*Intendant*), into a family with sugar plantations on Saint-Domingue in the Caribbean and extensive shipping interests. At age 15, sailed from Bayonne in the last year of the Seven Years War (1756–63), charged by his father with joining his brother in Saint-Domingue to fit out a privateer for operations against the British – a project aborted by the signing of peace preliminaries. Embarked on a peacetime career in the merchant service.

By mid-1770s, French entrepreneurs like the Vence family were becoming keen to cash in on the growing conflict between Britain and her American colonists. War of American Independence began at Lexington, 19 April 1775; 13 October, colonial Congress voted to form a 'Continental Navy' to fight Britain at sea, with privateering an initial essential. After sailing from Martinique to the Chesapeake Vence was promptly granted a privateer's 'Letter of Marque', beginning his new career as a commerce-raider at age 29 in autumn 1776.

In the 18 months before France's entry into the American War (February 1778), Vence proved himself one of the greatest privateers in maritime history, becoming the terror of British Caribbean merchant shipping. He ran up a total of 211 prizes taken in 40 actions, pushing up British maritime insurance premiums by a hair-raising 23 per cent and ending with the British Government putting a price of £2 million on his head.

Notified in August 1778 that France was in the war, Governor de Bouillé of Martinique asked Vence to try a *coup de main* against neighbouring British Dominica. Vence used family funds and his own massive reserves of prize money to recruit a force of 400 freebooters against the threadbare British forces on Dominica. When they stormed Fort Cachacrou on 7 September, the island surrendered.

Capture of Dominica coincided with the arrival of the French battle fleet under the *Comte d'*Estaing, who promptly rewarded Vence with a Navy commission as lieutenant-commander (*lieutenant de frégate*). Served in d'Estaing's flagship during French capture of St Vincent (19 June 1779). Promoted commander (*lieutenant de vaisseau*) for the ensuing assault on Grenada, Vence led the storming party which captured the British battery on Hospital Bluff and clinched the surrender of the capital, Georgetown (4 July). Appointed Port Captain of Georgetown by d'Estaing.

D'Estaing's belated attack on Savannah, Georgia (9 October) was beaten off with heavy French losses (one in five of the attackers killed or wounded).[2] Vence's desperate assault on the Spring Hill defences earned him the nickname of 'Out-in-Front Vence' ('*Vence toujours devancé*'). Vence was created *Chevalier de Saint-Louis* on 24 January 1780.

From 1780–82, Vence was victimised by a whispering campaign by the enemies of his patron d'Estaing, falsely accusing Vence of amassing corrupt profits from his post at Georgetown. Recalled to France to answer these charges, autumn 1782; shipwrecked in Spain (losing his prize-money fortune); took ship to Cadiz to serve under d'Estaing during last weeks of the Franco-Spanish 'Great Siege' of Gibraltar (1778–83); Peace of Paris finally signed, 3 September 1783.

For next six years Vence tried in vain to rebut the charges against him, consistently denied the court-martial which would have cleared his name. July 1789, elected officer in the Paris National Guard but still denied justice by the Navy Ministry until the fall of the monarchy (10 August 1792). Finally (10 November 1792) informed by Republican Navy Ministry that all former charges against him were null and void, with promotion to *capitaine de vaisseau* and battleship command (*Heureux*) in Truguet's Toulon fleet.

After Truguet's failure to capture Cagliari, Sardinia (February 1793) and his replacement by Trogoff in May, Vence remained with the Toulon fleet, transferred to the 74-gun *Duquesne*. At the age of 46, Vence was now entrusted with the most fateful mission of his career: to relieve the crisis-racked Republic from imminent famine. He was required to amass a supply convoy from every available French merchantman in the central and western Mediterranean, load it with grain purchased from Tunis, and see it delivered safely to Toulon and Marseille.

With a myriad of difficulties still to be overcome, Vence was still at Tunis in September 1793. With Toulon now in revolt against the Republic, the Convention in Paris suspected Vence of counter-Revolutionary sabotage. Veteran Captain Pléville le Pelley was sent out to Tunis to arrest Vence and bring him back for trial by the Committee of Public Safety. After meeting Vence in October 1793 and hearing of his problems, Pléville left him in post and returned to Paris, defending Vence in glowing terms.

Vence finally sailed for France in March 1794 with a huge grain convoy of 100 sail, delivering 80 to Marseille and 20 to Toulon. It was a feat in every way comparable to Vanstabel's delivery of the American grain convoy to Brest three months later, saving Vence from the fate of his brother and nephew (both guillotined as 'aristos'). On 9 May 1794, reinstated and posted to Brest fleet. On 2 September, promoted rear-admiral with seniority backdated to the day of his exoneration by Pléville (16 November 1793).

Vence engaged in port duties at Brest over the winter of 1794–95. His last seagoing mission (March 1795) took him from Brest to Bordeaux, there to muster another supply convoy and bring it back to Brest. Intercepted by a British battle squadron (8 June) but escaped to Lorient with all but eight of his convoy. Returned to Brest in December 1795. Sacked from command of the Brest fleet's second squadron (November 1796) for objecting to the plan to land General Hoche's army in Ireland.

As Military Commander of Toulon (July 1797) helped prepare Bonaparte's Egyptian expedition (May 1798). Appointed Maritime Prefect of Toulon by First Consul Bonaparte (July 1800). Placed on Retired List (30 September 1803) for condemning the 'Army of England's' invasion fleet as 'nothing but nutshells' (*véritables coquilles de noix*'.) Died on his estate at Vaulichères on 11 March 1808, aged 61.

Pléville le Pelley (1726–1805)

By the time of his death, respected as the Grand Old Man of the French Navy after a wholly remarkable career (and the only naval officer to have had his right leg shot off three times).

Born at Granville, 26 June 1726; orphaned young, and an unhappy boyhood under a domineering uncle. Ran away to sea at age 12; tough schooling on the Grand Banks cod fishery (1738–40). In Austrian Succession War (1740–48), aged 18, sailed with Granville-based privateer *Françoise du Lac*. Captured off Jersey after a two-hour battle in which his right leg was shattered. Amputated and life saved by British surgeons; walking again by the time he was returned to France in 1745, determined to return to sea.

In First Battle of Finisterre (3 May 1747), captured in armed merchantman *Mercure* with his wooden leg smashed by a shot; joked that it had only made more work for the carpenter.[3] Repatriated to France by autumn, and straight back to sea. Served in two more privateers, rising to rank of first officer, but denied his first privateer command by the signing of peace (October 1748). After a spell of cross-Channel smuggling, returned to Canada for a four-year stint as a civilian skipper in the Newfoundland fishing trade.

Outbreak of Seven Years War (1756–63) found Pléville's latest ship at Marseille, requisitioned to support the naval expeditions against Minorca and Corsica. Won support of Marseille's top privateer sponsor, Jean Rambaud, marrying Rambaud's daughter in 1757. In 1757–58, commanded Rambaud's privateer *Colibri* until her requisition by the Navy and attachment to de la Clue's squadron as an auxiliary frigate (1758).

Between 1758–62, commanding the bark *Hirondelle* with the rank of lieuten-ant-commander (*lieutenant de frégate*), Pléville engaged in commerce raiding against homeward-bound British East Indiamen, the best-defended merchant ships afloat. He managed to capture three, losing his second wooden leg in one attack, but his last cruise in 1762 ended with Pléville forced to apply for port duty ashore in health grounds. January 1766, took post as Port Commander at Marseille for the next four years.

On the stormy night of 4 May 1770, the British frigate *Alarm*[4] was caught on a lee shore outside Marseille harbour and threatened with shipwreck. Pléville took personal command of the rescue operation, struggling out through the surf to carry a warp aboard *Alarm* which enabled her to be brought safely into Marseille. This feat earned him – uniquely – the formal thanks of the British Admiralty and a magnificent silver presentation trophy, but no reward from his own service until a belated promotion to *capitaine de port* in January 1776.

On France's entry into the American Revolutionary War (February 1778), Pléville was promoted commander (*lieutenant de vaisseau*) and posted to the flagship of the *Comte d'*Estaing, C-in-C of the French expeditionary fleet to America. On *d'*Estaing's staff, served as fleet revictualling officer, also entrusted with the sale of captured prize ships; astonished the Navy by his refusal to line his pockets from these traditionally lucrative sources; promoted *capitaine de vaisseau* by d'Estaing (August 1779). Returned to France with d'Estaing (1780) and resumed his former post at Marseille, resigning from ill health in 1789.

After coming of Revolution (May 1789) Pléville unavailingly besought the Constituent Assembly for active employment. After the fall of the monarchy (August 1792) swore allegiance to the new Republic and was elected Treasurer of Marseille's Jacobin Club.

By autumn 1793 Marseille's Jacobin rulers were desperate for the belated arrival of Vence's grain convoy from Tunis. Pléville was despatched to Tunis to arrest Vence and bring him back for interrogation in Paris. On meeting Vence and hearing his problems, Pléville left him in post and returned to Paris, defending Vence in glowing terms and clearing his name. This brave stance, justified by the arrival of Vence's grain-ships in March–April 1794, raised Pléville's stock still higher, earning him promotion to commodore (*chef de division*) and a posting to the Navy Ministry.

After Bonaparte's conquest of North Italy (1796–97), tasked with setting up the French Navy's first Adriatic base at Ancona; provided the wherewithal for the capture of Corfu and the Ionian Islands by Brueys (July 1797). Appointed Navy Minister (19 July 1797) and promoted rear-admiral (5 October); advanced to vice-admiral

(9 April 1798) but resigned on the 28th in protest against Bonaparte's forth-coming Egyptian expedition.

After the *Brumaire* coup of November 1799, Pléville was created Senator by First Consul Bonaparte (24 December 1799) and Grand Officer of the Legion of Honour (14 June 1804). In his 79th year, Pléville died at Paris on 2 October 1805 – 19 days before the Battle of Trafalgar, in which his nephew Dumanoir le Pelley commanded the Franco-Spanish Van Division.

Notes

1 Provided in full, in companion volume *Admirals of the Tricolour* (in preparation).
2 Five future 'Admirals of the Arc' served at Savannah: Ganteaume, Martin, Missiessy, Émeriau, and Truguet, both of the latter two being wounded.
3 *'Le boulet s'est trompé – il n'a donné de besogne qu'au charpentier'.*
4 Captain John Jervis, the future Earl St Vincent.

Bibliography

Alden, J. R., *History of the American Revolution,* Macdonald, London, 1969

Barnett, C., *Bonaparte,* Allen & Unwin, London, 1978

Bennett, G., *Nelson the Commander,* Batsford, London, 1972

Bordonove, G., *Les marins d l'an II,* Robert Laffont, Paris, 1974

Chevalier, E., *Histoire de la Marine Française pendant la guerre d'Independence Américaine,* Librairie Hachette & Cie, Paris, 1884

Chevalier, E., *Histoire de la Marine Française sous la 1e République,* Librairie Hachette & Cie, Paris, 1884

Cronin, V., *Napoleon,* Readers Union, Newton Abbot, Devon, 1971

Granier, H., *Histoire des Marins Français 1789–1815,* Marines editions Nantes, 1998

Guérin, L., *Les marins illustres de la France,* Dufour et Mulat, Paris, 1845

Howard, J. E., ed., *Letters & Documents of Napoleon, Vol. I: The Rise to Power,* Cresset Press, London, 1961

Hulot, F., *Suffren, 'l'Amiral Satan',* Editions Pygmalion/Gérard Watelet, Paris, 1994

James, W., *The Naval History of Great Britain, 1793–1827,* 6 vols., Cambridge 2010

Levot, P., *Les gloires maritimes de la France: notices biographiques sur les plus célèbres marins,* Bertrand, Paris, 1866

Mahan, A. T., *The Influence of Sea Power Upon History,* Bison Books, Lonodon, 1980

Marquand, H. Le, *Vie Du Contre-Amiral Amable-Gilles Troude, l'Horace Français,* A. Broulet, Brest, 1934

Martineau. G., *Madame Mère,* John Murray, London, 1978

Six, G., *Dictionnaire Biographique des Généraux & Amiraux Français de la Révolution et de l'Empire, 1792–1814,* Librairie Historique et Nobiliaire, Paris, 1934

Taillemite, E., *Dictionnaire des marins français,* Éditions Maritimes et d'Outre-Mer, Paris, 1982

Thomazi, A., *Les Marins de Napoléon,* Tallandier, Paris, 1978

Warner, O., *Trafalgar,* Batsford, London, 1959

Warner, O., *The Glorious First of June,* Batsford, London, 1961

Index

Abensburg, Battle of (1809) 180
Aboukir, Battle of (1799) 75, 84
Aboukir Bay ('The Nile'), Battle of (1798)
    x, xiii, 52, 58–59, 74, 76, 83, 89,
    103, 104
Acre, siege of (1799) 74, 83, 84
Adda river (1796) 170
Admiralty Islands (1792) 161
Adriatic Sea 67, 82, 87, 172
Africa, East (1784–87) 27; (1799) 200–1
Africa, West (1786–88) 32; (1795) 81
Ajaccio, Corsica 75, 149
Alava, Vice-Admiral Don Miguel de
    62, 112
Alcolea (1808) 177, 180
Alexandria, Egypt (1798) 58, 69, 74–5,
    82; (1801) 76–77
Algeciras, Battle of (1801) 118–20, 205
Algiers: (1794) 80; (1805) 152
conquest of (1830) 183, 194
Algoa Bay (1799) 200–1
Allemand, Rear-Admiral Zacharie 6, 18,
    81, 91–92, 104, 168, 207, 208
Almazan (1810) 180
Ambleteuse (1804) 97
Amboina (1792) 160
American Revolutionary War (1778–83)
    xii–xiv, xix–xx, 4, 10–11, 15–16,
    20–21, 32, 40, 49–50, 55–56,
    66–67, 72, 79, 87, 101–2, 108,
    129–30,139, 159–60, 169, 197,
    203–4

Amiens, Peace of (1802–3) x, xx, 6, 13,
    44, 59, 91, 97, 104, 121, 150, 184,
    201, 207
Amsterdam, French shipbuilding at
    (1806–13) 92
Ancona (1798) 74, 104, 155
Andréossy, General Antoine 75
Andujar (1808) 176–9
Anglo-Dutch War, 4th (1780) 96
Angola (1787–92) 139
Antigua (1805) 61, 133
Antwerp: (1809) 18, 98; French
    shipbuilding at (1806–13) 92
Arcola, Battle of (1796) 171
Aspern-Essling, Battle of (1809) 154, 180
Aswan, Egypt 83
Augereau, General Charles-Pierre 97
Austerlitz, campaign and battle of (1805)
    28, 144, 174–75
Austria: (1792–97) 102, 170–71, 198,
    204; (1798–1800) 12, 205; (1805)
    174–75; (1809) 180
Azores 40, 134

Baco, René-Gaston 41, 111
Badajoz (1812) 177
Bagration, Prince Peter Ivanovich 155
Bailén, French capitulation at (1808) 169,
    177–80
Bali Strait (1797) 43
Ballinamuck (1798) 52
Baltic Sea (1785–86) 16, 36

Bantry Bay (1796) 117, 141
Barbados (1805) 61; (1806) 153
Barbary Corsairs 15, 26, 66, 152, 194
Barcelona (1809) 136
Barclay de Tolly, Prince 155
Barham, Lord Charles 134, 166
Basque Roads (Île d'Aix), Battle of (1809) 6, 92, 168
Bassano, Battle of (1796) 171
BASTE, Rear-Admiral Count Pierre (1768–1814) xiii: merchant service origins 169: auxiliary lieutenant (1793) 170; with 1794 grain convoy 170; in Toulon fleet, supporting Army of Italy (1796) 170; with Mantua siege flotillas (1796–97) 171; with Lake Garda flotilla (1797) 171; with Egyptian expedition (1798) 172; in siege of Malta (1798–1800) 172–73; in Saint-Domingue expedition (1802) 173; in *Marins de la Garde* (1803) 173–74; with Boulogne flotilla (1804–5) 174; with *Grande Armée* (1805–7) 174–75; last naval exploit of (1807) 175; in Bailén campaign (1808) 169, 175–80 captain (1808) 180; in Wagram campaign (1809) 180; rear-admiral and general (1809–14) 180–81; killed at Brienne (1814) xiii, 181
Bastille, Fall of (14 July 1789) xi, xx
Batavia, Dutch East Indies: (1772) 26; (1791) 96; (1796–98) 43–44, 162; (1804) 122
Batavian Republic (1795–1806) 97, 162–63
Baudin, Nicolas, Australian expedition of (1801–03) 142–43
Bay of Bengal, (1799) 44; (1809–10) 145, 187–88
Bay of Tombeau (1799) 44, 201
Bayonne, Spanish royal family held at (1808) 176

Beauharnais, Hortense, Queen of Holland 93
Belle-Île: (1793) 21; (1795) 23
Benghazi, Libya (1801) 76
Beresford, Commodore John 208
Bergeret, Captain Jacques 184
Berlin Decrees (1806) 91
Berry, Commodore Edward 90
Berthier, General Alexandre 75
Berthollet, Claude 75
Berwick, HMS, capture of (1795) 33, 80–81, 140
Beugnot, Jacques 154
Blackwood, Captain Henry 28, 90, 163
Blanquet du Chayla, Vice-Admiral Armand-Simon 68–69
Blücher, Marshal Gerhard 156–57
BONAPARTE, Jérôme (1784–1860) xii: typifies Napoleon's nepotism 149; sails with Ganteaume (1801) 149–50; with Saint-Domingue expedition (1801–2) 13, 150; character and flight of, to United States (1803) 150; marriage of, quashed by Napoleon 151; junior captain (1805) 151; commands *Vétéran* (1805) 152; sails with Willaumez (1805–6) 152–53, 166; flight of, to France 153–54; rear-admiral, quits Navy (1806) 154; King of Westphalia (1807–12) 154–55; in Russia (1812) 155; in 1814 collapse, 155; at Waterloo (1815) 156–57; in exile (1815–47) 157; under Second Republic and Empire (1848–60) 158
Bonaparte, Joseph, King of Naples and Spain 149, 154
Bonaparte, Letizia ('Madame Mère') 150–51, 157–58
Bonaparte, Louis, King of Holland 97–98, 154, 215
Bonaparte, Louis-Napoleon, *see* Napoleon III

Bonaparte, Lucien, 149, 151, 157

BONAPARTE, NAPOLEON, General, First Consul and Emperor (1769–1821): family of 149; in Italy (1796–97) 83, 170–71; in Egypt and Syria (1798–99) 52, 58, 74–75, 82–84, 89, 103, abandons Army of Egypt, returns to France (1799) 75, 84–5; First Consul (1799–1804) 12, 24, 75, 91; approves Baudin expedition (1800) 142; blind to realities of sea power 57–58, 91, 208; plans of, to invade England (1804–5) 14, 17, 60, 77, 131, 143, 174, 165; and Ulm-Austerlitz campaign (1805) x, 28, 144, 174–75; Jena-Auerstädt campaign (1806) 154; peace with Russia after Friedland (1807) 175; provokes Peninsular War (1807–8) 175–76; Aspern-Essling and Wagram (1809) 154, 180; in Russia (1812) 154–55; Leipzig campaign (1813) 155, 181; first abdication of (17814) 78, 98, 124, 137, 155, 194, 202, 209; and the 'Hundred Days' (March–June 1815) x, 6, 18, 34,78, 92, 99, 104, 137, 194, 202; and Waterloo (1815) x, 6, 18, 78, 92, 99, 104, 124, 156–57; second abdication and exile of, 99, 104, 157; reburied in Invalides 158

Botany Bay: (1788) 160; (1802) 143

Bougainville, Comte Louis-Antoine de 29, 159

Boulogne, invasion flotilla at: (1801) 12–13; (1803–5) 54, 97, 111, 143, 174, 185; (1810) 181

Bourmont, General Louis-Auguste de 194

Bouvet, Captain Pierre-François 190–91, 193

Brazil (1795–96) 204

Brest; shipbuilding at (1806–13) 92

Brest fleet and commanders: (1792–93) Morard de Galles 21, 198; (1793–96) Villaret-Joyeuse 21–23, 36, 73, 116–17, 198, 204; (1796–97) Morard de Galles 5, 23, 57, 131, 141; (1797–99) Bruix 51–53, 59, 117, 204; (1800) Latouche-Tréville 12; (1800–4) Truguet 6, 201; (1804–5) Ganteaume 77, 165–66, 185, 202

Bridport, Vice-Admiral Lotd Alexander 117

Brienne, Batttle of (1814) 181

BRUEYS D'AIGALLIERS, Vice-Admiral François-Paul, Comte (1753–98): varied command experience of 65; first ships of 61; in Zélé, escapes Saints defeat (1782) 66–67; in Toulon fleet (1792) 67; jailed under Terror (1793) 67; commodore and rear–admiral (1796–97) 67; captures Ionian Islands (1797) 67, 82; in Egyptian expedition (1798) 68; relations of, with Bonaparte 68–69; takes Malta 69; flawed deployment of, in Aboukir Bay 69, 103; killed in action 70

BRUIX, Vice-Admiral Etienne-Eustache (1759–1805): born on Saint-Domingue 49; in American Revolutionary War 49–50; Saint-Domingue survey cruise of (1784–88) 50; captain (1793) 50; cashiered under Terror (1793) 50; in Brest fleet under Villaret (1794–95) 51; in Irish expedition (1796) 51; rear-admiral (1797) 51; Navy Minister (1798) 52; supports Irish rebels (1798) 52; leads 'Bruix's Cruise' to Mediterranean (1799) 49, 52–53, 59, 117, 131; fateful legacy of same 53, 59; last months of 54

Brumaire coup d'état (1799) xxi, 75

Buller, Captain Sir Edward 134

Burgos: (1808) 175; (1810) 180

Burnel, Etienne-Laurent 41, 111

Bylandt, Rear-Admiral Lodewijk van 90
Byron, Admiral Sir John 101

Cadiz; and 'Great Siege' of Gibraltar
    (1778–83) 16, 204; and Richery's
    cruise (1795–96) 140–141; (1798)
    163; and 'Bruix's Cruise' (1799)
    52–53; and Algeciras, 'Gut of
    Gibraltar' battles (1801) 118–21,
    205–6; and Trafalgar campaign
    (1805) 27–28, 62, 112–13, 135,
    207; (1808) 28–29, 175–6,
    178–79; (1823) 147, 194
Cæsarea (1799) 84
Cagliari (1793) 4, 12, 56, 67, 130, 160
Cairo (1798–99) 74, 82–3
Calais (1805) 174
Calcutta, HMS, capture of (1805) 207
Calder, Vice–Admiral Sir Robert 61, 112,
    134, 207
Campana, General Francisco 95
Camperdown, Battle of (1797) x, xiii,
    93, 97
Canada: (1750) 220; (1752) x, 3; (1781)
    111; (1796) 141
Canary Islands: (1796) 41, 199;
    (1805) 207
Cancale Squadron (1794) 73
Cap-Français: (1793) 102, 170;
    (1803) 170
Cap Haïtien: (1793) 40; (1802) 111
Cape Bon (1799) 75
Cape Breton (1781) 11
Cape Finisterre, Battle of (1805) xxi, 61,
    112, 134
Cape Henry: (1781) 11; (1782) 160
Cape Leeuwin (1801) 142
Cape Lopez (Gabon) 124
Cape Noli, Battle of (1795) 33, 81,
    130, 140
Cape of Good Hope: (1772) 26; (1783)
    108; (1792) 160; (1796) 162, 199;
    (1799) 200; (1805) 123
Cape St Vincent, Battle of (1797) x
Cape Town (1805) 123–24

Cape Verde Islands (1806) 124, 153
Cartagena: (1799) 53; (1801) 120; (1805)
    17, 61, 131
Cassel 154–55
Castaños, General Xavier 178–79
Castiglione, Battle of (1796) 171
Catherine of Württemberg, Queen
    154, 157
Cayenne: (1765) 20; (1787) 102;
    (1806) 153
Ceylon (1805–6) 122–23
Chabreis (Chobra Kyt) 82–83
Chaptal, Jean (1802), 150
Chabreis (Chobra Kyt) 82–83
Chaptal, Jean, on Jérôme Bonaparte 150
Charbonnier, Captain 81
Charles, Archduke of Austria (1809) 180
Charles III of Spain, Order of 194
Charles X, King of France 194–95, 157
Chausey Islands 197
Cherbourg: (1784–89) 11, 203–4; ship–
    building at (1806–13) 92, 144;
    (1809–14) 209
Chesapeake Bay (Virginia Capes), Battle of
    (1781) 50, 56, 66, 87, 197, 204
Chlopicki, General Gregor 95
Choiseul, Duc de 55
Christophe, Henri 164
Cincinnatus, Order of 11, 102
Civitavecchia (1798) 69
Cochrane, Rear-Admiral Lord Thomas:
    (1801) 118; (1806) 153;
    (1809) 209
Collingwood, Vice-Admiral Sir Cuthbert:
    at Trafalgar (1805) 63, 113, 135;
    victory despatch of, censored by
    Admiralty 63; never relieved, death
    of at sea x, 136–37
Colli-Ricci, General Luigi 95
Combined fleets, Franco-Spanish:
    (1778–83) xx, 204, 219; (1779)
    xxi, 52–53, 118, 131; (1801) xxi,
    118–21, 131, 205–6; (1805) 28,
    60–63, 77, 112–14, 131–35, 207
Committee of Public Safety 4, 12, 67

Comores Arch (1810) 188–89

Compagnie des Indes: Villaret-Joyeuse 20; Ganteaume 72; Magon 108

Concarneau (1806) 186

Constantinople: (1787) 4; (1796) 82

Constitutional monarchy, French (1789–92) xi, 3, 6, 11–12, 51, 88, 102, 130, 198

Consulate, French (1799–1804) xi–xii, 5, 12, 24, 59, 75, 91, 97, 142, 150–51

Continental System (1806) 28, 98

Convention, National xi–xii, 4

Copenhagen, Battle of (1801) x, 191

Cordoba (1808) 176–77, 179

Corfu: (1797) 67; (1798) 74; (1808) 77, 136

Cornic, Rear-Admiral Pierre-François xiii

Cornwallis, General Lord Charles, at Yorktown (1782) 50, 66, 108, 197

Cornwallis, Admiral Sir William (1805) 166

Coromandel Coast: (1785) 100; (1796) 42; (1804) 122

Corsica: (1794–95) 33–34, 80; (1799) 75

COSMAO-KERJULIEN, Rear-Admiral Julien-Marie (1761–1825): in American Revolutionary War 129–30; under Truguet (1792–93) 130; and Martin (1795) 130; in 'Bruix's Cruise' (1799) 131; under Villeneuve (1805) 131–32; captures Diamond Rock 132–33; in Cape Finisterre battle 134; Trafalgar and aftermath 135–36; rear-admiral (1806) 136; in Toulon fleet under Ganteaume (1808–10) 136–37; last actions of (1813–14) 137

Crimean War (1854–56) xiii

Curtis, Captain Lucius 192

Dance, Commodore Nathaniel 122

Dannebrog, Danish Royal Order of 194

Danzig (1807) 175

Dardanelles (1784) 4

Daugier, Captain François-Henri 174–75

D'Auribueau, Lieutenant Jean-Louis 161

Davout, Marshal Louis-Nicolas 155

Decaen, General Charles, Governor: (1803) 121–22; (1810) 190–1, 193; surrenders Île-de-France (1810) 194

Decouz, General Pierre 181

DECRÈS, Vice-Admiral Denis, Duke (1761–1820) xi, xiii: in American Revolutionary War 87–88; to Île-de-France, under Saint-Félix 88; under Villeneuve (1796) 89; rear-admiral (1798) 89; commands frigates under Brueys (1798) 82, 89; in siege of Malta (1798–1800) 89–90; captured in *Guillaume-Tell* (1800) 90–91; Napoleon's longest-serving Navy Minister (1801–14) 87, 91–92; in 'Hundred Days' (1815) 92; murder of (1820) 92

Den Helder, Ver Huell defends (1813–14) 98

D'Entrecasteaux, Rear-Admiral Joseph-Antoine-Bruni, Chevalier 3, 160–61, 164

Derna, Libya (1801) 76, 205

Desaix, General Louis-Charles 205

Dessalines, Jean-Jacques 164

D'Estaing, Admiral *Comte* xi, 4, 15, 32, 41, 51, 101

Destouches, Rear-Admiral Charles-René Sochet 10–11

Diamond Rock, 'HMS' 17: captured by Cosmao (1805) 132–33, 186

Directory, French (1795–99), xi, 23, 41, 51, 67, 71, 74, 88, 111, 142

Dogger Bank, Battle of (1781) 96

Dombrowski, General Jan 95

Dominica: (1779) 32; (1780) 204

Dordelin, Rear-Admiral Alain-Joseph 131

Dorsenne, General Jean-Marie 180

Dos de Mayo (1808) 176

Duckworth, Vice-Admiral Sir John 153

Duguay-Trouin, Admiral René 26

Dumanoir le Pelley, Vice-Admiral 63, 140–41, 207
Duncan, Vice-Admiral Adam xiii
Dunkirk (1804–5) 174
DUPERRÉ, Vice-Admiral Guy-Victor, Baron (1775–1846): joins wartime Navy (1793) 183; captured (1796) 184; commander (1802) 184; and Jérôme Bonaparte (1805–6) 185–86; East Indies cruise of (1809–10) 187–8; and Grand-Port battle (1810) 189–93; in Île-de-France capitulation (1810) 194; defends Venice (1814) 194; blockades Cadiz (1823) 194; captures Algiers (1830) 194; last honours of 195
Dupont, General Pierre; and Bailén capitulation (1808) 175–79
Dutch East Indies: (1772) 26; (1785) 108; (1791) 96; (1796–99) 4, 43–45, 162, 200; (1803) 122
Dutch Republic 95–96, 102, 161; conquest of (1795) 97, 162

East India Company, British 43, 108–9, 122–23, 145, 162, 187, 199
Eckmühl, Battle of (1809) 180
Egypt; Truguet's mission to (1786) 4; French expedition to (1798) 12, 52, 58, 68–69, 82–84, 89, 103; attempts to relieve Army of 52–53, 59, 76–77, 85–86, 149–50
El Arish (1799) 83
Elba: (1801) 118; (1815) 155
ÉMERIAU, Vice-Admiral Maxime-Julien (1762–1845): in American Revolutionary War 101–2; commander (1792) 102; captain (1794) 103; under Villeneuve (1796) 103; to Malta and Egypt, wounded at Aboukir Bay (1798) 103–4; with Ostend invasion flotilla (1803) 104; commands Toulon fleet (1811–13) 104; last honours of 104–5

Empire, French: proclaimed (1804) 6, 59, 77; spread of (1806–13) boosts French naval construction x, 92
Encounter Bay (1802) 143
England, plans to invade: (1797–8) 73–4; (1803–5) 53, 59–60, 77, 97, 111–12, 131
Eylau-Friedland campaign (1807) 175

Ferdinand VII, King of Spain 194
Ferino, General Pietro 95
Ferrand, General Jean-Louiis 18
Ferris, Captain Solomon 119
Ferrol (1805) 62, 112, 134–35, 207
Fielding, Commodore Charles 96
First of June, campaign and Battle of (1794) 21–23, 36–37, 73, 103, 140, 198, 204
Flinders, Matthew 143
Flotte de Beuzidou, Rear-Admiral Paul de 66
Flottes, Rear-Admiral Marquis Joseph de xi, 3
Forfait, Pierre-Alexandre, Navy Minister 91
Fort Chambray, Malta 173
Fort Culabo, India 88
Fort Dauphin, Saint-Domingue 49, 111
Fort Desaix, Martinique 24
Fort Lamalgue, Toulon 67
Fort Ricasoli, Malta 173
Fort Royal, Martinique: (1805) 132–33; (1806) 153
Fouché, Joseph 157
Foul Point, Madagascar 108
Fréjus (1795) 34, 131
Friedland, Battle of (1807) 175

Galiano, Commodore Don Diego 113
GANTEAUME, Vice-Admiral Honoré-Joseph (1755–1818): 'Napoleon's Admiral' 71; merchant service origins 71–72; in American Revolutionary War 72; receives first command from Suffren 72; in

First of June campaign and battle 73; under Villeneuve (1796) 73; in Egyptian expedition (1798) 74; promoted admiral by Bonaparte 74; conveys Bonaparte back to France (1799) 75; attempts to relieve Army of Egypt (1801) 76–77; takes over Brest fleet from Truguet (1804) 6, 77; key player in Napoleon's invasion plan (1805) 77, 165–66; commands Toulon fleet (1808–10) 77, 136; supports abdication of Napoleon (1814) 78; final honours of 78

Garde de Paris (1808) 176–77

Gardner, Admiral Lord 165

Gaza (1799) 83

Genoa: (1795) 33; (1799) 53; French shipbuilding at (1806–13) 92, 137

Genoa Gulf (Cape Noli), Battle of (1795) 33, 81, 130

Germany: (1800) 12; (1807) 154; French loss of (1813) 155

Gibraltar: 'Great Siege' of (1778–83) 16, 204; (1795) 140; (1799) 52–53; (1801) 76, 118–20, 205; (1805) 61–62, 135

Gold Coast (1790) 139

Gorée (1786) 32

Gourdon, Vice-Admiral Adrien-Louis 194

Granada (1808) 178

Grande Armée: (1803–5) 91, 173; in Ulm-Austerlitz campaign (1805) 174–75; in Jena-Auerstädt campaign (1806) 144, 154; in Eylau-Friedland campaign (1807) 175; in Aspern-Wagram campaign (1809) 154, 180; destroyed in Russia (1812) 155, 181

Grand-Port, Batttle of (1810) 146, 188–93

Grande Rivière (1810) 190–91

Granger, Captain William 201

Grasse, Admiral *Comte* de xii, 4, 50, 55–56, 66–67, 87, 102, 108, 160, 197

Graves, Admiral Sir Thomas, 66

Gravina, Admiral Don Federico 13, 61–63, 112–13, 132–34, 136

Grenada: (1778–79) 15, 32, 72, 101; (1805) 61

Grimouard, Vice-Admiral Nicolas-René, *Comte,* guillotined xi, 3, 41, 51

Grodno (1812) 155

Groix, Battle of (1795) xx, 23, 51, 117

Guadeloupe: (1772) 35; (1782) 67; (1798) 204; (1801) 13; (1805) 17, 61, 133–34; (1806) 152; (1809) 208–9; (1814–15) 124

Guiana: (1763) 9; (1780) 129; (1787) 102; (1797) 24

Guichen, Vice-Admiral *Comte* de 4, 27, 40, 66, 108, 204

Guillaume-Tell, last fight of (1800) xxi, 90–92, 134

'Gut of Gibraltar', Battle of (1801) 120–21, 206

Haifa (1799) 83

HAMELIN, Rear-Admiral Jacques-Félix Emmanuel (1768–1839): merchant service, origins of 139; in First of June battle (1794) 140; and recapture of *Censeur,* Canadian cruise of, under Richery (1795–96) 140–41; in Irish expedition, under Dumanoir (1796) 141; and Baudin expedition (1800–3) 142–43; in *Marins de la Garde* (1803–5) 143–44, 174; to the East Indies in *Vénus* (1808) 144–45; East Indies cruise of (1808–10) 145–46; and Grand-Port battle (1810) 146, 188, 192–93; captured (1810) 146; last appointments of (1811–23) 146–47

Hannibal, HMS, capture of (1801) 119, 205

Hartog, Dirk 143

Harvey, Captain John 36–37

Havana, Cuba (1806) 167

Hawke, Admiral Lord Edward xii, 9

Hoche, General Lazare 5, 117, 141
Hohenlinden, Battle of (1800) 12
Holland, Kingdom of (1806–10)
    97–98, 154
Holy Spirit Order of 18
Hood, Admiral lord 33
Hood, Captain Samuel 70,130
Hotham, Admiral Lord 33–34, 37, 80–81,
    130–31, 140
Hougoumont (1815) 156
Howe, Admiral Lord Richard xiii, 21: in
    First of June campaign and battle
    (1794) 22–23, 36, 73, 116,
    140, 198
Hughes, Admiral Sir Edward 20
Humbert, General Jean-Joseph (1798) 52
'Hundred Days' (March–June 1815) x, 6,
    18, 34, 78, 92, 99, 104, 137,
    194, 202
Hyères Islands (Fréjus), Battle of (1795)
    34, 37, 81, 131

Île-Bourbon (Réunion, 1809–10) 145–46
    187–88
Île-de-France (Mauritius): (1773–83) 20,
    26; (1783–89) 108; (1792–93) 50,
    109, 161; (1794–95) 110, 161;
    (1796–99) 41–44 110–11, 162–3,
    199–201; British capture, of (1800)
    201; second capture of (1810) 45
Île de Groix (1808) 186
Île d'Oléron (1797) 24
Île de la Passe, Île de France (1810)
    89–91, 193
Île-du-Roi, Mergui Arch. (1796) 42, 199
Îles des Saintes, Battle of (1809) 208–9
Imperial Guard 78, 143, 157, 173–74,
    180–81
India: (1781–3) 20–21, 27, 72, 108–10,
    (1796–99) 5, 41–44, 199–200;
    (1803) 121–22; (1809) 145, 187
Indies station, French: (1777–83) 20–21;
    (1781–83) 72; (1783–92) 108–9;
    (1793) 50, 88; (1793–96) 109–10,

161; (1796–99) 41–44, 110–11,
    162, 199–201; (1803–6) 121–2;
    (1809–10) 144–46, 187–94
Ionian Islands, captured by Brueys (1797)
    34, 52, 58, 67, 82, 221; (1808) 77
Ireland: Brest fleet expedition to (1796)
    5, 12, 23, 51–52, 57, 73, 89, 103,
    117, 141; (1798) 52
Isles of Loss (1798) 163
Italy; Bonaparte conquers North (1796–
    97) 58, 82, 170–71; (1800) 12, 118

Jaen (1808) 178, 180
Jaffa (1799) 83
Jamaica (1782) 66; (1783) 88; (1806) 153,
    166
James, William 90
Jena-Auerstädt campaign (1806) 154, 175
July Revolution (1830) 157, 195
Junot, General Andoche 175

Keats, Captain Richard 120
Keith, Admiral Lord George 76, 84–85
Keppel, Admiral Augustus 27
Kerguelen, Rear-Admiral Yves-Joseph 26
Kersaint, Vice-Admiral Armand-Guy,
    guillotined xi, 12, 41, 51
Killala (1798) 52
Kilmaine, General Charles 95
Kinsbergen, Admiral Jan Hendrik Van 96
Kniazewicz, General Carl 95
Königsberg (1807) 175

La Carolina (1808) 177
La Force prison (1793) 12
La Pérouse, Commodore Jean-François,
    Comte 11; search for (1791–93)
    160–61
La Rochelle: (1796) 162; (1798) 163
Lafayette, Marquis de 10
Lagrange, General Joseph 17
Lake Garda (1796–97) 171
Lambert, Captain Henry 192–93
Lampedusa (1799) 84, 172

Landais, Rear-Admiral Pierre xiii

Landshut, Battle of (1809) 180

Lannes, General Jean 75

LATOUCHE-TRÉVILLE, Vice-Admiral Louis-René-Madeleine Levassor, *Comte de* (1745–1804): in Quiberon Bay battle (1759) 9; colonial Army service of (1768–72) 10; in American Revolutionary War (1776–82) 10–11; prisoner of war (1782–83) 11; and Revolutionary politics (1789–91) 11–12; in Toulon fleet under Truguet, jailed under Jacobin Terror (1792–94) 12; commands Boulogne flotilla, defeats Nelson (1801) 12–13; commands Rocherfort squadron, In Saint-Domingue expedition (1801–2) 13; commands Toulon fleet, duel of wits with Nelson (1803–4) 14; early death of (1804) 14

Lavilléon, Rear-Admiral Jean-Baptiste, *Comte de* 3

Lazowski, General Josef 95

Leander, HMS, capture of (1798) 59, 90

Leclerc, General Victor-Emmanuel 13, 111, 150

Leeward Islands (1768) 10

Le Feretier, Acting Captain Jean-Baptiste 145, 187

Le Gardeur de Tilly, Rear-Admiral Armand 3

Le Havre: (1786) 11; (1800) 142; (1803–4) 143, 174; shipbuilding at (1806–13) 144

Legion of Honour 83: Baste 180; Bruix 54; Cosmao 137; Decrès 92; Duperrée 195; Émeriau 104; Ganteaume 77; Hamelin 147; Latouche-Tréville 14; Lhermitte 202; Linois 125; Magon 111; Martin 34; Missiessy 18; Rosily 29; Sercey 45; Truguet 6; Ver Huell 98; Villaret-Joyeuse 24; Willaumes 168

Legnago 170

Leipzig campaign (1813) 155, 181

Leissegues, Rear-Admiral Corenti-Urbain xiii, 152, 185

Lennox, Commodore Charles 43, 122, 162

Leoben, Treaty of (1797) 171

L'Hermite, Rear-Admiral Pierre-Louis 197

LHERMITTE, Rear-Admiral Jean-Mathieu-Adrien (1766–1826): boy Navy volunteer (1780) 197; in American Revolutionary War (1780–83) 197; peacetime service (1784–92) 198; first captain of captured *Thames*, in First of June Battle (1794) 198; to Île-de-France with Sercey (1796) 199; commands *Preneuse* (1798–99) 44, 199–201; captured (1799) 201; commands *Regulus,* last war cruise of (1805–6) 201–2; last years and honours of 202

Libya: (1799) 75; (1801) 76

Ligny, Battle of (1815) 156

LINOIS, Vice-Admiral Charles-Alexandre Léon Durand, *Comte* (1761–1848): in American Revolutionary War (1778–83) 115; to Île-de-France under Decrès (1793) 116; commands *Atalante*, captured (1795) 116–17; captain (1795) 117; in Irish expedition (1796) and 'Bruix's Cruise' (1799) 117; in Toulon fleet under Ganteaume (1800) 118; sails for Cadiz (1801) 118; victor at Algeciras 118–19; in 'Gut of Gibraltar' battle 120–21; in Saint-Domingue expedition (1802) 121; to Île-de-France in *Marengo* (1803) 121; Indies war cruise of (1803–5) 122–23; in captivity (1806–14) 124; court-martial and acquittal of (1816) 124; last honours of 125

Lisbon: (1805) 151; (1807) 175

Livorno: (1794) 33; (1801) 118

Lonato, Battle of (1796) 171
Lorient: (1780) 159; (1790) 21; (1796)
    57, 103; (1804) 165; (1805) 202;
    ship-building at (1806–13) 92;
    (1808) 186; (1809) 167, 208
Louis XV, King 3
Louis XVI, King 3, 11–12, 102
Louis XVII 16, 32
Louis XVIII, King 6, 78, 99, 104, 124,
    147, 194, 209
Louis, Captain Thomas 103
Louis-Philippe, King 6, 45, 105, 147, 168,
    195
Louisbourg (1750–58) 31
Louisiade Archipelago 161
Louisiana 13
Lucas, Captain Jean-Jacques 113
Luckner, General Nikolas 95
Luxembourg prison 41

Macdonald, General Etienne-Jacques 53
Madagascar 108, 188
Madras, Battle of: (1782) 20; (1782–83)
    20–21; (1804–5) 122–3;
    (1809) 145
Madrid: (1797) 5; (1805) 28, 62; (1808)
    27, 176–77, 179
MAGON DE MÉDINE, Rear-Admiral
    Charles-René (1763–1805): Île-de-
    France planter family of 107, 109;
    in American Revolutionary War
    108; to Île-de-France under Rosily
    (1784–92) 108–9; and Saint-Félix
    (1792–93) 109; in action under
    Renaud (1793) 110; under Sercey
    (1796–98) 110–11; flag captain
    to Villaret (1801) 111; to Saint-
    Domingue (1801–2) 111; captures
    Fort Dauphin, promoted rear-
    admiral (1802) 111; commands
    Rochefort squadron (1803) 111;
    with Boulogne flotilla (1803) 111;
    joins Combined Fleet at Martinique
    (1805) 112; after Cape Finisterre
    battle, friction with Spaniards at

Cadiz 112–13; killed at Trafalgar
    113–14
Mahé, India 108
Malacca Strait (1796) 42
Malartic, Comte de, Governor 41–44, 109
    162–3
Malher, General Jean-Pierre 176
Malta: French capture of (1798) 58, 69,
    103, 172; blockade and siege of
    (1798–1800) 52, 59, 84, 89, 172;
    attempts to relieve (1799–1800)
    85, 172–73; surrender of (1800)
    59, 173
Mangalore (1798) 44, 199–200
Mantua, sieges of (1796–97) 171
Marabout (1798) 69, 82
Marengo, Battle of (1800) 12, 118,
Marie-Louise, Empress 155
Marins de la Garde 143–44, 173–74:
    (1805) 174–75; in Bailén campaign
    (1808) 175–80; (1809) 180;
    (1810–11) 180–81
Marmara, Sea of (1784) 4
Marmont, General Auguste-Frédéric 75
Martinique: (1767–70) 10, 26; (1777–83)
    32, 40, 49, 66, 101; (1788) 67;
    (1790–93) 102; (1801–3) 13, 150;
    (1804–5) 17, 24, 60–1, 112,
    132–33; (1806) 153; Villaret
    surrenders (1809) 24, 167, 208
MARTIN, Vice-Admiral Pierre, Comte
    (1752–1820): Canadian birth
    of x, 31; joins Navy (1769) 31;
    in American Revolutionary War
    (1778–83) 32; West African
    service of (1786–92) 32; early
    promotion to rear-admiral (1793)
    32; achievement of, commanding
    Toulon fleet (1794–97) 32–33;
    in Cape Noli (Genoa Gulf) battle
    (1795) 33, 81, 130, 140; and
    Hyères (Fréjus) battle (1795) 34,
    81, 131; succeeded by Brueys
    (1797) 34; last honours of 34
Marulaz, General Jacob 95

Mascarene Islands, *see* Île Bourbon
Massena, General André 53, 170
Mathilde of Württemberg, Princess 158
Maurice, Captain James 132–33
Mauritius, *see* Île-de-France
Mayotte Is, Comores (1810) 188
Mazzaredo, Admiral, Don José de 52–53
Mergui Arch. (1796) 42
Messina Strait (1801) 76
Milan (1796) 170
Military Merit, Order of 99
Miller, Captain Ralph 103
Mincio River (1796) 171
Minorca: (1795) 81; (1799) 53; (1800) 91
MISSIESSY, Vice-Admiral Edouard-
    Thomas de Burgues, *Comte*
    (1756–1837): early service of
    (1766–77) 15; in American
    Revolutionary War (1778–83)
    15–16; Mediterranean frigate service
    (1789–92) 16; imprisoned under
    Terror (1793) 16; unemployed
    after Toulon revolt (1794–1800)
    16; Maritime Prefect (1802) 16;
    commands Rochefort squadron
    (1804–5) 16–17; Caribbean cruise
    of (1805) 17–18; commands Scheldt
    Flotilla, defends Antwerp (1808–14)
    18; last honours of 18
Monge, Gaspard 75
Montagu, Rear-Admiral George 23
Montalban (1792) 4, 56, 67, 139
Montserrat (1805–6) 17, 153
Morard de Galles, Vice-Admiral Justin 3,
    5, 21, 23, 57, 72, 117, 141
Moreau, General Jean-Victor 53
Moreno, Vice-Admiral Don Juan de
    120–21, 205–6
Morice, Captain Nicolas 189–90
Morla, General Tomas de 29, 178
Moscow, retreat from (1812) 155, 181
Motte-Picquet, Admiral de la 26, 72, 101
Mozambique Channel: (1797) 43; (1804)
    122; (1810) 188

Murad Bey 83
Murat, Marshal Joachim 176–77
Muscat (1803) 121
Mysore 43, 108, 199

Naples; (1799) 37, 53, 75; (1805) 61–62
Napoleon I, Emperor, *see* BONAPARTE,
    NAPOLEON
Napoleon II 157
Napoleon III 96, 158, 215
Negapatam, Battle of (1782) 20
Nelson, Vice-Admiral Lord Horatio ix–x,
    xiii; in Cape Noli battle (1795) 33;
    and Hyères (Fréjus) battle 34; and
    Aboukir Bay battle (1798) 12, 58,
    69–70, 74, 89, 103–4, 119; and
    capture of *Généreux* (1800) 85–86;
    repulsed at Boulogne (1801) 13,
    118; at Copenhagen (1801) 191;
    blockades Toulon fleet (1803–5)
    14; and Trafalgar campaign and
    battle 61–63, 112, 133–45; killed
    at Trafalgar x, 63, 113
Nevis (1805) 17
New Britain (1793) 161
New Caledonia (1792–93) 160–61
New Guinea (1793) 161; (1802) 143
New Hebrides (1792) 161
New South Wales (1801) 142
New York: (1782) 10; (1793) 40
Newfoundland: (1764–70) 26; (1784–91)
    198; (1793) 40; (1796) 140–41;
    (1805–6) 152, 166
Newport, Rhode Island (1781) 10–11
Ney, Marshal Michel: at Quatre Bras
    (1815) 156; execution of 78, 124
Nice (1792) 4, 12, 56, 67, 139
Nicobar Islands (1809) 145
Nielly, Vice-Admiral Joseph-Marie 21–2,
    50, 116–17, 216–17
Niemen River (1812) 155
Nile, Battle of the, *see* Aboukir Bay
Norfolk, Va: (1793) 40; (1803) 150
North Sea: (1785) 36; (1795) 199

Norway (1795–96) 199

Oneglia (1792) 4, 12, 56, 140
Oran 80
Orvilliers, Admiral *Comte d'* 101, 108
Ostend (1803–5) 174
Ouverture, Toussaint l' 12, 164

Padang (1809) 145
Palermo (1799) 53, 75
Paris, Peace of: (1763) 10; (1783) 11, 21,
    102, 130, 160, 197
Parker, Admiral Sir Hyde 96
Patterson, Elizabeth 151
Peard, Captain Shuldham 85
Pellew Captain Sir Edward 25, 184
Peninsular War (1807–13): origins and
    outbreak of 28, 136, 175–77
Penmarch Point (1805) 207
Pensacola (1781) 40
'People's Representatives' 12, 21, 37,
    50, 109
PERRÉE, Rear-Admiral Jean-Baptiste-
    Emmanuel (1761–1800): welcomed
    by Republican Navy (1793) 79;
    frigate captain with Toulon fleet
    (1795) 80, 140; captures *Berwick*
    (1795) 80–81, 140; captured and
    released (1795) 81; raids West
    African coast (1795) 81; to Egypt
    under Brueys (1798) 82; commands
    Nile flotilla 74, 82–83; promoted
    rear-admiral by Bonaparte 83;
    supports siege of Acre (1799) 84;
    capture, release and court-martial
    of 84–85; leads Malta relief convoy
    (1800) 85; killed in action 86
Peschiera (1796) 170–71
Petit, Rear-Admiral Jean-Nicolas 208
Philippine Company, Spanish 43, 111, 163
Philippine Islands: (1783) 108; (1790) 27;
    (1796–99) 41, 43, 111; (1805) 123
Piacenza (1796) 170
Pichegru, General Jean-Charles 64

Pillau (1807) 175
Pléville le Pelley, Rear-Admiral Georges-
    René 51–52, 220–22
Pointe du Diable, Île-de-France (1810) 189
Pondichéry: (1788) 27, 108; (1793)
    109–10; (1803) 121
Poniatowski, Marshal Josef 95
Po River (1796) 170
Port-au-Prince, Saint-Domingue: (1786)
    116; (1802) 13, 150
Port Jackson, NSW (1802) 143
Port-Louis/Napoleon, Île-de-France (1810)
    146, 188–91, 193–94
Port Mahon, Minorca 91
Porto-Ferraio, Elba (1801) 118
Portugal: (1807–8) 28, 175
Prigny, Captain Mathieu 113
Primarolo, Battle of (1796) 171
Provédien, Battle of (1782) 20
Prussia: (1792–93) 102, 116; (1806) 154,
    175; (1813–14) 181; (1815) 156
Pulo Auro, Sumatra (1804) 122
Puységur, *Comte* Antoine de 50
Pym, Captain Samuel 190–2
Pyramids, Battle of (1798) 83

'Quadrilateral' fortresses (1796) 170–71
Quatre-Bras (1815) 156
Quiberon Bay, Battle of (1759) 9–10

Red Sea (1786) 4, 27
régiment de la Rochefoucauld 10
Reichstadt, Duke of *see* Napoleon II
Reille, General Honoré-Charles 156
Renaud, Commodore Jean-Marie 110, 161
RENAUDIN, Rear-Admiral Jean-François
    (1750–1809): early service of 35–6;
    commander and captain, in Brest
    fleet under Villaret (1794) 36; hero
    of last fight of *Vengeur,* in First of
    June battle 36–37; rear-admiral,
    reinforces Toulon fleet 37; in
    Hyères (Fréjus) battle (1795) 37;
    last appointments of (1799) 37

Réunion, *see* Île Bourbon
Richery, Rear-Admiral Joseph de 140–41
Rio de Janeiro (1762–63) 26
Rivière, Rear-Admiral Charles-Joseph-
    Mascarennes, *Chevalier* de 3
Rivière-Noire, Île-de-France
    (1809–10) 146
Rivoli, Batttle of (1797) 171
Robespierre, Maximilien, tyranny and fall
    of (1794) xi, 4, 21–22, 41, 57, 80,
    88, 116
Rochambeau, General Donatien-Marie,
    Vicomte 165
Rochefort: shipbuilding at (1806–13) 92
Rochefort Squadron: (1761–62) 10;
    (1796) 199; commanders of, Bruix
    (1799–1802) 53; Latouche-Tréville
    (1801) 13; Missiessy (1804–5)
    16–18, 60, 207; Allemand (1805–
    9) 18, 207–8; Truguet (1809) 6;
    Willaumez (1809) 167–68
Rochegude, Rear-Admiral Henri, *Marquis*
    de 39
Rodney, Admiral Lord George 40, 50, 56,
    66, 102, 108, 160, 197, 204
Rodriguez Island (1810) 187–88
Rondeau, Commodore Jacques-Mélanie 73
ROSILY-MESROS, Vice-Admiral François-
    Etienne de (1748–1832); in Seven
    Years War (1762–63) 26; sails with
    Kerguelen (1770–73) 26; captured
    in Channel (1778) 27; in American
    Revolutionary War (1780–83) 27;
    prolonged Indies station survey by
    (1784–88) 27; Director of Charts
    and Maps (1795–1805) 27; chosen
    as Villeneuve's successor (1805)
    27–28; at Cadiz (1805–8) 28;
    surrenders French Cadiz squadron
    (1808) 29, 178; last posts and
    honours of 29
Rosily-Vieuxbourg, Rear-Admiral
    Guillaume-François 25

Rotterdam: French shipbuilding at
    (1806–13) 92; Truguet defends
    (1813) 3, 6, 98
Roveredo, Battle of (1796) 171
Rowley, Commodore Josias 146, 193
Rusca, General Giovanni 95
Russia: (1799) 5, 52; (1805–7) 28, 175;
    (1812) 98, 155, 181; (1813–14)
    155, 181

Sables d'Olonne (1806, 1809) 208
'Sabres of Honour': Bonaparte presents to
    Perrée 83; Decrès 91; and Linois
    121
Saint-André, Jeanbon 21–23, 37, 152
Saint-Domingue (Haiti): (1759) 49; (1760–
    70) 10, 20, 26, 35; (1772–73) 66;
    (1781–82) 169; (1784–88) 50, 116,
    160; (1790–93) 21, 36, 102, 139,
    170, 204; (1801–3) 13, 24, 77, 111,
    121, 150, 164–65; (1805) 17
Saint-Félix, Vice-Admiral Armand-
    Philippe, *Marquis* de 3, 20, 88, 109
Saint-Louis, Order of: Brueys 67; Cosmao
    137; Decrès 92; Duperré 194;
    Ganteaume 78; Hamelin 147;
    Latouche-Tréville 10; Lhermitte
    202; Linois 124; Martin 32;
    Missiessy 16; Rosily 27; Sercey 45;
    Troude 209; Truguet 4; Villaret-
    Joyeuse 21; Willaumez 160, 168
Saint-Malo: (1768) 73; (1798–99) 108,
    142; (1799–1800) 164; ship-
    building at (1806–13) 144
Saint Nicolas Mole, Saint-Domingue
    (1803) 164–65
Saintes Archipelago (Guadeloupe) 208–9
Salé (1763) 26
San Fiorenzo Bay (1795) 34, 80
San Ildefonso, Treaty of (1800) 13
San Salvador (Bahia) 153
Santa Cruz Arch. (1793) 161
Santa Cruz (Canary Islands) 199

Sardinia, Kingdom of, war with (1792) 4, 56, 67, 102, 130

Saumarez, Rear-Admiral Sir James, at Algeciras (1801) 118–20, 193

Savannah, Georgia (1779), failed French attack on 4, 15, 32, 72, 101

Savary, Rear-Admiral Daniel 13, 52

Savona (1799) 53

Scheldt flotilla: under Missiessy (1808–12) 18, 137, 146

Schiarino-Rizzino, Convention of (1814) 194

Schimmelpenninck, President Rutger Jan 97

Schönbrunn, Peace of (1809) 180

Second Coalition (1798–1800) 5, 12, 52, 205

Second Empire, French (1852) 158, 215

Second Republic, French (1848) 158

Sellabar, Sumatra (1803) 122

Senegal (1786) 32

SERCEY, Vice-Admiral Pierre-César-Charles-Guillaume *Marquis* de (1753–136): early career of 39; sails with Kerguelen (1772–74) 39; in American Revolutionary War (1778–83) 40; at Saint-Domingue (1793) 40; jailed under Terror (1794) 41; Indies squadron of (1796) 41; hostility of Île-de-France Governor and planters 41–44; attacks *Arrogant* and *Victorious* 42; retreats from China convoy (1797) 43; frigate losses of (1798–99) 43–44; end of Indies cruise (1799) 44; last years of 44–45

Sérurier, General Jean-Mathieu 171

Seven Years War (1756–63) xii, 3, 10, 15, 26, 32, 55, 159

Seville (1808) 176–77, 179

Sicily: (1799) 84; (1801) 76; (1808) 136

Sierra Leone (1798) 111

Sierra Morena (1808) 176, 178

Siméon, Joseph 154

Simon's Bay (1805–6) 123

Smith, Rear-Admiral Sir Sydney 75

Smyrna (1795) 73

Soult, Marshal NicolasJean-de-Dieu 3, 174

Spain: in First Coalition against France (1793) 102; and San Ildefonso Treaty (1800) 13; assists Saint-Domingue Expedition (1801) 13; renews alliance with France (1805) 123; revolt of (1808) 176–77; and Bailén victory of (1808) 177–79; (1810) 180; (1823) 147, 194; *see also* Combined fleets, Franco-Spanish

St Agustin, Madagascar (1810) 188

St Barthélemy (1781) 160

St Eustachius (1781) 160

St Helena: (1806) 152; Napoleon exiled to (1815) 157

St Kitts-Nevis: (1781–82) 66, 102; (1805) 17

St Lucia; (1778) 15; (1805) 17

St Paul, Île Bourbon (1809–10) 145, 187

St Pierre and Miquelon (1796) 141

St Vincent (1805) 61, 133

Staatsbewind, Dutch 97

States-General, French (1789) 11, 102

Stewart, Captain John 145–46

Stopford, Rear-Admiral Sir Robert 208

Strachan, Captain Sir Richard 207

Suffren, Admiral the Bailli de, Indies campaigns of (1781–83) 5, 20–21, 27, 72

Sumatra: (1796) 42, 110; (1803–4) 122; (1809) 145

Surcouf, Robert 23

Surveying cruises (1783–89): Truguet 4; Rosily 26; Bruix 50; Brueys 67

Swiftsure, HMS, capture of (1801) 76, 150

Switzerland (1799) 5

Syria, Bonaparte invades (1799) 83–84

Talleyrand-Périgord, Charles de 53

Tappanouti (1809) 145

Taranto (1801) 59

Tasmania: (1792) 160–61; (1801–2) 142–43

Tellicherry (1798) 44, 199–200

Tenerife (1805) 207

Terror, Jacobin (1793–94): xi, 21,50, 80, 130; Brueys 51, 67, Bruix 50–51, Decrès 88, Latouche-Tréville 12, 51, Magon 109, Missiessy 16, 51, Sercey 41, 51, Truguet 4, 51, Villeneuve 57

Tetuan 75

Thames, HMS, capture of (1793) 198

Thebes, Egypt (1799) 83

Thévenard, Vice–Admiral Antoine-Jean 3, 51, 85

Tilly, Rear-Admiral Gardeur de 3

Timor (1801–2) 143

Tipu Sultan, French support for 5, 43, 108, 199–200

Tobago (1781) 56, 204

Tombeau River, Île-de-France (1799) 44, 201

Tonga (1792) 161

Tortola (1806) 153

Toulon: revolt and reconquest of (1793) 4, 16, 57, 130; shipbuilding at (1806–13) 92

Toulon fleet and commanders: Truguet (1792–93) 4, 12, 16, 56, 130; Trogoff (1793) 16, 57; Martin (1794–97) 32–34, 57, 80–82, 89, 103, 130–31; Brueys (1797–98) 67–8; Ganteaume (1801–2) 77; Latouche-Tréville (1803–4) 13–14; Villeneuve (1804–5) 17, 60–62, 131–32; Ganteaume (1808–10) 77, 136; Cosmao (1810–11, 1812–14) 137

Trafalgar, Battle of (1805) x, 25, 28, 62–63, 113, 135, 166, 202, 207–8

Trieste (1815) 155

Trincomalee (1782) 20

Trinidad: (1789) 88; (1805) 61

Trogoff de Kerlessy, Rear-Admiral Jean-Honoré, *Comte* de 16, 57, 130

Troubridge, Rear-Admiral Sir Thomas 123

TROUDE, Rear-Admiral Amable-Gilles (1762–1824): merchant service origins 203; in American Revolutionary War 203–4; in First of June battle (1794) 204; in Brest fleet under Bruix (1799) 204; in Algeciras, 'Gut of Gibraltar' battles (1801) 205–6; to Saint-Domingue (1803) 207; with Rochefort squadron under Missessy, Allemand (1804–5) 207–8; commands at Lorient (1806–14); in Îles des Saintes battle (1809) 208–9; rear-admiral (1811); returns Louis XVIII to France (1814) 209

TRUGUET, Admiral Laurent-Jean-François (1752–1781): in American Revolutionary War, wounded at Savannah (1779) 4; survey cruise in *Tartelon* (1784) 4; rear-admiral, commands Toulon fleet (1792) 4, 12, 56, 67, 130, 139; leads first operation of naval war 3–4; replaced by Trogoff after failure at Cagliari (1793) 4, 130; jailed under Terror (1794) 4; Navy Minister (1795–97) 5; and Irish expedition (1796) 5, 57; Ambassador to Madrid (1797–98) 5; exiled (1799) 5; commands at Brest (1803) 6; protest resignation of, against proclamation of Empire (1804) 6; replaces Allemand at Rochefort (1809) 6; defends Rotterdam (1813) 6, 98; last honours of 6

Tunis: (1770) 66; (1794) 80

Turkey, joins Second Coalition (1798) 52, 74–75, 84

Tyler, Captain Charles 1123

Ulm-Austerlitz campaign (1805) 28, 44, 174–75

'United Irishmen' (1798) 52

United Provinces, *see* Dutch Republic

United States of America 26, 88; Jérôme
    Bonaparte in (1803–5) 150–51
Ushakov, Admiral Feodor 75
Ushant: (1794) 23; Battle of (1778) 102

Vado Bay (1799) 53
Valladolid (1808) 175–76
Valletta, Malta (1798–1800) 85, 172–73
Valmy, Battle of (1792) 116
Van Diemen's Land, see Tasmania
Vanikoro (1793) 161
Vanstabel, Rear-Admiral Pierr-Jean 21–23,
    41, 50, 73, 103
Vaubois, General Charles-Henri 59,
    89, 173
Vaudreuil, Admiral Marquis de, 4, 11,
    32, 102
Vedel, General Dominique 178–80
Vengeur (ex-Marseillais), last fight of (1794)
    36–37, 73 113
Venice: (1797) 82, 172; French ship-
    building at (1806–13) 92; Villaret-
    Joyeuse Governor of (1811) 24;
    Duperré defends (1814) 194
VER HUELL, Vice-Admiral Carel
    Hendrik, Count (1764–1845): early
    career of, in Dogger Bank battle
    (1781) 96; quells mutiny (1785)
    96; in retirement after fall of Dutch
    Republic (1795) 97; rear-admiral
    (1802), at Boulogne 97; Dutch
    Navy Minister (1805) 97; supports
    Louis Bonaparte as King of Holland
    (1806) 97–98; defends Walcheren
    (1809) 98; favoured by Napoleon
    (1807–12) 98; defends Den Helder
    (1813–4) 98; last honours of , as
    Peer of France 99
Verona (1796) 170–71
Vienna: (1805) 174; (1809) 180
Vieux-Port, Guadeloupe (1809) 208–9
Vigo (1805) 62, 134, 207
Villafranca (1792) 4, 56, 67, 139

VILLARET-JOYEUSE, Vice-Admiral
    Louis–Thomas, Comte (1748–
    1812): family and social pretensions
    of 19–20; under Suffren (1781–83)
    20–21; profits from mutinies
    under Morard (1793) 21 Brest fleet
    commander, rear-admiral 21, 32,
    36,; and First of June campaign
    and battle (1794) 21–23, 73,
    140, 198, 204; defeated at Groix
    (1795) 23, 117; protests against
    Irish expedition, sacked (1796) 5,
    23, 117; Deputy (1797), defends
    Surcouf 23; proscribed and exiled
    (1797) 24; leads Saint-Domingue
    expeditionary fleet (1801) 13, 24;
    Captain-General of Martinique
    (1802–8); 17, surrenders (1809)
    24, 208; Governor-General of
    Venice and death of (1811–12) 24
Villavicencio, Commodore Rafael de 134
VILLENEUVE, Vice-Admiral Pierre-
    Charles-Jean-Baptiste-Silvestre
    de (1763–1806): in American
    Revolutionary War (1778–83)
    55–56; in Toulon fleet under
    Truguet (1792–93) 56–57;
    cashiered under Terror (1793)
    57; port commander at Toulon
    (1795); rear-admiral, leads battle
    squadron to Lorient (1796) 57,
    73; in Egyptian expedition (1798)
    58, 82; escapes from Aboukir Bay
    disaster 58–59, 89; in siege and
    surrender of Malta (1798–1800)
    59, 89–90; vice-admiral, commands
    Rochefort squadron (1804) 59–60;
    replaces Latouche-Tréville as Toulon
    fleet commander 60; rôle of, in
    England invasion plan 60–61, 77,
    165; cruises to Caribbean with
    Combined Fleet (1805) 61,
    131–32; only fleet victory of 61,

133, in Cape Finisterre battle 61, 134; at Cadiz, Rosily picked to succeed 27–28, 62, 112–13; in Trafalgar battle 63, 113, 135; 'suicide' of (1806) 64

Vinegar Hill (1798) 52

Violette, Rear-Admiral Pierre-François 13, 208

Vizagapatam (1804) 122

Vlaminck, Willem de 143

Vlissingen (1803–5) 97

Wagram campaign and battle (1809) 154, 180

Walcheren (1809) 98

War of 1812, Anglo-American x, 96

Warren, Vice-Admiral Sir John Borlase 124

Washington, General George..66

Waterloo, Battle of (1815) x, 92, 99, 124, 156–57

Wellesley, Lord Richard (1803)121

Wellington, Arthur Wellesley, Duke of 156

Westphalia, Kingdom of (1807) 154

WILLAUMEZ, Vice-Admiral Jean-Baptiste-Philibert, *Comte* (1763–1845): to sea with Bougainville (1777); 159; in American Revolutionary war (1778–83) 159–60; with d'Entrecasteax in search of La

Pérouse (1791–93) 160–61; prisoner of Dutch at Batavia (1794) 161; at Île-de-France, in action under Renaud 1795; sails for Indies with Sercey (1796) 162; with Magon, escorts Spanish treasure ships home (1798) 163; with Rochefort squadron on Saint-Domingue (1801) 164; escape of, from Saint Nicolas Mole (1803) 164–65; Brest fleet squadron commander under Ganteaume (1804–5) 165–66; war cruise of from Brest, with Jérôme Bonaparte (1805–7) 166–67; commands Brest fleet (1808–9) 167; blockaded in Rochefort, replaced by Allemand (1809); with Zuider Zee flotilla (1811–12) 168; last honours of 168

Willem V, Dutch *Stadhouder* 97–8

Willoughby, Captain Nisbet Josiah; in Grand-Port battle (1810) 189–93

Windward Islands (1768) 10; (1803) 59

Winter, Admiral Jan Willem de xiii, 95

Wurmser, Marshal Dagobert Sigmund 171

Yorktown, Va. (1782) 50, 56, 66, 108, 197

Zayonchek, General Josef 95

Zuider Zee: (1785) 96; (1794–95) 97; (1811) 168

Index of Ships

British

Adamant (1799) 201
Agamemnon (1794) 33–34
Aigle (1808) 186
Alert (1778) 27
Alexander (1800) 85
Amazon: (1796) 184; (1806) 124
Anson (1806) 167
Arrogant (1796) 41, 110, 162, 199
Astell (1810) 188
Audacious: (1800) 85; (1801) 119–20

Barnaby (1804) 122
Belleisle (1805) 135
Bellerophon (1798) 70
Berwick (1794–95) 33, 80–81, 140
Blenheim (1805) 123
Boadicea (1810) 146, 188–193
Brilliant (1798) 111
Brilliant (1798) 163
Britannia (1805) 62
Brunswick: (1794) 23, 36–37, 113;
  (1805) 123

Calcutta (1805) 207
Cæsar (1801) 119–20, 206
Camel (1799) 200
Carysfort (1796) 41
Centurion: (1794) 11, 161; (1804) 122–23
Ceylon (1810) 146, 188
Charlton (1809) 145
Culloden (1794) 37

Concorde (!796) 184
Cumberland (1803) 164
Curieux (1805) 134, 165

Daedalus (1799) 44
Dido (1795) 81
Diomede (1794) 110, 161

Europe (1809) 145, 187

Favourite (1806) 202
Foudroyant: (1800) 85–86, 90–91;
  (1806) 124

Gibraltar: (1806) 154; (1806) 185
Goliath (1803) 164

Hannibal (1801) 119–21, 205–6
Hector (1782) 11
Hercule (1803)
Hound (1795) 199

Incendiary (1801) 76
Illustrious (1795) 33, 130
Impetueux (1808) 186
Indefatigable (1796) 184
Iphigenia (1810) 188, 191–93
Iris (1780) 10

Jason (1798) 44

King George (1779) 50

Lion (1800) 85, 90–91
London (1806) 124
Lowestoffe (1795) 81

Magicienne (1810) 188, 191–92
Malta (1805) 134
Mars (1805) 135
Minerva (1793) 110
Minorca (1800) 90
Minotaur (1798) 103
Narcissus (186) 186

Néréide (1810) 146, 188–93
Northumberland (1800) 85–86

Orient (1809) 145
Otter (1810) 146

Pearl (1798) 111
Penelope (1800) 90–91
Pique (1798) 44
Pitt (1781) 160
Polyphemus (1805) 152
Pompée (1801) 119–20
Princess–Charlotte (1804) 122

Queen Charlotte: (1794) 22, 36; (1795) 117; (1800) 85

Rattlesnake (1799) 200
Royal Sovereign (1805) 62

St Albans (1794) 117
Sans Pareil (1795) 117
Sarah (1805) 123
Saturn (1808) 186
Sceptre (1783) 21
Sibylle (1799) 44
Sirius: (1805) 152; (1810) 188, 190–92
Speedy (1801) 118, 205
Sphynx (1796) 41
Spencer (1801) 119
Sprightly (1801) 76
Staunch (1810) 146

Streatham (1809) 145, 187
Success (1800–1) 76, 85
Superb (1801) 120, 206
Swiftsure: (1794) 116; (1801) 76, 150, 205

Thames (1794) 198
Theseus: (1798) 103; (1799) 84; (1801) 120
Tigre (1799) 84
Tonnant (1805) 113
Tremendous (1799) 201

United Kingdom (1809) 145

Vanguard (1798) 103
Venerable (1801) 119–21, 206
Victorious (1796) 41, 110, 162, 199
Victory (1805) 62–3

Warrior (1805) 165
Windham (1809) 145–6, 188–90

Zealous (1798) 70

French
Aber-Vrach (1770) 26
Achille: (1788) 198; (1805) 112, 133; (1793) 204
Actionnaire (1772) 66
Agamemnon (1813) 104, 137
Aigle (1782) 11
Aigrette (1776) 129
Aimable-Dorothée (1790) 139
Aimable-Victor (1777) 203
Alceste: (1794) 80–1; (1798) 75, 83
Alcide: (1794) 33; (1795) 81
Alerte: (1796) 42; (1798) 83
Alexandre: (1795) 117; (1805) 165–6; (1803) 201
Algésiras: (1804) 165; (1805) 112–14, 133, 135; (1808) 29
Alouette (1786) 88
Amazone (1781) 160
Ambition (1773) 26

América (1793) 32, 40
Amphion (1766) 26
Amphitrite: (1775) 40; (1786) 108
Annibal (1779) 108
Apollon (1783) 72
Aquilon (1798) 82
Argonaute (1808) 29
Argus (1805) 132
Artémise: (1795) 81; (1798) 82, 89
Asie: (1786) 139; (1789) 204
Astrée: (1781) 11; (1786) 102, 160; (1810) 146, 188, 193
Astrolabe (1791) 160–61
Atalante: (1770) 66; (1775) 20; (1793) 88, 116–17; (1802–3) 121–23, 173
Atlas (1805) 134
Auguste (1781) 49–50
Aventurier (1803) 122

Badine: (1792) 56; (1794) 80; (1800) 85
Barbeau: (1784) 115; (1787) 116; (1788) 67
Belette (1789–92) 16
Belle-Poule: (1778) 40; (1803) 121–24
Bellone: (1782) 20; (1806–10) 144, 146; (1808–10) 186–93
Berceau (1803) 121–22
Bergère: (1795) 162 (1798) 204
Berwick: (1795) 140; (1805) 132
Bien-Aimé (1777–8) 115, 159
Blonde (1783) 56
Bolonaise (1804) 174
Bonne-Citoyenne (1796) 41, 162
Borée (1809) 136
Boudeuse: (1778) 40; (1780) 49
Boulonnaise: (1785) 79; (1787) 130
Boussole (1791) 160–61
Bretagne (1778) 108
Bricole (1774) 31
Brillant (1781) 20
Brûle-Gueule (1797) 43–44, 200
Brune: (1794) 80; (1796) 82
Bucentaure: (1804) 14; (1805) 63, 112, 135

Calypso (1809) 208
Ça Ira (1795) 33, 81, 130
Carrère (1798–99) 74–5
Caroline (1806–9) 144, 187
Cassard: (1797) 117; (1805–6) 152–53, 166–67
Caton (1780) 108
Causse (1798) 74
Cayennaise (1783) 88
Censeur: (1782) 16; (1794–95) 33, 81, 130, 140
Centaure (1793) 16, 130
Cérès: (1781) 32; (1782) 40
Cerf (1793) 102
César (1776–7) 66, 115
Ceylon/Ceylan (1810) 146, 188–90
Chameau (1787) 102
Chien de Chasse (1783) 67
Chimère (1771) 66
Citoyen (1780–83) 4
Cléopâtre (1783) 27
Cocarde (1796) 41, 162, 199
Concorde (1781) 40
Conquérant: (1798) 82; (1795) 103; (1798) 103
Cornélie (1805) 136
Cormoran (1798) 142
Coromandel (1774) 20
Couleuvre (1762) 10
Courageuse (1798) 83
Courageux (1806) 208
Coureur: (1777) 26; (1787) 67
Couronne (1778) 40
Courtier (1776) 10
Cousine (1786–91) 32
Coventry (1785) 21
Créole (1809) 145
Crescent (1782) 204
Cybèle: (1792–3) 88, 109; (1794) 110; (1796) 41, 43–44, 110, 162; (1805–6) 202; (1809) 208

Dauphin-Royal (1781) 27, 102
Dauphine (1778–79) 20

David (1791) 170
Desaix (1801) 118–20
Destin (1782) 56
Diadème: (1781) 101; (1782) 115
Diane: (1796–97) 81–82; (1798–1800) 59, 76, 82, 89, 172–73
Didon (1805) 133
Diligente (1780) 87
Donauwerth (1809) 136
Dorade: (1779) 36; (1786) 130
Dragon (1759) 9
Dromedaire (1791) 198
Dryade (1788) 109
Dubois (1798) 74
Duc-de-Bourgogne (1791) 198
Duguay-Trouin (1793) 130; 164
Duquesne (1794) 81
Durance (1786) 16

Ecluse (1785) 88
Eléonore (1791) 139
Éléphant (1766) 20
Embuscade (1793) 103
Engageante: (1773–74) 15; (1792) 198
Entrepenant: (1792) 139; (1810) 146
Éole: (1790) 88; (1793) 40; (1793–94) 51; 204 (1797) 117; (1805–6) 152–53, 166–7; (181) 188
Epervier: (1794) 116; (1801) 150
Espérance (1791) 160–1
Espoir (1792) 32
Europe (1789) 204

Fantasque (1783) 102
Fauvette: (1783) 50; (1800) 85
Félicité (1809) 208–9
Fendant (1781) 27
Fidélité (1792) 198
Fine (1790) 130
Flamand (1778) 159
Flèche (1777) 66
Fidèle (1783) 130
Fier Rodrigue (1778) 72
Fine: (1790) 102; (1805) 132

Flamand (1778) 159
Flore: (1774) 66; (1776) 15; (1779) 55
Formidable: (1795) 117; (1796) 57, 89, 103; (1800) 142; (1801) 118–20, 205–7
Forte: (1785) 160; (1796–98) 41, 44, 110, 162
Fortune (1773) 120
Foudroyant: (1801) 13, 150; (1805–6) 152–53, 166–67
Fougueux (1805) 135
Fourmi (1778) 159
Fox (1779) 49
Franklin (1798) 58, 69, 82
Fraternité (1797) 141
Friponne (1794) 33
Furieuse (1809) 208–9

Galathée: (1787) 169–70; (1795) 199
Généreux: (1798) 52, 58–59, 82; (1800) 76, 85–86, 89–90, 172
Génois (1809) 136
Gloire (1782) 11
Glorieuse (1773) 79
Glorieux (1782) 87
Goéland (1791) 198
Gracieuse (1779) 66
Guerrier (1798) 69, 82, 103
Guillaume–Tell: (1796) 67; (1798, 1800) 58–59, 82, 89–91, 163, 172
Guyane (1786) 16
Gros-Ventre (1772) 26, 39

Hardi (1781) 55
D'Haultpoult (1809) 208–9
Hazard (1774) 35
Hector (1778–79) 4
Héliopolis (1801) 76
Henri IV (1791) 183
Heureux (1798) 82
Hercule (1780) 204
Hermione: (1780) 10–11; (1793) 32; (1805) 133, 136
Héros: (1781) 49; (1808) 29

Heure du Berger (1767–69) 39
Hirondelle: (1767) 26; (1781) 129;
    (1793) 170
Hortense (1805) 133, 136

Île-de-France (1772–73) 26
Impétueux (1805) 152–53, 166–67
Indefatigable (1802) 207
Indienne (1801) 120
Indivisible (1801) 76, 149
Indomptable: (1794) 22, 73; (1797) 51;
    (1801) 118–19, 205; (1802) 104;
    (1805) 136
Infante (1795) 170
Intrépide: (1762) 10; (1778) 101;
    (1802) 121
Italienne: (1808) 186; (1809) 208

Jason (1796) 82
Jean-Jacques Rousseau: (1796) 103;
    (1798) 117
Jemappes: (1794–97) 37; (1796) 103;
    (1798) 131; (1801) 111;
    (1805) 208
Jeune-Minna (1788) 139
Joséphine (1797) 171
Junon (1798–99) 74, 84
Jupiter (1793) 40, 72
Justice (1798, 1800) 59, 82, 89, 172–73

La Pucelle (1794) 170
Laharpe (1797) 172
Languedoc: (1780–83) 4; (1792) 12
Laverdy (1773) 26
Légère: (1766–67) 39; (1800) 172
Les Amis (1780) 159
Levrette: (1781) 40; (1794) 116
Lion (1809) 136
Lionne 1785) 160
Lively (1781) 27
Louise (1760–61) 10
Lourde (1786) 130

Magnifique (1778) 32
Magnanime (1805) 208

Maire-Guiton (1793) 183
Malicieuse (1763) 26
Manche (1806) 144–46, 187–88, 193
Manon (1773) 66
Marengo (1803) 121–24, 144
Marlborough (1781)
Marquis-de-Castries (1785) 108
Marseillais: (1781) 55–56; (1782) 108
Medée (1792) 197
Méduse (1790) 27
Mélanide (1762) 10
Mercure (1798) 82
Mérope (1797) 172
Minerve: (1791) 109; (1794–95) 80–81;
    84, 140; (1808) 179; (1810) 146,
    188–90
Modeste: (1784) 198; (1789–92) 16
Moineau (1796) 41
Mont-Blanc: (1794) 72–73; (1796) 103;
    (1805) 134; (1801–2) 111, 131
Montagne (1794) 21–22, 36, 198
Montréal (1779) 55
Muiron (1798–99) 74–75; (1801)
    118–19, 205
Mulet: (1782–83) 36; (1789) 102
Mutine (1796) 41, 162

Naïade (1783) 20–1
Naturaliste (1800–3) 142–43
Nativité (1798) 104
Nécessaire (1785) 108
Neptune: (1805) 136; (1808) 29
Nestor (1795) 117
Northumberland (1780) 197
Nourrice (1765) 20
Nymphe: (1778) 129; (1782) 40, 88;
    (1789) 88

Océan: (1799) 117; (1801) 111, 131
Oiseau: (1778) 129; (1783) 197
Orient (1798) 58, 68–70, 74, 82
Orion (1790–91) 36, 140

Pactole (1781) 169
Palinure (1805) 17

Pandour (1789) 109
Patriote: (1787) 102; (1792) 198 (1805)
    152–53; (1806) 166–7
Pégase (1781) 129–30; (1790) 16;
    (1796) 141
Pélagie (1800) 184–85
Perdrix (1792–93) 36
Perle (1768) 26
Petit-Jacobin (1793) 170
Peuple-Souverain: (1795) 57; (1798) 82
Pilote des Indes (1780) 197
Pintade: (1778) 20; (1783) 197
Pivert (1784–88) 50
Pluton: (1779) 202; (1795) 162; (1805)
    61, 131–32, 134–36; (1808) 29
Pluvier (1783) 88
Polonais (1809, 1814) 209
Pomone: (1793) 32; (1805) 151
Poulette (1790) 67
Poursuivante (1803) 164–65
Précieuse: (1791) 30; (1797) 141
Présidente (1805–6) 202
Proserpine: (1787) 116; (1794) 80, 140
Preneuse (1797–99) 43–44, 199–201
Protecteur: (1766) 66; (1782) 130
Protée (1776) 115
Provence (1776) 66
Prudente: (1790) 21; (1794) 110, 161;
    (1796) 41, 44, 110, 162
Pulvérisateur (1781–82) 20
Pygmée (1782) 16

Railleuse: (1782) 50; (1785) 21
Recherche (1791) 160–61
Redoutable (1805) 63, 113
Réfléchi: (1782) 16; (1785) 115–16
Régénérée (1796–98) 41, 43, 110–11,
    162–3, 199
Régulus (1805–6) 201–2
Républicain: (1798–99) 37; (1804) 201–2
Résolue (1794) 170, 198
Révolution (1796) 141
Rhin (1805) 136
Richemond (1780) 87

Robuste (1809) 136
Romulus (1813) 137
Rossignol: (1778–89) 10; (1785–86) 32

Sage (1762) 26; (1780) 27
Saint-Antoine (1801) 120, 206
Saint-Esprit: (1764) 31; (1779) 108
Saint-Joseph (1767–68) 35
Sainte-Catherine (1776) 203
Salamine (1798) 83
Sans-Culottes (1794) 33
Sans-Pareil: (1780) 40; (1800) 85
Sardine (1795) 73
Scévola (1796–97) 141
Scipion: (1779) 115; (1813) 137
Seine (1796–99) 41, 110, 162
Sémillante: (1783) 108; (1792) 50;
    (1803–5) 121–23
Sensible (1795) 73
Sérieuse (1798) 82
Serpent (1780) 40
Sincère (1792) 130
Sirène (1805–6) 132, 186
Six-Corps (1763) 26
Solitaire (1780) 108
Spartiate (1798) 82, 103–4
Suffren (1803) 207
Sultane (1777) 15
Superbe (1792) 198
Surveillante: (1780) 15; (1783) 72; (1787)
    198; (202)
Sylphe: (1776) 101; (1785) 160

Tamise (1793) 198
Tartelon (1784–87) 4, 32
Tartu (1795) 183
Terpsichore (1775) 32
Terrible (1780) 66
Tharon (1784) 160
Thémise (1805) 133, 136
Tigre (1795) 117
Tilsitt (1811) 137
Timoléon: (1798) 58, 82, 89; (1796) 103

Tonnant: (1762) 10; (1792) 56; (1798) 58, 69, 82; (1795) 130–31
Tortue (1793) 32
Tourville (1797) 117
Trajan (1793) 21
Trente-et-un–Mai (1794) 73
Tricolore (1792) 67
Triolmphant (1781) 102
Triton (1778) 40
Tyrannicide: (1794) 22; (1796) 103; (1800) 204–5

Union (1784) 204

Vaillant (1778–79) 15
Valeureuse (1805) 152–53
Vengeance (1797) 73
Vengeur (1794) 23, 36–37, 73, 113
Vénus: (1784–88) 27; (1806–10) 144–46
Vertu: (1796–98) 41–43, 110–11, 162–3, 199
Vestale: (1781) 67; (1794–95) 33, 81
Vétéran (1805–6) 152–54, 166, 185–86
Vicomte-Talleyrand (1773) 26
Victor (1810) 146, 188–91
Victoire (1790) 88, 116
Vigilante: (1784–85) 32; (1786) 130
Ville-de-Marseille (1800) 85
Ville de Paris: (1778) 40; (1780) 159
Virginie (1795) 184
Volage (1774–75) 35
Volontaire (1805) 152
Voltigeante (1796) 171

Zélé (1781) 66–67
Zizette (1788) 170
Zombi (1783) 88

Dutch
Argo (1779) 96

Heemskerk (1804) 97
Hollandia (1781) 96

Spanish
Argonauta (1801) 120, 206
España (1805) 134

Firme (1805) 134

Neptuno (1805) 136

Principe de Asturias (1805) 62–63, 112–13

Rayo (1805) 62, 112, 136
Real Carlos (1801) 120, 206

San Agustin (1801) 120, 206
San Fernando (1801) 120, 206
San Francisco de Asis (1805) 136
San Hermenegildo (1801) 120, 206
San Rafael (1805) 134
Santa Ana (1805) 62–63, 112, 135–36
San Fernando (1801) 120
Sabina (1801) 120
Santa Madalena (1805) 133
Santissima Trinidad (1805) 62–63, 112